Communications
in Computer and Information Science   242

Stefan Müller Arisona
Gideon Aschwanden   Jan Halatsch
Peter Wonka (Eds.)

Digital Urban Modeling and Simulation

 Springer

Volume Editors

Stefan Müller Arisona
Singapore-ETH Centre
Future Cities Laboratory, Singapore
E-mail: arisona@arch.ethz.ch

Gideon Aschwanden
Singapore-ETH Centre
Future Cities Laboratory, Singapore
E-mail: aschwanden@arch.ethz.ch

Jan Halatsch
ETH Zurich
Chair of Information Architecture
Zurich, Switzerland
E-mail: halatsch@arch.ethz.ch

Peter Wonka
Arizona State University
Department of Computer Science and Engineering
Tempe, AZ, USA
E-mail: pwonka@gmail.com

ISSN 1865-0929   e-ISSN 1865-0937
ISBN 978-3-642-29757-1   e-ISBN 978-3-642-29758-8
DOI 10.1007/978-3-642-29758-8
Springer Heidelberg Dordrecht London New York

Library of Congress Control Number: 2012941233

CR Subject Classification (1998): H.4, H.5, I.2, H.3, C.2, H.2

Typesetting: Camera-ready by author, data conversion by Scientific Publishing Services, Chennai, India

Printed on acid-free paper

Springer is part of Springer Science+Business Media (www.springer.com)

Preface

In the last few years, the use of computers to study and solve urban planning and design problems has become widespread. More recently, and also thanks to the advances of computer technology, the focus has shifted toward integrative approaches that attempt to look at urban systems at multiple scales, both in terms of space and time. However, such approaches also imply being connected to a growing number of fields, and it can be hard to keep track of the connections and – more importantly – of the connection points. Thus, many solutions computer and information science might have to offer are simply not recognized.

This book is thematically positioned at the intersections of urban design, architecture, civil engineering and computer science, and it aims to provide specialists coming from respective fields with a multi-angle overview of state-of-the-art work currently being carried out. It addresses both newcomers who wish to obtain more knowledge about this growing area of interest, as well as established researchers and practitioners who want to keep up to date. In terms of organization, the volume starts out with chapters looking at the domain from a wide angle and then moves focus toward technical viewpoints and approaches.

We wish to thank all authors – without them, this volume could not have been realized. Particular thanks go to Gerhard Schmitt, Chair of Information Architecture and Director of the Singapore-ETH Centre, who supported this work from the very beginning and provided valuable input throughout. Finally, we would like to thank Leonie Kunz and Stefan Göller of Springer for the excellent assistance during the editing process.

July 2011   Stefan Müller Arisona

Table of Contents

Part IV: Visualization, Collaboration and Interaction

Part I
Introduction

A Planning Environment for the Design of Future Cities

Gerhard Schmitt

Chair of Information Architecture
ETH Zurich
gerhard.schmitt@sl.ethz.ch

Abstract. In the global context, the population of cities and urbanized areas has developed from a minority to become the majority. Now cities are the largest, most complex and most dynamic man-made systems. They are vibrant centres of cultural life and engines that drive local and global economies. Yet, contemporary urbanized areas are environmentally, socially and economically unsustainable entities laying increasing pressure on the surrounding rural areas. Traditional methods of planning and managing large cities that lead to this situation have reached their limits. The planning and design processes therefore need a radical re-thinking. On the computational side, this necessitates the integration of new methods and instruments. On the planning and design side, this requires the involvement of stakeholders and decision makers much earlier than normally done in the past. The combination of interactive design and computation will demonstrate the effects and side effects of urban-rural planning or re-development. We build our design research approach on dynamics and scale: viewing cities and settlements as entities with dynamic urban metabolisms, we propose to apply stocks and flows simulations to the building scale (small, S-Scale), to the urban scale (medium, M-Scale), and to the territorial scale (large, L-Scale). Our long-term goal is the sustainable urban-rural system. Planning and implementation examples from Switzerland and ETH Zurich Science City serve as test cases, with the intent to use the findings for developments in other parts of the world.

1 Introduction

For too long and increasingly so, the transformation of existing and the planning of new cities have been following specific interests, ideologies or imagined constraints. Especially the growing apart of urban design and urban planning has lead to less desired results (Lampugnani, 2010). It appears that compared to science and engineering, not much progress has occurred in this field – or has even been reversed – in view of the seemingly overwhelming complexity of modern cities. For example, local heat and pollution islands as a result of the increasing number of mega cities reduce the quality of life in those centres and lead to increased vacation mobility of those who can afford it – a vicious circle. Neither market forces alone nor top-down planning have lead to the creation of sustainable cities. On the other hand, the "integrated" or "holistic" approaches towards city planning often turn out to be fairly arbitrary in their result, lacking clear models or neglecting local context and shaping forces. The virtualization of the city, as expected by some in the 1990s and beyond, did not occur and will most likely become part of the physical and real city (Boyer, 1996).

S. Müller Arisona et al. (Eds.): DUMS, CCIS 242, pp. 3–16, 2012.

Therefore, it is necessary to combine modern instruments and methods or to invent new ones to allow for the simulation of successful scenarios for sustainable future cities (Bettencourt and West, 2010). We propose to see and model cities as urban-rural systems and as material and information organisms with their own metabolism. And we propose the method of stocks and flows with the associated instruments to create scenarios for transforming existing and for designing new cities. Special care must be taken to incorporate the local stakeholders, the legislative authorities, politics and economy, as well as the geographic, social and environmental context in the process. As a consequence, the transformation towards sustainability of Singapore or cities in Switzerland, East Africa or South America should lead to similar positive effects for the inhabitants, but the physical appearance may be radically different. For the development and transformation of future cities, this design view defines the requirements for the model, the methods and the instruments.

2   Future Cities

We require future cities to be attractive, sustainable and in balance with their rural surroundings. The most crucial criterion is long-term social sustainability. This requires that urban design and architecture are of high quality; that transportation and the mobile parts of the city are integrated with the static, structural and spatial elements of the city; that as little external, non-renewable energy enters and leaves the city, resulting in low greenhouse gas emission settlements; that building materials and water are recycled continuously; and that the city is designed and built not only for the affluent and active, but also for the very young and the elderly. If the future city starts with an over-fulfilling of these positive requirements, chances are high that these positive indicators will strengthen with the growth of the city and lead to long-term sustainability (Bettencourt et al., 2010).

While it is relatively easy to specify these demands, it is hard to propose a re-design or a design for a city that can fulfil them. Once started, a city is never completed and constantly changes: it is a dynamic system for which a complete model needs yet to be found or defined. In spite of the importance of the starting conditions, a city is probably the system that is influenced and changed most by its own development. Imposing grand master plans for new cities on the scale of Le Corbusier's un-built Ville Contemporaine from 1922, his partially built Chandigarh design from 1951 (Sharma, 2009) or Oscar Niemeyer's Brasilia from 1957 has not been attempted for decades. Yet the idea of grand master planning with the goal of sustainability re-emerges in Foster + Partners' proposal for Masdar City in Abu Dhabi or in several Eco-City plans in China.

3   The Role of Context

The transformation of existing or the design of new cities is never an abstract, context-free activity. Context – understood as the surrounding societal, governmental, economical, environmental and technological conditions – is a fundamental factor to consider in the transformation of existing and in the design of new sustainable cities. Just looking at the examples of the Ville Contemporaine, Brasilia or Masdar, it becomes obvious how strongly the context of culture and national identity (society), climate (environment), and economy have influenced the design. Yet none of these designs, with the exception of Masdar, could benefit at their time from integrated modelling of the quantitative aspects of sustainability or other properties – they relied more on declaration than on simulation. One reason of course was that during the design of the earlier examples, no powerful computers were available to simulate the outcome of design decisions and their possible side effects. Also, there was a hierarchical rather than a team or stakeholder planning process in the earlier examples that precluded possible synergies. It is this schism between architects, urban designers and the other disciplines, which widened over time and lead to different languages and expressions that are difficult but necessary to reconcile today for a new planning environment.

In order to be useful for computer supported design and simulation, the real context needs a representation in the computational realm. We acknowledge that the resulting model and description of the real context in the computational world will be incomplete in the beginning and will not fully describe all aspects of the real context. But a definition of the model representing the context in its crucial aspects is the precondition to compute meaningful scenarios. It is also the precondition to extend the "digital chain" process to the urban and territorial scale. The digital chain process ties together the design, construction and management phase of a structure in digital representations that are compatible and are preserved for use in the next phases. The Department of Architecture of ETH Zurich has tested the approach in teaching (Schoch, 2005), and at the building level (D-ARCH, 2011).

For the planning environment to design sustainable future cities, we propose to begin with the modelling of the most relevant contexts, namely the local conditions relating to population, demographics and health (society), economy, water, energy, material, space and information.

4   Setting Priorities

The first priority in the transformation of existing and for the design of new sustainable cities must be the creation of a common communication base, common aims, and a common model. Precondition for this is bridging the widening gaps between architects, urban designers, planners, engineers, sociologists and other disciplines. Implementing this priority is best achieved by defining the common goal of sustainable urban-rural systems and a communication based on the common model. The platform associated with this model must deliver added value to all participants. Such a platform does not exist today, but could be the contribution of Information Technology to the re-design or design of future urban-rural systems. We therefore propose to define and build such a digital simulation platform.

Government organizations are well suited for this approach as they can tender large projects top-down. Examples for this are the Australian Commonwealth Scientific and Industrial Research Organisation (CSIRO, 2011) or the Singaporean Inter-Ministerial Committee on Sustainable Development (Singaporean Inter-Ministerial Committee on Sustainable Development, 2010) with its plans for "a lively and liveable Singapore – strategies for sustainable growth". Yet the

Fig. 1. Sustainable urban planning oriented examples in Addis Ababa (left) and Singapore (right). Construction status in October 2009, both cities have around 5 million inhabitants.

top-down approaches might miss the synergies that a bottom-up organization could bring to the task: in this case, excellent specialists from different disciplines would get together and define the common platform and model from the inside out.

It is the inside-out approach that ETH Zurich has taken together with the National Research Foundation of Singapore, to found the Future Cities Laboratory FCL (Future Cities Laboratory, 2011) as the first programme within the Singapore ETH Centre for global environmental sustainability SEC (Asiaone, 2009). The FCL members, an interdisciplinary team of professors and researchers, are committed to the common goal to transform and create cities towards sustainability.

5   Planning Environments: Case Studies

Planning environments are highly dependent on the context they developed and exist in, and in return they shape this context in the long term. To illustrate this fact, we present the case study of a traditional or existing planning environment, and based on the findings, propose an outline for future planning environments.

5.1   Traditional Planning Environments

As the planning of cities is a most complex issue, the governmental bodies in charge have broken it down into distinct processes and responsibilities. In well-developed planning environments, each step is clearly defined and a typical process can take several years. The overall contribution of digital instruments to traditional planning processes is restricted, as they primarily tend to support the individual, vertically organized processes.

Master Plan Hochschulgebiet Zurich. In 2000, the author approached the President of the University of Zurich to engage in a coordinated expansion of the two adjacent campus areas in the inner city of Zurich and to develop them, together with the Zurich art museum "Kunsthaus", into a cultural mile. The internal process to gain the support of the respective university boards took only 3 months. The first negotiations with the city and the Canton of Zurich took one year. A wise employee of the Canton of Zurich recommended moving the process with possible stakeholders carefully through all steps in order to prevent later unpleasant surprises and protests. We took this advice and the result was positive, yet the process took another two years. The international competition for the master plan took six months, as it is a highly formalized process that most city governments have experience with. In addition, the city planning department of Zurich had introduced the so-called test planning process, in that the teams in a competition present their intermediate work once during the competition process.

While most proposals concentrated on new urban elements or urban renewal, the introduction of landscape architecture and rural elements on a city scale and re-interpreting the university buildings as villas in a park-like city scape convinced the jury (see Figure 2). The winning team, headed by the landscape architect Christophe Girot, proposed a park-like structure of the "Hochschulgebiet Zürich" as it was officially named (Stadt Zürich, 2009).

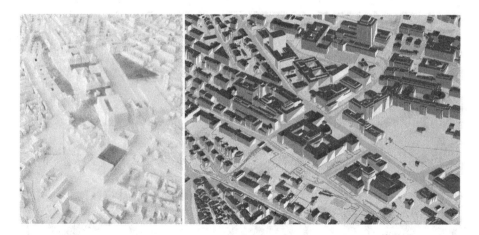

Fig. 2. Reintroducing landscape and terraces in the inner-city situation of Zurich. Analogue model used for display, Christophe Girot, 2004. Digital model of the same area, used for animation, Armin Grün, 2004.

Finally, 6 years after the original idea, the resulting master plan passed the official decision bodies. And it took 10 years after starting the process for the first building to begin construction according to the master plan. At this point in time, the initial reasoning and plans were already difficult to locate, and the connection between the original ideas and the planned construction are hard to maintain. This is where a simulation platform for the entire process could have contributed positively: As a digital repository of the work produced, including the discussions and interviews, representing the "soft", but deciding factors of the entire process.

5.2 Future Planning Environments

To overcome the shortcomings of existing planning processes, future planning environments must be based on initial stakeholder participation, common goals, and a common model. They also should be based on the digital chain, a concept that is emerging on the architectural scale for the design, construction and facility management of buildings (Schoch, 2005). Applying the digital chain to urban-rural system design is a promising research challenge and will for the first time allow the continuous overview over the design, construction and management processes of a city.

Monte Rosa. An early example for a future planning environment and for the application of the digital chain is the new Monte Rosa Building in the Swiss Alps, which at an altitude of almost 10'000 feet achieves a more than 90% resource autonomy with minimal impact on the pristine alpine environment (see Figure 3). Monte Rosa serves as a demonstration project for the future priority of low greenhouse gas emission construction and energy production on the building technology scale.

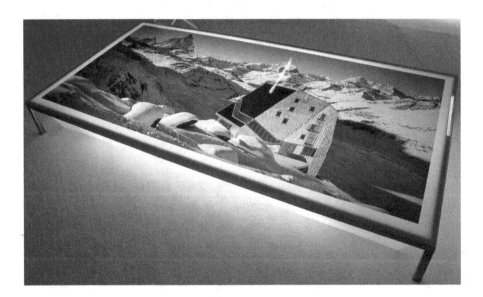

Fig. 3. Illustration of a digital chain process on the architectural scale: the new Monte Rosa shelter of the Swiss Alpine Club. Andrea Deplazes and students, ETH Zurich, 2009. Exhibition Philippe Carrard, ETH Zurich, 2010.

The digital chain started with the design phase of the shelter in a design research studio and the selection of a winning scheme, continued with the simulation and optimization of the design for resource autonomy, with the delivery of the resulting digital model to the production facility, to the CNC production of the wooden elements, including ornamentation, to the completion and continuous monitoring of the building to optimize the facility management (ETH Zurich, 2010).

6 ETH Zurich Science City

The Science City strategy for the new campus of ETH Zurich originated in 2003, three years after the Hochschulgebiet project for the original site of ETH in downtown Zurich. It serves as an example for the priorities of social sustainability and for the drastic reduction of greenhouse gas emissions. We had experienced the importance of initial stakeholder integration and we were also aware of some of the bottlenecks in the process. As a result, the project moved faster and a master plan competition took place already one year after the first ideas (Schmitt, 2007).

The intensive integration of many possible stakeholders had the effect of creating high public interest. And while most comments ranged from enthusiasm to constructive criticism, the Science City management team also was involved in intense negotiations with a group that wanted to keep the landscape and park character of the campus. Yet less than 2 years after the first idea, the city and the canton of Zurich approved the overall master plan (see Figure 4), 3 years later the ETH Board approved the sustainability concept (see Figure 5) and the first building was under construction.

The Science City project makes much more use of digital representations, simulation and communication than previous planning approaches. In fact, it involved the internal and external stakeholders from the very beginning in the definition and design process through its web site and meetings with more than 3000 people from neighbourhoods, political parties and NGOs. The process demonstrated the importance of a continuous digital repository of the input of all partners involved.

What we achieved with the mixture of analogue and digital design and decision making processes for the Monte Rosa Shelter and to a degree with the Science City planning, construction and management, we envision for the transition and planning processes for sustainable future cities: they must employ the digital chain from the beginning of the design phase to the construction phase and then to the facility management phase; they maintain a digital repository of all design steps and decisions; and they document the role and contribution of each partner in the overall process.

7 Planning Partners, Values, Languages

In establishing the digital chain for urban design, the partners must define, coordinate and translate their discipline-based languages. They need to describe syntax and semantics and, more importantly, they must study the effects of their own decisions on the other partners and on the values that have priorities for them. When planning and designing for sustainability, the single criterion optimization towards low first costs, affordability, efficiency or any other parameter will be of less interest in the future, as its irrelevance or even detrimental effects on sustainability become obvious today. Instead, multi-dimensional sustainability criteria should be the measure for the overall optimization. The following paragraphs sketch out in which direction the disciplines need to move in order to arrive at a common value system, language, and consequently at a common model.

Architectural education ranges from very practical to poetic aspects of designing new structures – including mostly buildings to some urban to few territorial projects

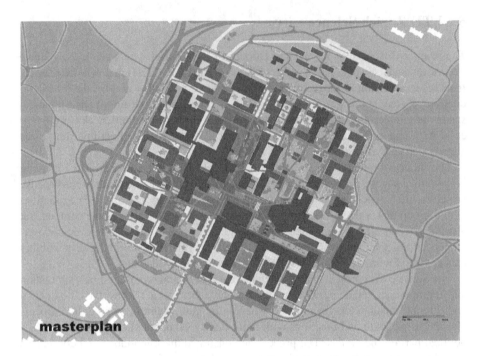

Fig. 4. ETH Zurich Science City master plan. Shown in dark grey: existing structures as of 2011, shown in light grey: proposed structures. Yet more important than the structures is the network of spaces and paths connecting them. Kees Christiaanse, 2005.

(D-ARCH, 2011). A strong grounding in history is part of the architectural education, as well as mathematics and building physics in some of the schools. Increasingly, management aspects for the profession become part of the curriculum, as well as sustainability compounds.

Engineering education, especially civil and transportation engineering, used to concentrate on analysis and quantitative aspects of structures. Yet there is a growing tendency towards design, towards environmental considerations and towards the building of interfaces between the natural and the artificial technical systems (D-BAUG, 2011).

Science education is fundamental, yet interdisciplinary by nature as it attempts to go to the bottom of things, to explore and explain the inner workings of processes and objects (Harvard University Department of Physics, 2011). Physics, mathematics, chemistry and biology increasingly shed light on the functioning of complex systems. Systems biology, for example, attempts to understand the functioning of living systems (SystemsX, 2010).

Although sketchy, exaggerated and not always correct, these observations are indications of educational tendencies and therefore impact future leaders. Each education provides its students with a view on the world that is sometimes difficult to reconsolidate with other views. But re-consolidation between different views is a necessary step towards the design of urban-rural systems.

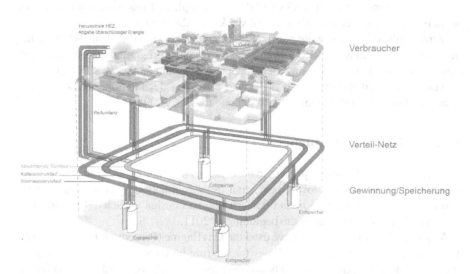

Fig. 5. Energy supply concept of Science City: a low temperature network connects all buildings and active alternative energy elements, excess heat is stored during the summer in a dynamic earth storage system and retrieved in winter. ETH Zurich, 2007

8 Models and Methods

For many years, there is a dispute between those who propose a unified model as a base for the highly complex simulation of cities (Bettencourt and West, 2010) and those who claim that such a methodology is futile. The latter propose a stepwise and modular approach instead, in which humans provide the necessary interfaces. For the sake of a clear argument, the long-term goal of the Simulation Platform in the Future Cities Laboratory will be an overall and integrated model and will come as close to its implementation as possible.

We chose to use the model of the Urban Metabolism (Deilmann, 2009). Abel Wolman describes the "metabolic requirements of a city" already in 1969 "as all the materials and commodities needed to sustain a city's inhabitants at home, at work, and at play" (Wolman, 1969). This early definition has evolved over time and we suggest expanding the model to that of an urban-rural metabolism, thus incorporating the territorial scale in addition to the building and city scale.

The dimension of time is highly relevant to the development of sustainable cities. Brunner and Rechberger (Brunner and Rechberger, 2001) point out the striking increase in material turnover per person from prehistoric to modern times by more than one order of magnitude and focus on material stocks that have grown most spectacularly, from less than 0.1 tons per capita per year to more than 260 tons per capita per year in modern cities. Materiality, of course, is the realm of architecture and urban planning. Stocks and Flows (Rotmans et al., 2000) and the Material Flow Analysis (MFA) are the methods we propose to use to analyse the transformation or planning of future cities. In addition, the Future Cities Laboratory has a very strong design base and direction that needs to incorporate the modelling of stocks and flows of people and space – elements that are not normally considered in the traditional stocks and flows model.

Increasingly, this model gains acceptance in large-scale projects on sustainable cities and systems, such as the CSIRO Urban Systems research program that attempts to address stocks and flows of, among others, people, water, and energy (CSIRO, 2010). At the building level, this research is much advanced and has lead to important knowledge creation for designers and planners (Hassler and d'Ayot, 2009).

9   Models and Instruments

We suggest placing the design process in the centre of the Future Cities Laboratory. This is necessary to constantly provide new input in the simulation processes and to keep a balance between optimization and powerful human design capacity. The following models and instruments refer to the beginning of 2011.

As a versatile instrument, we have used the CityEngine (Procedural Inc., 2011) software in research and teaching. It allows for the rule based and procedural generation of complex networks and city models and their use for analysis, simulation and further development.

We propose to use CityGML (CityGML, 2011) as shared information model to represent 3D urban objects, as well as the classes and relations for topographic objects including geometry, topology, semantics and appearance. It is intended to support simulation, urban data mining, facility management and thematic inquiries.

To study the interactions between land use, transportation, economy and the environment, we propose to use the simulation system UrbanSim (UrbanSim, 2009). It has been expanded over the past years and lead to interesting applications (Vanegas et al., 2009). These simulations bridge the gap to architectural or urban design environments and can be exported to the CityEngine environment, thus allowing modelling and visualization to the scale of the building.

Finally, on a level of fine granularity, we involve new interactive human machine interfaces based on multi-touch technology. A prototype developed by the Swiss company VASP (Burkhard and Merz, 2009) shows a promising approach to generate crucial parameters needed for CityEngine or UrbanSim input.

10   The Future Cities Laboratory Planning Model

Given the decision for the Stocks and Flows method under the expanded Urban Metabolism model, we propose to organize the Future Cities Laboratory in the following manner (see Figure 6).

The research takes place on three spatial scales: Building (S), city (M) and territory (L). It also occurs on three time scales: Short-term, medium-term and long-term. The content is concentrated into 9 research streams and an all-encompassing simulation platform. The research streams stretch across one or more scales:

Stocks and flows of people and space deal with urban sociology and urban design strategies and resources – space and capital; Stocks and flows of material and energy will conduct research in low exergy, new construction materials and digital fabrication;

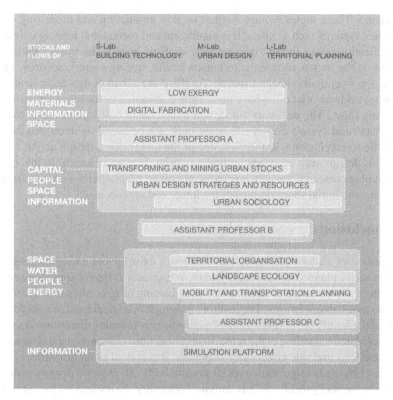

STOCKS AND FLOWS OF	S-Lab BUILDING TECHNOLOGY	M-Lab URBAN DESIGN	L-Lab TERRITORIAL PLANNING

ENERGY MATERIALS INFORMATION SPACE
- LOW EXERGY
- DIGITAL FABRICATION
- ASSISTANT PROFESSOR A

CAPITAL PEOPLE SPACE INFORMATION
- TRANSFORMING AND MINING URBAN STOCKS
- URBAN DESIGN STRATEGIES AND RESOURCES
- URBAN SOCIOLOGY
- ASSISTANT PROFESSOR B

SPACE WATER PEOPLE ENERGY
- TERRITORIAL ORGANISATION
- LANDSCAPE ECOLOGY
- MOBILITY AND TRANSPORTATION PLANNING
- ASSISTANT PROFESSOR C

INFORMATION
- SIMULATION PLATFORM

Fig. 6. The Future Cities Laboratory stocks and flows model. Three spatial scales (columns S, M, L) and 9 research streams (rows) define the research space.

Stocks and flows in space, water and capital deal with landscape ecology, water infrastructure, and transforming and mining urban stocks. Stocks and flows in material and space deal with territorial organization, mobility and transportation planning, and spatial density; and finally the simulation platform will form the data and information base for all research streams.

11   Notions to Overcome – Consequences for Education

Although new simulation software is powerful and seems to be able to create 3D scenarios on a whim and in a playful way, urban design is not a game. Neither are the transformation of existing and the planning of new urban-rural systems administrative tasks that can be solved by breaking them down into subtasks that will automatically lead to a solution. Rather, they are interactive and participatory processes combining knowledge and technology. The main process should be lead by designers who have the overall picture in mind. They are often visionaries, but they are also educated to invent and guarantee functioning systems.

At the same time, design education needs renovation and expansion. The role and position of systems design and management in architectural research and education must expand. These topics require support by new simulation and modelling courses for complex systems such as cities. It is significant and correct that leading universities and organizations place urban topics on their strategic agenda. In most of these cases, the reason is the increased interest in human health, ageing society, security, energy, or water – not primarily design aspects. Yet there are urban design and planning departments worldwide that often have no or little connection to the more scientific areas surrounding them. The necessity for design and science based curricula is therefore clear. Urban-rural system design education must not be based on anecdotal evidence or scientific research alone. Rather, it is one of the most critical design activities in the future. This design must be based on findings from rigorous research. In this context, urban sociology research has a high priority, as human adaptation is a strong possibility to overcome the initial shortcomings of the integrated approach.

12   Conclusions

The definition of sustainable future cities includes existing and emerging settlements as well as newly planned urban-rural systems. A radically different approach is needed towards the transformation of existing and the planning of new cities in order to arrive at overall sustainable solutions. The cultural, geographic, strategic and climatic contexts are crucial to identify the optimal transformation or new planning directions. As we start with a limited understanding of the actual interconnections in the urban-rural metabolism and of the effects and side effects they may have, it is crucial to set priorities.

The first priority is to guarantee social sustainability. The second priority is the mid-term achievement of greenhouse gas emission neutrality. To implement these priorities, we need to drastically change the planning environments. Whereas traditional planning is based on decisions arrived at through different, mostly separated processes and municipal departments that are bound to their individual goals and thus are less able to support the overall desired developments, we propose an integrated design and planning environment in that decisions are arrived at in a scientifically supported participatory process, and where the results of proposals and decisions are visible in real-time for the stakeholders. To arrive at this situation, computer based design and decision support systems will increasingly complement and support the human interaction and provide an interface that is necessary in the beginning of the process.

As approach, we chose the stocks and flows model and dynamic urban metabolism simulations on the small, medium and large scale. As instruments, we employ and extend tools such as UrbanSim and CityEngine. Preliminary results are most exciting and in some ways unexpected. In the process, it will become clear that the "one fits all" approach towards urban planning is out-dated and that only strongly contextual developments will have a chance to provide long-term high quality and sustainable urban-rural environments.

Acknowledgments. The author wants to thank Mark Angélil, Franz Oswald, Kees Christiaanse, Armin Grün, Kay Axhausen, Stefan Müller Arisona and Jan Halatsch for their essential support in the definition, preparation and start of the Future Cities Laboratory.

References

Asiaone. New centre to tackle problem of growing cities (2009),
   http://www.asiaone.com/News/Education/Story/
   A1Story20091029-176555.html (accessed March 1, 2011)
Bettencourt, L., West, G.: A unified theory of urban living. Nature 467(7318), 912–913 (2010)
   ISSN 0028-0836
Bettencourt, L.M.A., Lobo, J., Strumsky, D., West, G.B., Añel, J.A.: Urban scaling and its devi-
   ations: Revealing the structure of wealth, innovation and crime across cities. PloS one 5(11),
   e13541 (2010) ISSN 1932-6203
Boyer, M.C.: CyberCities: visual perception in the age of electronic communication. Princeton
   Architectural Press (1996) ISBN 1568980485
Brunner, P.H., Rechberger, H.: Anthropogenic metabolism and environmental legacies. Encyclo-
   pedia of Global Environmental Change 3, 54–72 (2001)
Burkhard, R.A., Merz, T.: A visually supported interactive risk assessment approach for group
   meetings. In: 9th International Conference on Knowledge Management and Knowledge Tech-
   nologies, Graz, Austria, September 2-4 (2009)
CityGML (2011), http://www.citygml.org/ (accessed March 1, 2011)
CSIRO (2010), http://www.csiro.au/science/UrbanSystems.html
   (accessed March 1, 2011)
CSIRO. Australian commonwealth scientific and industrial research organisation (2011),
   http://www.csiro.au/ (accessed March 1, 2011)
D-ARCH. Education at the Faculty of Architecture of ETH Zurich (2011),
   http://www.arch.ethz.ch/darch/studium_start.php?lang=en (accessed
   March 1, 2011)
D-BAUG. Department of Civil, Environmental and Geomatic Engineering of ETH Zurich (2011),
   http://www.baug.ethz.ch/index_EN (accessed March 1, 2011)
Deilmann, C.: Urban metabolism and the surface of the city. In: Guiding Principles for Spatial
   Development in Germany, pp. 1–16 (2009)
Zurich, E.T.H. (ed.): Neue Monte-Rosa-Hütte SAC. Ein autarkes Bauwerk im hochalpinen Raum.
   gta Verlag (2010)
Future Cities Laboratory (2011), http://futurecities.ethz.ch (accessed March 1,
   2011)
Harvard University Department of Physics (2011), http://www.physics.harvard.edu/
   (accessed March 1, 2011)
Hassler, U., d'Ayot, C.: Bauten der Boomjahre Paradoxien der Erhaltung / Architectures de la
   croissance Les paradoxes de la sauvegarde. Institut für Denkmalpflege und Bauforschung,
   ETH Zurich, Zurich (2009)
Lampugnani, M.V.: Die Stadt im 20. Jahrhundert - Visionen, Entwürfe, Gebautes. Klaus Wagen-
   bach, Berlin (2010)
Procedural Inc. CityEngine (2011), http://www.procedural.com/ (accessed March 1,
   2011)
Rotmans, J., van Asselt, M., Vellinga, P.: An integrated planning tool for sustainable cities. Envi-
   ronmental Impact Assessment Review 20(3), 265–276 (2000) ISSN 0195-9255
Schmitt, G.: Espace de savoir interactif. Un projet pour l'ETH: Science City. In: Chatelet, V. (ed.)
   Interactive Cities, Editions Hyx, Orleans, France, pp. 172–195 (2007)
Schoch, O.: Applying a digital chain in teaching CAAD and CAAM. In: Digital Design: The
   Quest for New Paradigms (23nd eCAADe Conference Proceedings/ISBN 0-9541183-2-4),
   Lisbon (Portugal), pp. 21–24 (2005)

Sharma, S.: Corbs Capitol: A Journey Through Chandigarh Architecture. Chandigarh (2009) (accessed March 1, 2011)

Singaporean Inter-Ministerial Committee on Sustainable Development (2010), http://www.sustainablesingapore.gov.sg (accessed March 1, 2011)

Stadt Zürich. Hochschulgebiet Zürich-Zentrum – Bericht Entwicklungsgebiete Stadt Zürich (2009) (accessed March 1, 2011)

SystemsX. What is systemsx.ch (2010), http://www.systemsx.ch/about-us/what-is-systemsxch/mission/ (accessed March 1, 2011)

UrbanSim (2009), http://www.urbansim.org/ (accessed March 1, 2011)

Vanegas, C.A., Aliaga, D.G., Beneš, B., Waddell, P.A.: Interactive design of urban spaces using geometrical and behavioral modeling. ACM Transactions on Graphics (TOG) 28(5), 1–10 (2009) ISSN 0730-0301

Wolman, A.: The metabolism of cities. In: Water, Health and Society, pp. 276–296. Indiana University Press (1969)

Calculating Cities

Bharat Dave

Faculty of Architecture, Building and Planning, The University of Melbourne, Australia
b.dave@unimelb.edu.au

Abstract. Places exercise imagination and exert power. Measuring and representing places was privileged and highly guarded in the antiquity. The rise of quantification and global mercantile traffic that ushered in the Renaissance in Europe fostered development of increasingly unambiguous and detailed representations of space and urban environments. The rise of increasingly sophisticated and precise measures at various points in time and place underpinned descriptive representations (i.e. records of how things are), concretized meanings (i.e. set forth ideals for how things could be in future), and provided instrumental prescriptions (i.e. codes to be conformed to). This chapter provides a very brief overview of selected developments in urban modeling to highlight changing roles of representations and purposes they served with a view to contextualise many lineages that inform the very notion of virtual urban modelling.

1   Introduction

But what if we are actually at the end point of network logic?

Network Fever: Mark Wigley (2001)

A fever indeed seems to have been adrift in the few years prior to and following the 1960's. The state of urban environments needed urgent interventions, especially as cities appeared to be mushrooming out of control with problems that were complex and increasingly appeared intractable using traditional thinking and design approaches. Instead what one needed, so the one particular argument went, were more systematic approaches that took into account multiple, interacting variables and could help devise a way out of these problems into new desirable order of urban environments. These sentiments run through a number of key texts that appeared around the time in architecture and urban design. For example, Chermayeff and Alexander in *Community and Privacy* (1965) laid out a systematic approach to decomposition of urban environments into a set of requirements that could then be recomposed into other patterns responsive to different needs. Yona Friedman followed a similar trajectory in *Towards a Scientific Architecture* (1975), whereas Nicholas Negroponte developed some of these arguments further in *The Architecture Machine* (1972) and *Soft Architecture Machines* (1975). And somewhere in between the 1960's and 1970's an enigmatic group named Archigram (1999) furiously drew and published graphic visions of urban futures in a range of projects with intriguing titles such as the Walking City, Plug-In City, Instant City, Control and Choice living, Metamorphosis, Computer City.

S. Müller Arisona et al. (Eds.): DUMS, CCIS 242, pp. 17–23, 2012.
© Springer-Verlag Berlin Heidelberg 2012

The ideas and language that frame these and other writings of the time drew upon concepts from the emerging domains of operations research, systems thinking, cybernetics, control and feedback systems and information systems, all of which had proved invaluable during the war years. These newly founded disciplines illustrated how to cope with complexity; surely they could be just as applicable to combat urban issues. It is against this background that we encounter the first tentative steps towards urban modeling using digital information systems.

Increasingly in the discourse that unfolded in these early projects, we witness explicit and implicit intersections between urban thinking and information and communication technologies. The language of urban design gets infused with notions of networks and flows, dependencies between variables, mathematization of decision making processes, and much more. And we encounter also in these early studies manifestation of subtle differences in how computing and communications technologies were marshaled differently to respond to urban issues. Negroponte, for example, conceptualized *The Architecture Machine* as a tool to assist in generation of design possibilities, not just to record and process information but also as an active participant in the man-machine dialogue about exploration of spatial compositions or design futures. The *Computer City* of Dennis Crompton, on the other hand, did not employ computing to generate fixed alternatives but embedded these technologies as the very constitutive and integral elements of continuously evolving and shifting urban infrastructure and environments. These are not opposing positions but only two early conceptualizations about how to shape urban environments using digital technologies. The former employed computer representations and modeling to facilitate exploration of alternative urban futures, the other imagined representations and what was represented as but one and the same.

The early body of work from the 1960-70s provided foundations and impetus for developments in a number of cognate disciplines in urban modeling in the subsequent years with advances in computer aided modeling systems, geographic information systems, digital photogrammetry, and networking infrastructure that linked dispersed repositories of data. To better understand and frame the role and scope of future virtual urban modeling systems, it may be instructive to briefly review the spectrum of lineages that inform thinking in urban modeling literature.

2   Urban Modelling Trajectories

Although digital technologies began to infuse urban design and planning literature during the 1960s, the very idea of conceptualizing, representing and imagining extant and alternative urban forms and futures appeared much earlier at different times and places to serve different needs. The diversity of ideas may be illustrated by following three broad significant trajectories in urban modeling literature. First, the descriptive or pictorial-cartographic tradition in which the focus is on modelling and describing existing urban environments with as much verisimilitude as possible. Second, the idealistic tradition in urban literature which focuses on not just here and now of existing environments but primarily on imagined futures and idealized urban settings. Third, the instrumental tradition that revolves around codification of design and planning standards to mediate between present and future urban developments.

3   Descriptive Traditions

The patterns incised on spears or dot patterns recorded on canvas to mark landscape and natural features by the indigenous Australians or the shells and sticks strung together to mark relative location of islands by the Marshall Islanders are just two of the many ways to model and communicate knowledge of natural environments. With the passage from such abstract descriptions to pictorial ones, there followed increasing verisimilitude between environments being described and their graphic representations. However, these pictorial descriptions are selective and heavily invested with a view to communicate relative significance of features; even when they describe some part of the existing world they are interpretive acts, not documentary in nature. The pictorial traditions then gave way to cartographic ones wherein uniform scale operates throughout information rendered and establish mapping and maps as a way to measure, record, and describe the world. Harvey (1980) notes this trajectory from symbols to picture-maps to scale maps and surveys as illustrative episodes in development of topographical maps or episodes in the evolution of descriptive models of the world.

Moving closer to the recent times in the descriptive tradition, there appear increasing levels of symbolic conventions which allow both abstraction and details at various scales of information. Thus navigation maps become more detailed and systematised just as town plans and bird's eye-view so popular in pictorial tradition become even more dense and realistic. It is quite astounding that prior to the advent of aerial photography in the mid 18th nth century, descriptive models relied upon the world as understood, measured and experienced from the ground.

The recent advances in long-range photogrammetry matched with high fidelity terrestrial scanning technologies now make possible digital modelling of indoor, outdoor and terrestrial environments at any level of details. They represent contemporary descriptive models using compositional elements of pixels, points and vectors, located in a selected coordinate space as a frame of reference. These models offer not just more detail and accuracy; they also enable simultaneous juxtaposition of information from different times in the same descriptive model and continuous update of models in real time.

4   Idealistic Traditions

A famous passage in *The Book of Zhou* dated to the 1st millennium B.C. describes Wangcheng or the "ruler's city" articulated in the seven principles for imperial planning. It was not a plan for an ordinary city or even for an existing one but a plan for an ideal city, one that reflected the higher order of how the world should be according to the Chinese worldview of the time. Unlike the descriptive city models, the ideal city plans delineate a dominant worldview informed by either divine, princely or some other political force or value systems to drive spatial distribution of both social and material worlds (Rosenau, 1974).

With the gradual rise of centres of power and aggregation of people around these centres, the growth of urban communities was inevitable. And so was the speculation and need to guide the form they should take. The ideals espoused during various ages and places reflect a variety of themes. For the Chinese, the grid provided a way to orient and align the cosmic order with the earthly one. In the Indian tradition of *Vastu-Purusha*, similar sentiment informs subdivision of a square aligned with cardinal directions. The Greek thinking on ideal city models is reflected in Plato's *Timaeus* and *Critias* including the legendary island of 'Atlantis' as a prototype of these ideals. The Romans and their military preoccupations are reflected in the writings of Vitruvius in *De Architectura Libri Decum*. The same spatial device of grid though is marshaled in different cultures to serve diametrically opposed worldviews of either creating graduated and differentiated spaces or encoding relative equality of any point in grid to any other.

The decisive turn in ideal city models comes with the rise of quantification following the expansion of global mercantile traffic and the need for quantification and measuring which ushered in the Renaissance in Europe. It is against this background that Alberti pens *De Re Aedificatoria*, the theory of town planning and Filarete writes *Treatise on Architecture* which described and illustrated the imaginary city of Sforzinda as an ideal model.

Whereas these writings on ideal cities revolved around formal spatial configurations as their prime focus, Sir Thomas More's *Utopia* reflected on the dual nature of urban environments, social and formal both and set the stage for thinking about urban developments that followed in Europe.

As urban centres expanded, the focus on cities as seats of royal or industrial power magnified the need to (re)think not just the existing state of urban agglomerations but what they should aspire to. It is in that vein that a number of early treatises and projects were articulated on urban planning and design in France in the 18th century. From Pierre Pate's plans for Paris to Ledoux's plans for the ideal city of Chaux, the interest and dominant viewpoint shifts from royal interests to the needs of the citizens and community.

These changes almost anticipate what transpired in the aftermath of the Industrial Revolution. For example, Fourier's *Phalanstery*, a community of consumption and production, or Ebenezer Howard's *Garden City* responded to needs of urban conditions of the 19th century. These communities and ideals came unstuck in the early 20th century with technologies of mass production and succession of wars and set the stage for Le Corbusier's vision for high-rise units Ville Radieuse (1935) dotted among green landscapes.

These ideals too were then engulfed by the subsequent developments in the late 20th century, bringing us closer to the current notions of 24-hour city, real-time city, crash-test metropolis, wired city, or smart cities. Each of these monikers invokes a particular assemblage of technologies and infrastructure, simultaneously acting both as ideals to aspire to and as vehicles for explaining ongoing shifts in urban thinking and modelling.

5   Instrumental Traditions

Between the descriptive models of how things are and the idealistic models of how things ought to be operate the instrumental models codified in the form of design and planning standards and guidelines. This tradition is best exemplified in the work of Baron Haussmann of Paris, later dubbed also as the standard bearer of "state science".

Between the time that he was hired in 1852 and fired in 1870 by his benefactor Napoleon III, Haussmann set out a new plan for Paris that affected nearly 60% of the existing building stock. The city had grown by a process of accretion resulting in narrow, dense network of streets overflowing with refuse and sewage. Haussmann's response was methodical and decisive (Saalman, 1971). His plan to "let air and men circulate" cut through large swathes of buildings and created wide boulevards and squares at intersections of streets. The regulatory framework of urban design that enabled Haussmann spelt out specific design rules, e.g. buildings with street frontage required roofs with eaves angled at 45^0, and prefigured the subsequent expansion in codification of urban development of cities around the world.

The growth of urban agglomerations in the past was guided by implicit and explicit planning interventions of the kind that Haussmann exercised at a large scale in Paris. As discussed by Ben-Joseph (2005), all the early exemplar urban settlements in early China, India, Greece or Rome, resulted from urban design rules – explicit or implicit, used as instruments by the ruling power. Some of these design guidelines were concerned not only with formal aspects of shapes and symbolism but also as instruments to fulfill utilitarian and pragmatic needs. A notable example of the latter is Julian of Ascalon who wrote a treatise on urban design rules dealing with view sheds, drainage and planting issues. The rulebook contained, what Ben-Jospeh calls, "*a large measure of performance outcomes and a small dose of prescribed rules.*"

Following Haussmann's interventions in Paris, there emerged greater recognition of the complexity of urban settlements and the need to manage and regulate further growth. In London, it resulted in passage of the London Building Act in 1844 with a mandate to stipulate town-planning principles which included, among other issues, street widths to ensure better ventilation and air quality and improved drainage. The Model By-Laws that resulted from the Building Act marked the beginning of regulatory codes as a means to transform existing urban environments to approximate an ideal (or desirable) model. This regulatory legacy would only become stronger in the subsequent decades with the spread of new means of transportation including rail and automobiles, the tantalizing glimpses of which first emerged in the series of World Exposition fairs. With the *First National Conference on City Planning and the Problems of Congestion* held in Washington in 1909, the ground was paved for by-laws dealing with land subdivision and zoning some of which became ever more prescriptive and rigid.

6   Urban Modelling Futures

The preceding cursory survey of the landscape of ideas in urban modelling provides a rich background against which to contextualize current and future developments in virtual urban modelling. Although only selected trajectories in urban modelling were briefly sketched earlier, it is worth emphasizing that historically there have existed a number of diverse and useful perspectives from which urban issues may be framed and approached. And that will be true in the case of emerging clusters of projects loosely organized around the idea of virtual urban modelling. The prominence and rise of software-mediated spatiality in a number disciplines ranging from human and social geography to cyber geography underpin Batty's characterization of *The Com-*

putable City (1997) with many variations in virtual urban modelling agendas they pursue now and in future however they all are likely to share some common threads.

All urban models are vehicles for understanding the real so as to realize the ideal. Whereas techniques of representation in virtual urban modelling may be moving towards universal adoption, the ideals they serve remain contingent on local specificities of place and culture. The duality of local and global, universal and specifics, persistent and evolving purposes, will always remain contested elements in future virtual urban modelling.

The early work reflected two distinct ways to embrace computing technologies in urban modelling: as generative tools exemplified, for example, in the *Architecture Machine* by Negroponte, and as an integral part of urban infrastructure exemplified, for example, in the *Computer City* by Crompton. If the former approach revolved around space as the primary structuring variable, the latter one focused on time as the more significant dimension of urban issues. Although these distinctions only serve to highlight specific emphases between these two approaches in urban modeling, the current and future developments already suggest realignment of these emphases. These shifts have become visible over the last few decades wherein relative stability or permanence of spatial configurations and temporal fluidity of urban processes collide and the idea of urban modelling transforms into a more amorphous, complex, dynamic and distributed undertaking.

Some contemporary examples of these shifts already illustrate outlines of emergent technology-mediated urban modelling futures. For example, real-time traffic data collected using distributed sensors reroute traffic flows and thereby continuously reorder topologies of urban corridors and territories. Temporal fluctuations in shifting demands and markets registered via data loggers trigger real-time and variable costs and distribution of goods and services over urban territories which, in turn, reshape the very demands and markets for services and consumption. Smart metering systems make possible variable apportionment of utilities and costs and may lead to even more segmentation in access to services perhaps in direct contradiction to the very motivating factors that underpin development of smart metering systems. New communication systems fuel formation of fluid communities such as flash mobs and mobile social interactions that make it ever more complex to locate persistent centers and boundaries in urban spaces. Geo-tagging technologies give rise to new ways to perceive and experience space and time in urban environments.

The preceding eclectic list of examples begins to suggest some features of urban modeling futures wherein social transactions become unhinged from spatial fixity and urban modelling increasingly takes a turn to *process-centric* conceptualizations. To some extent, these shifts in perspective will build upon earlier traditions of urban modelling using descriptive, idealized or instrumental approaches. However these shifts may well herald a more nuanced articulation of the notion of *'urban metabolism'* conceptualized by Abel Wolman (1965) as a way to model, analyze and act upon urban environments as interconnected spaces and flows of materials, energy and information. With increasing recognition of environmental issues and interconnectedness of systems- human, natural and artificial, urban modeling futures then will need to simultaneously address territory, time, technologies and human agency at varying scales as part of the dynamic phenomena that are urban environments.

With the spread of pervasive and embedded technologies, we are inching closer to a new ecology of urban fabric comprising men, machines, and flows of information and materials wherein it becomes increasingly difficult to separate virtual models from what is being acted upon, processes from outcomes, or cities from silicon. The task of calculating cities becomes ever richer with more complex representations supported by new computational and communication technologies, a development that Thrift and French (2002) characterize as '*automatic production of space*' and '*turn to the noncognitive*', paralleled by the rise of cities that are themselves more calculating than before and feeding their very representations.

References

1. Batty, M.: The computable city. International Planning Studies 2(2), 155–173 (1997)
2. Ben-Joseph, E.: The Code of the City. The MIT Press, Cambridge (2005)
3. Chermayeff, S., Alexander, C.: Community and privacy: toward a new architecture of humanism. Doubleday, Garden City (1965)
4. Cook, P. (ed.): Archigram. Princeton Architectural Press, New York (1999)
5. Friedman, Y.: Toward a scientific architecture. MIT Press, Cambridge (1975)
6. Harvey, P.A.D.: The History of Topographical Maps. Thames and Hudson, London (1980)
7. Negroponte, N.: The architecture machine: toward a more human environment. MIT Press, Cambridge (1972)
8. Negroponte, N.: Soft architecture machines. The MIT Press, Cambridge (1975)
9. Rosenau, H.: The Ideal City. Studio Vista, London (1974)
10. Saalman, H.: Haussmann: Paris transformed. G. Braziller, New York (1971)
11. Thrift, N., French, S.: The Automatic Production of Space. Transactions of the Institute of British Geographers 27(4), 309–335 (2002)
12. Wigley, M.: Network Fever. Grey Room (4), 82–122 (2001)
13. Wolman, A.: The metabolism of cities. Scientific American 213(3), 179–190 (1965)

The City as a Socio-technical System: A Spatial Reformulation in the Light of the Levels Problem and the Parallel Problem

Bill Hillier

Bartlett School of Graduate Studies University College London
Gower Street London WC1E 6BT U.K.
b.hillier@ucl.ac.uk
www.spacesyntax.org
www.spacesyntax.com

Abstract. On the face of it, cities as complex systems are made of (at least) two sub-systems: a physical sub-system, made up of buildings linked by streets, roads and infrastructure; and a human sub-system made up of movement, interaction and activity. As such, cities can be thought of as socio-technical systems. Any reasonable theory of urban complexity would need to link the social and technical sub-systems to each other. Historically, most urban models have sought to make the link through the concept of distance in the physical system as a cost in the social system, defining the physical sub-system as a set of discrete zones. Such models have proved practical tools, but over the years have contributed relatively little to the development of a more general theory of the city. Here we propose a more complex and, we believe, true-to-life model based on the definition of the physical sub-system of the city as a network of spaces – streets and roads - linking buildings, rather than as a system of discrete zones. This allows us to approach urban complexity in a new way.

Two key issues – theoretically perhaps the two key issues - in the study of complexity in general are the levels problem: how organised complexity at one level becomes elementary the next level up; and the parallel problem: how systems with different internal dynamics interact with each other. In (Cohen & Stewart 1993) a general framework for conceptualising these two problems is outlined: complex phenomena at one level commonly produce lawful (though rarely mathematically describable) emergent simplicities one level up which then have their own emergent dynamic, independent of the complex processes that created them. They call such emergent simplicities, in which 'chaos collapses', 'simplexities'. Simplexities of different kinds then interact and modify each other to create 'complicities', or complexes of simplexities, to construct the complexity of the real world. Here it is argued that this formulation captures the problem of complexity in cities as socio-technical systems, and that we need vertical theories to capture the relations across levels, and lateral theories to capture the relations of parallel systems. We outline a vertical and a lateral theory to account for generic aspects of the emergent complexity of cities.

However, both theories require an account of the linking mechanism, and here we show that since all actions that create cities are taken by human agents, the vertical and lateral linking mechanisms necessarily involve human minds, not in

S. Müller Arisona et al. (Eds.): DUMS, CCIS 242, pp. 24–48, 2012.

the sense of real historic individuals, but in the sense of a generalised individual acting according to spatial laws which are both objective and intuitively known, in the same sense that an individual who throws a ball of paper so that its parabola leads it to land in a waste paper basket intuitively 'knows' the law of physics. We call this generalised human subject the 'objective subject' of the city, and show that by virtue of being everywhere in space and time in the formation and working of the city, it everywhere imposes its point of view on it, so that cities are cognitive formations in an even more fundamental sense than they are socio-economic formations. The cognitive sets the envelope of possibility within which socio-economic processes create the city.

1   Vertical and Lateral Theories

On the face of it, cities as complex systems are made of (at least) two sub-systems: a physical sub- system, made up of buildings linked by streets, roads and infrastructure; and a human sub-system made up of movement, interaction and activity. As such, cities can be thought of as socio- technical systems. Any reasonable theory of urban complexity would need to link the social and technical sub-systems to each other. Historically, most urban models have sought to make the link through the concept of distance in the physical system as a cost in the social system, defining the physical sub-system as a set of discrete zones. Such models have proved practical tools, but over the years have contributed relatively little to the development of a more general theory of cities. Here we propose a more complex and, we believe, true-to-life model based on the definition of the physical sub-system of the city as a network of spaces – streets and roads -linking buildings, rather than as a system of discrete zones. This allows us to approach urban complexity in a new way.

Two key issues – theoretically perhaps the two key issues - in the study of complexity in general are the *levels* problem: how organised complexity at one level becomes elementary the next level up; and the *parallel* problem: how systems with different internal dynamics interact with each other. In (Cohen & Stewart 1993) a general framework for conceptualising these two problems is outlined: complex phenomena at one level commonly produce lawful (though rarely mathematically describable) emergent simplicities one level up which then have their own emergent dynamic, independent of the complex processes that created them. They call such emergent simplicities, in which 'chaos collapses', 'simplexities'. Simplexities of different kinds then interact and modify each other to create 'complicities', or complexes of simplexities, to construct the complexity of the real world.

Here it is argued that this formulation captures well the problem of complexity in cities as socio- technical systems. To understand cities we need theories, which deal with relations across levels, and theories that deal with relations between parallel processes. We might call the former *vertical* theories, and the latter *lateral*. A *vertical* theory will be one, which works across levels of emergent phenomena, showing how complex distributed processes produce emergent simplicities, which then ignore the complexity of their creation and become independent forces at the emergent level in creating a further level of complexity. A *lateral* theory will then be one which shows how parallel but dynamically independent process, each with its own emergent simplicities, interact to shape each other.

Singularly clear examples of each can be found in the two most basic processes that create the city: the *vertical* emergence of a network of space from the process of aggregating buildings to create the physical city; and the *lateral* interaction of this emergent pattern with the processes by which different types of economic and social activity locate and organise themselves in space. The *vertical* process, we might say, creates the *spatial* city, the *lateral* process the *functional* city. The outcome of these vertical and lateral processes is the city, which is at once a form of *spatial* patterning and at the same time a form of *social* and *economic* patterning.

These two processes, and the relations between them, are the subjects of this paper. The ultimate focus is on a central question: what is the *mechanism* by which the vertical and lateral connections, on which the operation of the system depends, are made? The answer proposed is the same in both cases: the *human mind*, using intuitive knowledge of *spatial* and *spatio-functional* laws, is the key mechanism. By this we mean that there exist spatial and spatio-functional laws which while being wholly objective and describable by simple mathematics, are intuited by people in the same sense that when we throw a ball of paper so that its parabola leads it to land in a waste paper basket we are intuiting the laws of physics. We do so in both cases because these are the laws of the world, and our bodies and minds then learn to operate under the constraints imposed by these laws. An implication of this is that we cannot understand the city without understanding the interaction between human minds and the form of the material world. This is why we must redefine the city as a socio-technical system if we are to develop effective theories about it.

Now this may seem at first a strange pair of ideas: that the emergence of the spatial *form* of the city and the emergence of its pattern of *functioning* both involve laws, and that these laws are somehow imposed on the city through *human cognition*. But both seem to be the unavoidable conclusions of the application of space syntax analysis to study cities over the past two decades. Here we show the research, which has led us to these conclusions. First we show how the use of the space syntax methods to study cities has brought to light a remarkable series of spatial and spatio-functional *regularities* which are pretty well *invariant across cities*, suggesting that there is some kind of *universal city* underlying the diversity of real cities - a remarkable reflection if we bear in mind the heterogeneous social, economic and temporal circumstances in which the world's cities have been created. These regularities are for us the theoretical *explicandum* – that which is to be explained – of cities. Second, the use of space syntax as an *experimental tool* has brought to light simple *configurational* laws of space which deal precisely with the effect on emergent patterns of space of different kinds of physical intervention in it, such as placing blocks of buildings in space. We call this the law of *spatial emergence*, and have elsewhere called it the *law of centrality*. This is the law governing the *vertical* process through which the spatial form of the city emerges. Third, the use of space syntax as a tool to study *functional patterns* in cities has brought to light a fundamental relation between the *form* of the city and its *functioning*: that the network of space is in and of itself the primary influence on movement flows in different parts of the network, and through this, on emergent patterns of land use and densities, including the shaping of the pattern of centres and sub-centres. This is the law of *spatial agency*, and it governs the *lateral* process by which the form of the city shapes its functional patterns. We propose in effect that the *regularities* in cities – the *universal city* – can be explained by the *laws*, but that this happens in such a way as to be show that *human cognition* is the primary linking mechanism in both processes.

In what follows, we first show how space syntax has brought to light the regularities in the structures of the spatial networks of cities. Then we set out how the laws of the vertical and lateral processes came to light, and show how they have shaped the city into a spatio-functional whole. We then show how both processes can be seen in terms of this Cohen-Stewart model, and why this leads to the conclusion that the key mechanism in both the vertical and lateral processes is the human mind - not in the sense of real historic individuals, but in the sense of a *generalised individual* acting according to spatial laws which are both objective and intuitively known to humankind in general. We call this generalised human individual the *objective subject* of the city, meaning, in effect, *all of us*, and how we use our minds in making and use the city. By virtue of being everywhere in space and time in the formation and working of the city, the *objective subject* everywhere imposes its point of view on it, so that cities are cognitive formations in an even more fundamental sense than they are socio-economic formations. The cognitive sets the envelope of possibility within which socio-economic processes create the city. This is why we must revise our definition of the city as *socio-technical* system.

2   Regularities in Urban Spatial Form

To bring to light the *regularities* in the spatial form of urban networks we must make use of the standard space syntax representation of the network, the *least line map*, or the smallest number of straight lines that cover the system while making all connections. These can in small scale cases be created algorithmically by using the UCL DepthMap software (Turner 2002, Turner, Penn & Hillier 2005, Turner et al 2006) but for large scale urban systems this is computationally prohibitive, so least line maps are commonly digitised using the rules for creating and checking maps set out in (Hillier & Penn 2004).

Examining least line maps for cities at all scales and in all parts of the world we find:

-   That at all scales, from local areas to whole cities, cities are made up of a very small number of long lines and a very large number of short lines (Hillier 2002), so much so that in terms of the line length distributions in their least line maps cities have been argued to have scale- free properties (Carvalho & Penn 2004). This is just as true of more geometric cities such as Chicago and Athens, as it is for more 'organic' (meaning lacking obvious geometry) such as Tokyo or London.
-   That in 'organic' cities (as defined above), the longer the line the more likely it is to be end- connected to another by a nearly straight connection (between about 5 and 25 degrees), creating sequences of such lines, which the eye instinctively identifies *Figure 1 and 2* when look at a least line map; the shorter the line the

more likely it is to intersect with others at near right angles, creating local clusters of such lines. In geometrical cities, a similar pattern can be found but with straight rather than nearly straight long lines.

- Through these metric and geometric regularities, cities street networks acquire a *dual* structure, made up of a dominant *foreground network*, marked by linear continuity (and so in effect *route continuity*) and a background network, whose more localised character is formed through shorter lines and less linear continuity.

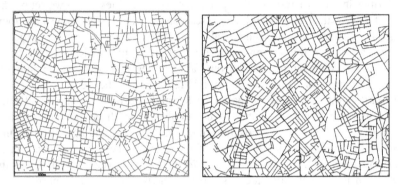

Fig. 1./2. Arbitrary sections of the least line maps of a section of Tokyo (left) and London (right)

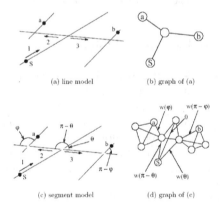

Fig. 3. Line and segment representation of street networks and their graphs

Using the UCL Depthmap software, we can then bring to light *configurational* regularities in city structures. DepthMap breaks up the least line map into the street segments between junctions, allows 3 definitions of the distance between each segment and its neighbours: : *metric*, that is the distance in metres between the centre of a segment and the centre of a neighbouring segment; *topological*, assigning a value of 1 if there is a change of direction between a segment and a neighbouring segment, and 0 if not; and *geometric* - assigning the degree of the angular change of direction between a segment and a neighbour, so straight connected are 0-valued and a line is a sequence of 0-valued connections. It then uses these 3 concepts of distance to calculate two kind of measure: syntactic *integration*, (mathematical *closeness* with the normalisations set out in Hillier & Hanson 1984), which measures how close each segment is to all others under each definition of distance;; and syntactic *choice,* or mathematical *betweenness*, which calculates how many distance- minimising paths between every pair of segments each segment lies on under different definitions of distance. So using the *metric* definition of distance we find the system of *shortest path* maps for integration and choice, with the *topological* definition we find the system of *fewest turns* maps, and with the *geometrical* definition we find the system of *least angle change* maps. Each of the 6 measures (2 measures with 3 definitions of distance) can then be applied with the 3 definitions of distance used as definitions of the *radius* from each segment at which the measures can be applied, giving a total of 18 measures, which can of course be applied at any radius, so yielding a potentially very large set of possible measures - for example least angle change choice at a metric radius of 800 metres – which would be infinite if we count the smallest variation in metric radius.

Applying these measures to cities, we bring to light further regularities. For example:

- by colour banding mathematical values from red (dark) through orange and yellow to green and blue (light), meaning to strong to weak, we find in case after case, least angle integration (normalised closeness) analysis without radius restriction (so the most 'global' form of the analysis), identifies a dominant structure in the form of what we call a *deformed wheel*, meaning a 'hub' of lines in the syntactic centres, strong 'spoke's linking centre to edge and strong 'rim' lines(closely reflecting the patterns brought to light by the earlier syntactic analysis of topological closeness of the least line map). *Figure 4* and *Figure 5*, for example, show the underlying deformed wheel pattern in both London within the M25 and metropolitan Tokyo (with multiple rims).

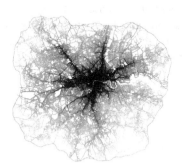 

Fig. 4./5. Showing least angle integration (normalised closeness) for London within the M25 (left) and metropolitan Tokyo (right), in each case showing a variant of the 'deformed wheel' structure, with multiple rims in the case of Tokyo

- Using the same colouring techniques, the least angle choice (betweenness) measure commonly identifies a network spread through the system, though strongest in the more syntactically central locations (see *Figure 5 and 6*).

Fig. 6./7. Least angle choice (betweenness) analysis of London (left) and Tokyo (right) showing the network pattern in both cases

In other words, in spite of the differences in socio-economic and temporal circumstances in which cities grow, they seem to converge on common generic forms, which have metric, geometric and configurational properties in common.

However the similarities between cities does not stop there. On close examination, for example, all cities seem to exhibit a property we call *pervasive centrality*, meaning that 'central' functions such as retail and catering concentrations diffuse throughout the network at all scales, from the city as a whole to the local network of streets. For example, *Figure 8* is Mike Batty's image of the 168 largest centres in London within the M25. By comparing *Figure 8* to *Figure 6* we find a strong 'eyeball' correspondence. However, the image also makes clear that the global properties shown in the map are not sufficient in themselves to identify the location of centres. We typically find for example that along the length of a high global movement potential alignment we find the centre occurring only in certain locations. For example, if we take the Edgeware Road between the North Circular Road and Oxford street, *Figure 8* there are three high streets with the rest fairly free of shops. In each case, the centre occurs where local *grid intensification* (a dense and smaller scale local grid) coincides with the globally strong alignment. The pattern is far more complex than envisaged in theories of *polycentrality*. It is notable also that pervasive centrality seems spatially sustainable because it means that wherever you are you are close to a small centre and not far from a much larger one. (Hillier 2009)

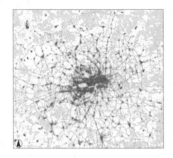

Fig. 8. Mike Batty's map of the 168 main centres and sub-centres in London within the M25

These belong in the boxes in the figure

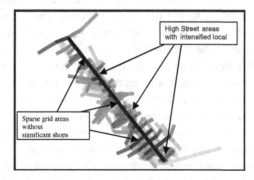

Fig. 9. Grid intensification coincides with the high street areas in a London alignment

If we then reduce the metric radius of the measures we then find the – much more numerous - smaller scale centres. For example, at radius 750 metres, all of the 'urban villages' in a section of north west London are picked out in red (dark). *Figure 9*

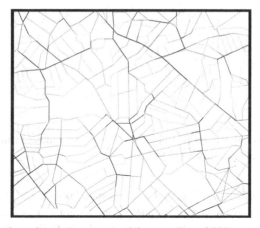

Fig. 10. Least angle through movement potential at a radius of 750 metres in an area of north west London with the dark lines approximating the urban villages

These effects are not confined to London or organic grids in general. The same kind of pattern of pervasive centrality was recently found in the historic grid based city of Suzhou in China. We have also shown it to be the case in Brasilia. But it is critical that these effects are found in the least angle map and disappear if we substitute metric for least angle distance in the model. For example, Figure 10 (not shown - to be shown at conference) shows the pattern of shops in one of the unplanned areas of Jeddah in Saudi Arabia and Figure 11 (not shown) shows the least angle choice measure at a radius of 3.5 kilometres. The match between the two red patterns is remarkable. If we substitute metric for least angle distance Figure 12 (not shown) we find no relation to the functional patterns. The reasons are simple. In Figure 13, we consider three ways of diagonalising a grid. In the top case, the diagonal is regular and so the length of the diagonal route is identical to that of the right side peripheral route. Bottom left, we then create an upward kink on of the line elements, with the effect of marginally increasing the length of the diagonal route compared to the peripheral route. Bottom right, we create a downward kink on one line, so marginally shortening the diagonal route compared to the peripheral route, which we show following our usual colouring convention. It follows that with the most marginal changes of this kind, shortest routes will find complex diagonals or simple peripheral routes more or less arbitrarily. This is confirmed in the right figure where we construct a system in which the two diagonals compete, and movement shifts decisively to the downward link and so the shortest path route. Which route is selected by the shortest path algorithm will often then depend on very minor differences in angles, and so be virtually arbitrary.

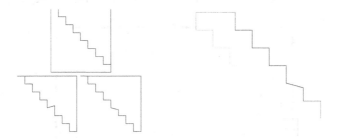

Fig. 13. Different ways of diagonalising the grid, showing why minor geometrical changes can lead to near arbitrary changes in shortest paths

This arbitrary selection of complex diagonals as shortest paths will feature particularly strongly where a more regular grid system is associated with complex internal structures within grid islands. For example, in Beijing, shortest path choice analysis – right above - does not find the eight-lane boulevard between the Forbidden City and Tiananmen Square, a boulevard which crosses Beijing east to west and is one of the busiest routes in Beijing. This is then a remarkable failure. In the case of Jeddah, least angle choice analysis without radius restriction (and so with reference to Jeddah as a whole) picks out the pattern of shops, though more weakly than with the local analysis, *Figure 14,* but substituting metric for least angle distance we find *Figure 15,* highlighting a nonsense route through the system, with innumerable changes of direction, and with no relation to the functional pattern. At best, we might say that metric analysis helps to identify taxi driver's routes!

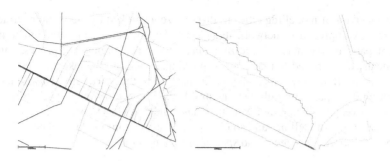

Fig. 14./15. Least angle choice (left) of an area of Jeddah and metric choice analysis(right), both at radius-n

3   A New Definition of the City

The regularities that we find in cities with least angle analysis suggest a new definition of the city. Cities of all kinds, however they originate, seem to evolve into *a foreground network of linked centres at all scales, from a couple of shops and a café through to whole sub-cities, set into a background network of largely residential space*. The *foreground* network is made up of a relatively small number of longer lines, connected at their ends by open angles, and forming a super-ordinate structure within which we find the *background* network, made up of much larger numbers of shorter lines, which tend to intersect each other and be connected at their ends by near right angles, and form local grid like clusters. We suggest this is the proper generic definition of what a city is as a large object.

So what forces give the city this shape. We believe the answer lies in two key new phenomena which research using space syntax has brought to light. The first we call *spatial emergence*: the network of space that links the buildings together into a single system acquires emergent *structure* from the ways in which objects are placed and shaped within it. This process is law-governed, and without an understanding of these laws the spatial *form* of cities cannot really be deciphered. How the city is physically *built* is critical. Cities are not simply reflections of socio-economic processes, but of the *act of building* in the light of these processes. The 'fact of the act' imposes a new framework of lawful constraints on the relation between socio-economic activity and space. It is the *law of spatial emergence, which* governs the *vertical* process through which the form of the city's spatial network emerges. The second phenomenon is *spatial agency*: the emergent spatial structure *in itself* has lawful effects on the functional patterns of the city by, in the first instance, shaping movement flows, and, through this, emergent land use patterns, since these in their nature either seek or avoid movement flows. Through its influence on movement, the urban grid turns a collection of building into a living city. Movement is literally the lifeblood of the city. The *law of spatial agency* governs the *lateral* process through which cities fit functional to spatial patterns.

It is these two linked processes of *spatial emergence* and *spatial agency* that set in train the self- organising processes through which cities acquire their more or less *universal* spatial form. These two processes are rendered more or less invisible by the standard method of modelling cities as discrete zones linked by Newtonian attraction. In the syntax approach to network modelling, the differences in attraction found in different parts of the network are *outcomes* of the self-organising process, and so theoretically (as opposed to practically) speaking, should not be taken as a given. But perhaps more than any other factor, it has been the - equally Newtonian ! - assumption that space can only be a neutral background to physical processes, rather than an active participant in them, that has rendered these space-based dynamics invisible to urban modelling, and so obscured the path from model to theory. We will now look at *spatial emergence* and *spatial agency* in turn.

4   A Vertical Theory: Spatial Emergence as a Law Governed Process

To understand the emergence of the spatial form of the urban network – the vertical problem - we need first to understand its topology then its geometry. The basic form of all cities is one of discrete groups of contiguous buildings, or 'blocks', usually outward facing, defining a network of linear spaces linking the buildings. How can this arise? In fact very simply.

Fig. 16. Aggregating dyads of open and closed cells by a restricted random process

If we take cell dyads (*Figure. 16*, top left), representing buildings linked by entrances to a bit of open space, and aggregate them randomly apart from a rule that each dyad joins its open space cell to one already in the system (forbidding vertex joins for the buildings, since no one joins buildings corner to corner), a pattern of buildings and spaces emerges with the topology of a city - outward facing blocks defining a linking network of linear space - but nothing like its geometry, in spite of being constructed on a regular grid (Hillier & Hanson 1984). The 'blocks', and so the spaces, are the wrong shape. Where then does the characteristic urban geometry come from?

To understand this we need first to think a little about the network of space in cities and how we interact with it, and the role that different notions of distance might play. Space in cities is about seeing and moving. We interact with space in cities both through our bodies and our minds. Our bodies interact with the space network through moving about in it, and bodily the city exists for us as a system of *metric distances*.

Our minds interact with the city through seeing. By seeing the city we learn to understand it. This is not just a matter of seeing buildings. We also see space, and the city comes to exist for us also as a visually more or less complex object, with more or less visual steps required to see all parts from all others, and so as a system of *visual distances*. This warns us that distance in cities might mean more than one thing.

But we also need to reflect on the fact that cities are collective artefacts, which bring together and relate very large collections of people. Their critical spatial properties of cities are not then just about the relation of one part to another, but of *all parts to all others*. We need a concept of distance, which reflects this. We propose that if *specific distance* means the common notion of distance as the distance, visual or metric, from *a* to *b*, that is from an origin to a destination, *universal distance* means the distance from each origin to all possible destinations in the system, and so from all origins to all destinations (Hillier 1996). Why does this matter? Because universal distance behaves quite differently from the normal metric and geometric concepts of distance that we use habitually. For example, if, as in *Figure 17* we have to place a cell to block direct movement between two cells, the closer we place it to one of the outer cells the less the total distance from each cell to all others will be, because more cell-to-cell trips are direct and do not require deviations around the blocking object.

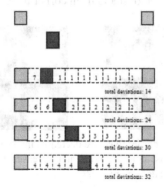

Fig. 17. Moving an object between two others from edge to centre increases the sum of distances from all cells to all others

The same applies to intervisibility from all points to all others *Figure 18*. As we move a partition in a line of cells from centre to edge, the total inter-visibility from each cell to all others increases, though of course the total area remains constant.

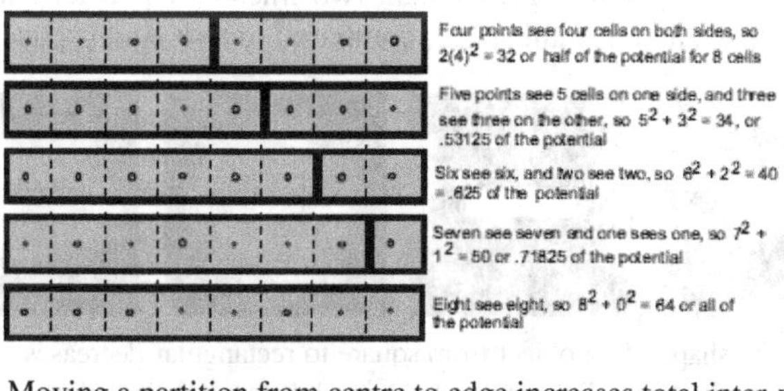

Fig. 18. Moving a partition from centre to edge increases total inter-visibility

Both metric and visual effects arise from the simple fact that to measure inter-visibility or inter- accessibility we need to square the numbers of points on either side of the blockage. So all we need to know is that twice the square of a number, n, will be a smaller number than $(n - 1)2 + (n + 1)2$ and that in general:

$$2n2 <(n-x)2 +(n+x)2 \qquad (1)$$

We can call this the 'squaring law' for space. It applies when, instead of being interested in, say, the distance from a to b, we are interested in the distance, metric or visual, from each point in the system to all others. In space syntax these 'all to all' properties are called *configurational* to distinguish them from simple relational or geometric properties.

So why does this matter? Because how we place and shape physical objects, such as urban blocks, in space, determines the emergent configurational properties of that space. For example, one consequence of the squaring law is that as we move objects from corner to edge and then to central locations in bounded spaces, total inter-visibility in the system decreases, as does visual integration (or universal visual distance) defined as how few visual steps we need to link all points to all others *Figure 19 (left)* The same applies to metric integration (or metric universal distance) defined as the sum of shortest paths between all pairs of points in the ambient space, which increases as we move the obstacle from corner to centre *(right)*.

Fig. 19. Moving an object from corner to centre decreases intervisibility (left – light means less visual distance to all other points, and dark more) and increases the mean length of trips (right – light is less metric distance, and dark more)

The same squaring law governs the effect of shape *Figure 20*: the more we elongate shapes, keeping area constant, the more we decrease inter-visibility and increase trip length in the ambient space. The effect of a long and short boundary is to create greater blockage in the system through the squaring law. Even at this stage, this spatial law has a critical implication for cities: in terms of configurational metrics a short line and a long line are, other things being equal, metrically and visually more efficient in linking the system together than two lines of equal length. *Figure 21*, as would be a large space and a small space, compared to two equal spaces.

Fig. 20. Changing the shape of an object from square to rectangular decreases inter-visibility and increase mean trip length. Again, light means less visual distance (left) and metric distance. (right)

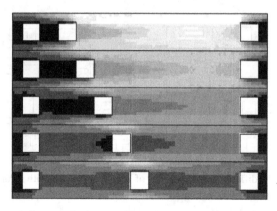

Fig. 21. Other things being equal, short and long lines integrate more than two lines of equal length. Again, dark means less visual distance

Another consequence is for the mean length of trip (or metric integration) from all points to all others in different types of grid, holding ground coverage of blocks, and therefore total travelable distance in the space, constant. In the four grids in *Figure 22*, darker (for clarity) means shorter mean trip length to all other points. Compared with the regular orthogonal grid (top left), interference in linearity on the right slightly increases mean trip length. But more strikingly, if we reduce the size of central blocks and compensate by increasing the size of peripheral blocks, we reduce mean trip length compared to the regular grid. This of course is the 'grid intensification' that we often note in looking at centres and sub-centres in cities. As so often, we find a mathematical principle underlying an empirical phenomenon.

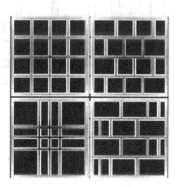

Fig. 22. Changing the scaling of a grid changes mean trip length. In this case, for graphical clarity, dark means less metric distance from each point to all others. The mean distances for each system are: top left 2.53, top right 2.59, bottom right 2.71, bottom left 2.42.

How we place and shape objects in space then determines the emergent configurational properties of that space. But what kind of block placing and shaping make space urban?

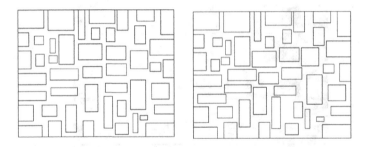

Fig. 23. Two slightly different arrangements of identical blocks, with strong linear relations between spaces on the left and weak on the right

On the left of *Figure 23*, we aggregate buildings in an approximately urban way, with linear relations between spaces, so we can see where we are going as well as where we are. On the right we retain the identical blocks but move them slightly to break linear connections between the spaces. If we then analyse metric and visual distances within the two complexes, we find that all to all metric distances (not shown) increases in the right hand case, so trips are on average longer, but the effect is slight compared to the effect on all to all visual distances, which changes dramatically (shown in *Figure 24*). Showing visual integration – dark mean less visual distance as before - we see that the left case identifies a kind of main street with side and back streets, so an urban type structure has emerged. But the right case has lost both structure and degree of inter- visibility. Even though the changes are minor, it feels like a labyrinth. We can see where we are but not where we might be.

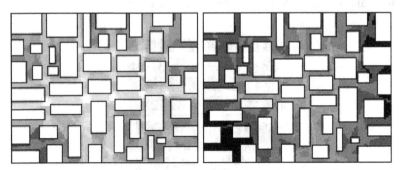

Fig. 24. Visual integration analysis (light is high, and so low visual distances from all points to all others) showing how non-urban layout on the loses both integration and structure through the slight block changes

The effect on computer agents moving around the system is striking, if obvious. In *Figure 25* we move 10000 computer agents with forward vision in the space, again using the software by Alasdair Turner (Turner 2002). The agents randomly select a target within their field of vision, move 3 pixels in that direction, then stop and repeat the process. On the left, the traces of agent movement 'find' the structure of visual integration. On the right, they wander everywhere and tend to get trapped in fatter spaces. This is an effect purely of the configuration, since everything else is identical.

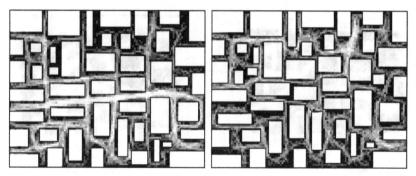

Fig. 25. Traces of 10000 forward looking agents moving nearly randomly in two slightly different configurations. Light means many traces, dark few.

But what about human beings? Human beings do not of course move randomly, but purposefully, and successful navigation in an unfamiliar environment would seem to depend on how good a picture of the whole pattern we can get from seeing it from a succession of points within it. One way we might plausibly measure this property is by correlating the size of the visual field we can see from each point with the visual integration value (its visual distance from all others), so in effect measuring the relation between a *local* property that we can see from each point, and a *non-local* one that we cannot see (*Figure 26*)

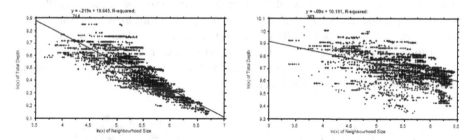

Fig. 26. Intelligibility scattergams for the two layouts in Figure 15

In space syntax this is called this the *intelligibility* of the system. The r2 for the 'intelligible' layout on the left is 0.714 while for the right case it is 0.267. Defined this way, the intelligibility of a spatial network depends almost entirely on its linear structure. Both field studies (Hillier et al 1987) and experiments (Conroy-Dalton 2001) suggest that this does work for humans. For example, Conroy Dalton took a linearised 'urban' type network (*Figure 27 left below*) and asked subjects to navigate in a 3D immersive world from left edge to 'Town Square' and back. As the traces show, they manage to find reasonable routes. But she then moved the (identical) blocks slightly to break the linear structure and reduce intelligibility (*Figure 27 right below*), and repeated the experiment. The subjects found the modified layout labyrinthine and many wandered all over the system trying to perform the same way-finding task.

Fig. 27. Trace of human agents navigating in an intelligible (left) and unintelligible (right) layout

So if, coming back to our aggregative process, we modify it by requiring those adding cells to the system to avoid blocking a longer local line if they can block a shorter one (*Figure 28*, left) – we might call it a *preferential avoidance* rule ! - we find a layout emerges, which, while still not yet recognisably urban, approximates the mix of long and short lines we find in real systems (Hillier 2002). With the contrary rule — always block long lines (*Figure 28*, right) — we construct a labyrinth in which lines are of much more even length.

Fig. 28. A layout generated by a 'conserve longer lines' rule (left) and one generated by the inverse rule

5 A Lateral Theory of Spatial Agency

The *vertical* process of *spatial emergence* is then shaped by the *squaring law* though which the placing and shaping of objects in space creates emergent patterns, and this is why, simply to be intelligible to, and usable by, human beings, spatial networks must include enough long alignments, in proportion to the scale of the settlement itself Hillier 2002) The *lateral* process of *spatial agency* is then about the consequences of these emergent structures for the *functionality* of the system. As spatial emergence depends on a spatial law, so spatial agency depends on a spatio-functional law we call the law of *natural movement* (Hillier et al 1993): that other things being equal, the main determinant of movement rates in different parts of a network will be a function of the structure of the network itself.

To clarify this we may first reflect on human movement. Spatially speaking, every human trip is made up of two elements: an origin-destination pair—every trip is from an origin space to a destination space—we can call this the *to-movement* component; and the spaces passed through on the way from origin to destination—we can call this the *through-movement* component. It is exactly these two elements of movement, which are captured in the closeness (integration) and betweenness (choice) measures. Integration measures the accessibility of nodes as destinations from origins, so from the principle of distance decay (and other things being equal), we must statistically expect more movement potential for nodes that are closer to all others at some radius. Likewise, since choice measures the sequence of segments we pass through so we must expect a similar bias in real movement. In effect integration measures the to-movement, and choice the through-movement, potential of spaces and since we have used these to measure movement potentials of both kinds in urban networks, it would be surprising if these potential did not to some degree reflect real movement flows.

But this will depend on how people calculate distances in complex spatial networks, and this is a question, much discussed in the cognitive literature (for example Winter 2002, Timpf et al 1992, Hochmair & Frank 2002, Conroy-Dalton 2003, Duckham & Kulik 2003, Golledge 1995, Montello 1992, 1997, Sadalla 1980, Duckham, Kulik & Worboys 2003, Kim & Penn 2004) All three measure of distance used in DepthMap - shortest paths, fewest turns, paths and least angle change have all been canvassed. But in (Hillier & Iida 2005) we suggest this can be resolved by correlating real flows with the spatial values produced in DepthMap by the three different definitions of distance. Accordingly, we applied the three weightings to the two measures of to and through movement potentials to make six different analyses of the same urban system, and correlated the resulting patterns of values for each segment with observed movement flows on that segment (Tables 1, 2), arguing that if across cases there were consistently better correlations with one or other weighting, then the only logical explanation would be that this weighting reflects better how people are biasing spatial movement choices, since everything else about the system is identical. In fact, across four separate studies in areas of central London, we consistently found that geometric, or least angle weightings yields the strongest movement prediction, with an average of around 0.7 for vehicular movement and 0.6 for pedestrian, closely followed by the topological or fewest turns weighting. Metric shortest paths are markedly inferior in most cases, and in general, to-movement potentials are slightly stronger than through- movement potentials, though this varies from case to case. (Hillier & Iida 2005)

Table 1. 2. Showing r2 values for observed movement and spatial values

VEHICULAR MOVEMENT r² values for correlations between vehicular flows and shortest path, least angle and fewest turns analysis applied to accessibility and choice measures. Best correlations are marked *. Numbers in brackets indicate best radius in segments for accessibility measures.

	Gates	Measure	Least Length	Least angle	Fewest turns
BARNSBURY	116	accessibility	.131(60)	.678(90)	.698(12)
		choice	.579	.720*	.558
CALTHORPE	63	accessibility	.095(93)	.837*(90)	.819(69)
		choice	.585	.773*	.695
SOUTH KEN	87	accessibility	.175(93)	.688(24)	.741*(27)
		choice	.645	.629	.649
BROMPTON	90	accessibility	.084(81)	.692*(33)	.642(27)
		choice	.475	.651*	.588

PEDESTRIAN MOVEMENT r² values for correlations between pedestrian flows and shortest path, least angle and fewest turns analysis applied to accessibility and choice measures. Best correlations are marked *. 'a' or 'c' for combined multiple values indicates whether accessibility or choice is dominant. Numbers in brackets indicate best radius for accessibility measures.

	Gates	Measure	Least length	Least angle	Fewest turns
BARNSBURY	117	accessibility	.119(57)	.719*(18)	.701(12)
		choice	.578	.705	.566
CALTHORPE	63	accessibility	.061(102)	.637(39)	.624*(36)
		choice	.430	.544*	.353
SOUTH KEN	87	accessibility	.152(87)	.523*(21)	.502(15)
		choice	.314	.457	.526*
BROMPTON	90	accessibility	.111(81)	.623*(63)	.578(63)
		choice	.455	.513*	.516

Once the law of natural movement is understood, it is clear that the link between the network configuration and movement flows is the key to the *lateral* dynamics and evolution of the system. Because the network shapes movement, it also over time shapes land use patterns, in that movement-seeking land uses, such as retail, migrate to locations which the network has made movement-rich while others, such as residence, tend to stay at movement-poor locations. This creates multiplier and feedback effects through which the city acquires its universal dual form as a foreground network of linked centres and sub-centres at all scales set into a background network of residential space. Through its impact on movement, the network has set in train the self- organising processes by which collections of buildings become living cities.

A key element of this will be the formation of centres and sub centres on something like the following lines. Every centre has a centre. Each centre starts with a spatial seed, usually an intersection, but it can be a segment. The seed of a centre will have *destination* and *route* values at both local and global levels. Some - usually small - centres start because they are the focus of a local intensified grid – a local case – others because they are at an important intersection – a global case. Both global and local properties are relevant to how centres form and evolve. The spatial values of the seed for the centre will establish what we can all a *fading distance* from the seed, which defines the distance from the seed up to which e.g. shops will be viable. This is a function of metric distance from the seed proportionate to the strength of the seed. The centre will grow beyond the fading distance established by the initial seed to the degree that further seeds appear within the fading distance, which reinforce the original seed. Again these can be local or global, and stronger or weaker. A centre becomes larger to the degree that it is reinforced by what are, in effect, new seeds created by the grid, which allow the shopping to be continuous.

Centres then expand in two ways: linearly and convexly. Linear expansion, the most common case, will be along a single alignment or two intersecting alignments, and occurs when the reinforcers are more or less orthogonal or up to 45 degrees to the original alignment or alignments. Convex expansion will be when the shopping streets form a localised grid, and this occurs when reinforcers occur on the parallel as well as the orthogonal alignment. So centres vary in the strength of their local and global properties and reinforcers, and the balance between them will tend to define the nature of the centre. Most centres will be in some sense strong in both in local and global terms, but differences in the balance between local and global will be influential in generating the scale and character of the centre. Centres also grow or fail through interaction with neighbouring centres at different scales, and some potential locations for centres fail to be realised due to the existence of a centre close by, but the way in which the urban grid evolves tends to ensure that seeds for potential centres occur only at certain distances from each other.

6   The Dual City of Economic and Social Forces

Building on the *vertical* process, then, the *lateral* process is the means through which economic and social forces put their different imprints on the city. The foreground structure, the network of linked centres, has emerged to maximise grid-induced movement, driven by micro-economic activity. Micro-economic activity takes a universal spatial form and this type of foreground pattern is a near-universal in self-organised cities. The residential background network is configured to restrain and structure movement in the image of a particular culture, and so tends to be culturally idiosyncratic, often expressed through a different geometry which makes the city as a whole look spatially different. We call the first the *generative* use of space since it aims to generate co-presence and make new things happen, and the second *conservative* since it aims to use space to reinforce existing features of society. In effect, the dual structure has arisen through different effects of the same laws governing the emergence of grid structure and its functional effects. In the foreground space is more random, in the background more rule governed, so with more conceptual intervention.

We can illustrate this most clearly in a city with more than one culture (now unfortunately separated): Nicosia *Figure 29*. Top right is the Turkish quarter, bottom left the Greek quarter. Their line geometry is different. In the Turkish quarter, lines are shorter, their angles of incidence have a different range, and there is much less tendency for lines to pass through each other. Syntactically, the Turkish area is much less integrated than the Greek area. We can also show that it is less intelligible, and has less synergy between the local and global aspects of space. Yet in spite of these strong cultural differences in the tissue of space, we still find Nicosia as a whole is held together by a clear deformed wheel structure. This shows how micro-economic activity spatialises itself in a universal way to maximise movement and co-presence, while residence tends to be reflect the spatial dimension of a particular culture, and the expression is in the first instance geometrical. Since residence is most of what cities are, this 'cultural geometry' tends to dominate our spatial impressions of cities.

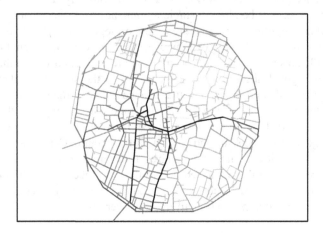

Fig. 29. The old city of Nicosia (left) and its integration analysis, showing the deformed wheel core in spite of culturally differentiated residential space

7   The Vertical and Lateral Processes as a Simplexity-Complicity Duo

We see then that the form of the city and its characteristically urban functional patterns emerges from the *vertical* process of *form emergence* and the *lateral* process of *function emergence*. This is why in self-organised cities; things always seem to be in the right place. It is in the nature of the evolutionary processes through which cities acquire their spatial and functional form. But it is also clear that the vertical and lateral processes form a *simplexity-complicity duo* in the Cohen- Stewart sense. The low-level, step by step, aggregation of buildings, with the requirement that they be linked to continuous pattern of space, form an emergent pattern of space with its own independent structure – a *simplexity* -, and this independent structure, without regard for the complexities of its creation then shapes the spatial relation between economic and social processes, which have their own internal dynamics, but which become spatialised in the city through the movement law, so constituting a *complicity* formed by the interaction of socio- economic and spatial processes.

As we have seen, both the vertical, or simplexity, and the lateral, or complicity, processes are articulated through the intervening medium of spatial and spatio-functional laws. We see this in the fact that only a very small class of spatial forms are created by cities, a vanishingly small proportion of the possible forms that could be constructed with the same raw materials. This is all the more surprising if we bear in mind that almost all large scale random aggregates produced by the 'basic generative process' I described, are labyrinths, and labyrinths are nowhere found in cities, although we sometimes like to imagine that they are. On the contrary, cities tend towards an improbably high level of integration and intelligibility, and do so through the dual structure, which arises in the first instance from the distribution of line lengths. We can be in no doubt about this, because all cities exhibit dual structures related to the line length distribution, and in all cases the relation to functional processes is of the same kind. Cities are highly improbable forms, but of the same generic kind.

Since the astonishingly tight set of regularities that render cities non-labyrinthine are all expressions of the same basic laws of space, and all the actions that create cities are taken by human beings, it is hard to avoid the inference that the mechanism through which the laws of space reach the spatial form of the city is the human mind, and that this implies that human beings in general understand the laws of space. In fact careful observation of human behaviour easily shows that we do intuitively know the laws of space. Consider this. A group of people is sitting in armchairs in my daughter's flat. My two year old grandson comes into the room with two balloons attached to weights by two pieces of string about two and a half feet long, so that the balloons are at about head height for the sitting people. Looking mischievous, he places the balloons in the centre of the space defined by the armchairs. After a minute or two, thinking he has lost interest, one of the adults moves the balloons from the centre of the space to the edge. My grandson, looking even more mischievous, walks over to the balloons and places them back in the centre of the room. Everyone understands intuitively what is going on, including you. But what is actually happening? What my grandson knows is that by placing an object in the centre of a space, it creates more obstruction from all points to all others in that space than if the object is placed anywhere else. In this way, he seeks to draw attention to himself, so that people will interact with him rather than each other. In other words, at the age of two Freddie knows the laws of space and can use them to achieve social objective.

Or consider the politics of table shapes. If you take a simple shape, fill it with a fine grid and measure the distance from the centre point of each grid square to the centre point of all other grid squares, the mean distance from central locations to all others is less than those of edge or corner locations. We make the pattern clear by colouring low mean distances in red through to blue for high, using the same range in all cases. As we elongate the object, keeping area constant, we can see that mean distances increase, but the general centre to edge pattern is conserved. If we look at the first elongation process, we find that although the overall shape has higher mean distances, the mean distance in the centre of the long side is for a while less than in the centre of the sides in the square shape. This is lost as we elongate more. So there is a certain point in the elongation of a square to a rectangular shape at which an optimal – in the sense of closer to all other points - edge location is created. It is this simple mathematical fact that is exploited in what we might call the politics of tables shapes, as in the next image.

But this evidence of the intervention of human minds, knowledgeable of laws, in the processes of creating cities is circumstantial. We can find much more direct evidence for the intervention of minds in the lateral process through which the grid shapes movement and through this the overall functional patterns of the city. The fact that movement patterns reflect the objective distribution of least angle integration and choice in the system has clear implications. In choosing routes through the urban network, and so in all likelihood estimating distances, people must be using some kind of mental model of the urban grid involving geometric and topological elements, and since urban space can only be experienced as a set of discrete experiences, either of places or routes, these must then be synchronised into a larger scale pattern for this model to be formed. However, this is exactly the process described by cognitive sciences in moving from knowledge of routes to map-like knowledge (or 'survey' as they call it). So here we see that this kind of knowledge in human minds, by shaping movement patterns through the network, is shaping the emergent functional patterns in the city itself.

In other words, the key mechanism by which the vertical and lateral processes are linked is actually the human mind itself – in effect, all of us, taking decisions about how to move in the city. This in turn leads to another unavoidable conclusion: that because movement patterns reflect the large scale geometrical and topological structure of the network and not the local properties of space, the human mind is actually the means through which cities are created bottom up by the aggregation of building and spaces, but function top-down through the influence of the larger scale grid on movement patterns. And the mechanism, by which this remarkable reversal takes place, at the moment when the vertical process first engages the lateral process, is the human mind itself. The vertical-lateral process, which creates the city, is then indecipherable without this knowledge of the intervention of human minds.

8   The Objective Subject

The proper theoretical conclusion of these explorations is, I believe, that the human cognitive subject is at its heart of the vertical and lateral processes that create the city, not simply in the sense of a series of real historical individuals located at specific points in time and space, but in terms of the invariance of the cognitive apparatus that those historical individual bring to the task of creating the city. We are talking in effect of a generalised individual located at all points in time and space in the city and everywhere imposing its cognitive apparatus on the ambient city. We might call this generalised individual the *objective subject* of the city creating process, and therefore of the city.

If, then, it is the case that the city has an objective subject which plays a critical role both in the 'vertical' form-creating process by which the accumulation of built forms creates an emergent spatial pattern, and in the 'lateral' form-function processes by which the emergent spatial pattern shapes movement and sets off the process by which an aggregate of buildings becomes a living city, then what does this imply for our paradigms of the city? The field is broadly split between the social physics paradigm, which seeks to understand the formation of the physical city as the product of spatialised economic processes, and the humanistic or phenomenological paradigm, which seeks to understand the city through our direct experience of it. The social physics view is essentially a mathematical view of the city, while the phenomenological view more or less precludes mathematics. The effect is to create paradigms, which are as irreconcilable methodologically as they are theoretically. The split is made to appear natural by the way we conceptualise our field meta-theoretically as being about the relations between environments simply as material objects and human beings as experiencing 'subjects'.

If the argument in this paper corresponds in any sense to what really happens in cities, then it is clear that environmental 'objects' and human 'subjects' are deeply entangled with each other, with the 'subjective' appearing in the 'objective' world as much as the objective world appears in the human subject. Nor is it the case that the object side of the urban system can be dealt with mathematically and the subject side only qualitatively. The fact that the city is shaped by the human cognitive subject does not lessen its mathematical content since the cognitive processes by which the subject intervenes reflect mathematical laws (Hillier 2005, 2007). We cannot understand the generation of the material form of the city without understanding the formal aspects of the cognitive subject's role in shaping the city, nor understand the experience of the city without knowledge of the formal shape the city acquires under the influence of cognitive subjects.

It follows that we cannot progress while the paradigm split remains. Space syntax was originally created to try to find links between the two previously irreconcilable domains of the city, the city of people and the city of things, hence the 'social' logic of space. The project for space syntax research must now be to engage with the problematic of both the mathematical and humanistic paradigms in the hope and expectation that by finding how each is present in the other we will progress towards synthesis (Hillier 2005). It could also be instructive for the study of human- mediated complex systems in general, not excluding society itself (see Hillier 2010).

References

1. Carvalho, R., Penn, A.: Scaling and universality in the microstructure of urban space. Physica A 332, 539–547 (2004)
2. Cohen, J., Stewart, I.: The Collapse of Chaos. Viking, Penguin (1994); Conroy, R.: Spatial Navigation in Immersive Virtual Environments PhD thesis University of London (UCL) (2000); Conroy Dalton, R.: The secret is to follow your nose: route path selection and angularity. Environment and Behavior 35, 107–131 (2003)
3. Duckham, M., Kulik, L.: "Simplest" Paths: Automated Route Selection for Navigation. In: Kuhn, W., Worboys, M.F., Timpf, S. (eds.) COSIT 2003. LNCS, vol. 2825, pp. 169–185. Springer, Heidelberg (2003)
4. Duckham, M., Kulik, L., Worboys, M.F.: Imprecise navigation. Geoinformatica 7, 79–94 (2003)
5. Golledge, R.G.: Path Selection and Route Preference in Human Navigation: a Progress Report. In: Frank, A.U., Kuhn, W. (eds.) COSIT 1995. LNCS, vol. 988, pp. 207–222. Springer, Heidelberg (1995)
6. Hillier, B., Hanson, J.: The Social Logic of Space. Cambridge University Press, Cambridge (1984)

7. Hillier, B., et al.: Natural movement: or configuration and attraction in urban pedestrian movement. Environment & Planning B: Planning & Design 19 20, 29–66 (1993)
8. Hillier, B.: Space is the Machine. Cambridge University Press, Cambridge (1996)
9. Hillier, B.: The hidden geometry of deformed grids: or, why space syntax works, when it looks as though it shouldn't. Environment and Planning B: Planning and Design 26(2), 169–191 (1999)
10. Hillier, B.: A theory of the city as object. Urban Design International 7, 153–179 (2002); Hillier, B., Penn, A.: Rejoinder to Carlo Ratti. Environment & Planning B: Planning and Design 31, 501–511 (2004)
11. Hillier, B., Iida, S.: Network and Psychological Effects in Urban Movement. In: Cohn, A.G., Mark, D.M. (eds.) COSIT 2005. LNCS, vol. 3693, pp. 475–490. Springer, Heidelberg (2005)
12. Hillier, B.: Spatial sustainability: organic patterns and sustainable forms. Keynote paper to the Seventh Space Syntax Symposium, Stockholm (2009)
13. Hillier, B.: What do we need to add to a social network to get a society? answer: something like what we have to add to a spatial network to get a city. Journal of Space Syntax 1, 1 (2010)
14. Hochmair, H., Frank, A.U.: Influence of estimation errors on way finding-decisions in unknown street networks — analyzing the least-angle strategy. Spatial Cognition and Computation 2, 283–313 (2002)
15. Kim, Y.O., Penn, A.: Linking the spatial syntax of cognitive maps to the spatial syntax of the environment. Environment and Behavior 36, 483–504 (2004)
16. Montello, D.R.: The Geometry of Environmental Knowledge. In: Frank, A.U., Campari, I., Formentini, U. (eds.) GIS 1992. LNCS, vol. 639, pp. 136–152. Springer, Heidelberg (1992)
17. Montello, D.R.: The Perception and Cognition of Environmental Distance. In: Hirtle, S.C., Frank, A.U. (eds.) COSIT 1997. LNCS, vol. 1329, pp. 297–311. Springer, Heidelberg (1997)
18. Sadalla, E.K., Burroughs, W.J., Staplin, L.J.: Reference points in spatial cognition. Journal of Experimental Psychology: Human Learning and Memory 6, 516–528 (1980)
19. Timpf, S., Volta, G.S., Pollock, D.W., Frank, A.U., Egenhofer, M.J.: A Conceptual Model of Way Finding Using Multiple Levels of Abstraction. In: Frank, A.U., Campari, I., Formentini, U. (eds.) GIS 1992. LNCS, vol. 639, pp. 348–367. Springer, Heidelberg (1992)
20. Turner, A.: Depthmap, v2.11 (computer program) UCL', London (2002); introduced in Turner, A.: Depthmap: a program to perform visibility graph analysis. In: Proceedings of the Third International Symposium on Space Syntax 2001, Atlanta, GA, pp. 31.1–31.9 (2001)
21. Turner, A., Penn, A., Hillier, B.: An algorithmic definition of the axial map. Environment and Planning B: Planning and Design 32(3), 425–444 (2005)
22. Turner, A.: Angular analysis. In: Proceedings of the Third International Space Syntax Symposium, pp. 30.1– 30.11. Georgia Institute of Technology, Atlanta (2001)
23. Winter, S.: Modelling costs of turns in route planning. GeoInformatica 6, 345–360 (2002)

Technology-Augmented Changes in the Design and Delivery of the Built Environment

Martin Riese

Partner, Front
mriese@frontinc.com

Abstract. The evolution of integrated design and delivery processes combined with the adoption of various emerging building lifecycle information management technologies is steadily bringing measurable improvements to the industry of the built environment. Not only is this increasing the efficiency and the quality of project outcomes, but it is enabling substantial new possibilities for innovation in design and delivery. This chapter explores some of the areas of interest, the highlights and the new possibilities brought about by the adoption of these new technologies and working practices in design and construction.

Keywords: Building Lifecycle Information Management, Automation in Design and Fabrication, Information Technology as an Enabler of Sustainable Development.

1   Introduction

"One of the principal ways in which modern societies generate new value is through projects which create physical assets that can then be exploited to achieve social and economic ends – factories for manufacturing goods, offices and shops for delivering services, hospitals for health care and tunnels for transport. Societies even create assets that are exploited largely for symbolic purposes, such as opera houses and cathedrals. In a typical modern society, around half of all physical asset creation (fixed capital formation) is the responsibility of the construction industry, thereby generating around 10% of national wealth (gross domestic product). These figures are much higher for rapidly developing countries. The creation of these assets is the principle force in the dynamics of cities and change in the built environment and, therefore, one of the major sources of social and economic change."[1]

The evolution of integrated design and delivery processes combined with the adoption of various emerging building lifecycle information management technologies is steadily bringing measurable improvements to the industry of the built environment. Traditional industry practices employing 2 dimensional paper-driven design and delivery methods are being replaced by 3 dimensional internet-based building lifecycle information and knowledge management processes that integrate and improve many key aspects of the design and delivery processes. This enables enhanced efficiencies, improved project outcomes, and dramatic new possibilities for

S. Müller Arisona et al. (Eds.): DUMS, CCIS 242, pp. 49–69, 2012.
© Springer-Verlag Berlin Heidelberg 2012

innovation that are helping to drive the evolution of a new global language of architecture. This chapter explores some of the specific highlights of the emerging technology-driven design and building processes.

The power of the sketch has long been one of the architect's primary and most powerful tools for exploring and communicating ideas at any level of development. Emerging technologies combine the same potentially subjective possibilities of the beginnings of a design sketch with the necessary precision of delivery. Just as in a sketch, new possibilities are not eliminated until they have to be, therefore retaining the explorative power of the sketch at the very beginning of the fabrication process.

2   Preliminary Design

The preliminary design process seeks to appropriately integrate vast amounts of project information and industry knowledge to create an initial design intent that is ready for further development towards delivery. The degree to which technology influences the preliminary design process varies from project to project, and it can manifest itself at this stage in a number of ways. The efficient exploration of complex, large scale abstract geometry can be automated and combined at an early stage with knowledge-based attributes and parametric generative rule sets that integrate various engineering, cost and delivery objectives for the project. This semi-automated process implies that fabrication, delivery and lifecycle performance information is already present in the initial considerations of the design. "Design for fabrication" is common place in other industries and is increasingly influencing the evolution of the built environment.

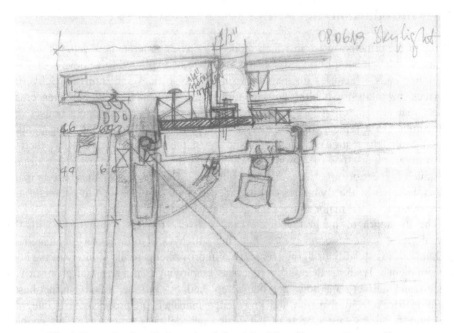

Fig. 1. Example of preliminary hand sketch by Marc Simmons, Partner, Front

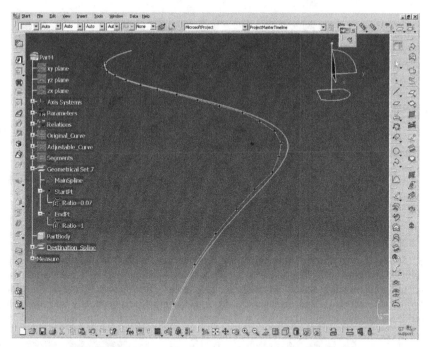

Fig. 2. Front defining plan sketch of LSS project elevation drives the entire façade BIM directly - all the way to CNC fabrication

Fig. 3. In this image created by the Laboratory for Explorative Architecture & Design, the building structure is generated automatically according to a rich rule set that is driven by geometric, spatial and engineering parameters. Hundreds of options driven by many variables can be generated quickly and reviewed by the project designers. The relatively effortless iterative exploration of large scales and complexities using fabrication-friendly data often yields fascinating results that would be unimaginable without the use of this technology.

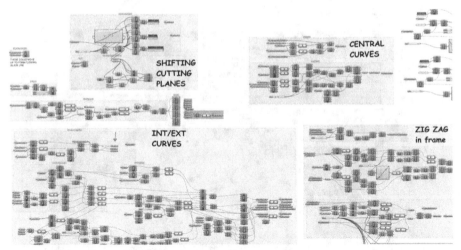

Fig. 4. This is a portion of the script that generated the model of the structure in Fig. 3. Logically and graphically improved user interfaces are beginning to make powerful advanced computing functionality accessible to a larger user group. This increase in the power of design information exploration and management tools will continue exponentially and the seamless interface with fabrication and delivery will become increasingly integral to that toolset.

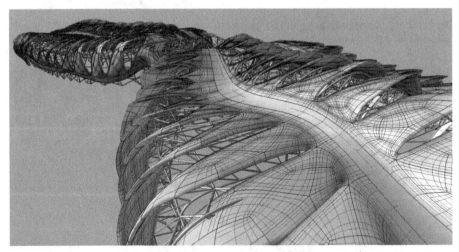

Fig. 5. Illustrated here is an example of how the preliminary design exploration of the building skin can be directly connected to the separate process of the exploration of building structure. This image produced by Dylan Baker Rice at Affect_t, shows how a different collaborator can contribute another element of the project to a central project model over the internet. The analysis of building structure is still predominantly reduced to the management of static centerline forces, and although the form may be driven by abstract, non-uniform ideas, these are all too often not initially sufficiently generated by driving engineering considerations. Using the BIM model as a common knowledge sharing and management platform, engineers and architects can progress the design together in the same environment. The aggregate power of various software solutions can be brought to bear simultaneously on the same model, which in itself opens up new possibilities for innovation.

The building skin may be more readily adaptable to abstract forms. The mode of delivery of these forms is more easily explored and integrated into the design using automation techniques. Fabrication and delivery rules can already be introduced as defining parameters at this early stage.

"Digitization of both design and building methods are the key problems of the day for architects and builders. Our technologists and programmers will succeed in inventing highly inclusive digital design methods which will be built using Computer Numerically Controlled (CNC) machines.

Today's design tools bring elements that were reserved to the functionalist province of the engineer and fabricator into the realm of architects at the earliest conceptual stages of the design process. Highly intuitive graphic interfaces provide direct and real-time feedback of physical, structural and environmental performance from the very start. This close integration of a design's performativity aspects allows for a responsible use of resources and reinstates the architect in his role as creative director of a multi-disciplinary design team.

Where today customizable parts are made in automated factories ("file-to-factory") and work on site consists of their pre-programmed assemblage at high speed, soon fabrication will happen directly and entirely on site in a fully integrated "file-to-site" process. This will not only reduce building cost: it will allow for the emergence of a new architectural language previously thought unpractical or uneconomical – a language which mode of conception shifts towards the procedural design of system logics.

Computer augmented design processes provide the architect nimbleness in creatively tackling today's design challenge where projects demand unprecedented construction speed, scale, and complexity.

Only when the methods of our time are fully integrated into the design process and the architect takes hold of the unprecedented control they bring back into his realm, can this new architecture come to its own." - Kristof Crolla, *Laboratory for Explorative Architecture & Design.*[11]

"The design of the roof shell is the result of a highly iterative exchange and integration process between the functional requirements of the brief and a desired aesthetic affect. The intent of the process was to bring about a type of mimesis of the biological through the efficiency of the digital. However, the parallels between digital and biological run deeper than merely the formal outcome. The process of design itself evolved as numerous environmental triggers and responses shaped what seemed to be an eventuality more than pre-determined aim. To some extent this can be said of all design processes, but in this particular case the project team had initial ideas about what the building required that were nevertheless accompanied with genuine surprise with how the final design looked.

The building began with the notion of a light weight skin stretched over a structural system; an outcome that the project team wanted to achieve because of the cost of raw materials and construction, transit, and the carbon footprint. The constraints of passive cooling, ventilation and day-lighting created the need for a porous skin which needed to be highly calibrated to the particular climate of Hong Kong and Shenzhen. Analytical models of the site were constructed using various programs such as "Ecotect". This narrowed the focus of the technical aim providing the team with a more specific design goal; a building that is both flooded with natural light and yet open enough to feel as if the occupants were not in a building. These constraints were merged with the idea of a light-weight structure and the first sketch models and drawings quickly focused on a shell structure.

The evolutionary process of the digital started with iterative attempts to bring the gestural qualities of the sketch and feelings of movement and change to the surface of the building. Blending the pedestrian and vehicular movement through its skin or surface created a notational building not unlike the Library of Henri Labrouste, in which the exterior would allow one to read or at least infer the purpose of the interior. Utilizing, first fluid dynamics with "nurbs modeling" in "Maya" software, and later "subdivisions modeling" in Maya, computer models were constructed which had aspects of dynamism and interpenetrating spaces but none of the precision and rigor that made the skin feel like it was more than a crude sketch for covering a steel superstructure. As holes were punched and the surface became increasingly a minimal mathematically defined surface, the model became more complex. Simplifying construction of the small scale elements worked to add depth to the overall object as variation became more discernable and the light scoops acted as a field instead of singular entities.

Perhaps the small Eureka moment where it took on its own logic was when the day lighting apertures became analogous to funnels, and then jet-engines, and then the air-intakes on a muscle car, becoming ever more evocative with subtle changes. The evolutionary moment in the design process took over and the surface came into being or achieved a sort of critical complexity in which it began to create its own logic and constraints rather than simply responding.

The question that the design team struggled with in its collaborative process was whether to be man or machine. The question was whether to set up a free running scripted program or to model iterations through manual process. In the end the team selected a hybrid of the two. Sometimes "gesture" was more important as in the Maya modeling of the lighting scoops, but alternatively the structure and organization of the field needed to have the rigor best achieved through scripted variations. What was most critical was the team's decision in judging which method of making is the best-fit for each particular task and what needs to go into the process of making or design that will allow a sort of micro-ecology where the thing which is being made takes on its own agency and aids in determining what it should be. Ultimately the team was seeking a result that was not predetermined, and was more than the sum of its constituent parts." – Dylan Baker-Rice, Principal, Affect_t.[12]

3   Design Development

The commonly used formal titles of project stages continue to delineate the phases of the actual development of the design. As the project evolves beyond the scheme design phase the cost to the stakeholder of the collaborative process increases proportionally. Stakeholders are called upon to make substantial financial commitments to progress the design beyond this point, and therefore they need to be able to make adequately informed decisions about the course of the project.

The role of information technology and automation at this stage of a project is to expand the exploration and documentation of the information about the design towards the objective of reasonable certainty of cost and deliverability. The ultimate objective of this phase of the project is to prepare the necessary information to secure the parties that will deliver the project - at an agreed cost. All of the elements of the design have cost and delivery time attributes directly associated with them in the BIM model in this phase, and that increases project cost certainty and reduces risk. A direct link between project geometry and time management tools helps project teams to determine and optimize an initial delivery sequence strategy.

This is the point when the power of machine automation starts to improve the efficiency and accuracy with which the increasing amount of information is managed. In the past, this is the stage in which aggregate human errors resulting from the collaborative process itself, used to start to cause cost and time penalties on projects. It was simply humanly impossible to track so much information manually, but mechanized information management strategies can not only handle the information, they can enhance the outcome of the process. The kaleidoscopic ease with which computers manipulate information and knowledge frees up large amounts of human time to do other things.

With the adoption of automated information management technologies comes the possibility to formally engage and integrate *mathematics* – with all of its beauty and ability to explore complexity – and with its limitless *possibilities*. One of the many useful applications of mathematics is the inherent ability to analyze and optimize geometry. "The realization of freeform shapes in architecture poses great challenges to engineering and design. The complete design and construction process involves many aspects, including form finding, feasible segmentation into panels, functionality, materials, statics and cost. Geometry alone is not able to provide solutions for the entire process, but a solid geometric understanding is an important step toward a realization of such a project. In particular, it is essential to know about the available degrees of freedom of shape optimization". [2]

4   Virtual Prototyping

Virtual prototyping involves the construction of a complete 3 dimensional representation of a project – including all of its information attributes – in the computer before the stakeholder commits to the procurement of the real thing. This brings the "try before you buy" philosophy that is prevalent in other industries, to the built environment.

"Architects and other designers inhabit a curious borderland between the virtual and the physical. They have always been concerned with conjuring up things that don't exist but might, imagining them in detail, and eventually finding ways to translate these visions into physical reality. Over the last half-century, computer-generated virtual worlds have played an increasingly crucial role in this process." [3]

Virtual prototyping adds value at all stages of a project – and with whatever information that is available at that time. The critical path of a project in the design phases is not as significantly influenced by virtual prototyping as it is by the generation of the design information itself. It is not disruptive, does not affect the critical path, and provides an ideal framework on which to organize the project. Virtual prototyping seeks to help to integrate all known aspects of the design at any given stage, but the actual formative decisions about the project are still made by the project team in collaboration with the stakeholder. The project team may include a constructability advisor from the onset, and that consultant could turn out to be the actual constructor of the project. The virtual prototype may be passed to the constructor at the time of the construction contract award and this further strengthens the bi-directional flow of information between design and the delivery. Ultimately the virtual prototype should be the only "contract document" governing the scope and cost of the project.

Some of the advantages of virtual prototyping are; improved 3 dimensional coordination of building elements earlier on, quicker and more accurate access to quantities and costs, automated production of 2 dimensional drawings, delivery sequence simulation and optimization, and lifecycle performance simulation. The optimization of the build sequence and lifecycle performance - necessarily - inform the preliminary design. The virtual prototype can also be used after completion for various facilities management purposes and the re-use of knowledge gained on the project. The rules that helped to define the virtual prototype can be automatically carried forward to the next project, making it a vehicle for knowledge management

Fig. 6. Actual Working Virtual Prototype of Barclay's Arena cladding produced by Front. This is the same paperless information that drives the fabrication and delivery process.

5   Integrated Coordination

"The traditional process for planning and designing facilities is under attack from many directions. Facility owners are tired of the waste and errors. The news media attack cost overruns and mismanagement of projects. Architects struggle with tight fees and standards of care that do not fairly assign risks and rewards. The attacks all spring from a process that has not adapted to changes in our society." [4]

Design professionals from all disciplines need to collaborate closely as a team to ensure that the project is coordinated optimally. Only an all-inclusive iterative coordination process can bring a building design to the status of "the whole is greater than the sum of the parts." Notwithstanding the sharing of information over the internet, face to face meetings are still the best forum in which to progress the coordination of the design. Everybody needs to take full responsibility for their own work. The integration of more project knowledge into the design earlier on in the process will result in a reduction in unknowns and cost and time penalties later on during the delivery.

The integration into the Building Information Modeling process of advanced analysis and simulation, enhanced supply chain engagement and reusable project knowledge during all phases of the project is increasingly unifying design and construction into a more singular process, thereby eliminating the inefficiencies that have traditionally compromised the industry.

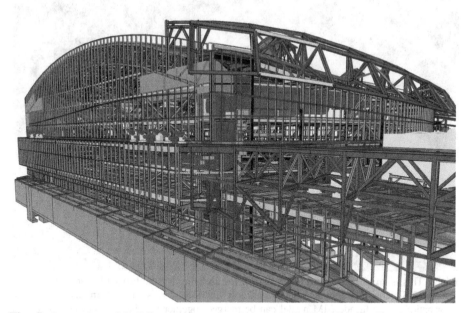

Fig. 7. Integration of building structure, services and cladding into a singular Building Information Model by the Barclay's arena project team. Different elements of the project have been modeled by the appropriate project team member and merged into a virtual prototype of the project. In the case of – at least - the structure and façade, this is fabrication level information which is also used to drive CNC machines and other automated manufacturing processes.

6   Design for Fabrication

Following are examples of Front projects that have evolved and progressed preliminary design information directly through to fabrication. Necessarily, the fabrication process demands sub-millimeter accuracy, and this has to be reconciled with the need for the progressive transition from broad initial concepts that do not require such accuracy. Emerging technologies and user interfaces are able to easily merge and carry along high levels of accuracy without imposing the kind of time penalties that sustaining this level of information would normally impose on humans. Technology brings to the process its strengths of performing millions of small and repetitive tasks accurately and quickly, leaving humans more time to make broader associations and decisions – based on the improved quality and quantity of global project information available. In fact, in its ideal implementation, technology helps humans to work better by performing tasks in a way that humans cannot. This is where the implementation of technology can yield exciting results that are simply not achievable without it.

The history of technology is full of examples of new tools yielding innovative and previously unimagined results, but with the new generation of lifecycle knowledge management technology, the entire process becomes empowered with the benefits of a purpose-conceived tool set.

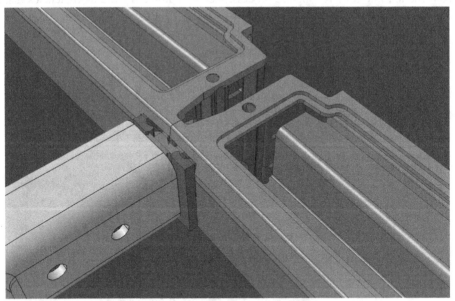

Fig. 8. This is an assembly that forms part of the cladding for the Front LSS project. Unlike discrete 2 dimensional drawings which can only be viewed in isolation from each other, the information in the façade BIM model can be merged together into hundreds of combinations, contexts and coordination forums, and can then also inform and drive the fabrication and delivery machinery. One of the key aspects of the management and delivery of the built environment is the culture of tolerances. BIM technology enables the appropriate and enhanced management of tolerances. Clash detection and fabrication tolerances can be specified and / or changed, coordinated or tested, thereby helping to bring under better control one of the traditional risks of fabrication and delivery.

Fig. 9. A key component of Front's DVF project in the final moments before it makes the transition from the façade BIM model into actual fabrication

Fig. 10. This image shows the moment in which the long line of DVF project representational design, exploration and coordination, makes the actual transition into the real world

7   Curtain Wall Lifecycle Modeling at Front Inc.

Neil Thelen is an architect who leads the BIM process for Front. Following is a summary written by Neil describing the role of automation and virtual prototyping at Front. "Front Inc. is a multi-disciplinary group of creative individuals with professional backgrounds in Architecture, Structural Engineering, and Mechanical Engineering. Front specializes in architectural facade systems for new construction including curtain wall, bespoke cladding systems, and the use of structural glass and related lightweight structures. With offices in Brooklyn, Hong Kong, San Francisco and Tacoma, Front has a dispersed network of client-facing facade consultants providing professional services to estate developers & owners, architects, contractors, and fabricators. Given that Front is a small consultancy with a high degree of specialization, the team often finds itself working on larger global aggregate project teams made up of other small businesses. An ever expanding digital toolkit benefits Front's agility and effectiveness within these teams, but digital tools are only effective to the extent that one can negotiate the political, legal, and cultural complexities of these project teams.

A unitized curtain wall is an engineered suite of structural framing members, connections and infill panels that are designed to fulfil architectural design intent while achieving performance benchmarks - effectively a parametric kit of parts. Notwithstanding widespread implementation of 3D & 4D BIM technologies, the curtain wall industry remains firmly entrenched in a paper-based world where facade consultancies provide a handful of typical 2D details and specifications, and the contractor builds to minimum standards for maximum profit. As "BIM evangelists" have been espousing for decades, this delivery method provides too much room for error, inefficiencies and redundancy, ultimately affecting the project's profitability and performance. It is ironic that while curtain wall manufacturing bears a superficial resemblance to other manufacturing sectors such as automotive or aerospace, it seems to be the least inclined to leverage advanced technologies for lifecycle management. This hesitation to embrace innovation originates at the industry's centres of profit - curtain wall contractors are not motivated to uproot a traditionally lucrative status quo.

It is clear that owners will see huge benefits from mandating BIM and lifecycle management technologies in the design, prefabrication, construction, and commissioning of curtain walls. The innovation necessary to realize these potentials will not come from the largest curtain wall contractors or consultancies. Instead, it will come from ad-hoc partnerships between owners, designers, and technology providers. As with other social movements and technological advances, the most powerful and disruptive innovation originates with grass-roots efforts.

Collaborative facade models with company-specific project standards, set-outs and exchange formats have been successfully developed and deployed within Front's project teams, primarily enabled by software produced by French solution provider Dassault Systemes. Libraries of facade-specific points, wires, and surfaces are designed as intelligent BIM objects representing structural framing members & infill panels. Each element is embedded with sets of tags or attributes that correspond to specific model views: architectural design and production, scheduling and construction logistics, structural analysis, environmental analysis, cost estimation, trade coordination, clash detection and delivery sequence optimization. Rule-based configurations of these elements are built to locate facade framing & infill. Automation routines "instantiate" (create instances) of these parametric templates which adjust to unique conditions based on variable inputs (mullion centrelines, anchor locations, sills, parapets, etc.) Concurrent with panel "instantiation," Front's templates and automation routines can output 2 dimensional assembly and part drawings for each unique unit, bills of materials, quantity take-offs, glazing schedules etc. Any measurable metric can be built into the templates and extracted during the instantiation process. Change is managed through server-based versioning software so that collaborators always have the most current version of the model for their own particular task. This digital chassis provides real-time access to detailed project information for the entire project team.

The specific scope of a project and level of detail required are driving factors in how this digital chassis is designed. Contracts distributed by the American Institute of Architects (AIA) that are specific to BIM modelling, provide useful guidelines to the level of detail required for specific project phases. BIM objects and automation routines can be specifically designed around these categories, corresponding to specific contractual deliverables. Additionally, organizations such as "buildingSmart Alliance" are actively developing standardized digital formats and exchange documents for the AEC industry, including building envelopes and curtain walls.

Technology-enabled management and distribution of coordinated sets of project information have resulted in innovative collaborations between Front and its clients, and it would be possible to design a workflow that accounted for every single stage of a curtain wall's lifecycle. However, it is highly unlikely that any single organization would ever control the entire process. Value is achieved in a competitive marketplace where various organizations are able to showcase their capabilities and submit bids for products and services. Forward-looking owners and developers are gradually starting to recognize that the ability of a particular bidder to truly collaborate with the project team's BIM model represents a significant value for the project. In this changing marketplace, companies that are able to participate with standards such as those developed by "buildingSmart" will have a huge market advantage.

This is especially true in the curtain wall industry. Large curtain wall contractors with standardized product offerings are able to deliver value through repetition and reuse. Design & engineering, testing, manufacturing, installation & servicing - nearly the full lifecycle of a curtain wall - are integrated and streamlined within a single organization, allowing them to offer a competitive product. However, emerging technologies are enabling smaller design and consulting organizations to control larger parts of this lifecycle to benefit owners and smaller businesses. This is invariably a good thing for the industry of the built environment and for the global economy - making the whole process more democratic and ultimately resulting in a better performing, more profitable product for building owners." [13]

8   Building Information Modeling Scale and Complexity

The scale and complexity of the information which defines typical building projects is normally very large. The rate of change of the influence of information technology on the management of the built environment is directly linked to the evolution of information technology itself. "Moore's Law" quantifies the rate of the evolution of information technology. Digital representation will always fit in, fully engage and normally exceed the available capacity to contain it. The more capacity that is available for representation, the larger and more complex the digital models will become. This trend toward exponential growth of BIM model size and detail is in itself a source of innovation. The ad-hoc philosophy of "because we can" increasingly influences innovation. One can now imagine that at some point in the not too distant future a unified model could be created that simulates the management of the entire urban built environment and even some aspects of the behaviors of society in it.

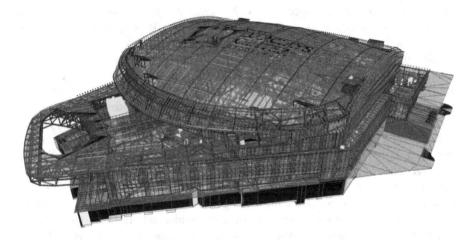

Fig. 11. This Image of the façade BIM model of the Barclay's stadium project in New York illustrates the level of scale and complexity of a typical modern building project. All elements of the building down to screw-hole chamfers are managed in the centralized BIM model.

9   Internet-Based Collaboration

Centralized internet-based project knowledge databases can contain all of the information about a project. The management of access to data, version control and project documentation are best managed over the internet ("on the cloud,") because it is the safest and most convenient place to store and access information. Technology vendors are increasingly offering the added value of wholly internet-based solutions. The technology can be maintained, continually updated and revised there, and usage can be tracked and paid for on a "pay as you go" basis.

Project team members and stakeholders can share real time access to the process of aggregating the knowledge about the project over a centralized database. As long as project team members regularly commit revised design and delivery information to the database, then the entire team has instant access to the most current state of the project. Previous versions can be restored and countless project metrics can be tracked and managed.

10   Integrated Supply Chain and Manufacturing

"Architecture requires control, deep control, not merely of an idea, but also of the stuff we use to give form to the idea. The architect has been much diminished in the now centuries-old splintering and segregation of the former role of master builder. Ironically, by narrowing its realm of significant interest to appearance only, architecture sacrificed control of its one remaining stronghold: appearance." [5]

Following are examples of actual Front projects in which the preliminary design has been informed and influenced by the actual supply chain that produced the projects. Substantial improvements in efficiency and new dimensions of innovation are available to the entire industry by working in this way.

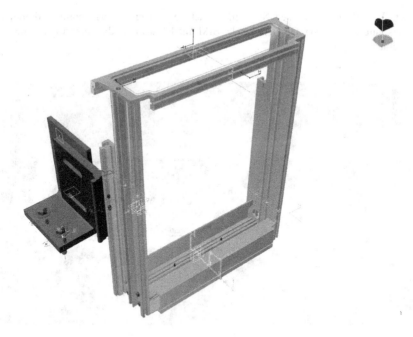

Fig. 12. This image shows a CNC produced part modeled by Front on the LSS project using Dassault Systemes' CATIA software. The part is modeled employing automation techniques that merge company experience, industry knowledge and design intent specific to the project.

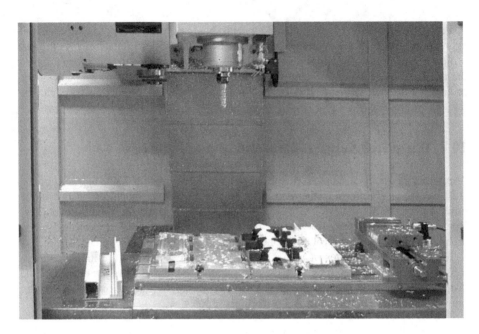

Fig. 13. This image shows the CNC milling machine producing actual coordinated production elements direct from the CATIA façade BIM model without the intermediary step of 2 dimensional drawings

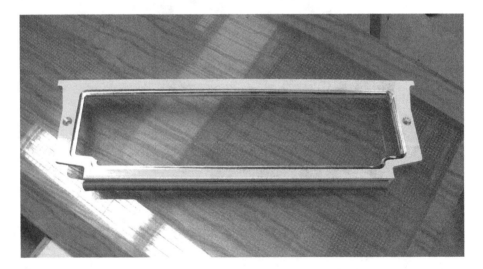

Fig. 14. The final LSS project façade production element produced by CNC milling straight from the BIM model

Fig. 15. The fabricated elements are then immediately tested to ensure that they are fit for purpose within the context of the overall system that they help to comprise

11   Building Lifecycle Knowledge Management

Information technology is a key enabler of overall building lifecycle knowledge management. As the granularity and sophistication of digital knowledge representation increases, it can surpass the representational capacity of any analog. One of the powers of digital representation is its ability to surpass analog representation in scale and complexity. The broadest mathematical potential becomes directly accessible to and applicable to representation that describes – and prescribes the real world that we wish to create. Ultimately, the human imagination itself becomes the only limitation to the boundaries of design and construction.

At this point, it is worth defining the words information and knowledge.

"Information, in its most restricted technical sense, is an ordered sequence of symbols that record or transmit a message. It can be recorded as signs, or conveyed as signals by waves. Information is any kind of event that affects the state of a dynamic system." [6]

"Knowledge is a familiarity with someone or something, which can include information, facts, descriptions, and/or skills acquired through experience or education. It can refer to the theoretical or practical understanding of a subject. It can be implicit (as with practical skill or expertise) or explicit (as with the theoretical understanding of a subject); and it can be more or less formal or systematic." [7]

"Technical progress in computing power, remote sensing technologies, computer-controlled production machinery, distributed computing, information exchange technologies, and other technologies will open new possibilities that software vendors will exploit to their own competitive advantage. Another technical area that may introduce further developments and that influence BIM systems is euphemistically referred to as *artificial intelligence*. BIM tools are convenient platforms for a renaissance of expert system developments for a range of purposes, such as code checking, quality reviews, intelligent tools for comparing versions, etc. design guides and design wizards. Many of these efforts are already underway but will take another decade to become standard practice. Information standardization is another driver for progress. Consistent definitions of building types, space types, building elements and other terminology will facilitate e-commerce and increasingly complex and automated workflows. It can also drive content creation and aid in the management and use of parametric building component libraries, both private and public. Ubiquitous access to information, including component libraries, makes the use of computable models more attractive for a wide variety of purposes." [8]

75 per cent of the cost of a building comes in its post-completion phase. Facilities management and asset management processes can be managed on the BIM infrastructure used during the design and delivery of a building. The possibility exists to standardize and inter-connect facilities management processes between individual buildings and larger portions of the urban environment. This would bring improved efficiencies on an urban scale.

The knowledge gained managing individual buildings and even entire cities could become available to inform preliminary designs. The effective management of the building lifecycle is a key element of overall sustainable development.

12   Sustainable Development Enabled by Information Technology

Information technology is a key enabler of sustainable development. By integrating and unifying the process of managing the information and knowledge underlying the lifecycle of the built environment, the entire outcome can be iteratively simulated, analyzed and optimized. Large scale outcomes can be tested before projects go beyond the design phase. Decisions of substantial impact can be informed by the result of reliable and fully calibrated tests of the final outcomes. This process accelerates the 'trial and error" nature of innovation and therefore – in combination with the other advantages of technology-augmented design and delivery – accelerates the evolution of innovation.

"Better and faster" have always been catch phrases associated with the advancement of technology. However, consensus on what is actually "better" does not always immediately follow on from the adoption of new technology. As the richness and sophistication of prototyping and testing increases proportionally with the adoption of new technologies and working practices, the ability to deliver outcomes that are measurably "better" will increase as well.

In particular, the move to increase engineering-informed or even engineering-led design and delivery will bring with it more measurable improvements in efficiency and "fit for purpose" outcomes. The emerging field of "design science" is a manifestation of the need to bring quantifiable calibration to the collaborative technology-augmented design and construction industry.

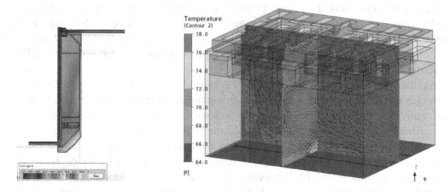

Fig. 16. The simplified iterative integration of case-specific engineering information into the preliminary design is the key to improved lifecycle performance outcomes in the evolution of the built environment. One of the key objectives of sustainable development is the fair and efficient distribution of energy and resources across the human population.   Information technology brings the power and precision of the machine to the task of managing vast, "super-human" amounts of information and resources.

13   Conclusion: The Future of the Technology-Augmented Design and Building Process

"The availability and rapid colonization of architectural design by computer-aided techniques presents the discipline with yet another opportunity to retool and re-think itself as it did with the advent of stereo-metric projection and perspective. If there is a single concept that must be engaged due to the proliferation of topological shapes and computer-aided tools, it is that in their structure as abstract machines, these technologies are animate." [9]

"The introduction of the concept of *autopoiesis* reflects the premise that the discipline of architecture can be theorized as a distinct *system of communications*. Autopoiesis means self-production. The concept was first introduced within biology to describe the essential characteristic of life as a circular organization that reproduces all its most specific necessary components out of its own life-process. This idea of living systems as self-making autonomous unities was transposed into the theory of social systems understood as systems of communications that build up and reproduce all their necessary, specific communication structures within their own self-referentially closed process. It is this total network of architectural communications, a gigantic, self-referentially closed parallel process, that is referred to in the title of the book: the *autopoiesis* of architecture is this overall, evolving system of communications". [10]

To some degree, the future of the design and building process is here now. As William Gibson said, "The future is already here, it's just unevenly distributed". Whilst there is no question that the generating kernel of the design process will continue to be human-centric, the integration of evolving technologies and working practices into the process will – in itself - increasingly influence and help to define design and construction.   The possibilities brought about by the automated exploration, optimization and management of the information underlying design, fabrication and delivery will increasingly and more quickly permeate back into preliminary design thinking. This can only happen – in part – as a result of some level of automation.

As the set of parameters that can be considered, coordinated and simulated increases in granularity and richness, more sophisticated possibilities can be explored and delivered.   Eventually, all of the resources available on the planet could incrementally be brought into the realm of the virtual prototype and managed in this way. Ultimately, the objective of managing the entire planet with a more equitable and sustainable distribution of wealth across the population will only be achievable through the adoption and further evolution of large scale information management technologies and with them - higher degrees of automation and even "machine intelligence".

What will appear to be almost magically self-perpetuating "automatisms" of entire knowledge patterns on an urban, even global scale – self-replicating, self-referencing and multiplying exponentially as they evolve, will be interconnected directly to infinitely sophisticated production chains that complete a helical logical connection back to the original "generating spark of human imagination," that will remain the ultimate driver of the entire process at every level. Assuming for the moment that nearly anything that we can imagine – and virtually prototype – can and will become real, we probably do need, as they say, to be careful about what we wish for.

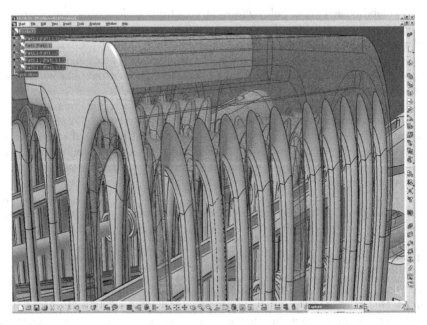

Fig. 17. Experimental Architectural Design for Fabrication – Martin Riese

Acknowledgments

11. From an e-mail text by Kristof Crolla, Laboratory for Explorative Architecture & Design (2011)
12. From an e-mail text by Dylan Baker-Rice, Affect_t (2011)
13. Section 7 was written by architect Neil Thelen, Front (2011)

References

1. Winch, G.M.: Managing Construction Projects An Information Processing Approach, 2nd edn., p. 3. John Wiley & Sons (2008)
2. Pottman, H., Asperl, A., Hofer, M., Kilian, A.: Architectural Geometry, p. 671. Bentley Institute Press (2007)
3. Mitchell, W.: Virtual Futures for Design, Construction and Procurement. Blackwell Publishing Limited edited by Peter Brandon and Tuba Kokaturk (2008)
4. Jernigan, F.E.: Big BIM Little BIM The Practical Approach to Building Information Modeling Integrated Practice done the right way! 4 Site Press (2007)
5. Timberlake, K.: Refabricating Architecture, p. 29. McGraw-Hill (2004)
6. http://en.wikipedia.org/wiki/Information
7. http://oxforddictionaries.com/view/entry/ m_en_us1261368#m_en_us1261368
8. Eastman, C., Teicholz, P., Sacks, R., Liston, K.: A Guide to Building Information Modeling for Owners, Managers, Designers, Engineers and Contrctors. John Wiley & Sons (2008)
9. Lynn, G.: Animate Form, p. 41. Princeton Architectural Press (1999)
10. Schumacher, P.: The Autopoiesis of Architecture. John Wiley & Sons Ltd., London (2010)

14   Image Credits

All images printed with the permission of Front except Images 3, 4, 5 and 17.
Image 3 & 4: printed with permission of Kristof Crolla, Laboratory for Explorative Architecture & Design.
Image 5: printed with permission of Dylan Baker Rice at Affect_t
Image 17: by Martin Riese, Front.

Part II

Parametric Models and Information Modeling

City Induction: A Model for Formulating, Generating, and Evaluating Urban Designs

José P. Duarte[1], José N. Beirão[1,2], Nuno Montenegro[1], and Jorge Gil[2]

[1] Technical University of Lisbon, Faculty of Architecture, Rua Sá Nogueira,
Pólo Universitário, Alto da Ajuda, 1349-055 Lisboa, Portugal
{jduarte,jnb,nmontenegro}@fa.utl.pt
[2] Delft University of Technology, Faculty of Architecture, P.O. Box 5043,
2600 GA Delft, The Netherlands
{J.N.Beirao,j.a.lopesgil}@tudelft.nl

Abstract. Urban planning and design have a considerable impact on the economic performance of cities and on the quality of life of the population. Efficiency at this level is hampered by the lack of integrated instruments for formulating, generating, and evaluating urban plans. This chapter describes the theoretical foundations of a research project, called *City Induction*, aimed at the creation of a model for the development of such an instrument, departing from existing theories, which are integrated through a discursive grammar. The proposed model is composed of three sub-models: (1) a model for formulating urban programs from the analysis and interpretation of the context, based on Alexander's pattern language; (2) a model for generating urban plans that match the program, based on Stiny's shape and description grammars; and (3) a model for evaluating urban plans, that can be used for analyzing, comparing and ranking alternative solutions, departing from Hillier's space syntax. A common urban space ontology guarantees the syntactic and semantic interoperability among the three sub-models. This ontology will be used to structure and codify information into a Geographic Information System (GIS), which will be the kernel for the computer implementation of the larger model. A CAD system is used to construct 3D models from contextual information stored in the GIS. In short, following Stiny and March's design machines concept, the goal is to create an urban design machine that is able to produce flexible urban plans at the site planning level.

Keywords: urban design, ontology, pattern language, shape grammars, space syntax, GIS, CAD.

1 Introduction

The growth of cities is a complex phenomenon, partially spontaneous and partially planned. There have been several attempts to uncover the laws that rule such a complexity. The underlying idea is if one understands these laws, one can control them to generate better urban environments, that is, environments that satisfy the needs of the community, have less socio-economic costs, and use less natural

S. Müller Arisona et al. (Eds.): DUMS, CCIS 242, pp. 73–98, 2012.

resources. In addition, recent developments in urban design theories point towards flexible design practices to increase the operability of urban planning. [1][2] The work described in this chapter is concerned with the development of a rule-based approach to urban design to support the development of sustainable and flexible urban plans.

In 1969, in his book 'The Sciences of the Artificial,' [3] Herbert Simon postulated that as natural sciences have successfully discovered the laws governing natural systems, it could be possible to uncover the laws underlying human design activity. Since then, an important part of design research has been devoted to uncover such laws. This effort is part of the endeavor to develop artificial intelligent (AI) systems. There are two approaches to AI, called weak and strong AI. The first defends the possibility of developing general problem-solving programs, whereas the second advocates the development of programs with intensive domain knowledge. Approaches to model urban growth and planning also fall into these categories. The publication in 1957 of Chomsky's work on natural languages grammars was very influential to the emergence of strong approaches to design. [4] According to Chomsky, a grammar consisted of a set of substitution rules that applied recursively to an initial assertion to produce a final statement. Influenced by Chomsky, in 1972 Stiny and Gips [5] proposed the idea of shape grammars. They were one of the earliest algorithmic systems for creating and understanding designs directly through computations with shapes, rather than indirectly through computations with symbols. In 1981, Stiny developed the concept of description grammars to address the semantic aspects of design. While in shape grammars [6] the assertions are shape descriptions, in description grammars they consist of symbolic descriptions. [7] Thus, the first deals with syntax and the second with semantics.

In 1981, in a paper called 'Design Machines', [8] Stiny and March proposed a theoretical model for the automated production of design objects. The model encompassed both the automated generation of designs and the fabrication of the corresponding objects. In 2002 this model was implemented by Wang and Duarte [9] who developed a program that permitted to generate 3D models of abstract objects based on shape grammars and to fabricate them using rapid prototyping. Later, Duarte [10] proposed a model for the automatic production of housing called discursive grammar. This model combined shape and description grammars with a set of heuristics to find the design in the language defined by the shape grammar that matched criteria given a priori.

In the 1970s, Alexander published two books describing a new theory of urban design. One of these books, 'A Pattern Language,' [11] provided a language for building and planning that included detailed patterns for things ranging from rooms to towns. The other book, 'The Timeless Way of Building,' [12] provided the theory and the instructions to use the language, that is, the methodology that made it possible to use the patterns to create a building or a town. The work of Alexander stirred the field but had little practical impact. Later, Gamma et al. [13] used this theory to develop programming patterns for software design. They added to Alexander's pattern structure a generic code that could be applied to solve the problem encoded by the pattern. These were called design patterns and they have since been successfully used in the software industry.

In 1984, in the 'Social Logic of Space', [14] Bill Hillier set out a new theory of space as an aspect of social life, called space syntax. This theory proposed a series of parameters to characterize syntactically buildings and urban environments and linked them to aspects of social behavior. The theory developed into an extensive research program into the spatial nature and functioning of buildings and cities. More recently, Carlo Ratti [15] pointed out some inconsistencies in the theory. Among other aspects, Ratti criticized its inability to take into account other features that are relevant for urban description, including building height and land use. The theory has since been extended by Hillier and Iida [16] to incorporate the geometry of designs in angular segment analysis, and with its integration into a Geographic Information System (GIS) framework by Gil et al., [17] space syntax is now applied in academia and practice as one of the layers that compose a comprehensive spatial analysis methodology [18][19].

In 2004, Heitor et al. [20] proposed to integrate space syntax and shape grammars into a coherent model for formulating, evaluating, and generating designs, and illustrated this by extending the concept of discursive grammar. The idea was to use space syntax parameters as features of the description part of the discursive grammar. This permitted to specify the desired syntactic features of the designs to be generated and to evaluate such designs against the initial specifications, thereby using space syntax to control the generation of designs by the grammar.

Over the years, shape grammars have been explored through applications addressing a variety of design problems. However, the use of shape grammars for urban design has been limited. Teeling [21] designed a grammar to encode the generation of urban form using as a case study a specific section of the docklands in Friedrichshafen, Germany. Later developments, such as those of Parish and Muller [22], Mayall and Hall [23], and Duarte et al. [24] among others, have shown the growing interest in the potential of shape grammars to deal with urban design problems. In 2005, Beirão and Duarte [25] described the use of urban grammars in design studios at the TU Lisbon Faculty of Architecture. Their goal was to use grammars for allowing flexible urban design. The idea was that urban planning could evolve by first defining a system of rules and then by designing solutions based on such rules in response to particular contexts. The shape grammar methodology used in this studio is detailed in Duarte and Beirão. [26]

The 'City Induction' research project aims at developing a computer platform to support such urban design methodology. Following the concept of discursive grammar, this requires the development of models for urban design formulation, evaluation, and generation. The idea is to use the theories mentioned above—pattern language, space syntax, and shape grammars—as the starting points for developing such models. To guarantee the interoperability among these partial models it is necessary to develop an ontology of urban environment adequate to site planning. Ontology has been the subject of intensive research in recent years, [27] [28] and it will be used to encode urban information into a Geographic Information System GIS, which will be the core of the computer implementation. A CAD system will be used to construct 3-dimensional digital models from the information stored in the GIS. Recent software platforms, such as AutoCAD Civil 3D, already integrate GIS and 3D CAD capabilities.

Other approaches to urban modeling fall into the category of weak AI. For instance, in 1971 Michael Batty [29] suggested the use of cellular automata, agent-based models, and fractals to model urban growth. The idea behind these approaches is that urban form emerges from the complex behavior of dynamic systems. More controlled versions of this approach build on Darwin's idea of evolution. [30] The concept is to give a dynamic system the ability to respond to changes in the environment so that the configuration of the system is shaped by the environment. Genetic algorithms [31] and their design extensions [32] fall into this category. However, most of these models have been used to simulate urban growth rather than utilized as design tools, although the work of König [33] stands out as an interesting exception.

Whether a specific approach will fall into the strong or a weak side of the spectrum depends on the amount of domain knowledge that is known at the outset. The model envisioned in the *City Induction* project falls in between, as search can be used to evolve urban design solutions towards desired goals. In the previous discursive model, heuristic search controlled the generation of designs by the shape grammar. In the current model, other search techniques will also be tested, including evolutionary approaches. The idea is to use such techniques, at least in partial aspects of the problem, for instance, in the adaptation of the urban grid to the topography, to find solutions that are more appropriate to the context. In this sense, the proposed system would function like a dynamic system that evolves solutions until it reaches the equilibrium (finds a fit solution). A small change in the environment would prompt the system to reach a new equilibrium (to find a new solution). Once implemented, such a machine would constitute a powerful simulation tool that allowed the exploration of design alternatives, thereby supporting the design process and the dialogue between the various participants in the urban development process.

2   *City Induction* and *Discursive Grammars*

Urban planning and design affects the economic performance of cities and regions and the quality of life of their population. Performance largely depends on the capacity to identify community needs and recognize the potential of the territory to satisfy such needs, and then to plan the built space to maximize their satisfaction using the least resources. However, such a capacity is currently limited by the lack of integrated instruments for creating urban plans.

The goal of the *City Induction* project is to create a model for the development of such instruments using new technologies. The project departs from existing partial theories, namely Alexander's pattern language, Hillier's space syntax, and Stiny's shape grammars, among others, and it attempts at integrating these theories to create the desired model. Accordingly, the project foresees the development of three partial models.

The first sub-model is concerned with the formulation of urban problems—the formulation model. It lays its foundations on Alexander´s pattern language and departs from existing urban design guidelines and geo-spatial databases to create a system for generating the specifications or the ingredients of a plan given a site and a community. It will take into account both the physical features of the site and the social and economic characteristics of the population and sets the programmatic specifications for that context.

The second sub-model aims at creating a system for generating alternative design solutions from a generic urban design language which is progressively constrained and manipulated along the design process—the generation model. It looks into Stiny's shape and description grammars formalisms to codify the rules of syntax of the plan so that it generates solutions that match specifications set by the formulation model and are appropriate for the given design context.

The third sub-model is targeted at the development of an urban design evaluation system—the evaluation model. It departs from Hillier's space syntax theory, which focuses mainly on topological and geometric space configurations, and incorporates it in theories of sustainable urban form, such as the compact city.. The new features will address social, environmental, and infrastructural aspects applying a range of spatial analysis techniques, including network analysis, data mining and pattern recognition. The goal is to provide the basis for comparing and ranking alternative design solutions.

The development of a common ontology to describe urban space and design guarantees the syntactic and semantic interoperability and integration among the partial models. This ontology is used to structure and codify information into a Geographic Information System, which will constitute the core of the computer implementation of the larger model. A CAD system is used to construct 3-dimensional digital models from the information stored in the GIS.

The project aims at sketching the prototype of an interactive computer system for exploring urban design solutions, which will facilitate the dialogue between the various participants in the urban development process, such as community members, town halls, financing institutions, designers, promoters and developers. The project is targeted at the site planning scale and the goal is to promote the generation of better urban environments.

In short, following Stiny and March's design machines concept, the project defines a structure for urban design machines, called *urban grammars*, [34] and describes how to define a specific machine, that is a specific *urban grammar*, for a given design context. This machine should be able to produce flexible and adaptable site plans for evolving design contexts. The proposed structure for urban design machines is an extension of the concept of discursive grammar and adapted to urban design. From the technical viewpoint a discursive grammar includes a shape grammar to describe the formal properties of the context and the design; a description grammar to describe their other, non-formal but relevant properties; and a set of heuristics to guide generation towards designs that match the program. From the operative viewpoint, a discursive grammar includes a formulation grammar that generates the program from an interpretation of the context and a generation grammar that generates design solutions that match the program. An evaluation mechanism is invoked to ensure that the program fits the context and the design matches the program. The basic conceptual model of the computer platform envisioned in the City Induction project is diagrammed in Figure 1.

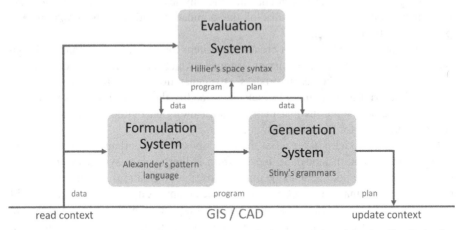

Fig. 1. Basic conceptual model of the computer platform envisioned in the City Induction project

3   Ontology

In computer science, according to Gruber [35], ontology is a formal representation of concepts, from real or imagined domains, and the relationships between them. The ´City Induction' project includes two types of ontology: environment ontology and process ontology. The first describes urban environment; first the context, and then the context with the solution. The second ontology reflects the underlying urban development methodology, that is, the process of generating solutions that respond to the context, and it provides the structure for the envisioned platform. Together, these ontological types provide the necessary protocols for the three modules to communicate with each other.

3.1   Urban Environment Ontology

The urban environment ontology defines and organizes the significant relations among the various types of objects and features found in the urban environment. It is divided into five main classes or sub-ontologies, each corresponding to a specific domain of the city structure, namely 'Networks', 'Blocks', 'Zones', 'Landscapes' and 'Focal Points', partially inspired in Lynch's basic elements. [36] 'Networks', for instance, describe the connectivity domain and the city morphology, [37] which includes several systems. We call systems the autonomous semantic units of the ontology that describe well known sub-domains. The 'street network' is one of such units within the 'Networks' sub-ontology. Other systems in this sub-ontology are 'railways networks' and 'waterways networks,' among others.

Figure 2 diagrams the urban environment ontology, highlighting its five main classes. Systems are subdivided in object classes (e.g. axial network), each class has object types (e.g. highest level axis) and each object type has a set of dimensional parameters (e.g. width) and qualitative attributes (e.g. the label a_1 to identify an axis as a main axis). The objects types are defined through shape representations and shape descriptions, and they are subclasses of their object classes. Classes are denoted with two bold capitals. Systems are branches or interlaced branches of the ontology, depending on the specific relationships between classes, and they represent a particular way of understanding cities (e.g. city as a street system).

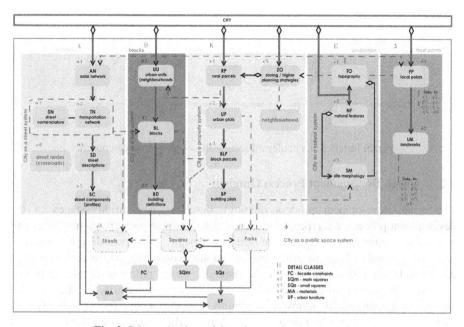

Fig. 2. Schematic view of the urban environment ontology

A previous paper [38] focuses on the description of the street system. It defines a hierarchy of classes to describe the street system with different levels of abstraction. The top class corresponds to a very abstract, axial representation of the street network called *Axial Network*. Axes in this representation can be assigned different labels to denote hierarchic levels; for instance a_1, meaning a higher level street. Another class defines a street's role as part of the *Transportation Network*, for instance, a street can be set as a distribution street in the *Transportation Network*. Cultural definitions or interpretations of streets are defined through a *Street Nomenclature*; for instance, a distribution street can be called a boulevard. In order to obtain a detailed representation of streets, axial descriptions can be detailed through a set of *Street Descriptions* specifying which *Street Components* form the street section, thereby defining its physical features. For example, a main axis a_1 may be defined as a distribution street called boulevard and then described as being composed of a minimum set of street components, for instance, a sidewalk, a bicycle lane, a side street composed of a parking space and a car lane, a green stripe with vegetation, and a tree alignment separating the side street from the central way of the boulevard, which is composed of three traffic lanes in each direction and possess a symmetrical structure as shown in Fig. 3. Specific instances of object classes (e.g. axial network) may be obtained by assigning specific values to parameters and attributes of specified object types (e.g. highest level axis such as a boulevard).

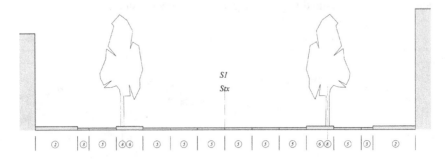

Fig. 3. Instance of a boulevard section showing its street components

3.2   Urban Development Process Ontology

The urban development process ontology describes the various stages of the development process, the type of data manipulated and the participants involved. [39] It considers three main stages: 'pre-design', 'design', and 'post-design'. Figure 4 provides a detailed diagram of the pre-design stage ontology, which corresponds to the formulation process model. In the diagram, boxes represent elements, that is classes, of the model, whereas labeled arrows between boxes clarify the relationships among such elements in terms of taxonomy and partonomy (is, is part of), and mereology (has, belongs to, interacts with). Arrows also indicate the information flow in the formulation process.

The diagram permits vertical and horizontal readings. The gray boxes at the bottom of the diagram represent the core classes of this model, namely, 'stages', data 'categories', 'processes', and 'users'. Related subclasses are represented by white boxes placed above in a vertical line. The 'stages' class, for instance, includes two sub-classes: 'pre-design phase 1' (contextual data collection and analysis) and 'pre-design phase 2' (interpretation of the analysis). According to the horizontal reading of the diagram 'pre-design phase 2', for instance, includes three elements: 'language', 'design patterns' (DP), and 'designer language'. 'Language' corresponds to the urban pattern language concept defined by Alexander, which 'design patterns' are a 'part of' and which a designer can 'interact with' to form a 'designer['s] language', that is, his own design language.

While the vertical reading refers to the thematic domains of the formulation process drawn in chronologic order, the horizontal reading corresponds to a scale decomposition of the elements that are essential to produce an urban program.

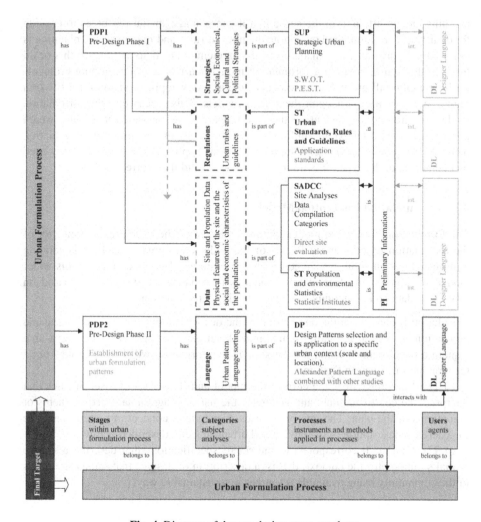

Fig. 4. Diagram of the pre-design stage ontology

4   Formulation Model

As we have seen above, the urban development process includes several stages. The formulation process corresponds to a specific stage of the design process called pre-design stage, which consists in the analysis and interpretation of contextual data that occurs before design begins [40]. The goal of this stage is to analyze the context to identify the requirements, constraints, and opportunities for a given site [41]. For this purpose, the planner (or designer) follows a set of guidelines to define strategies to be followed in the design stage in order to obtain appropriate design solutions.

Attempts to use planning to bring urban settlements under the control of a planner have not entirely resulted yet. [42] However, there is a relatively common belief that planning can be efficient in the sense that it can manage spatial resources to provide for quality of life. Embodied by a large quantity of rules and requirements, planning is essentially algorithmic, and made up of if-statements like 'if something do this or do that'. In this sense, creating a formulation model is a matter of developing protocols for how a city will grow. Such protocols support a development vision for a site or a region and they are built upon theoretical models. This means that the formulation model is extremely dependent on the type of paradigms on which it is built, which poses a risk; [43] if the paradigm fails so fails the program. The proposed formulation model is being developed after a survey of various approaches that are currently used by planners and, therefore, it is no more or no less valid than current practices.

4.1   Formulation Conceptual Model

The formulation conceptual model (Figure 5) describes the structure and behavior of the formulation process and it is part of the wider conceptual model for generating customized design solutions called discursive grammar. [44] According to this wider model, the role of the formulation model is to produce the design brief based on contextual data and it encompasses the following three components:

a) Input: It consists in the description of the design context and it includes site and population, as well as regulations and higher level plans, or any other documents that contain a development vision for the site. This information will be available from a Geographic Information System.

b) The Interpreter: It is the core of the model and it consists of a set of rules that interprets the contextual data and generates the list of programmatic requirements or ingredients of the plan. The interpreter uses Alexander's concept of pattern language to generate a description of the envisioned urban space as described below.

c) The Output: It corresponds to the set of specifications that describe adequate spatial solutions for the context, that is, a description of designs that satisfy the needs of the community using available resources in a sustainable way.

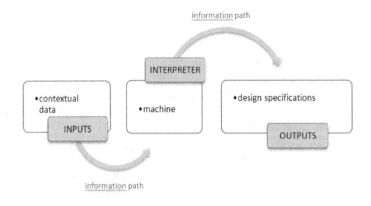

Fig. 5. Formulation conceptual mode

4.2   Formulation Methodology

The goal of the formulation model is to generate the program for the urban intervention or design brief. The mechanism by which the program is generated from the context is the core of the model. In the proposed model, such a mechanism captures the methodology used in the design studio mentioned in Section 1. The basic methodology can be described in a very simplified way as follows. In 'pre-design phase 1', one surveys the site and collects all the information required to depict the existing situation. The resulting picture includes existing population data, urban indexes, housing types, public facilities, services, industries, and so on. It also includes a detailed survey of the natural physical features of the site such as topography, soil type, weather conditions, and so on. Finally, it takes into account that the site is part of a wider context to which apply several national and local regulations, including higher level plans. In 'pre-design phase 2', one generates the design brief taking into account the collected data. Higher level plans establish several urban indexes that constrain population and construction density. Projections of population growth and composition are used to estimate the amount of people who will live on the site and household profiles. These figures then determine the amount of housing required. By relating this figure with urban and socio-economic indexes and physical features, one can determine the housing types and related information like the number of floors. With population figures and following existing guidelines, one can also determine the type and number of public facilities required. In addition, existing economic surveys can help to define the breakup of services and industrial facilities. The algorithm just described depicts the overall flow of information from the context to the urban program.

In the proposed model, this algorithm is supported by a language that can be used to describe solutions that fit the context. This language is based on Alexander's urban pattern language. An urban pattern represents recurrent spatial features found in the urban environment, for instance, 'high density housing' or 'public square.' Patterns are akin to recipes in which by considering contextual data and following specified routines, one may arrive, first, at descriptions of solutions and, then, at solutions themselves. Each pattern describes a particular recurrent urban problem and provides a set of precise instructions to generate a solution for that problem. Each pattern has a name, a description of the context in which the pattern may occur, links to smaller and higher patterns related with the specific pattern, and links to other patterns, called city induction patterns, (UIP) that contain the rules for instantiating the pattern. When the precise context in which the pattern may occur is found in the design context, the pattern is triggered. The aim in using a pattern language is to allow the participants of the formulation process to manipulate triggered patterns creatively to develop programs that are adequate to the context. The language underlying the formulation model included patterns from Alexander's original language and patterns added in the context of the City Induction project. By adding or removing patterns one may adjust the proposed language to specific wider contexts (e.g. a region or a country) or particular theoretical models of the city preferred by the designer (e.g. garden city or high density city). The formulation model is, thus, extensible and customizable.

4.3   Knowledge Representation and Implementation

In theory, the rules of the formulation model can be encoded into a description grammar, this means to use a description grammar as the knowledge representation device for the model. This was the process used to encode the rules for generating housing programs, which was then implemented in JESS, a Java expert or knowledge-based system shell, using the Clips language. [45] Nevertheless, in practice this endeavor faces two major problems. The first is the complexity of the urban formulation problem and the other is the lack of an interpreter for description grammars. Given the variety and amount of information that is required to formulate urban programs, it would be rather difficult, tedious, and cumbersome to write the rules in the format of description grammars rules. Add to this the lack of a description grammar interpreter and the task becomes virtually impossible. So, in the City Induction project a different strategy is being used that consists in representing patterns as ontologies and then use an ontology editor for the implementation. In this case, the ontology is the urban knowledge representation device, and the ontology editor, Protégé-OWL [46] becomes the interpreter of the formulation rules. This strategy naturally followed from the effort of developing the urban process ontology.

Ontologies are created to facilitate the understanding of a specified domain by defining its entities, classes, functions and relationships among them. [47] Some of the reasons to create an ontology are to share a common understanding of the structure of information among people or software agents, to enable the reuse of the domain knowledge, to make domain assumptions explicit, to separate concepts knowledge from operations knowledge, and to facilitate the analysis of domain knowledge. In the context of the formulation model such process permits to create a common shared structure of information to support the development of urban programs; to retrieve such information and use it recurrently in different urban contexts; to make the formulation concepts explicit by defining the way entities operate within the ontology; to separate the taxonomic description of urban concepts from the rule-based description of the formulation process; and to facilitate the assessment of the data model, thereby promoting a continuous improvement of the ontology. [48]

The urban formulation ontology is conceived to increase qualitative inputs by reducing ambiguities, through a flexible but automated process applied to urban planning. An ontology editor is an integrated software tool used by system developers and domain experts to develop knowledge-based systems. The applications developed with an ontology editor are generally used in problem-solving and decision-making in a particular domain. In this case, the problem is focused on urban environment phenomena and decision-making to implement solutions to promote sustainable communities.

At the end, to develop an ontology is formally equivalent to develop a description grammar; both are knowledge-based systems and both require one to identify the categories of the domain and the operative relationships among them – the rules.

5   Generation Model

The generation module produces designs according to the specifications defined by the formulation module and the designers reflective input. Recall that these specifications are a collection of urban patterns, which contain links to one or more city induction patterns (UIP) that contain rules to instantiate the pattern. It is the designer's task to select urban induction patterns to instantiate the urban pattern. Design generation stems from the sequential application of the rules that correspond to the selected urban induction patterns. This sequence is progressively defined along the design process allowing for continuous design responsiveness. Urban induction patterns are design patterns, that is, they encode recurrent design moves with a very broad application range. [49] Technically, these patterns are generic discursive grammars, which are shape grammars provided with heuristics to search for design solutions matching goals defined by a description grammar. [10] These generic discursive shape grammars can be manipulated by the designer to define a specific discursive grammar. This manipulation may involve reducing rule sets and constraining their parameters. By selecting urban induction patterns and manipulating the corresponding rules, the designer defines a design language. By applying the resulting rules, the designer generates a design solution.

The design solution has a shape part and a description, which follow the ontological structure described in Section 3. The shape part includes 3-dimensional and 2-dimensional representations. This enables the solution to be written on the same GIS system used to read the context. As such, the grammars are defined in a way that layered representations are generated following the ontological structure. They are parallel grammars where each shape set corresponds to a class in the ontology. In general, the grammars generate layered representations that reflect the five top levels of the ontology, namely, 'networks', 'blocks', 'zones', 'landscape' and 'focal points'. [38] The partial shape representations that correspond to these five ontological levels are geo-referenced to a particular reference system, are made of points, lines and polygons and may include symbolic data associated to these shape entities. [50]

5.1   Formal Definition of Urban Grammars

Each object class is a set of object types divided into geometry (shapes and parameterized shapes), attributes (labels). The ontology guarantees that all the shape and label sets that compose an urban plan have the same structure, thereby allowing grammars to take them as parameterized labeled shapes in the application of rules to generate urban designs. Each set of parameterized shapes in the ontology is noted with S_i where the index i defines the position of the set in the ontology from 1, 2,..., n and n is the total number of shape sets in the ontology.

As a generic definition, an urban induction pattern (UIP) is a recurrent urban design move encoded into a generic grammar that can be applied to replicate the design move in various contexts and an urban grammar is a specific arrangement of UIPs. The generation module contains all the Urban Grammars that can be defined from all the possible arrangements of UIPs and all their parameter variations.

Therefore, we will call Urban Pattern Grammar to the set Γ, a very generic grammar containing all urban grammars Γ' available in the generation module.

The current version of the generation model was developed after a set of four urban plans used as case studies to extract urban induction patterns. [51] The strategy was to identify the design moves used by designers in the four plans and include them in the model. Some moves are common to one or more plans, whereas others are specific to one plan. The model can be extended by increasing the set of available UIPs using additional case studies. The grammars encoding common design moves were developed in such as way as to permit variations to account for different design expressions. To guarantee a wide range of application, UIP grammars were kept as generic as possible by considering a wide range of rules and parameter values that can be manipulated in design exploration.

Formally, an Urban Grammar Γ' is the Cartesian product of parallel grammars $\Gamma_1 \times \Gamma_2 \times \Gamma_3 \times ... \times \Gamma_n$ that take a set of parameterized shapes from the city ontology, respectively $S_1, S_2, S_3, ..., S_n$, to design an urban plan. Generically, four design phases produce four sub-designs with different levels of detail. Each design phase uses some of the parallel grammars, Γ_1 to Γ_n of an urban grammar Γ' to generate the several layers that define the sub-design corresponding to the design phase. Label sets $L_1, L_2, L_3, ..., L_n$ are the label sets in grammars $\Gamma_1, \Gamma_2, \Gamma_3, ..., \Gamma_n$, respectively, and they correspond to the attribute classes in the ontology. [52]

Any urban grammar Γ' is built up from a sequence of UIPs. It is the sequence of design decisions behind the selection of UIPs that in the end reflects the design language of the urban plan. The same urban grammar Γ' can be used to produce different instantiations of the UIP by assigning different parameter values to the parametric shape rules. The urban pattern grammar Γ is, in fact, an algorithmic implementation of part of a Pattern Language as Alexander [11] conceived it, but done in a way that permits the designer to define his own pattern language (Γ'). In terms of computer implementation, the concept is closer to that of Gamma et al.'s design patterns [13] and as such we may call UIPs as design patterns for urban design.

Following the previous definitions, a UIP is a sub-grammar of Γ'. A UIP uses some of the parallel grammars in Γ', a subset Γ'' of Γ', namely some components of the set $\{\Gamma_1, \Gamma_2, \Gamma_3, ..., \Gamma_n\}$. A UIP is a compound grammar Γ'' composed of a set of parallel discursive grammars Γ_i of the form $\Gamma_i = \{D, U, G, H, S_i, L_i, W, R, F, I_i\}$ where S_i is the set of parameterized shapes corresponding to the ith shape object class in the ontology, L_i is the set of labels corresponding to the ith attribute object class in the ontology and I_i is the initial shape. The initial shape I_i is always a shape in S_i generated by a previous UIP or a shape in I_0 in the case of initial UIPs where I_0 is the set of initial labeled shapes. These initial labeled shapes are objects found in the representations of the existing context which are used by the initial UIPs to start the design. There are only two types of initial shapes, I_s, the intervention site limit and R_{ef} objects which are labeled shapes representing selected elements from the site context. R_{ef} objects are selected by the designer for being perceived as referential elements in the context and, therefore, suitable candidates for defining the main guidelines of the plan. Each UIP addresses a goal G which is to be achieved through a set of description rules D starting from an initial description U. A set of heuristics H decides which of the rules in the rule set R to apply at each stage of the design process. W is a set of weights and F a set of functions used to constrain the generation to comply with existing regulations and quality standards.

5.2   Controlling the Generation

The specifications defined by the formulation module can be generically defined as being of two different kinds: *input data* and *control data*. These two kinds of data play a different role in the context of the generation module. Furthermore and because the generation of designs is part of the urban design process, decision making is a reflective and responsive process that takes time and evolves progressively through several design phases. Four different design phases are considered in the design process: phase 1, where rules are applied to generate design guidelines based on selected territorial features; phase 2, where the main grids and networks are generated; phase 3, where the characteristics of the urban units, such as neighbourhoods, city blocks and plots are defined and generated; and phase 4, which generates the urban details that characterize and materialize public space. [26] Therefore, not all the data is needed at the beginning of the design process, neither is this data completely known then. As such, a continuous register of outputs is also needed. In fact, the *output data* serves two purposes: checking the generation outputs against the inputs and feeding back information to complete the data needed for other steps of the design process. Therefore, the input database is conceived as an interactive and dynamic database which can be updated directly by the designer and by the outputs.

Input data can be quantitative or qualitative and different kinds of input data maybe needed in different phases of the design. *Input data* contain two data basis for each phase: one for quantitative input and another for qualitative input:

- for phase Ph1:

MBi_Qt-PlReq – defining quantitative plan requirements such as construction areas, density, indexes, etc.
MBi_Ql-PlReq – defining qualitative plan requirements such as required urban functions or components to be applied, etc.

- for phases Ph2 and 3:

MBi_Qt-NeiReq – defining quantitative neighborhood requirements (local requirements) such as construction areas, density, indexes, etc to be used at a local level, that is, at the neighborhood level.
MBi_Ql-NeiReq – defining qualitative neighborhood requirements (local requirements) such as required functions or components to be applied at a local level, that is, at the neighborhood level.

Input data can come from various sources: the stakeholders, the designer, the regulations, a master plan, from planning authorities or from other agents, depending on the context, but they all should provide a progressive fulfilment of requirements that the generative rules need for the generation of designs.

Control data is defined in two separate data basis, one concerning regulations and another concerning norms and quality standards. The idea is to separate items that are related with local regulations and prescriptions (which might vary from country to country or even according to municipality,) from items related with quality and performance standards (which might be organized in different quality levels.) Therefore we have:

MBc_Reg – for regulations.
MBc_QuaSta – for quality standards.

Control data and, specifically, quality standards data are responsible for guaranteeing that the generated solutions comply with certain qualitative criteria. The criteria might be set by the formulation module and reset by the designer.

Finally, *output data* is extracted from the generation outputs. Two different kinds of outputs are considered: data extracted from the representations – quantitative and qualitative – and a register of the sequence of applied UIPs (a kind of history of the derivation.)

The data extracted from the representations contains the same categories as the input data. That is, there is a data base for output data *MBo_Qt-PlDat* that has to be fulfilled with exactly the same parameters values as the data base for input data *MBi_Qt-PlReq*. In fact, the goal of the generation is to produce results such that each output data base *MBo* matches the equivalent input data base *MBi*. Therefore, in the end of the generation:

MBi_Qt-PlReq should match MBo_Qt-PlDat,
MBi_Ql-PlReq should match MBo_Ql-PlDat,
MBi_Qt-NeiReq should match MBo_Qt-NeiDat,
MBi_Ql-NeiReq should match MBo_Ql-NeiDat.

The register of the sequence of applied UIPs simply registers the sequence of instructions, namely, the sequence of UIPs that were used to produce the design in order to reuse them (or not) in the feedback loop. The data base for pattern sequences (*MBo_PatSeq*) stores the sequence of patterns per design phase. It is a list containing the sequence of application of UIPs and the corresponding rule choices and rule parameters. Each time a pattern is applied it adds a list containing its ID, rules and parameters to the main list. This allows for the generation to respond to feedback from both the evaluation module and the formulation module in order to improve the design solution.

As a component of City Induction, the generation module may receive most of the input and control data from the formulation module. It is the integration of the three modules that makes City Induction an interesting design tool because it allows for the generation of context sensitive input and control data by the formulation module and the evaluation of the output data by the evaluation module. However, it is also conceived to function independently from the other two modules, and rely simply on designer's interaction. As an independent application the generation module constitutes a conventional design tool with no decision support systems. Nevertheless, even in this case, it offers a few advantages over regular urban design tools:

- it contains generative rules encoding current design moves, which enables the fast generation of design and supports enhanced design exploration;
- it generates plans in a format that can be exported and linked to a geo-referenced context in a GIS, which enables the use of GIS assessment tools and, therefore, gives feedback on the results; and
- it generates output data that includes part of the information that the designer needs to assess the design, which facilitates a reflective design exploration.

In short, the generation module consists of a rule-based CAD environment linked to a GIS environment.

6   Evaluation Model

Evaluation is present at various phases of the urban development process, i.e. in site and context analysis to identify priorities, in evaluating the development vision or in monitoring the plan's performance after implementation, with each phase providing different input elements to and requiring different output options from an evaluation process, leading to specific evaluation principles and strategies each time.

The evaluation module developed for the City Induction project addresses the evaluation of urban design options during the early design phase of the urban development process. It is responsible for assessing the performance potential of alternative designs based on principles of sustainable urban development (SUD) to support the difficult decision and design tasks of selection and evolution towards a final design solution.

The evaluation process is synthesized in Figure 6, representing its stages and its links to the other modules of the City Induction project.

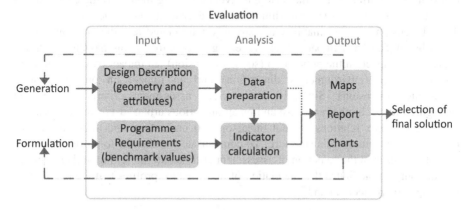

Fig. 6. The evaluation process and its operation within the City Induction project

6.1   Evaluation Principles and Structure

The evaluation framework follows a structure based on the elements commonly found in other SUD evaluation tools, as identified in a detailed review of the field conducted by the authors [53], and on previous experience with similar urban evaluation methods involving space syntax theory [54]. The general structure consists of five levels with increasing detail and specificity, namely:

a) **Sustainability Dimensions**: the high level goals of environmental, social and economic sustainability;
b) **Urban Sustainability Issues**: the topics of concern to sustainable urban development, e.g. improve access to socio-economic opportunities;
c) **Assessment Criteria**: a set of aspects that need to be assessed in order to verify the response of the plan to the issues, e.g. access to public transport, access to local services;
d) **Performance Indicators**: measurements of design attributes with a specific calculation method and a unit, e.g. percent of residents within 400m walking distance of a public transit stop, average distance to the nearest doctor;
e) **Performance Benchmarks:** values that are indicative of the performance of the design in relation to a specific design indicator, e.g. 50% of residents, average distance shorter than 400m.

In order to develop an evaluation framework based on sound theoretical principles and empirical evidence, the elements in the various levels are derived from existing tools currently being used worldwide to evaluate urban plans and other research projects including HQE^{2}R [55] and the European Common Indicators [56], which involved a consultation of experts in the field and city representatives about the key concerns for addressing SUD. The assessment criteria are largely based on the principles set in "Shaping Neighborhoods" by Barton et al. [57] and expanded with criteria from other sources [53].

For the sake of simplicity and usability of the tool we only implement a simple hierarchical classification of the different levels assigning them into the categories of the level above, e.g. issues into dimensions and criteria into issues. However, the three dimensions of sustainability are strongly interrelated and the elements of the levels below can have impact on all three, e.g. access to schools has an health and educational impact on the population (social dimension), an impact on CO_2 emissions and congestion (environmental dimension) and an impact on property values (economic dimension). Similarly, the various assessment criteria can present synergies with each other and have an impact on various urban sustainability issues.

These complex relations are not linear or well understood and therefore are not implicit in the framework's structure. To compensate for this, the tool offers a degree of customization in the selection of assessment criteria and the setting of their weights and in doing so facilitates the calculation of performance profiles that are meaningful to the specific project at hand.

6.2   Input Requirements

There are two types of input for the evaluation process, coming from each of the other two modules of the City Induction process. The formulation module provides the set of performance benchmarks to be achieved by the designs and the generation module provides the description of one or more complete designs.

The performance benchmarks are a direct result of the formulation phase of the project, and the process of setting these values should involve teams of experts in the various issues of SUD, as well as public participation to bring local interests and knowledge into the equation. When the goals agreed in the development vision do not map directly onto the available assessment criteria, one needs to translate these goals into quantitative values to obtain performance benchmarks. To ensure an adequate translation, this process should involve at least one representative of the stakeholders involved in the development of the program and someone familiar with the available assessment criteria and the corresponding design indicators.

The benchmarks can be a single value representing the minimum acceptable condition, or three ranges of values for acceptable, good and excellent conditions. The setting of benchmark values automatically selects which assessment criteria and performance indicators to use in the evaluation process. There are no default benchmark values because these are extremely sensitive to the type of project, to the geographic location, to the socio-economic and cultural conditions of the population and to the moment in time. A few reference cases are provided that offer specific benchmark values that can be used to test the tool but only to evaluate how a proposed design would perform under the exact same conditions.

The design description is the product of the generation module and is stored in a spatial database containing the geometry of the design entities, together with their attribute data. The spatial database structure is defined by the shared ontology described earlier in the chapter.

For the purpose of evaluation, the designs need a certain degree of completeness in terms of information, but they need not be the final solution of the design phase. This evaluation process exists to support the selection and evolution of alternative designs from the early stages of the design phase. To properly assess the plan in its multi-dimensional nature there is a minimum of information required, including urban layout, building type, land use, and mobility infrastructure. The tool will inform the designer about the completeness of the information for the selected assessment criteria and benchmarks. At early stages of the design process, these can be set for lower information requirements using simpler performance indicators (Figure 7).

6.3   Design Analysis

The design analysis stage calculates the performance indicators that inform the selected assessment criteria and involves two main tasks: a semi-automated preparation of the input data sets and the calculation of the indicators.

After the data input requirements have been fulfilled, the design data is prepared for analysis by creating auxiliary data tables that contain design attributes used in indicators calculation, e.g. the location of schools, the walking distance of every property to the nearest school. The design attributes can be extracted directly from the design's geometry or can be read directly from the design's memory banks. In some cases the extraction of design attributes involves complex spatial analysis calculations or data processing algorithms that take a considerable amount of time, such as space syntax network analysis.

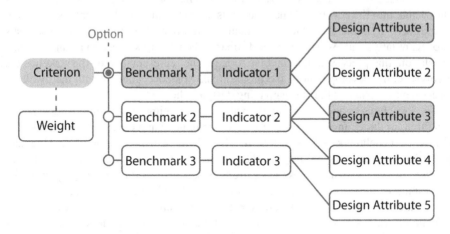

Fig. 7. Diagram of the components in the calculation of assessment criteria

Once all the design attributes have been determined, the tool can calculate the performance indicators according to their specific equations. Some assessment criteria can be fulfilled by different performance indicators, and this selection is based on the performance benchmarks set by the user (Figure 7). This choice of indicators can accommodate different levels of detail in terms of input data or specific interests of the stakeholders involved in the evaluation process.

The raw output of the design analysis stage of the evaluation process is a large amount of quantitative data that is stored in the project's spatial database, resulting from the calculation of the various performance indicators and the design attributes. The generation model can use this quantitative data to drive design evolution or optimization algorithms following design strategies based on formulation requirements and/or in response to the evaluation results. For example, it can choose to manipulate the street layout aiming to obtain a specific space syntax integration value that supports the vitality defined for specific areas of the plan, such as the high street or quieter residential areas, or choose to insert specific street and building typologies based on the street network hierarchy determined by the integration value.

6.4   Output Options

The final stage of the evaluation process takes the design analysis data for output in three different formats: maps, summary charts and a quantitative report. It is important to offer a range of output options that cater for the requirements of the different stakeholders of the planning process and that support the use of this information in different ways.

Maps are the first output option as they provide important visual design support to planners and other stakeholders. These maps present performance information at the highest level of spatial detail, such as buildings, plots or street segments. A map can be produced for every performance indicator or design attribute that is calculated at this spatial resolution, using, whenever available, a color range based on the performance benchmark values. This helps to identify strengths and weaknesses in the plan, specific areas for improvement, e.g. density is below the requirements, or specific areas where the impact of the design is most negative, e.g. accessibility to schools is lowest therefore the street layout or the school's location need to be addressed.

Summary charts present the performance of the neighborhood design according to the selected assessment criteria and aggregated at the other levels of the evaluation structure, i.e. urban sustainability issues and sustainability dimensions, using simple linear equations of assessment criteria. These charts are multi-level pie charts for presenting a single design option and spider charts for comparing multiple design options simultaneously. Their interpretation is qualitative and indicative of the fulfillment of the higher-level SUD concerns.

The quantitative report is a CSV text file containing the values aggregated at neighborhood level that are used to produce the summary charts, including the values of assessment criteria, performance benchmarks and weights. This numeric output can be used to produce alternative summary charts or to calculate performance rankings for semi-automated design option selection processes.

The City Induction evaluation model supports the early stages of the design process by being able to operate with the limited information available in the early stages of planning and by feeding information about the various design options back into the generation module. It can also provide valuable support to the design decision-making process involving multiple stakeholders. It is not a rating system applied at the end of the design process, as this requires extremely elaborate non-linear equations to address the complexity of the problem and the synergies between assessment criteria. Furthermore, at the end of the design phase one should consider the use of sophisticated but also expensive – in terms of time and cost - simulation methods to evaluate more rigorously the performance of the proposed development.

7   Conclusion

We have described the theoretical foundations of a project called City Induction, whose ultimate goal is to develop a computer platform for assisting urban planning and design at the site planning scale. The project encompasses two steps: first, the development of the theoretical model, which will define the structure and operation of the computer platform, and then, the computer implementation of the model. The first step includes the development of three partial models – formulation, generation, and evaluation – and an ontology to unify them into a common general model, where as the second step foresees the development of a proof-of-concept implementation of this model. As such, the expected short-term impacts or immediate benefits of the project are:

- A formulation model that will permit the generation of rigorous specifications for urban plans based on community and site features. These specifications embody a given development vision, provide the guidelines for the design of a plan, and constitute a chart against which to evaluate its performance. This sub-model stems from Alexander's pattern language theory.
- A generation model that will provide the means for producing design solutions that are adapted to variations in the design context motivated by evolution or changes in urban development factors. This will make it easier to accommodate such changes and extend the life-time of urban plans. This sub-model model is based on Stiny's shape and description grammars theory.
- An evaluation model that will permit the analysis and comparison of alternative urban plans. This will constitute a rigorous basis for decision support during the development process, involving its various stakeholders including local authorities, community leaders, financing institutions, promoters, developers, designers, and builders. This sub-model incorporates Hillier's space syntax theory in accepted models of sustainable urban development, such as the compact city.
- An ontology that will permit to describe the concepts and the operations within each partial model and work as a protocol for communication among the three sub-models. This ontology includes an ontology of the urban environment and an ontology of the urban development process.
- A general model that will contain a set of guidelines to follow in the formulation, evaluation, and generation of urban plans, and that can be used to inform both the teaching and practice of urban planning and design. The prototype of a computer implementation, which will take the form of an interactive system for exploring urban design programs and solutions.

The novelties and contribution of the project are:

- A formulation model that permits to ground the definition of urban programs on wider contextual information, and to generate flexible urban programs, formed by a set of patterns that can be selected and defined by the designer;
- A generation model that associates Alexander's concept of patterns with algorithms for instantiating them, thereby including a mechanism that permits to develop an urban grammar, that is, an urban language that is, at the same time, a pattern language and a shape grammar, using the formalism of shape grammars in such a way that there is no need to know a specific design language a priori, but to construct one iteratively and reflexively from a generic grammar during the design process;
- An evaluation model that permits, in addition, to validate design goals by evaluating the output of the formulation model against the context, and to validate design decisions by evaluating the output of the generation model

against the program, to validate the plan within the widen context of the city by evaluating its performance in absolute terms;
- The processes associated with the three models may be distributed in terms of time and scale by different moments and detail levels of the urban development process, as this process is not formed by a single formulation-generation-evaluation cycle, but rather by a composition of such cycles.

Finally, it is our hope that long-term impacts of the project may be:
- At the knowledge production level, contribute for extending and integrating the theories on which each partial model is based, which usually are considered separately, thereby laying the foundation for a unifying theory.
- At the ethical and professional level, contribute for improving the communication between the various participants in the urban development process, thereby facilitating the underlying negotiation process; and helping to ground the design process on contextual information and to assess the outcomes against such information; and providing a tool that may augment the designer's ability to respond to complex problems and generate quality urban environments.
- At the socio-economic and environmental level, contribute for increasing community participation in the urban development process, thereby acknowledging its role as a city-making agent; increasing users satisfaction thereby consolidating the sense of identity with their own urban environment; diminishing the social costs associated with the inadequacy of urban environments to their users; decreasing the urban development costs by making the process more efficient; increasing urban quality and the quality of life; using natural resources in a more sustainable way; and generating more efficient cities that facilitate economic activities.

The results of the City Induction project will be available at http://www.cityinduction.com from January 1st 2011.

Acknowledgements. The authors wish to thank George Stiny and Terry Knight from MIT, Rudi Stouffs, Henco Bekkering, Sevil Sariyildiz, Vincent Nadin, and Stephen Read from the Delft University of Technology, as well as Paulo Urbano from the University of Lisbon and Jeniffer Vendetti from Standord University for their contributions to the *City Induction* research. The *City Induction* research project is funded by Fundação para a Ciência e Tecnologia (FCT) with grant PTDC/AUR/64384/2006 and is hosted by ICIST at TU Lisbon. J. P. Duarte coordinates the project. N. Montenegro, J.N. Beirão and J. Gil are responsible for the formulation, generation and evaluation modules, respectively, and are funded by FCT with grants SFRH/BD/45520/2008, SFRH/BD/39034/2007, and SFRH/BD/46709/2008.

References

1. Friedman, A.: Design for Change: Flexible Planning Strategies for the 1990s and Beyond. Journal of Urban Design 2(3), 277–295 (1997)
2. Archer, F.: Metapolis: acerca do futuro da cidade. Celta Editora, Oeiras (1978)
3. Simon, H.: The Sciences of the Artificial. MIT Press (1969)
4. Chomsky, N.: Syntactic Structures. Mouton, The Hague (1957)
5. Stiny, G., Gips, J.: Shape Grammars and the Generative Specification of Painting and Sculpture. In: Freiman, C.V. (ed.) Information Processing, vol. 71, pp. 1460–1465. North-Holland, Amsterdam (1972)
6. Stiny, G.: Introduction to shape and shape grammars. Environment and Planning B: Planning and Design 7, 343–351 (1980)
7. Stiny, G.: A note on the description of designs. Environment and Planning B: Planning and Design 8, 257–267 (1981)
8. Stiny, G., March, L.: Design machines. Environment and Planning B: Planning and Design 8, 245–255 (1981)
9. Wang, Y., Duarte, J.P.: Automatic Generation and Fabrication of Designs. Automation in Construction 11(3), 291–302 (2002)
10. Duarte, J.P.: A discursive grammar for customizing mass housing. Automation in Construction 14, 265–275 (2005)
11. Alexander, C., et al.: A Pattern Language. Oxford University Press (1977)
12. Alexander, C.: A Timeless way of Building. Oxford University Press (1977)
13. Gamma, E., Helm, R., Johnson, R., Vlissides, J.: Design Patterns: Elements of Reusable Object-Oriented Software. Addison-Wesley, Reading (1995)
14. Hillier, B.: The Social Logic of Space. Cambridge University Press (1984)
15. Ratti, C.: Space Syntax: some inconsistencies. Environment and Planning B: Planning and Design 31, 487–499 (2004)
16. Hillier, B., Iida, S.: Network and Psychological Effects in Urban Movement. In: Cohn, A.G., Mark, D.M. (eds.) COSIT 2005. LNCS, vol. 3693, pp. 475–490. Springer, Heidelberg (2005)
17. Gil, J., Stutz, C., Chiaradia, A.: Confeego: Tool Set for Spatial Configuration Studies. In: Turner, A. (ed.) 6th International Space Syntax Symposium, New Developments in Space Syntax Software, pp. 15–22. Istanbul Technical University, Istanbul (2007)
18. Chiaradia, A., Hillier, B., Barnes, Y., Schwander, C.: Residential Property Value Patterns in London. In: Proceedings of the 7th International Space Syntax Symposium. KTH Stockholm, 015:01–015:12 (2009)
19. Chiaradia, A.: Profiling land use location with space syntax - angular choice and multi metric radii. In: Proceedings of the 7th International Space Syntax Symposium, KTH Stockholm (2009)
20. Heitor, T., Duarte, J.P., Marques, R.P.: Combining Grammars and Space Syntax. International Journal of Architectural Computing 2(4), 491–515 (2004)
21. Teeling, C.: Algorithmic design: Generating urban form. Urban Design Studies 2, 89–100 (1996)
22. Parish, Y.I.H., Müller, P.: Procedural modeling of cities. In: Fiume, E. (ed.) Proceedings of ACM SIGGRAPH 2001, pp. 301–308. ACM Press (2001)
23. Mayall, K., Hall, G.B.: Landscape grammar 1: spatial grammar theory and landscape planning. Environment and Planning B: Planning and Design 32(6), 895–920 (2005)

24. Duarte, J.P., Rocha, J., Ducla-Soares, G.: Unveiling the structure of the Marrakech Medina: A Shape Grammar and an Interpreter for Generating Urban Form. In: Gero, J., Dong, A. (eds.) AIEDAM Artificial Intelligence for Engineering Design, Analysis and Manufacturing, vol. 21, pp. 1–33 (2007)

25. Beirão, J.N., Duarte, J.P.: Urban grammars: Towards flexible urban design. In: Duarte, J.P., Ducla-Soares, G., Sampaio, A.Z. (eds.) Proceedings of eCAADe 2005, Lisbon, pp. 491–500 (2005)

26. Duarte, J.P., Beirão, J.N.: Towards a methodology for flexible urban design: designing with urban patterns and shape grammars. Environment and Planning B: Planning and Design (forthcoming)

27. Guarino, N.: Formal Ontology and Information Systems. In: Proceedings of FOIS 1998, Trento, Italy, June 6-8, pp. 3–15. IOS Press, Amsterdam (1998)

28. Fonseca, F., Egenhofer, M.: Ontologias e Interoperabilidade Semântica entre SIGs. In: II Workshop Brasileiro em Geoinformática – GeoInfo 2000, Proceedings, São Paulo (2000)

29. Batty, M.: Modelling Cities as Dynamic Systems. Nature 377, 574 (1971)

30. Darwin, C.: The Origin of Species. John Murray (1859)

31. Holland, J.: Adaptation in Natural and Artificial Systems. University of Michigan Press, Ann Arbor (1975)

32. Caldas, L.G.: An Evolution-Based Generative Design System. Ph.D. Dissertation, MIT (2001)

33. König, R., Bauriedel, C.: Computer-generated urban structures. In: 7th Generative Art Conference GA 2004, Milan, Italy (2004),
   http://www.entwurfsforschung.de/compStadt/compStadt.htm

34. Beirão, J.N., Duarte, J.P., Stouffs, R.: Structuring a grammar for urban design: linking GIS to shape grammars. In: Muylle, M., De Vos, E. (eds.) Proceedings of the 26th Conference on Education in Computer Aided Architectural Design in Europe, eCAADe 2008, Antwerpen, Belgium, pp. 929–938 (September 2008)

35. Gruber, T.B.: A translation approach to portable ontology specifications. Knowledge Acquisition 5(2), 257–267 (1993)

36. Lynch, K.: The image of the city. MIT press (1960)

37. Montenegro, N., Duarte, J.: Towards a Computational Ontology of Urban Planning. In: Colakoglu, B., Cagdas, G. (eds.) Proceedings of the 27th Conference on Education in Computer Aided Architectural Design in Europe, eCAADe 2009, Istanbul, Turkey (2009)

38. Beirão, J.N., Montenegro, N., Gil, J., Duarte, J.D., Stouffs, R.: The city as a street system: A street description for a city ontology. In: SIGraDi 2009 - Proceedings of the 13th Congress of the Iberoamerican Society of Digital Graphics, Sao Paulo, Brazil, November 16-18 (2009)

39. Gil, J., Duarte, J.P.: Towards an Urban Design Evaluation Framework: integrating spatial analysis techniques in the parametric urban design process. In: Muylle, M., De Vos, E. (eds.) Proceedings of the 26th Conference on Education in Computer Aided Architectural Design in Europe, eCAADe 2008, Antwerpen, Belgium, p. 257 (September 2008)

40. Best, R., De Valence, G.: Building in value: pre-design issues. Butterworth-Heinemann (1999)

41. McCallum, M.H., Ellickson, D.E., Goldberg, H.G.: 1996 Editions of AIA Design/Build Standard Forum Agreements. The. Constr. Law. 16, 38 (1996)

42. Hélie, M.: Conceptualizing the Principles of Emergent Urbanism. Archnet IJAR, 3 (2009)

43. Clark, T.N.: Old and new paradigms for urban research: Globalization and the fiscal austerity and urban innovation project. Urban Affairs Review 36(1), 3 (2000)

44. Duarte, J.P.: A Discursive Grammar for Customizing Mass Housing - The case of Sizaś houses at Malagueira. Ph.D. Dissertation, Massachusetts Institute of Technology, Cambridge (2003)
45. Duarte, J.P., Correia, R.: Implementing a Description Grammar for Generating Housing Programs Online. Construction Innovation Journal on Information and knowledge Management in Construction 6(4), 203–216 (2006)
46. Knublauch, H., Fergerson, R.W., Noy, N.F., Musen, M.A.: The Protégé OWL Plugin: An Open Development Environment for Semantic Web Applications. In: McIlraith, S.A., Plexousakis, D., van Harmelen, F. (eds.) ISWC 2004. LNCS, vol. 3298, pp. 229–243. Springer, Heidelberg (2004)
47. Fonseca, F.T., Egenhofer, M.J.: Ontology-driven geographic information systems. In: Proceedings of the 7th ACM International Symposium on Advances in Geographic Information Systems, pp. 14–19 (1999)
48. Noy, N.F., Sintek, M., Decker, S., Crubezy, M., Fergerson, R.W., Musen, M.A.: Creating semantic web contents with protege-2000. IEEE Intelligent Systems 16(2), 60–71 (2001)
49. Schon, D.A.: The Reflective Practitioner: How professionals think in action. Basic Books, New York (1983)
50. Beirão, J.N., Duarte, J.P., Stouffs, R.: Grammars of designs and grammars for designing, CAAD Futures, University of Montreal, Canada (2009)
51. Beirão, J.N., Duarte, J.P., Gil, J., Montenegro, N.: Monitoring urban design through generative design support tools: a generative grammar for Praia. In: Proceedings of the 15th APDR Congress on Networks and Regional Development, Cidade da Praia, Cape Verde (2009)
52. Beirão, J.N., Duarte, J.P., Stouffs, R.: Creating specific grammars from generic grammars: towards flexible urban design. In: Nexus 2010, Relationships between Architecture & Mathematics, Conference Edition of Nexus Network Journal (2010) (forthcoming)
53. Gil, J., Duarte, J.: A review of urban design sustainability evaluation tools. In: 10th International Conference on Design & Decision Support Systems in Architecture and Urban Planning. Eindhoven University of Technology, Eindhoven (2010)
54. Chiaradia, A., Schwander, C., Gil, J., Friedrich, E., Gosset, A.: Mapping the intangible value of urban layout (i-VALUL): Developing a tool kit for the socio-economic valuation of urban areas, for designers and decision makers. In: 9th International Conference on Design & Decision Support Systems in Architecture and Urban Planning. Eindhoven University of Technology, Eindhoven (2008)
55. Outrequin, P., Charlot-Valdieu, C.: The ISDIS system (Integrated SD Indicators System) and the INDI model: Assessment of neighbourhood regeneration scenarios, action plans. CSTB-La Calade (2003)
56. Ambiente Italia Research Institute: European Common Indicators - Towards a Local Sustainability Profile. European Commission, Milano (2003)
57. Barton, H., Grant, M., Guise, R.: Shaping neighbourhoods: a guide for health, sustainability and vitality. Spon Press, London (2003)

Sortal Grammars for Urban Design: A Sortal Approach to Urban Data Modeling and Generation

Rudi Stouffs[1], José N. Beirão[1,2], and José P. Duarte[2]

[1] Delft University of Technology, Faculty of Architecture, P.O. Box 5043,
2600 GA Delft, The Netherlands
`{r.m.f.stouffs,j.n.beirao}@tudelft.nl`
[2] Technical University of Lisbon, Faculty of Architecture, Rua Sá Nogueira, Pólo
Universitário, Alto da Ajuda, 1349-055 Lisboa, Portugal
`{jnb,jduarte}@fa.utl.pt`

Abstract. Grammar formalisms for design come in a large variety, requiring different representations of the objects being generated, and different interpretative mechanisms for this generation. At the same time, all grammars share certain definitions and characteristics. Building on these commonalities, we consider a component-based approach for building grammar systems, utilizing a uniform characterization of grammars. *Sortal* representations constitute the components for this approach. They implement a model for representations, termed *sorts*, that defines formal operations on *sorts* and recognizes formal relationships between *sorts*. Each *sort* defines an algebra over its elements; formal compositions of sorts derive their algebraic properties from their component sorts. This algebraic framework makes *sortal* representations particularly suited for defining grammar formalisms considering a variety of algebra, and match relations (or interpretative mechanisms). For urban design and simulation, *sortal* grammars may include, among others, descriptive grammars, shape grammars, GIS-based grammars and any combination thereof.

Keywords: data modeling, representations, grammars, generation, exploration.

1 Introduction

Grammar formalisms have been around for over 50 years and have found application in a wide variety of disciplines and domains, to name a few, natural language, architectural design, mechanical design, and syntactic pattern recognition. Grammar formalisms come in a large variety (e.g., [1], [2], [3], [4], and [5]), requiring different representations of the objects being generated, and different interpretative mechanisms for this generation. Altering the representation may necessitate a rewrite of the interpretative mechanism, resulting in a redevelopment of the entire system. At the same time, all grammars share certain definitions and characteristics. Grammars are defined over an algebra of objects, U, that is closed under the operations of addition, $+$, and subtraction, $-$, and a set of transformations, F. In other words, if u and v are members of U, so too are $u + f(v)$ and $u - f(v)$ where f is a member of F. In

S. Müller Arisona et al. (Eds.): DUMS, CCIS 242, pp. 99–116, 2012.

addition, a match relation, $\leq$, on the algebra governs when an object occurs in another object under some transformation, that is, $f(u) \leq v$ whenever u occurs in v for some member f of F, if u and v are members of U.

Building on these commonalities, we consider a component-based approach for building grammar systems, utilizing a uniform characterization of grammars, but allowing for a variety of algebras, and match relations (or interpretative mechanisms) [6]. *Sortal* representations constitute the components for this approach. They implement a model for representations, termed *sorts*, that defines formal operations on *sorts* and recognizes formal relationships between *sorts* [7]. Each *sort* defines an algebra over its elements; formal compositions of *sorts* derive their algebraic properties from their component *sorts*. This algebraic framework makes *sortal* representations particularly suited for defining grammar formalisms. Provided a large variety of primitive *sorts* are defined, *sortal* representations can be conceived and built corresponding to almost any grammar formalisms.

The need for varying grammar formalisms using varying representations is quite apparent in urban design. CAD systems are very powerful drawing tools and fit for design practice, also in urban design. On the other hand, GIS systems are very powerful systems for accessing large-scale urban data; hence they play an important role in urban planning as analytical tools. However, these tools were conceived as interactive maps and so they lack capacities for designing. Therefore, in urban design, the linking of GIS to CAD tools and representations becomes an important goal to allow designing directly on the GIS data.

For urban design and simulation, *sortal* grammars may include, among others, descriptive grammars, GIS-based set grammars, shape grammars and any combination thereof.

2   *Sortal* Representations

Stouffs [7] describes a semi-constructive algebraic formalism for design representations, termed *sorts*, that provides support for varying grammar formalisms. It presents a uniform approach for dealing with and manipulating data constructs and enables representations to be compared with respect to scope and coverage, and data to be converted automatically, accordingly. *Sorts* can be considered as hierarchical structures of properties, where each property specifies a data type; properties can be collected and a collection of one or more properties can be assigned as an attribute to another property. *Sorts* can also be considered as class structures, specifying either a single data type or a composition of other class structures.

Each *sort* has a behavioral specification assigned, governing how data entities combine and intersect, and what the result is of subtracting one data entity from another or from a collection of entities from the same sort. This behavioral specification is a prerequisite for the uniform handling of different and a priori unknown data structures and the effective exchange of data between various representations. The behavioral specification of a *sort* is based on a part relationship on the entities of this *sort*, with the *sortal* operations of addition, subtraction, and product defined in accordance to this part relationship. As such, a behavioral specification explicates the match relation (or interpretative mechanism) underlying a *sortal* algebra and grammar. The behavioral specification of a primitive *sort* forms part of the predefined template of this *sort*; composite *sorts* derive their behavioral specification from the component *sorts* in conformity with the compositional operation. In addition, a functional *sort* allows the specification of data (analysis) functions that automatically apply to *sortal* structures through tree traversal.

2.1   A Simple Example

Consider the following example: given a public transportation network, where the transportation nodes represent stations or stops and the edges represent transportation lines, how can we derive a transportation lines connectivity graph, where the nodes represent transportation lines and the edges exchanges between these lines? Basically, we are interested in knowing how many lines there are, which stations or stops are on which line, which lines connect to one another, etc., such that we can take into account the number of exchanges that might be necessary to get from one point to another. We assume that stations and stops have attribute information specifying the lines that stop here.

From a programming point of view, the derivation of a line connectivity graph from a transportation network or stop connectivity graph is not all that complex, but without proper programming knowledge, the task can still be very challenging. We show how one might approach this problem using *sortal* structures. First, we need to define the representational structure we will use as a starting point.

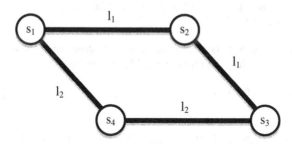

Fig. 1. A simple transportation network consisting of two lines and four stops

Fig. 1 illustrates the data that may be present in the stop connectivity graph. We ignore the format in which the data may be provided, and instead consider the basic data entities that are required. Firstly, we need to represent the stops themselves, e.g., "s1", "s2", "s3" and "s4". We can do so by their name, a string. We define a primitive *sort* with Label as *sortal* template:

```
sort stops : [Label];
form $stops = stops: { "s1", "s2", "s3", "s4"};
```

The first line defines the *sort* stops, with template Label. The second line defines an exemplary data form of *sort* stops and referenced by the *sortal* variable $stops. It defines a collection of stops or, more specifically, stop labels "s1" through "s4". Similarly, we can represent the transportation lines that use a stop also as strings with *sortal* template Label:

```
sort lines : [Label];
form $lines = lines: { "l1", "l2" };
```

Finally, we need to represent the connectivity relations. For this, we use the Property template. Unlike other templates, the Property template requires two primitive *sorts* as arguments, and defines not one but two new primitive *sorts*:

```
sort (connections, rev_connections) : [Property] (stops,
stops);
```

The two arguments define the representational structure for the tails and heads of the connectivity relationship. Since the Property template applies to directional relationships, we consider two resulting sorts: connections and rev_connections (reverse connections). An example is given below.

A complex representational structure is defined as a composition of primitive representational structures. *Sortal* structures offer us two compositional operators: an attribute operator, ^, specifying a subordinate, conjunctive relationship between *sortal* data, and a sum operator, +, specifying a co-ordinate, disjunctive relationship. Considering the room adjacency graph, we can define a corresponding *sortal* structure as follows:

```
sort input : stops ^ (lines + connections +
rev_connections);
```

Stops have lines, connectivity relationships and reverse connectivity relationships as attributes. A corresponding data form would be defined as:

```
form $input = input:
{ #me-stops-1 "s1"
  { (lines): { "l1" },
    (connections): { me-stops-2, me-stops-4 } },
  #me-rooms-2 "r2"
  { (lines): { "l1" },
    (connections): { me-stops-3 } },
  #me-rooms-3 "r3"
  { (lines): { "l1", "l2" },
    (connections): { me-stops-4 } },
  #me-rooms-4 "r4"
  { (lines): { "l2" } } };
```

Of course, this data form may be generated from the original data format, rather then specified in textual form. Especially, the connectivity relationships may be generated automatically from a sequentially-ordered list of stops on a transportation line. `#me-stops-1` is a reference ID for "s1" that can be used later, in the form `me-stops-1`, to reference "s1" in an connectivity relationship from a different stop. The specification of reverse connectivity relationships is optional; the *sortal* interpreter will automatically generate these.

Similarly, we can define a representational structure for the output we need to produce. Consider the goal to group stops on the same line. For this, we can consider lines with stops as attributes; the stops themselves may still have (reverse) connectivity relationships as attributes:

```
sort output : lines ^ stops ^ (connections +
rev_connections);
form $output = output: $input;
```

The second line defines a variable of *sort* `output` with `$input` as data. Since `$input` is defined of sort `input`, the data must be converted to the new *sort*. This conversion is done automatically based on rules of semantic identity and syntactic similarity. The result is:

```
form $output = output:
{ "l1"
  { #me-stops-1 "s1"
    { (connections): { me-stops-2, me-stops-4 } },
    #me-stops-2 "s2"
    { (connections): { me-stops-3 },
      (rev_connections): { me-stops-1 } } },
    #me-stops-3 "s3"
    { (connections): { me-stops-4 },
      (rev_connections): { me-stops-2 } } },
  "l2"
  { #me-stops-1 "s1"
    { (connections): { me-stops-2, me-stops-4 } },
    #me-stops-3 "s3"
    { (connections): { me-stops-4 },
      (rev_connections): { me-stops-2 } },
    #me-stops-4 "s4"
    { (rev_connections): { me-stops-1, me-stops-3 } } } }
};
```

This is a collection of transportation lines, with for each line a list of stops (ordered alphabetically, rather than sequentially), with stop connectivity relationships (and reverse relationships). It does not yet constitute a transportation lines connectivity graph. For this, we need to define relationships (and reverse relationships) between transportation lines:

```
sort (exchanges, rev_exchanges) : [Property] (lines,
lines);
```

We can now consider lines with exchange relationships (and reverse relationships); the lines may still have stops as attributes but for the automatic conversion of the relationships to take place, we must omit the stop connectivity relationships.

```
sort graph : lines ^ (stops + exchanges + rev_exchanges);
form $graph = graph: $ouput;
```

The result will be:

```
form $graph = graph:
{ #me-lines-1 "11"
  { (stops): { "s1", "s2", "s3" },
    (exchanges): { me-lines-1, me-lines-2 },
    (rev_exchanges): { me-lines-1 } },
  #me-lines-2 "12"
  { (stops): { "s1", "s3", "s4" },
    (exchanges): { me-lines-2 },
    (rev_exchanges): { me-lines-1, me-lines-2 } } };
```

Using functional entities integrated in the representational structures, we can also calculate the number of lines, the number of stops per line, etc. For this, we define a new primitive *sort* with Function as *sortal* template, and define a representational structure of counting functions with lines as attribute, where the lines themselves have stops as attributes, though we ignore any relationships:

```
sort counts : [Function];
sort number_of_lines: counts ^ lines ^ stops;
// func count(x) =   c : {c(0) = 0, c(+1) = c + 1};
ind $count = number_of_lines: count(lines.length)
$output;
```

The last line defines a data form as an individual (a single data entity, not a collection of data entities or individuals) contained in the variable $count of *sort* number_of_lines. This individual consists of the count function applied to the length property of the *sort* lines. The function count is pre-defined in the *sortal* interpreter but, otherwise, could be specified as shown in the comment (preceded by '//'). A function always applies to the property of a *sort*. In this case, the exact property doesn't matter as its value is not actually used in the calculation of the result of the count function. The length property of a *sort* with Label as *sortal* template specifies the length—the number of characters—of the corresponding label. The result is:

```
ind $count = number_of_lines: count(lines.length) = 2.0
{ "11"
  { #me-stops-1 "s1",
    #me-stops-2 "s2",
    #me-stops-3 "s3" },
```

```
  "12"
{ #me-stops-1 "s1",
  #me-stops-3 "s3",
  #me-stops-4 "s4" } };
```

Similarly, in order to calculate the number of stops per line, we can apply the function count to the length property of the *sort* stops. We reuse the *sort* number_of_lines for now.

```
ind $count = number_of_lines: count(stops.length)
$output;
```

However, the result will be incorrect as stops belonging to multiple lines will be counted as many times. In order to correct the result, we need to alter the location of the count function in the representational structure to be an attribute of the *sort* lines. We can achieve this simply by creating a new *sort* and relying on the automatic conversion of one data form (or individual) into another.

```
sort number_of_stops: lines ^ counts ^ stops;
form $stops_per_line = number_of_stops: $count;
```

The result is:

```
form $stops_per_line = number_of_stops:
{ "11"
  { 3.0
    { #me-stops-1 "s1",
      #me-stops-2 "s2",
      #me-stops-3 "s3" } },
  "12"
  { 3.0
    { #me-stops-1 "s1",
      #me-stops-3 "s3",
      #me-stops-4 "s4" } } };
```

3   *Sortal* Grammars

Grammars are formal devices for specifying languages. A grammar defines a language as the set of all objects generated by the grammar, where each generation starts with an initial object and uses rules to achieve an object that contains only elements from a terminal vocabulary. A rewriting rule has the form *lhs* → *rhs*; *lhs* specifies the similar object to be recognized, *rhs* specifies the manipulation leading to the resulting object. A rule applies to a particular object if the *lhs* of the rule 'matches' a part of the object under some allowable transformation. Rule application consists of replacing the matching part by the *rhs* of the rule under the same transformation. In other words, when applying a rule $a \rightarrow b$ to an object s under a transformation f such that $f(a) \leq s$, rule application replaces $f(a)$ in s by $f(b)$ and produces the shape s − $f(a)$ + $f(b)$. The set F of valid transformations is dependent on the object type. In the case of geometric entities, the set of valid transformations, commonly, is the set of all Euclidean transformations, which comprise translations, rotations and reflections, augmented with uniform scaling. In the case of textual entities, or labels, case transformations of the constituent letters may constitute valid transformations.

The central problem in implementing grammars is the matching problem, that of determining the transformation under which the match relation holds for the *lhs*. Clearly, this problem depends on the representation of the elements of the algebra. *Sorts* offer a representational flexibility where each *sort* additionally specifies its own match relation as a part of its behavior. For a given *sort*, a rule can be specified as a composition of two data forms, a *lhs* and a *rhs*. This rule applies to any particular data form if the *lhs* of a rule is a part of the data form under any applicable transformation *f*, corresponding to the behavioral specification of the data form's *sort*. Rule application results in the subtraction of *f*(*lhs*) from the data form, followed by the addition of *f*(*rhs*) to the result. Both operations are defined as part of the behavioral specification of a *sort*.

As composite *sorts* derive their behavior from their component *sorts*, the technical difficulties of implementing the matching problem only apply once for each primitive *sort*. As the part relationship can be applied to all kinds of data types, recognition algorithms can easily be extended to deal with arbitrary data representations, considering a proper definition of what constitutes a transformation. Correspondingly, primitive *sorts* can be developed, distributed, and adopted by users without any need for reconfiguring the system. At the same time, the appropriateness of a given grammar formalism for a given problem can easily be tested, the formalism correspondingly adapted, and existing grammar formalisms can be modified to cater for changing requirements or preferences.

The specification of spatial rules and grammars leads naturally to the generation and exploration of possible designs; spatial elements emerging under a part relation is highly enticing to design search [8] and [9]. However, the concept of search is more fundamental to design than its generational form alone might imply. In fact, any mutation of an object into another, or parts thereof, can constitute an action of search. As such, a rule can be considered to specify a particular compound operation or mutation, that is, a composition of operations and/or transformations that is recognized as a new, single, operation and applied as such. Similarly, the creation of a grammar is merely a tool that allows a structuring of a collection of rules or operations that has proven its applicability to the creation of a certain set (or language) of designs.

3.1   *Sortal* Behaviors

The simplest specification of a part relationship corresponds to the subset relationship in mathematical sets. Such a part relationship applies to points and labels, e.g., a point is part of another point only if they are identical, and a label is a part of a collection of labels only if it is identical to one of the labels in the collection. Here, *sortal* operations of addition, subtraction, and product correspond to set union, difference, and intersection, respectively. In other words, if x and y denote two data forms of a *sort* of points (or labels), and X and Y denote the corresponding sets of data elements, i.e., sets of points (or labels), then ($x : X$ specifies X as a representation of x)

$$x : X \wedge y : Y \Rightarrow x \leq y \Leftrightarrow X \subseteq Y$$
$$x + y : X \cup Y$$
$$x - y : X/Y \tag{1}$$
$$x \cdot y : X \cap Y.$$

An alternative behavior applies to weights (e.g., line thicknesses or surface tones) as is apparent from drawings on paper—a single line drawn multiple times, each time with a different thickness, appears as if it were drawn once with the largest thickness, even though it assumes the same line with other thicknesses (see also [11]). When using numeric values to represent weights, the part relation on weights corresponds to the less-than-or-equal relation on numeric values;

$$x : \{m\} \wedge y : \{n\} \Rightarrow x \leq y \Leftrightarrow m \leq n$$
$$x + y : \{\max(m, n)\}$$
$$x - y : \{\} \text{ if } m \leq n, \text{ else } \{m\} \tag{2}$$
$$x \cdot y : \{\min(m, n)\}.$$

Thus, weights combine into a single weight, with its value as the least upper bound of the respective individual weights, i.e., their maximum value. Similarly, the common value (intersection) of a collection of weights is the greatest lower bound of the individual weights, i.e., their minimum value. The result of subtracting one weight from another depends on their relative values and is either the first weight, if it is greater that the second weight, or zero (i.e., no weight).

Another kind of part relationship corresponds to interval behavior. Consider, for example, the specification of a part relationship on line segments. A line segment may be considered as an interval on an infinite line (or carrier); in general, one-dimensional quantities, such as time, can be treated as intervals. An interval is a part of another interval if it is embedded in the latter; intervals on the same carrier that are adjacent or overlap combine into a single interval. Specifically, a behavior for intervals can be expressed in terms of the behavior of the boundaries of intervals. Let $B[x]$ denote the boundary of a data form x of intervals and, given two data forms x and y let I_x denote the collection of boundaries of x that lie within y, O_x denote the collection of boundaries of x that lie outside of y, M the collection of boundaries of both x and y where the respective intervals lie on the same side of the boundary, and N the collection of boundaries of both x and y where the respective intervals lie on opposite sides of the boundary (Fig. 2) [12]. Then,

$$x : B[x] \wedge y : B[y] \Rightarrow x \leq y \Leftrightarrow I_x = 0 \wedge O_y = 0 \wedge N = 0$$
$$x + y : B[x + y] = O_x + O_y + M$$
$$x - y : B[x - y] = O_x + I_y + N \tag{3}$$
$$x \cdot y : B[x \cdot y] = I_x + I_y + M.$$

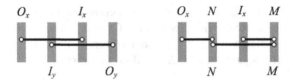

Fig. 2. The specification of the boundary collections I_x, O_x, I_y, O_y, M and N, given two data forms of intervals x (above) and y (below)

This behavior applies to indefinite intervals too, providing that there is an appropriate representation of both (infinite) ends of its carrier. Likewise, behaviors can be specified for area intervals (plane segments) and volume intervals (polyhedral segments). The equations above still apply though the construction of I_x, O_x, I_y, O_y, M, and N is more complex [12].

3.2 Exemplar Grammar Systems

A uniform characterization for a variety of grammar systems is given in [1]. Krishnamurti and Stouffs [13] survey a variety of spatial grammar formalisms from an implementation standpoint. Here, we consider the specification of some of these examples using *sorts*.

3.2.1 Structure Grammars

Structure grammar is an example of a set grammar. "A structure is a symbolic representation of parts and their relationships in a configuration" [3]. A *structure* is represented as a set of pairs, each consisting of a symbol, e.g., a spatial icon, and a transformation. The resulting algebra corresponds to the Cartesian product of the respective algebras for the set of symbols and the group of transformations. Both symbols and transformations define *sorts* with discrete behavior, i.e., respective sets match under the subset relationship. These combine into a composite *sort* under the attribute relationship; each symbol in a set may have one or more transformations assigned as an attribute.

```
sort symbols : [ImageUrl];
sort transformations : [Transformation];
sort structures : symbols ^ transformations;
```

The *sort* symbols is specified to use the *sortal* template ImageUrl, a variant on the template Label that allows the label to be treated as a URL pointing towards an image that can be downloaded and displayed.

3.2.2 Tartan Worlds

Tartan Worlds [14] is a spatial grammar formalism that bestrides string and set grammars. We consider a simplified string grammar version of the *Tartan Worlds*: each symbol in a string corresponds to a geometrical entity represented as a graphical icon and located on a grid. A rule in these *simplified Tartan Worlds* [13] consists of one symbol on the *lhs* and symbols on the *rhs* given in their spatial relation. An equivalent *sortal* grammar may be defined over a *sort* composed over a grid of a *sort* of graphical icons. On a fixed-sized grid, the behavior of the composite *sort* breaks down into the behavior of the *sort* of graphical icons, e.g., ordinal or discrete, over each grid cell. The matching relation is defined in the same way.

```
sort icons : [ImageUrl];
sort tartan_worlds : icons {30, 20};
```

Again, the *sort* `icons` is specified to use the *sortal* template `ImageUrl`, The *sort* `tartan_worlds` is defined as a composition of the *sort* `icons` over a fixed-size grid, similar to a two-dimensional array, of 30 by 20.

3.2.3 Augmented Shape Grammars

A *shape* [1] is defined as a finite arrangement of spatial elements from among points, lines, planes, or volumes, of limited but non-zero measure. A shape is a part of another shape if it is embedded in the other shape as a smaller or equal element; shapes adhere to the maximal element representation [15] and [16]. Shapes of the same dimensionality belong to the same algebra; these define a *sort*. A shape consisting of more than one type of spatial elements belongs to the algebra given by the Cartesian product of the algebras of its spatial element types. The respective *sorts* combine under the operation of sum, as a disjunctive composition.

A shape can be augmented by distinguishing spatial elements, e.g., by labeling, weighting, or coloring these elements. Augmented shapes also specify an algebra as a Cartesian product of the respective shape algebra and the algebra of the distinguishing attributes. However, the resulting behavior can better be expressed with a *sort* that is a subordinate composition of the respective *sorts*, i.e., combined under the attribute operator. A *sort* of labels may adhere to a discrete behavior, a *sort* of weights to an ordinal behavior; a weight matches another weight if it has a smaller or equal value.

Most shape grammars only allow for line segments and labeled points:

```
sort line_segments : [LineSegment];
sort labeled_points : (points : [Point]) ^ (labels :
[Label]);
sort shapes : line_segments + labeled_points;
```

3.3 *Sortal* Rules

When considering a simple *sortal* grammar, the grammar rules can all be specified within the same *sort* as defined for the grammar formalism. In the case of more complex *sortal* grammars, or when the grammar formalism may change or develop over time, it may be worthwhile to consider grammar rules that are specified within a different *sort*, for example, a simpler *sort* or a previously adopted *sort*, without having to rewrite these to the *sortal* formalism currently adopted. *Sortal* grammar formalisms support this through the subsumption relationship over *sorts*. This subsumption relationship underlies the ability to compare *sortal* representations, and assess data loss when exchanging data from one *sort* to another. When a representation subsumes another, the entities represented by the latter can also be represented by the former representation, without any data loss.

Under the disjunctive operation of sum, any entity of the resulting *sort* is necessarily an entity of one of the constituent sorts. *Sortal* disjunction consequently defines a subsumption relationship on *sorts* (denoted '≤'), as follows:

$$a \leq b \Leftrightarrow a + b = b; \qquad (4)$$

a disjunctive *sort* subsumes each constituent *sort*.

Most logic-based formalisms link subsumption directly to information specificity, that is, a structure is subsumed by another, if this structure contains strictly more information than the other. The subsumption relationship on *sorts* can also be considered in terms of information specificity, however, there is a distinction to be drawn in the way in which subsumption is treated in *sorts* and in first-order logic based representational formalisms. First-order logic formalisms generally consider a relation of inclusion (hyponymy relation), commonly denoted as an is-a relationship. *Sorts*, on the other hand, consider a part-of relationship (meronymy relation).

Two simple examples illustrate this distinction. Consider a disjunction of a *sort* of points and a *sort* of line segments; this allows for the representation of both points and line segments. We can say that the *sort* of points forms part of the *sort* of points and line segments—note the part-of relationship. In first-order logic, this corresponds to the union of points and line segments. We can say that both are bounded geometrical entities of zero or one dimensions—note the is-a relationship.

This distinction becomes even more important when we consider an extension of *sortal* subsumption to the attribute operator. Consider a *sort* cost_types as a composition under the attribute relationship of a *sort* types with template Label and a sort costs with template Weight:

```
sort cost_types : (types : [Label]) ^ (costs : [Weight])
```

For example, these cost values may be specified per unit length or surface area for building components. If we lessen the conjunctive character of the attribute operator by making the cost attribute entity optional, then, we can consider a type label to be a cost type without an associated cost value or, preferably, a type label to be part of a cost type, that is, the sort of types is part of the sort of cost types. Vice versa, the sort of cost types subsumes the sort of types or, in general:

$$a \leq a \wedge b. \qquad (5)$$

In logic formalisms, a relational construct is used to represent such associations. For example, in description logic [17], roles are defined as binary relationships between concepts. Consider a concept Label and a concept Color; the concept of colored labels can then be represented as Label ∩ ∃hasAttribute.Color, denoting those labels that have an attribute that is a color. Here, ∩ denotes intersection and ∃R.C denotes full existential quantification with respect to role R and concept C. It follows then that Label ∩ ∃hasAttribute.Color ⊆ Label; that is, the concept of labels subsumes the concept of colored labels—this is quite the reverse of how it is considered in *sorts*.

As such, a shape rule specified for a *sort* of line segments and labeled points remains applicable if we extend the formalism to include plane segments or even volumes (if all considered in three dimensions). Similarly, the shape rule would still apply if we adapt the formalism to consider colored labels as attributes to the points, or line segments for that matter.

Another important distinction is that first order logic-based representations generally make for an open world assumption—that is, nothing is excluded unless it is done so explicitly. For example, shapes may have a color assigned. When looking for a yellow square, logically, every square is considered a potential solution—unless, it has an explicitly specified color, or it is otherwise known not to have the yellow color. The fact that a color is not specified does not exclude an object from potentially being yellow. As such, logic-based representations are automatically considered to be incomplete. *Sorts*, on the other hand, hold to a closed world assumption. That is, we work with just the data we have. A shape has a color only if one is explicitly assigned: when looking for a yellow square, any square will not do; it has to have the yellow color assigned. This restriction is used to constrain the application of grammar rules, as in the use of labeled points to constrain the application of shape grammar rules. Another way of looking at this distinction between the open or closed world assumptions is to consider their applicability to knowledge representation. To reiterate, logic-based representations essentially represent knowledge; *sorts*, on the other hand, are intended to represent data—any reasoning is based purely on present (or emergent) data.

4   Urban Design Grammars

Beirão, Duarte and Stouffs [18] present components of an urban design grammar inferred from an extension plan for the city of Praia in Cabo Verde (Figure 3). The development of the urban grammar forms part of a large research project called City Induction aiming at integrating an urban program formulation model [19], a design generation model [20] and an evaluation model [21] in a 'computer aided urban design' tool. The central idea to the project is to read and interpret data from the site context on a GIS platform, generate program descriptions according to the context conditions, and from that program generate alternative design solutions guided by evaluation processes in order to obtain satisfactory design solutions. The architecture of the proposed tool considers urban grammars as an extension of the discursive grammar schema developed by Duarte [22] and adapted for urban design. From the technical viewpoint a discursive grammar includes a shape grammar to describe the formal properties of the context, the program, and the design; a description grammar to describe their other, non-formal but relevant properties [23]; and a set of heuristics to guide generation towards designs that match the program. From the operative viewpoint, a discursive grammar includes a formulation grammar that generates the program from an interpretation of the context and a generation grammar that generates design solutions that match the program. An evaluation mechanism is invoked to ensure that the program fits the context and the design matches the program. A common ontology provides a common protocol to describe the urban domain, in order to guarantee an effective communication between the three components of the tool.

Fig. 3. Plan for the city of Praia, Cabo Verde

The formulation of urban programs proceeds by manipulating an urban pattern language [24] defined as a description grammar. An urban pattern represents recurrent spatial features found in urban space, for instance, 'high density housing' or 'public square.' In addition to the name, which constitutes a descriptive identifier of the pattern, each pattern includes a description of the context in which the pattern may occur, links to other related patterns of higher or smaller scale, and links to one or more 'Urban Induction Patterns,' whose rules can be used to instantiate the pattern. When an urban pattern's context is found in the design context, it is added to the urban program and the corresponding urban induction patterns are triggered. The set of triggered urban induction patterns form a generic urban design grammar. The generation of urban designs involves the selection of urban induction patterns from those triggered by the urban program and their application to the design context, in an iterative process. Each urban induction pattern is encoded as a small discursive grammar (a descriptive grammar, a shape or spatial grammar and a set of heuristics). It is called urban induction pattern because it can be used to formalize a solution that matches the context, thereby inducing a specific urban solution. Each urban induction pattern is encoded by rules whose shape part replicates the design moves of urban designers when formalizing the pattern [25] and whose descriptive part generates a description that matches a part of the urban program. Therefore, in the envisioned tool, designing is a two-step process. The first step is the development of a specific urban grammar—or urban design language—from the generic grammar by choosing which urban induction patterns to apply and by restricting the parameter values of the selected patterns. The second step is the application of the selected urban induction patterns—or discursive grammars— to the context, which involves the application of urban design rules so as to match the requirements of the urban program. The 'shape grammar' part of the discursive grammar may itself be a compound spatial grammar that may include one or more (2D or 3D) shape grammars, but also a raster-based string or set grammar, in order to allow rule-based operations on both vectorized and rasterized GIS data, as well as any other spatial data. All spatial grammar manifestations considered here would allow for various attribute data to be associated with the spatial elements, not just labels as is strictly the case for shape grammars.

The urban design process transforms the urban space, specifically, a particular intervention area by reacting to data available from the design context. This may involve dealing with highly differentiated kinds of data, including data representing pre-existent landscape or urban elements, population data, economical data, historical data, higher scale planning goals, stakeholders' interests and other data, depending on the particular context. GIS platforms provide ways of relating geographical data and representational data together with other kinds of data that may be attached to the representations through a common reference system. Representing the complexity of urban structures has always been a difficult problem to solve. The domain is vast and complex. As a result of such complexity, urban analysis and urban design experts have been using different tools and the two processes of urban analysis and design have been almost separated, while running against the commonly accepted move-see-move cycle of a reflective design process, thereby preventing a higher degree of interactivity between analysis, design and the validation of design decisions (evaluation).

Sorts provide an efficient formalism for the representation of the urban domain relating spatial elements, attributes of these elements and several kinds of data on the site context that may be essential in decision-making during the urban design process. In the urban design domain, *sorts* are mainly defined as compositions of spatial types, specifying spatial elements such as points, line segments, plane segments or volumes, and attribute data types specifying values such as labels or numeric values.

A previous paper [26] shows part of an ontology for describing cities, which represents the interoperability protocol between the three models in the City Induction project. The paper focuses on the description of networks as one of the five top levels of the ontology and specifically on the description of streets. The five top-level classes are identified as *Networks*, *Blocks*, *Zones*, *Landscape* and *Focal_Points*. Each class can be structured as *sorts* and compositions thereof.

The network class distinguishes five different concepts involving the representation of networks, namely, *Axial_Network*, *Street_Nomenclature*, *Transportation_Network*, *Street_Descriptions* and *Street_Components*. In short, *Axial_Network* represents the city networks (e.g. street networks, bus networks, bicycle networks); *Street_Nomenclature*, the names of street types in a given culture; *Transportation_Network*, the classification of streets in terms of their hierarchical role in the transportation network (e.g., distribution street, local street); *Street_Descriptions* are descriptions of the components of a street type, basically a sequence of street components; and *Street_Components* is a set of parametric components of streets (e.g., sidewalk, car lane, bus lane).

Sorts of augmented shapes define different levels of detail of street representations and are defined as a composition under the attribute relationship of *sorts* of shapes and *sorts* of attribute values on different levels. For example, the *sort* `street_network`, considered as part of a *sort* `Axial_Network`, is a composition of the *sort* `axes` and the *sort* `street_hierarchies`, where the *sort* `axes` is itself composed of `axial_segments` and `axial_nodes`. The axial nodes connect the axial segments to form axes, which combined with street hierarchies form the street network. Axial nodes and axial segments are, respectively, represented by line segments and points, each with identifier attributes. The street hierarchies are represented by labels.

```
sort axial_segments : (segments : [LineSegment]) ^
(segmentIDs : [Key])
sort axial_nodes : (nodes : [Point]) ^ (nodeIDs : [Key])
sort axes : axial_segments + axial_nodes;
sort street_hierarchies : [Label];
sort street_network : axes ^ street_hierarchies;
```

Designs in this system are obtained through a procedural approach. At any stage of the design process certain conditions are verified against the existing context, which sets the available inputs for the generation model. However, not all the data is available in the beginning of the design process, nor is it possible to extract all input information from the design context as some of the design decisions may concern the designers personal design language or the reaction to a previous design move. Urban induction patterns produce designs using only some of the *sorts* from the total *sortal* structure available. Some might use new *sorts* while others may generate designs using only entities provided by *sorts* that have been used before. Such a process basically extends (or not) the amount of available features in the context and, as urban induction patterns are only made available when certain occurrences are found in the design (or design context), then each time a new *sort* is used new patterns become available to extend the design options to new levels of detail.

The advantages of such a structure are:

- Allows an incremental urban design process allowing customized design decisions.
- The use of grammar formalisms generates designs with predefined representational structures without interfering with the design decisions. This representational structure allows the integration of the designs within a GIS platform making available the advantages of the use of available GIS assessment tools.
- It provides the structure to link different types of grammar formalisms, which may link spatial elements with other data entities (attributes) allowing for higher standard semantics.
- Links analysis, design generation and evaluation in the same design process, providing an interactive information structure which is adequate for the holistic characteristics of design decisions while taking advantage of the available tools. It corresponds to the integration of decision support systems in the regular workflow of urban design.

5   Conclusion

Sorts specify a common syntax for the representation of urban design information, allowing for different vocabularies and languages to be created, and for a variety in grammar formalisms to be defined and adopted. This makes it specifically applicable to urban design generation considering a pattern-based approach, where urban design patterns may consider a variety of features to be represented in the design context and generate new kinds of features not previously used within the design process. The City Induction project considers such an approach for a computer aided urban design tool and considers *sorts* as a means to express and represent urban design and modeling information and rules.

Acknowledgments. The authors wish to thank Ramesh Krishnamurti for his contributions to the *sortal* research. The City Induction project is funded by Fundação para a Ciência e Tecnologia (FCT), Portugal (PTDC/AUR/64384/2006), hosted by ICIST at TU Lisbon, and coordinated by José P. Duarte. José Beirão is also funded by FCT, grant SFRH/BD/39034/2007.

References

1. Stiny, G.: Introduction to shape and shape grammars. Environment and Planning B: Planning and Design 7, 343–351 (1980)
2. Stiny, G.: A note on the description of designs. Environment and Planning B: Planning and Design 8, 257–267 (1981)
3. Carlson, C., McKelvey, R., Woodbury, R.F.: An introduction to structure and structure grammars. Environment and Planning B: Planning and Design 18, 417–426 (1991)
4. Duarte, J.P., Correia, R.: Implementing a description grammar: generating housing programs online. Construction Innovation: Information, Process, Management 6(4), 203–216 (2006)
5. Duarte, J.P.: A discursive grammar for customizing mass housing: the case of Siza's houses at Malagueira. Automation in Construction 14, 265–275 (2005)
6. Stouffs, R., Krishnamurti, R.: Sortal grammars as a framework for exploring grammar formalisms. In: Burry, M., Datta, S., Dawson, A., et al. (eds.) Mathematics and Design 2001, pp. 261–269. The School of Architecture & Building, Deakin University, Geelong, Australia (2001)
7. Stouffs, R.: Constructing design representations using a sortal approach. Advanced Engineering Informatics 22(1), 71–89 (2008)
8. Mitchell, W.J.: A computational view of design creativity. In: Gero, J.S., Mahel, M.L. (eds.) Modeling Creativity and Knowledge-Based Creative Design. Lawrence Erlbaum Associates, Hillsdale (1993)
9. Stiny, G.: Emergence and continuity in shape grammars. In: Flemming, U., Van Wyk, S. (eds.) CAAD Futures 1993, pp. 37–54. North-Holland, Amsterdam (1993)
10. Gips, J., Stiny, G.: Production systems and grammars: a uniform characterization. Environment and Planning B: Planning and Design 7, 399–408 (1980)
11. Stiny, G.: Weights. Environment and Planning B: Planning and Design 19, 413–430 (1992)

12. Krishnamurti, R., Stouffs, R.: The boundary of a shape and its classification. Journal of Design Research 4(1) (2004)
13. Krishnamurti, R., Stouffs, R.: Spatial grammars: motivation, comparison and new results. In: Flemming, U., Van Wyk, S. (eds.) CAAD Futures 1993, pp. 57–74. North-Holland, Amsterdam (1993)
14. Woodbury, R.F., Radford, A.D., Taplin, P.N., et al.: Tartan worlds: a generative symbol grammar system. In: Noble, D., Kensek, K. (eds.) ACADIA 1992 (1992)
15. Krishnamurti, R.: The maximal representation of a shape. Environment and Planning B: Planning and Design 19, 585–603 (1992)
16. Stouffs, R.: The algebra of shapes. Ph.D. dissertation. School of Architecture, Carnegie Mellon University, Pittsburgh, PA (1994)
17. Baader, F., Calvanese, D., McGuinness, D., et al.: The Description Logic Handbook: Theory, Implementation and Applications. Cambridge University, Cambridge (2003)
18. Beirão, J., Duarte, J., Stouffs, R.: An Urban Grammar for Praia: Towards Generic Shape Grammars for Urban Design. In: Computation: The New Realm of Architectural Design, pp. 575–584. Istanbul Technical University, Istanbul (2009)
19. Montenegro, N.C., Duarte, J.P.: Towards a Computational Description of Urban Patterns. In: Muylle, M. (ed.) Architecture 'in computro', Integrating Methods and Techniques, pp. 239–248. eCAADe and Artesis Hogeschool Antwerpen, Antwerp (2008)
20. Beirão, J., Duarte, J., Stouffs, R.: Structuring a Generative Model for Urban Design: Linking GIS to Shape Grammars. In: Muylle, M. (ed.) Architecture 'in computro', Integrating Methods and Techniques, pp. 929–938. eCAADe and Artesis Hogeschool Antwerpen, Antwerp (2008)
21. Gil, J., Duarte, J.P.: Towards an Urban Design Evaluation Framework. In: Muylle, M. (ed.) Architecture 'in computro', Integrating Methods and Techniques, pp. 257–264. eCAADe and Artesis Hogeschool Antwerpen, Antwerp (2008)
22. Duarte, J.P.: A Discursive Grammar for Customizing Mass Housing: the case of Siza's houses at Malagueira. Automation in Construction 14(2), 265–275 (2005)
23. Stiny, G.: A note on the description of designs. Environment and Planning B: Planning and Design 8(3), 257–267 (1981)
24. Alexander, C., Ishikawa, S., Silverstein, M.: A Pattern Language: Towns, Buildings, Construction. Oxford University, Oxford (1977)
25. Schön, D.: The Reflective Practitioner: How Professionals Think in Action. Basic Books, New York (1983)
26. Beirão, J., Montenegro, N., Gil, J., et al.: The city as a street system: A street description for a city ontology. In: SIGraDi 2009 - Proceedings of the 13th Congress of the Iberoamerican Society of Digital Graphics, São Paulo, Brazil, November 16-18, pp. 132–134 (2009)

Sort Machines

Thomas Grasl[1] and Athanassios Economou[2]

[1] SWAP, Lange Gasse 16/12, 1080 Vienna, Austria
tg@swap-zt.com
[2] College of Architecture, Georgia Institute of Technology,
247 4th St, Atlanta, 30332 USA
economou@coa.gatech.edu

Abstract. A graph grammar for the generation of topologies for the U.S. federal courthouse typology is introduced. Possible configurations are enumerated and a nomenclature is proposed.

Keywords: Shape Grammars, Graph Grammars, Typology, Courthouse design.

1   Introduction

Contemporary U.S. Courthouses pose unique design challenges. They have complex functional requirements and vary extensively in their size, volume, configuration, form, program and style. The courthouse design itself has received lots of attention in the past few years under the GSA Design Excellence Program, a program that has fostered a series of many innovative designs to be built and a corresponding interest in the theoretical debate about the design of these buildings. For recent accounts of the functional and formal organization of these buildings, see for example, Phillips and Griebel (2003); Gruzen, Daskalakis and Krasnow (2006); USCDG (2008); Leers (2011); Economou and Grasl (2011).

The tell-the-tale characteristic of the federal courthouses is their division in three distinct, independent zones and networks that all meet at the courtrooms of the courthouse. These three zones are: a) the public zone intended for the circulation and accommodation of the general public including attorneys, clients, witnesses and jurors; b) the restricted zone, intended for the circulation and accommodation of judges, court clerks, court employees and jurors; and c) the secure zone intended for the circulation and accommodation of the defendants in custody. The functional requirements of these three zones can be quite complex. For example, the public zone includes central public halls and waiting areas, as well as circulation corridors, staircases, elevators, restrooms etc. The restricted zone includes jury facilities, judges' chambers suites, court libraries, clerk's offices, probation and pre-trial offices, court units, as well as circulation corridors, staircases, elevators, restrooms, mechanical

S. Müller Arisona et al. (Eds.): DUMS, CCIS 242, pp. 117–137, 2012.

areas, maintenance areas, storage areas, and so forth. Finally the secure zone includes holding areas and circulation corridors, staircases, elevators and so forth. All zones include and terminate into the various courtrooms, that become thus, literally and figuratively, the core of the courthouse. A definitive and detailed account of the exact functions, area requirements and accessibility relations required for the federal courthouses is given in the U.S. Courts Design Guide (2008).

Still, while the programmatic decomposition of these buildings is thoroughly documented, currently there is no consensus on the nature and spatial characteristics of the underlying configurations that can accommodate such complex program. A first systematic attempt for the description, interpretation and evaluation of the existing federal courthouses and for the design of new ones is currently under way (Economou and Grasl, 2011). The study includes a formal description of the existing courthouses that have been built under the aegis of the GSA Design Excellence Program and an associated database that supports the model.

The model considers courthouses as binary compositions of two spatial systems: a) the courtroom system (hard system); and b) the administrative and support organization of the courthouse (soft system). The hard system is the most rigid and clearly defined part of the courthouse organization and it consists of all the courtrooms of a courthouse and their associated spaces. This system typically extends to one or more building plates to produce a two-dimensional or three-dimensional spatial organization respectively. The soft system is the most flexible and adaptable part of the courthouse organization and it consists of all the administrative and support functions needed for the proper function of the courthouse. This system typically extends as well to one or more building plates to produce a two-dimensional or three-dimensional spatial organization respectively. Both systems, the hard and the soft, consist of subsystems that are connected one to another and with the three independent network systems found in contemporary courthouses.

The corresponding database illustrates the model by providing an extensive documentation of the existing federal courthouses including figure-ground diagrams, accessibility diagrams, zone diagrams, numerical data, immersive images, photographs, drawings and so forth. All media allow for comparative views and evaluations of the courthouses in various representations. There are currently forty-nine case studies in the database and on-going work provides for more case studies and further expansion of the representations used for the description and evaluation of federal courthouses. A sample of the corpus in the system foregrounding the relation of the public zone to the courtroom zone is shown in Figure 1.

Fig. 1. Figure ground courthouse diagrams showing the relation of public zone and courtrooms

Embedded within this larger project on the analysis and generative description of federal courthouses, the aim of this work is to test and implement potential modelling techniques to account for a constructive description of the courtroom organization. More specifically, the work here reports on a specific graph-theoretic model that can generate and enumerate all possible topologies for the courtroom organisation typology given a specific methodological framework. The model includes: a) an initial graph representing an ensemble of two or three zones grouped around one, two or more courtrooms; b) a graph theoretic rule-set covering all legal combinations and modifications of the initial basic element; c) a rewriting process to apply a variable number of rules and generate rudimentary descriptions of possible courthouse designs in terms of accessibility graphs; and d) an expansion of the nodes of the graphs into detailed spatial descriptions.

Graph notation and terminology are according to Harary (1994), more specifically to the architectural interpretation of Steadman (1976). A comparative account of graph grammar formalisms with respect to production systems is given in Gips and Stiny (1980). The project is implemented using GrGen.Net (Geiß et al., 2006), a graph rewriting system which is formally based on the single push-out approach (SPO) (Rozenberg, 1997) extended by features such as negative application conditions (NAC), attributes and retyping. Although multigraphs can be handled by the system and they are thinkable in accessibility graphs, they make little sense at this level of detail and are hence suppressed where necessary using NACs. A more involved graph grammar taking advantage of multigraph representation for the automation of the Palladian shape grammar is given in Grasl (2011).

2   Topological Grammar

The graph theoretic model requires that all spaces of the courtroom organization are mapped upon discrete nodes. The accessibility relations between these spaces are represented by the edges of the graph. Adjacent nodes may be combined and/or concatenated to produce smaller or bigger spaces and zones but they can never be combined with nodes that belong in some other zone. Clearly the notion of a collapse of two nodes into one, or the corresponding expansion of one node into two, has architectural implications and both views suggest different insights into the structure of the courtroom organization. The graph grammar developed here can be applied at various representational levels of the courtroom organization. The granularity of the functions that comprise the zones of the courthouse follows the existing design guide specifications (USCDG, 2007). An example of a graph model of a hypothetical courtroom plate into three levels of detail for zones, components and subcomponents, is shown in Figure 2.

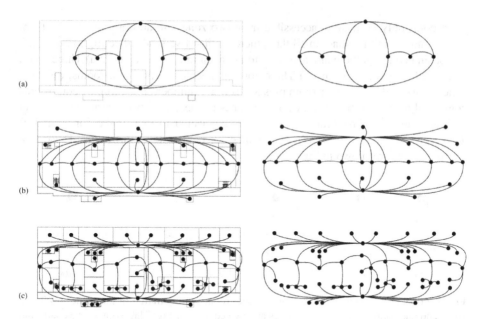

Fig. 2. Possible functional levels of details for a hypothetical courtroom plate: a) Zones; (b) Components; (c) Subcomponents

2.1   Model

A key problem in the design of the courtroom organisation is that all three zones of the courthouse require access to a courtroom. Since courthouses mostly contain numerous courtrooms the designer is often faced with the problem of finding layouts for three or more courtrooms on a floor. This problem corresponds to the $K_{3,3}$ complete bipartite graph, well known from Kuratowski's theorem. It has been proven that this graph cannot be laid out in the plane (see for example, Harary, 1994). Hence the maximal number of courtrooms one triple of zones can serve in the plane is two. Should three or more courtrooms be required on a particular floor additional vertical circulation elements must be inserted. A model of the $K_{3,3}$ bipartite graph for three courtrooms and three distinct zones is shown in Figure 3.

Fig. 3. The complete bipartite graph $K_{3,3}$. Z_1, Z_2 and Z_3 denote the three distinct zones of the courthouse, and C_1, C_2 and C_3 denote distinct courtrooms

Still, there are courtroom types, such as bankruptcy courtrooms, which do not require access from a secure zone (Greenberg, 1973; USCDG, 2007). Because these courtrooms only need to be accessible from two zones, an arbitrary number of them can be laid out in the plane. In all then, there are just five kinds of configurations, that can be embedded in the plane and need to be taken into consideration: a) Three zones connected to one courtroom; b) Three zones connected to two courtrooms; c) Three zones connected to one courtroom plus an arbitrary number of bankruptcy courtrooms connected to two of the zones; d) Three zones connected to two courtrooms plus an arbitrary number of bankruptcy courtrooms connected to two of the zones; and e) Two zones connected to an arbitrary number of bankruptcy courtrooms. These five configurations are shown in Figure 4.

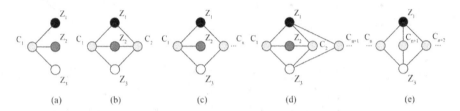

(a)   (b)   (c)   (d)   (e)

Fig. 4. Possible embeddings of the zones - courtrooms configuration in the plane: (a) Three zones and one courtroom; (b) Three zones and two courtrooms; (c) Three zones, one courtroom and an arbitrary number of bankruptcy courtrooms; d) Three zones, two courtrooms and an arbitrary number of bankruptcy courtrooms; and e) Two zones and an arbitrary number of bankruptcy courtrooms

For the sake of algorithmic and visual simplicity each of these five configurations can be collapsed to a single graph, the complete bipartite graph $K_{1,2}$. In this graph, one node, labelled here as an ensemble node (E_n), represents each of the five configurational cases of possible connections of a single zone with all possible types and numbers of courtrooms. The concatenation of the nodes of the graph representing zones and courtrooms onto the ensemble node is shown diagrammatically in Figure 5.

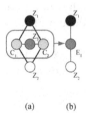

(a)   (b)

Fig. 5. The complete bipartite graph $K_{1,2}$. a) The unfolded version consisting of three zones (Z_n) for $n=3$ and two courtrooms nodes (C_i); (b) Its collapsed version.

There are examples were such conglomerates are both assignable to a specific courtroom and separated by circulation corridors. It is clear as well that arrangements of such conglomerates could produce heuristic patterns that may involve all possible configurational possibilities including point/central, linear and planar growth. Some hypothetical patterns involving possible arrangements of these concatenated spaces are shown in Figure 6.

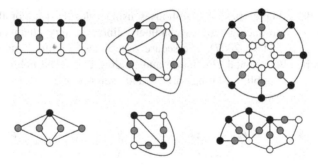

Fig. 6. Possible courthouse floor graphs with connected zones

2.2 Rules

The generation of topologies commences with the initial graph (Fig. 7). It is a single collapsed element as defined above.

Fig. 7. The initial graph consists of one collapsed basic element

The rules for the generating graph grammar are of two different kinds. Rules 1-4 add new triples to the already existing graph in all variations (Fig. 8). The main criterion for a legal addition is that the triples zone-nodes must be connected to like nodes of the graph. Rules 5 and 6 operate within a specific zone. They allow the addition of edges between like nodes in order to introduce circuits and additional circulation possibilities. These two rules contain NACs to prevent multigraphs.

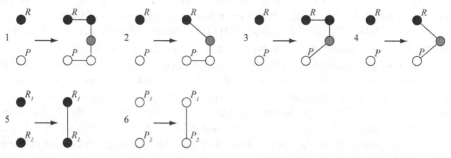

Fig. 8. The rules which generate the basic topologies. Labeled nodes are mapped from left to right during the rewriting process. All other nodes are either created or deleted.

Finally these rudimentary topologies can be refined to include more detail. The previously collapsed courtroom ensembles can be expanded into one of the five variants using rules 7-10 (Fig. 9). Moreover the zone nodes can be expanded to better approximate the complexities of courthouses using rules 11-13. For the restricted zone this means introducing judge's chambers, libraries, jury chambers and other essential spaces (USCDG, 2007). The secure zone is less manifold and usually only consists of vertical/horizontal circulation and holding cells. The public zone can be differentiated into public waiting areas and semi-public offices for various administrative purposes.

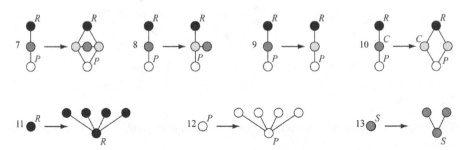

Fig. 9. Rules to expand the rudimentary topology graph and give the representation more detail

2.3   Enumeration

For the time being the main interest has been focused on finding topologies where the two obligatory zones are connected. Other configurations in which the two obligatory zones are not connected are conceivable and do exist, see for example, the Erie Federal Courthouse; still, these configurations are seldom. The following enumeration counts the number of possible rudimentary topologies, before the expansion is commenced.

Finding topological combinations according to the above limitations is no trivial task, thus far a subset of the problem could be solved using the Pólya Enumeration Theorem (PET) to count configurations, furthermore a procedural approach giving all configurations could be described. The appropriate method for this inquiry can be found in Pólya's theorem of counting non-equivalent configurations with respect to a given permutation group (Pólya et al, 1983). For architectural applications of the theorem, see Economou (1999), Din and Economou (2011). Essentially, Pólya's theory of counting specifies the structurally different ways that m elements can be distributed to the n vertices of a figure without considering any two arrangements as different if they can be transformed one to another by a symmetry operation. A fundamental assumption here is that any shape can be represented as a symbolic sentence representing the permutations of the vertices of the shape induced under the symmetry group of the figure. This symbolic sentence, the cycle index of the permutation group of the vertices of the shape, provides the blueprint for the enumeration of all possible non-equivalent arrangements of the m elements upon the n vertices.

In Pólya's notation a cycle of order k is represented by the variable f_k, and a combination of cycles of various orders, say a cycle of order k and a cycle of order l, is represented as a product of variables $f_k f_l$. For example, a permutation of the four vertices of a square induced by a half-turn rotation about the centre of the square produces two cycles of order 2 and is denoted as $f_2 f_2$ or f_2^2. The sum of all products of cycles of permutations induced by the elements of the symmetry group divided to the total number of the elements in the group is the cycle index of a permutation group of the vertices of the figure.

The core of Pólya's theorem lies on an ingenious substitution of the cycles of permutations with a figure inventory of elements that are to be permuted upon the structure. For f_k a cycle of order k and a figure inventory, say, $x + y$ equal to m this substitution is given in (1).

$$f_k = x^k + y^k \qquad (1)$$

This is not the usual algebraic expansion! And still this expansion combines with the regular algebraic expansion required for the computation of the products of cycles captured by the binomial and more generally, the multinomial theorem. For example, for a product of cycles f_k^l and a figure inventory of elements, say, $x + y$ equal to m, the substitution is given in (2).

$$f_k^l = (x^k + y^k)^l \qquad (2)$$

The computation of such products and expansions can be formidable but it is rewarding. The coefficients in any expansion of the form $(x+y)^n$, whereas n any natural number, can be taken from the Pascal's triangle or from the binomial theorem - and in general for any number $n>3$ of elements in the figure inventory from the multinomial theorem. The binomial theorem is given in (3), its expansion is given in (4) and the formula for each coefficient in (5).

$$(x + y)^n = \sum_{r+s=n} \frac{n!}{r!s!} x^r y^s \qquad (3)$$

$$(x + y)^n = \binom{n}{0}x^n y^0 + \binom{n}{1}x^{n-1}y^1 + \cdots + \binom{n}{n-1}x^1 y^{n-1} + \binom{n}{n}x^0 y^n \qquad (4)$$

$$\text{whereas } \binom{n}{k} = \frac{n!}{k!(n-k)!}, \text{ for } n > k > 0 \qquad (5)$$

The resulting coefficients of all the terms after the expansion of the cycle index in powers of x and y give the non-equivalent configurations of the elements x and y upon the structure. For example, the coefficient of a term, say, $x^r y^s$ for $r + s = n$ gives the distinct ways that r x-elements and s y-elements can be arranged on the structure.

Pólya's formalism provides the answer for $m>n$ as well; that is, in principle, it is possible to know the different number of ways any number of entities m can be permuted in an n-vertex figure without considering any two arrangements as different if they can be mapped one to another by a symmetry operation. And the generalization of the theorem can be further attained through a more general form of the figure inventory. Figure inventory in the standard format of the theorem is the sum of variables or choices in a design context. The idea is that each choice in the figure inventory is associated with a value that is not a unique variable. In the previous example, the figure inventory consists of two elements and is denoted as $x+y$. If for example, we cared to arrange these two elements in clusters of threes, and we wanted to know in how many different ways we can place in a vertex, say, *3 x-elements, 2 x-elements and 1 y-element*, and *1 x-element and 2 y-elements*, then these possibilities would be represented in the figure inventory as $x^3+x^2y+xy^2$. The extension of the theorem to any number of variables and any conceivable cluster formation is straightforward (Pólya et al, 1983 p.74-85).

In order to apply this theorem to the enumeration of courthouse topologies we will first of all restrict the enquiry to topologies with three ensemble elements. The graphs to be enumerated all exhibit the following pattern: Two graphs, each connected and with up to three nodes, are connected to each via three ensemble nodes. The four configurations the two obligatory zones can take on are shown in Table 1 along with their cycle indices and a string with corresponding symmetry properties.

Table 1. The four possible graphs for the obligatory zones, their cycle indices, and a string with corresponding symmetry properties

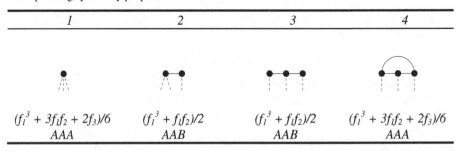

1	2	3	4
$(f_1^3 + 3f_1f_2 + 2f_3)/6$	$(f_1^3 + f_1f_2)/2$	$(f_1^3 + f_1f_2)/2$	$(f_1^3 + 3f_1f_2 + 2f_3)/6$
AAA	AAB	AAB	AAA

Essentially we have to count the number of ways to connect two such configurations via three ensemble nodes. These connections can also be represented as labels to aid us in applying Pólya's Enumeration Theorem (Fig. 10).

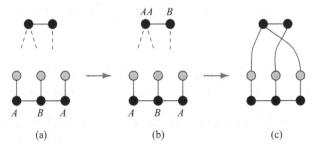

Fig. 10. Counting connections: (a) Frame of the graphs to be enumerated; (b) Labelling the nodes; (c) A valid topology

Each of the configurations according to the string representation in Table 1 has to be directly connected to the ensemble nodes and labelled (Fig. 10a). Using PET we can determine how many ways there are of labelling the remaining configuration (Fig. 10b), such that it results in a valid topology (Fig. 10c).

In order to find the number of combinations between two of the zone one now has to simple substitute the figure inventory $A+B$ into the cycle index of one of the configurations and take the coefficient of the string representation of the other as the number of solutions. The 16 possible combinations of configurations of the obligatory zones, numbered according to Table 1, are shown in Table 2. If the individual results are summed we arrive at a total of 20 possible configurations for three ensemble elements.

Table 2. The solutions to the 16 distinct combinations sum up to a total of 20

	1	2	3	4
1	1	1	1	1
2	1	2	2	1
3	1	2	2	1
4	1	1	1	1

While the given approach works for topologies with three ensemble elements and some configurations of higher order it is not a general solution. The problem is that not only the cycle index is used to describe the symmetry properties of a group, the string representation is misused to do the same. As soon as the group, which is being described by the figure inventory, becomes too complex to be described by a linear string of symbols the approach given above fails.

2.4   Configurations

Finding topological configurations is a graph theoretical problem. In order to gain a clearer understanding of the problem and to devise a solution it is essential to develop a model of the set of graphs being generated. First of all the graphs are divided into subsets according to n, the number of ensemble nodes. The model will be demonstrated on the set with $n=4$. The basic idea is that there is some sub-graph representing the restricted zone and some sub-graph representing the public zone. For $n=4$ these sub-graphs will consist of four nodes at most and they must be connected. Thus there are ten possible sub-graphs; these are shown in Fig. 11.

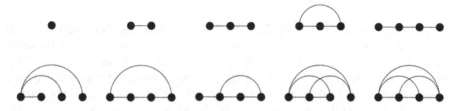

Fig. 11. The ten connected graphs with at most four nodes

Additionally these sub-graphs are connected to the four ensemble nodes by four edges; thereby each node of the sub-graph is attached to at least one of these edges. Therefore there are 12 distinct ways of connecting these sub-graphs to the ensemble nodes, which need to be taken into consideration; these are shown in Fig. 12.

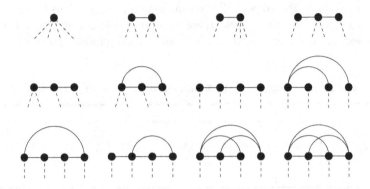

Fig. 12. Twelve possible ways of connecting the graphs in Fig. 11 to four nodes, such that each node is connected at least once

The details of these sub-graphs can be omitted for the moment, it is important to remember only that these two graphs are connected to each other via four ensemble nodes (Fig. 13a). In fact for the time being the ensemble nodes can be left away as well (Fig. 13b). If the connectors between the two sub-graphs are numbered from one to four, it becomes clear that each solution corresponds to a permutation on the set of four elements. Hence we know that there are 4!=24 possible solutions to connect the two sub-graphs.

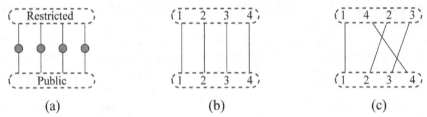

| (a) | (b) | (c) |

Fig. 13. Two undefined sub-graphs connected by four ensemble nodes (a). The model can be seen as permutations on the set of four elements (b,c).

Once the sub-graphs are re-introduced it becomes clear that there are at most 24 different solutions for each pair of sub-graphs. This is due to the symmetric properties of the sub-graphs which render certain solutions equal. Fig. 14 shows an example of this behaviour on a graph and the respective permutations in two line notation. Applying a symmetry operation, in this case a rotation by 180°, corresponds to the permutation product of *1243* (the original graph) and *4321* (the permutation corresponding to a 180° rotation). Permutation products are not always associative, so $a \circ b \neq b \circ a$. In the model this difference between a right and a left product corresponds to manipulating the restricted zone sub-graph versus manipulating the public zone sub-graph respectively. At first glance the graphs resulting from these operation (permutations *4312* and *3421*) may look different to the original graph (permutation *1243*), but in fact they are the same graph merely embedded differently in the plane.

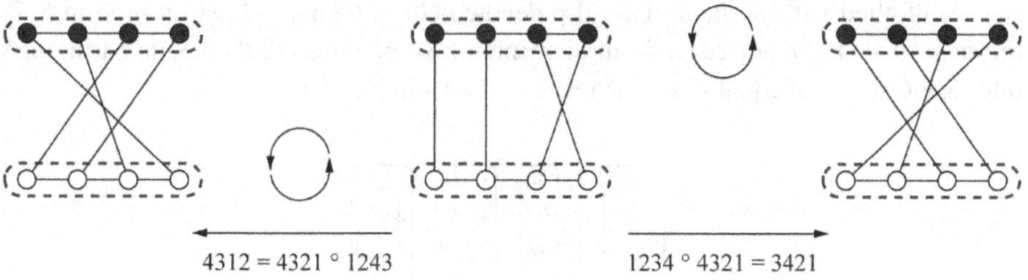

$$4312 = 4321 \circ 1243 \qquad\qquad 1234 \circ 4321 = 3421$$

Fig. 14. Applying the same symmetry operation to the restricted zone (right) vs. applying it to the public zone

So in order to compute non-equivalent solutions it is necessary to represent these properties as permutation groups, the sub-graph representing the restricted zone has a group G of operations under which it is equivalent, the sub-graph representing the public zone has a group H of operations under which it is equivalent, and finally the *24* possible permutations are represented by the symmetric group S_4. Fig. 15 shows these three groups using a more complex example. The restricted zone sub-graph is a star graph with four nodes, its symmetry sub-group G is of order *6*. On a side note this sub-group corresponds to the possible symmetry operations on a tetrahedron while keeping one vertex fixed. The public zone sub-graph more irregular, there is one node of degree 1, one node of degree 3 and two nodes of degree 2. Only the two nodes of degree 2 can be exchanged with one another to produce an isomorphic graph, resulting in a symmetry sub-group of order 2. This in turn corresponds to mirroring a tetrahedron trough an edge.

$$G = \begin{Bmatrix} 1\ 2\ 3\ 4 & 1\ 2\ 4\ 3 \\ 1\ 3\ 2\ 4 & 1\ 3\ 4\ 2 \\ 1\ 4\ 2\ 3 & 1\ 4\ 3\ 2 \end{Bmatrix}$$

$$S_4 = \begin{Bmatrix} 1\ 2\ 3\ 4 & 2\ 1\ 3\ 4 & 3\ 1\ 2\ 4 & 4\ 1\ 2\ 3 \\ 1\ 2\ 4\ 3 & 2\ 1\ 4\ 3 & 3\ 1\ 4\ 2 & 4\ 1\ 3\ 2 \\ 1\ 3\ 2\ 4 & 2\ 3\ 1\ 4 & 3\ 2\ 1\ 4 & 4\ 2\ 1\ 3 \\ 1\ 3\ 4\ 2 & 2\ 3\ 4\ 1 & 3\ 2\ 4\ 1 & 4\ 2\ 3\ 1 \\ 1\ 4\ 2\ 3 & 2\ 4\ 1\ 3 & 3\ 4\ 1\ 2 & 4\ 3\ 1\ 2 \\ 1\ 4\ 3\ 2 & 2\ 4\ 3\ 1 & 3\ 4\ 2\ 1 & 4\ 3\ 2\ 1 \end{Bmatrix}$$

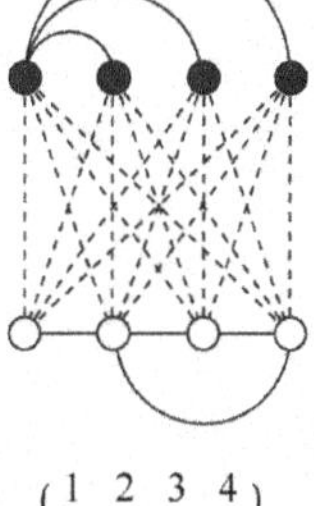

$$H = \begin{Bmatrix} 1\ 2\ 3\ 4 \\ 1\ 2\ 4\ 3 \end{Bmatrix}$$

Fig. 15. The symmetric group S_4 and two of its sub-groups G and H, which correspond to the symmetry operations on the shown sub-graphs

It has been shown how to find equivalent solutions using the symmetric properties of the sub-graphs, and this leads directly to the solution for finding all distinct solutions for a pair of sub-graphs. If an element $s \in S4$ and $s \notin G$ is taken and multiplied with

right multiplied with element of G, also denoted $G \circ s$, then a right coset of G in S_4 is returned. If this is repeated until all elements of S_4 are covered, then S_4 is partitioned into $/S_4//G/$ parts of equal size. The result is shown in Fig. 16.

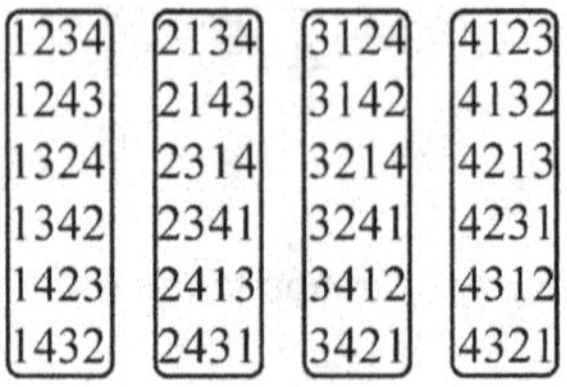

$$
\begin{array}{llll}
1234 & 2134 & 3124 & 4123 \\
1243 & 2143 & 3142 & 4132 \\
1324 & 2314 & 3214 & 4213 \\
1342 & 2341 & 3241 & 4231 \\
1423 & 2413 & 3412 & 4312 \\
1432 & 2431 & 3421 & 4321
\end{array}
$$

Fig. 16. The right cosets of G in S_4

Similarly the left cosets of H can be procuded by using left multiplications. The left cosets of H in S_4 are shown in Fig. 17.

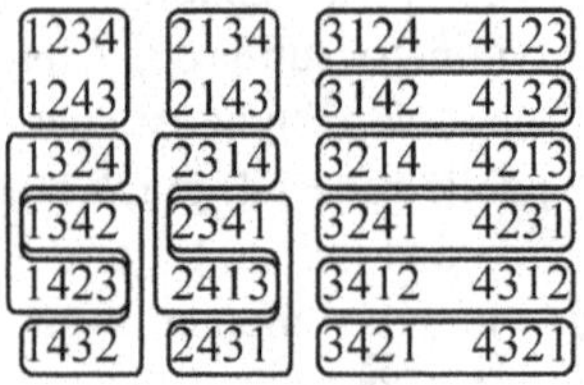

$$
\begin{array}{llll}
1234 & 2134 & 3124 & 4123 \\
1243 & 2143 & 3142 & 4132 \\
1324 & 2314 & 3214 & 4213 \\
1342 & 2341 & 3241 & 4231 \\
1423 & 2413 & 3412 & 4312 \\
1432 & 2431 & 3421 & 4321
\end{array}
$$

Fig. 17. The left cosets of H in S_4

To arrive at the final solution these two partitions have to be overlaid to produce the so called double cosets $H\backslash S_4/G$, these are shown in Fig. 18.

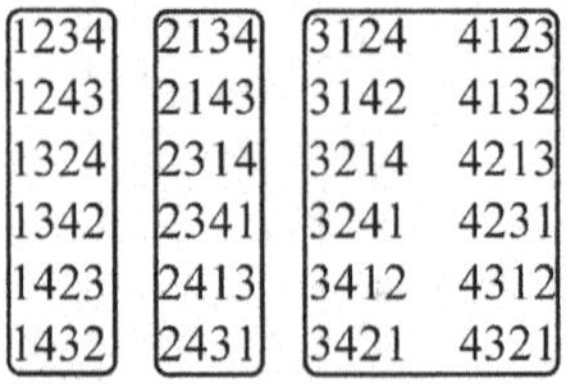

$$
\begin{array}{llll}
1234 & 2134 & 3124 & 4123 \\
1243 & 2143 & 3142 & 4132 \\
1324 & 2314 & 3214 & 4213 \\
1342 & 2341 & 3241 & 4231 \\
1423 & 2413 & 3412 & 4312 \\
1432 & 2431 & 3421 & 4321
\end{array}
$$

Fig. 18. The double cosets $H\backslash S_4/G$

It has been shown how to enumerate possible topologies for a given pair of sub-graphs. The advantage of the given solution is that it not only returns the number of solutions, but also their exact structure. In order to enumerate all solutions for n=4 the possible sub-graphs and their symmetric groups must be found. These are shown in Table 3.

Table 3. The ten possible sub-graphs for the obligatory zones. The table shows the 12 distinct ways of connecting the four edges and the respective symmetry group.

	1	2	3	4	5	6
Graph	K_1	K_2	K_2	$K_{1,2}$	$K_{1,2}$	C_3
Group	S_4	D_{2d}	C_{3v}	C_{2v}	C_v	C_{2v}
Abstract	S_4	D_4	D_3	$Z_2 \times Z_2$	Z_2	$Z_2 \times Z_2$
Order	24	8	6	4	2	4
Permutations	1234	1234	1234	1234	1234	1234
	1243	1243	1243			1243
	1324		1324	1324		
	1342		1342			
	1423		1423			
	1432		1432			
	2134	2134			2134	2134
	2143	2143				2143
	2314					
	2341					
	2413					
	2431					
	3124					
	3142					
	3214					
	3241					
	3412	3412				
	3421	3421				
	4123					
	4132					
	4213					
	4231			4231		
	4312	4312				
	4321	4321		4321		

Table 3. (*Continued*)

	7	8	9	10	11	12
Graph		$K_{1,3}$	C_4			K_4
Group	C_2	C_{3v}	D_{2d}	C_v	C_{2v}	S_4
Abstract	Z_2	D_3	D_4	Z_2	$Z_2 x Z_2$	S_4
Order	2	6	8	2	4	24
Permutations	1234	1234	1234	1234	1234	1234
		1243		1243	1243	1243
		1324				1324
		1342				1342
		1423				1423
		1432	1432			1432
					2134	2134
			2143		2143	2143
						2314
			2341			2341
						2413
						2431
						3124
						3142
			3214			3214
						3241
			3412			3412
						3421
			4123			4123
						4132
						4213
						4231
						4312
	4321		4321			4321

The solutions to the 144 possible pairs of sub-graphs are shown in Table 4. The numbers and actual configurations were derived using a short Mathematica script. If the individual results are summed we arrive at a total of 335 possible configurations for four ensemble elements.

Table 4. The solutions to the 144 distinct combinations sum up to a total of 335

	1	2	3	4	5	6	7	8	9	10	11	12
1	1	1	1	1	1	1	1	1	1	1	1	1
2	1	2	1	2	2	2	3	1	2	2	2	1
3	1	1	2	2	3	2	2	2	1	3	2	1
4	1	2	2	3	4	3	4	2	2	4	3	1
5	1	2	3	4	7	4	6	3	2	7	4	1
6	1	2	2	3	4	3	4	2	2	4	3	1
7	1	3	2	4	6	4	8	2	3	6	4	1
8	1	1	2	2	3	2	2	2	1	3	2	1
9	1	2	1	2	2	2	3	1	2	2	2	1
10	1	2	3	4	7	4	6	3	2	7	4	1
11	1	2	2	3	4	3	4	2	2	4	3	1
12	1	1	1	1	1	1	1	1	1	1	1	1

We have calculated the number of configurations for up to four ensemble elements (Table 5). The number of possible graph configurations rises steeply and few courthouses have more than four ensembles, hence for the time being no further computation has been required.

Table 5. Number of configurations for arranging n triples in the plane, if each of the two obligatory zones is to be connected without passing through a courtroom node

No. of Elements n	1	2	3	4
No. of Configurations	1	4	20	335

This is the approach to enumerating the number of topologies for this very specific problem. However, the general method of pruning and simplifying a complex class of topologies down to its quintessential base may well be of use for other problem domains as well.

2.5   Nomenclature

While a sequence of rules gives a rough idea about the structure of a graph, it is too ambiguous to use for naming. In order to name a graph it is necessary to map an inherently non-linear representation into a linear one. Once again the fact that we have broken down our class of graphs into a set of defining elements and a generative grammar will ease the task. Our approach is modelled on the nomenclature of organic chemistry, which most of us got to know at some stage of our education. We are concerned with the rudimentary topology before the expansion process only. Essentially we are trying to map one representation onto another, it does not necessarily have to be a 1:1 map, if at all possible it would require a long list of naming rules. All we are looking for is a possibility to unambiguously talk about configurations. A 1:n mapping will be sufficient, meaning that there may be several names for a graph, as long as there is only one graph per name.

Analogous to rules 1-4 of the graph grammar we have defined and named the following four variations of the original triplet: (a) full triplet F; b) ensemble and public zone P; c) ensemble and restricted zone R; and d) ensemble only E. The four variations of the triplet are shown in Fig. 19.

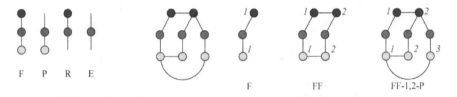

Fig. 19. Four named variations of the triplet and their application in the naming process

It is then a matter of stepping through the generation process, adding the letters for applied rules to a chain and numbering the nodes in their order of creation. If not noted otherwise it is assumed that a new triplet is attached to the two nodes with the highest numbers, else one must prefix the letter with the respective numbers.

Finally should rules 5 or 6 be applied the numbers of the connected nodes must be prefixed or suffixed to the entire string. In general it is desirable to start with the longest possible chain of Fs and keep the amount of required numbers at a minimum. A pictorial and discursive description of the 20 topologies of three ensemble elements is given in Figure 20.

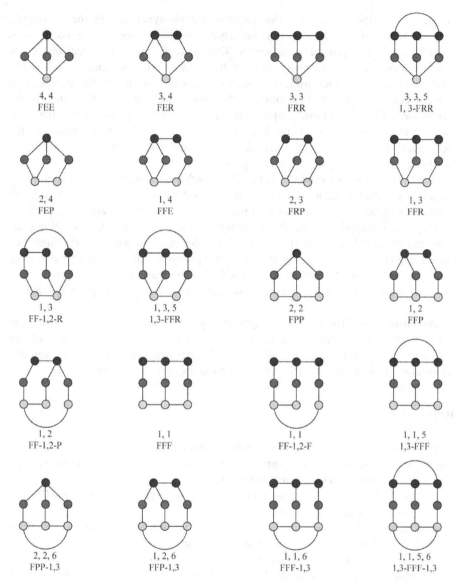

Fig. 20. The 20 topologies of size three. A sequence of rules and an unambiguous term is given for each.

3   Discussion

Graphs and graph grammars are well known as tools to explore abstract systems of objects and their relations. In architecture these are often interpreted to be programmatic functions and their interrelations or, more concrete, spaces and their adjacencies. This project is construed within this tradition and proposes a specific mapping – a triplet of sorts – that captures the idiosyncrasies of the courthouse program to generatively construct the underlying structure of the existing courthouses as well as other new possible courthouses. Since there are only few conceivable cases in which a courthouse floor will host more than, say, eight courtrooms, which would correspond to about four triplets, it seems practical answers to the enumeration problem could also have been achieved with a brute force approach. Nevertheless, the insight gained by decomposing topologies into graph grammar rules and using these for enumeration and nomenclature has proven to be invaluable in understanding the topic. Many assumptions which were taken for granted have had to be revisited due to topologies and insights gained from the grammar.

Furthermore it is interesting to notice the abundance of topological possibilities to the given problem, even more so since the applied variations are relatively limited. Even allowing for the fact that some of the theoretical variants are either not practical or not planar the applied solutions only cover a fraction of the possibilities. While the solutions presented here are specific to this rather narrow problem, we think that similar approaches could be valuable to other typologies. After all understanding the topological structure of a typology, being able to enumerate the theoretic possibilities and unambiguously communicate about them can only benefit typological research.

Acknowledgments. The work was supported by the General Service Administration (GSA), more specifically by the Office of the Chief Architect. We would like to particularly thank the Centre for Courthouse Programs for their invaluable help and architectural insight on the features and complexities of these buildings.

References

Greenberg, A.: Review of the American Courthouse. Architectural Record (1973)

Din, E., Economou, A.: Surface Symmetries: The Smith House Revisited. The International Journal of Architectural Computing, 485–506 (2011)

Economou, A.: The symmetry lessons from Froebel building gifts. Environment and Planning B: Planning and Design 26, 75–90 (1999)

Economou, A., Grasl, T.: CourtsWeb Development and Support: Research Report, 48066S5; # GS-00P-07-CY-C-0185; Georgia Institute of Technology (2011)

Geiß, R., Batz, G.V., Grund, D., Hack, S., Szalkowski, A.: GrGen: A Fast SPO-Based Graph Rewriting Tool. In: Corradini, A., Ehrig, H., Montanari, U., Ribeiro, L., Rozenberg, G. (eds.) ICGT 2006. LNCS, vol. 4178, pp. 383–397. Springer, Heidelberg (2006)

Grasl, T., Economou, A.: Spatial similarity metrics: Graph theoretic distance measurement and floor plan abstraction. In: Maver, T. (ed.) CAADFutures Conference Proceedings, Sydney, Australia, pp. 251–263 (2007)

Grasl, T., Economou, A., Branum, C.: Combining Triples: Using a Graph Grammar to Generate Courthouse Topologies. In: Gagdas, G., Colakoglu, B. (eds.) 27th eCAADe Conference Proceedings of Computation: The New Realm of Architectural Design, pp. 605–612. ITU /YTU, Istanbul, Turkey (2009)

Grasl, T., Economou, A.: Palladian Graphs: Using a Graph Grammar to Automate the Palladian Grammas. In: Schmitt, G., et al. (eds.) 28th eCAADe Conference Proceedings of Future Cities, pp. 275–284. ETH Zurich, Switzerland (2010)

Gruzen, J., Daskalakis, C., Krasnow, P.: The Geometry of a Courthouse Design. In: Flanders, S. (ed.) Celebrating the Courthouse: A Guide for Architects, Their Clients, and the Public. W.W. Norton & Company, New York (2006)

Gips, J., Stiny, G.: Production systems and grammars: a uniform characterization. Environment and Planning B 7(4), 399–408 (1980)

Harary, F.: Graph Theory. Perseus Books (1994)

Leers, A.: The New American Courthouse, Unpublished Notes in Executive Education Programs: GSD, Harvard University (2011)

Phillips, T.S., Griebel, M.: Building Type Basics for Justice Facilities. John Wiley & Sons, Inc., Hoboken (2003)

Pólya, G., Tarjan, R., Woods, D.: Notes on Introductory Combinatorics. Birkhauser, Boston (1983)

Rozenberg, G. (ed.): Handbook of Graph Grammars and Computing by Graph Transformation: Foundations, vol. 1. World Scientific Publishing Co., Pte. Ltd. (1997)

Steadman, P.: Graph-theoretic Representation of Architectural Arrangement. In: March, L. (ed.) The Architecture of Form, pp. 94–115. Cambridge University Press, Cambridge (1976)

USCDC: U.S. Courts Design Guide, Washington (2007)

Modeling Water Use for Sustainable Urban Design

Ramesh Krishnamurti, Tajin Biswas, and Tsung-Hsien Wang

School of Architecture, Carnegie Mellon University,
5000 Forbes Avenue, Pittsburgh PA 15317, USA
{ramesh,tajin,tsunghsw}@cmu.edu

Abstract. Achieving sustainability on an urban scale is an overwhelming problem. We can address this by dividing the problem into manageable proportions. Environmental impacts of urban design fall into measurable categories, for example, air quality, biodiversity, solid wastes, water and wastewater, hazardous materials, and impacts of nonrenewable energy use. Such measures are incorporated into building rating systems as a way of codifying sustainability. In this chapter, to illustrate such codification, we examine water use as well as generated wastewater according to the requirements of a specific sustainable building rating system. Conventional calculations are coupled with building information modeling to illustrate the overall effects of parametrically selecting fixtures, systems and materials to control the use of potable water. We further demonstrate how this approach of combining parametric building information modeling with measures of their environmental impacts can be employed on an urban scale, thereby, guiding the design of sustainable urban spaces.

Keywords: Sustainability, Sustainable Building Rating System, Building Information Modeling, and Parametric Design.

1 Introduction

In 2008 the number of urban dwellers surpassed those living in rural areas [1]. Cities and their residents occupy 2% of the terrestrial surface and consume a vast amount (75%) of the earth's natural resources. While these resources are becoming scarcer, the nature of the use and waste of resources contribute to environmental degradation. Among the resources to run our cities—energy, water, building materials—are some that can be reasonably quantified. Water consumption reduction, water recycling, and wastewater minimization are supported by almost all sustainability principles that are codified by sustainable building rating systems.

Urbanization is growing at a staggering scale, according to census 2000 population statistics, almost 80% of the total world's population live in urban areas today [2], and approximately 44.2 bgal/day of water withdrawals are used for public supply [3]. Rise in urban population shows an increase in the use of potable water from public supply from 62% in 1950 to 86% in 2005. Increase of population further complicates, with the geographical shift of population requiring rapid increase in water supply demand and maintenance of aging systems in areas of diminishing populations. In the last

S. Müller Arisona et al. (Eds.): DUMS, CCIS 242, pp. 138–155, 2012.

twenty years, communities have spent $1 trillion in 2001 dollars on drinking water treatment and supply, and on wastewater treatment; although this is a staggering amount; moreover, it may be insufficient for future needs [4].

Water conservation is more widely followed in the arid areas of the United States. However, using water efficiently is increasingly becoming an essential part of creating sustainable buildings and environment [5]. Ezel [6] cites a recent study by McGraw Hill's Construction [7], which indicates that after energy efficiency, water is treated with the next highest priority.

In order to study the effects of water use in the urban setting, we begin, firstly, by looking at water use in a residential building and then look at typical water use in commercial office buildings. According to Vickers [8], water use reduction in residences can be improved by efficiencies in water use, that is, by a combination of using less water with water efficient fixtures, and reusing wastewater generated by water use activities such as showers, baths, and laundry. Wastewater generated from bathtubs, wash basins, dishwashers and laundry is defined as *graywater* by the Uniform Plumbing Code (UPI) in its Appendix G [9]. Graywater reuse strategies and possibilities for rainwater collection and reuse have an effect on reducing overall water requirements. Reusing graywater and/or harvested rainwater pose technical problems. For example, adequate filtration, treatment facilities and water tank volumes would need to be determined during design. This requires additional modeling [5], for example, for water tank sizing. The same applies to rainwater reuse. However, although accounting for graywater and rainwater reuse is important, our focus in this chapter is to illustrate water savings. This is easily demonstrated by using data tables for efficient water fixtures. Likewise, if data tables for gray- and rainwater can be constructed, the same technique would still apply.

According to Mayer et. al. [10], toilets use 29% of total indoor water consumption. Water used for showering/bathing, dishwashing and laundry respectively account for approximately 36%, 14% and 21% of total indoor water consumption. In the urban scenario where we consider commercial office buildings, according to Dziegielewski [11], indoor water use falls into three main categories. These are: indoor use for toilets and wash basins; cooling systems; and outdoor use for irrigation based on the landscape and types of plants.

Outdoor water use depends on the site area around the building and type of landscaping. If the plants chosen for landscaping require only a small amount of water that can be provided by harvested rainwater, then the amount of outdoor water use is insignificant in comparison to indoor water use. Even when fixtures used indoors are efficient and even waterless, water is still required for flushing toilets and faucets. Under these water use conditions, without further research, it would be difficult to determine a typical outdoor versus indoor water use ratio. We are not aware of any literature on the subject.

In this research we focus on water use from the first category—these deal with water use for toilets and washbasins. For this, we consider an urban mass model centered on the office building. Previously we had developed a prototype to validate requirements for a green building rating system [12], linked to a commercial building information modeling software [13]. We implemented an application to visualize effects of using efficient water fixtures. Accordingly, we tested the model for a typical office building and then extended it to the urban area. It is important to point out that our original prototype application was primarily created for individual sustainable building projects—our aim is to expand its capabilities to meet needs at an urban scale. In this respect, there is other work, for example, by Müller et al on rule-based procedural modeling of cities [14]. However, it is not clear to us whether their shape rules can incorporate calculators and/or aggregations, for example, for sustainability related evaluations.

2   Background

Environmental Aspects. The total water withdrawn for use in buildings for toilets, faucets and showerheads are from rivers, streams and underwater aquifers. Reducing the amount of water for these uses would benefit potable water conservation. Reduction in potable water means that less water would need to be treated at municipal water treatment works. The accumulated effects of water use reductions go as far as allowing municipalities to defer or keep up with high investments in wastewater treatment infrastructure and supply of clean water.

In the case of rainwater harvesting for systems for reduction of potable water use in flushing, local weather conditions as well as local health ordinances should be taken into account. Quality of water supplied from rainwater collection or recycled graywater have to be accounted for in the selection of fixtures to ensure long-term fixture performance.

Economic Aspects. Reduction of water consumption at the source helps to minimize the overall operating costs of a building. According to USGBC, buildings that have been retrofitted with more efficient plumbing fixtures through incentives programs provide a cost effective way of deferring capital costs of water treatment and supply facilities. The US Environmental Protection Agency (EPA) estimates that public wastewater and supply infrastructure repair costs for the United States in the next 20 years will be about $745 billion to $1 trillion. Infrastructure repair and replacement costs to an already aging system will increase the cost average for water bills from 0.5% of the average household income to 0.9% [15]. Thus, water efficiency on a large scale will decrease the stress on current water management infrastructure such as water distribution networks, sewer lines, and treatment of both sewage and drinking water supplies.

Policy Aspects. Changing existing water fixtures with more efficient ones makes them more affordable; councils and organizations that promote green building rating systems have mobilized the industry to make efficient fixtures and water saving technologies more readily available in the general market. We could also consider harvesting rainwater and or graywater for use in water fixtures. For example, in this context, for flushing toilets in commercial buildings, there are many components that have to be taken into consideration such as roof, pipes, filtration, storage tank, pumps, controls, and available area [16].

2.1   Rating Systems and Water Efficiency

As a way of codifying sustainability, certain measures are incorporated in the form of green building rating systems. Historically, rating systems set requirements for buildings. In 1990 the British Research Establishment (BRE) was the first to develop an environmental impact assessment method, BREEAM, British Research Establishment's Environmental Assessment Method. Subsequently, other countries adopted the BRE approach in developing their own assessment method [17]. In the United States, the US Green Building Council (USGBC) created the Leadership in Energy, and Environmental Design (LEED) system. The latest release is version 3 commonly referred to as LEED v3 [19]. To the present day, there are approximately 1800 LEED certified buildings in the US mostly according to LEED 2.2 [20]. LEED v3 is a substantially different from LEED 2.2. For this paper, we work with LEED 2.2. It is interesting to note that BREEAM has started to expand their benchmarking to the community scale [18].

Table 1. Water efficiency requirements in different rating systems

Water Efficiency	LEED 3.0	Green Star	BREEAM	Green Globes
Water use reduction	WE pre, WE 3.1-3.3 Water use reduction by 20%, 30%, 40%, 50%	Wat-1 Occupant amenity water (reduction of water use)	Wat-1 Water consumption reduction for sanitary purposes	D1. Water consumption reduction
Water efficient landscaping	WE 2.1- 2.2 Reduce water use for irrigation	Wat-3 Landscape irrigation		D 2.3 Minimal use for irrigation D2.4 Efficient irrigation equipment
Waste water treatment	WE 2 Innovative waste water technologies			D3.1 Reduce offsite water treatment
Water use control		Wat-2 Water meters	Wat-2 Water meter for monitoring consumption Wat-3 Major leak detection Wat-4 Sanitary supply shut off	D2.1 Sub-metering for high use areas
Systems water use		Wat-4 Heat rejection water Wat-5 Fire system water use		D2.2 Minimal use for cooling towers

Water use reduction is considered as an essential measure in all building rating systems, generally measured by a percentage of water use reduction. Two cases provide the basis for comparison: water use in the design, and a baseline water use.

Table 1 illustrates water use from the perspective of four different rating systems. The rating systems shown correspond to those designated by Fowler [12] as providing inherently distinct ways of calculating water as an important resource in the building domain. The left-most column captures the broad categories in which water resource use is measured.

Each rating has a distinct way of allocating credits for meeting requirements. For instance, the LEED 2.2 rating system for New Construction has 4 credits dedicated to this criterion. Green Star, the rating system by the Green Building Council of Australia (GBCA) awards from up to a maximum of 5 points for water use reduction. BREEAM allocates 3 credits, while Green Globes, licensed by the Green Building Initiative, dedicates between 10-40 points depending on the amount of reduction in water use. It is important to note that although different weights and points are given to this category by the different rating systems, each considers water use reduction an essential component of green design.

2.2   Urban Water Use in Commercial Buildings

Reducing water use by installing efficient fixtures is a relatively simple criteria to follow in order to earn credits, for example, from a sample of LEED 2.1 Silver certified buildings in Pennsylvania, we found that 88% of the buildings achieved credits for water use reduction, and 56% of the same set achieved 4 out of 5 possible credits [19]. Figure 1 shows the samples, numbered from 1 to 25 on the x-axis, with the water efficiency credits on the y-axis, numbered from 1 to 5.

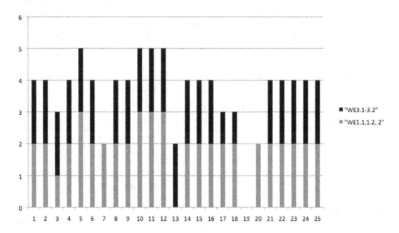

Fig. 1. Distribution of LEED water credits earned by certified buildings. The lighter and darker series respectively represents credits WE1.1, WE1.2 and WE2, and credits WE3.1 and WE3.2. These two kinds of credits essentially cover fixtures, water use and water use load calculations.

In a study of LEED certified buildings on the campus of Carnegie Mellon University, we found that all but one had acquired water reduction credits (Table 2). According to facilities management, the benefits can be seen not only in the use of less water but also in the overall operation and maintenance costs of the facilities. Although the campus has several differing types of buildings certified under LEED New Construction, calculations generally vary only in the allocation of types of fixtures, number of users and number of days in a year the buildings are used. The reason for the one of the buildings not having achieved LEED water credits can be attributed to the small footprint of the building. Water use reduction is reflected in the deployment of available efficient fixtures at the time.

Table 2. Water efficiency credits achieved for LEED certified buildings on the campus of Carnegie Mellon University

Project Name	Certification	LEED version	LEED water credits achieved
New House	Silver	LEED NC 2.0	WE 1.1, WE 1.2
Henderson House	Silver	LEED NC 2.0	WE1.1, WE 1.2, WE3.1, WE3.2
407 S Craig St	Silver	LEED NC 2.1	None
300 S Craig St	Silver	LEED NC 2.1	WE1.1, WE 1.2, WE 3.1
Collaborative Information Center	Gold	LEED CS	WE1.1, WE 1.2, WE2, WE 3.1, WE 3.2

3   Modeling Water Use

We employ two different methods to model water use in buildings. The first considers individual buildings to determine their water use. It is assumed that the number of occupants is known. Further, there is an urban information model containing the floor areas and numbers of floors in each building. Urban water use is then, an aggregation of water use by the occupants in each the selected buildings. The second approach works from 2D drawing of an urban area with known building heights. Numbers of occupants, fixtures and fixture flow rates are assigned and maintained in an external database.

We modeled the test case in a commercial design software, Revit® Architecture 2010 [13]. It provides designers with an architectural modeling environment, with a built-in collection of general objects or a family base of building elements such as walls, windows, floors, roofs, columns, beams, fixtures, zones, etc. Revit allows the user to parametrically manage, update and propagate changes in the model. It provides an Application Programming Interface (API) for writing specific functions according to need. It offers capabilities for ready design documentation with calculations that can be, ultimately, submitted for certification.

For water use requirements we employ criteria from LEED NCv2.2, and a building information model to make informed decisions on using certain fixtures for achieving sustainability goals set by LEED. The advantage in creating and using a building information model is its intrinsic characteristic of holding project information for all team members. This includes designers, planners, facility managers, and on a larger scale, policy and decision makers. To demonstrate the approach of designing towards specific LEED goals, we also employ Revit as the building information model. Figure 2 illustrates the test case, modeled in Revit® Architecture 2010.

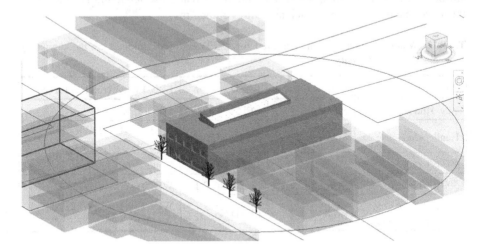

Fig. 2. Test case for modeling water efficiency for LEED

Building Information Model. There is no standard definition for a building information model (BIM). A BIM is a modeling technology with an associated set of processes to produce, communicate, and analyze building models [20]. From an information science perspective, a BIM is an instance of a populated data model of buildings that contains multidisciplinary data specific to a particular building, which can be described unambiguously.

According to Eastman [20], building models are made of

- Building components, (objects) that 'know' what they are, and can be associated with data attributes and parametric rules
- Components that include data that describe how they behave, as needed for analysis, e.g. scheduling, specification, and energy analysis
- Consistent and non-redundant data, such that component data are represented in all views such plan, section, elevation and schedules.
- Coordinated data, such that all views of a model are represented in a coordinated manner.

BIM has its roots in decades old computer-aided design research, but it is only recently that it is being adopted in different domains of the building industry. Some features sought in BIM software are the following—it must be digital, spatial (3D),

measureable (quantifiable, dimensionable and queryable), accessible to the entire
AEC/owner team; and durable (usable through all phases of the facility's life cycle).

Current implementations of BIM do not meet these criteria within any single
software [20]. Different BIM tools vary in their sophistication of their predefined
objects; ease of use and learning; ease with which users can define and customize new
object families; in their abilities to interface with other software. Figure 3 illustrates
Revit as an example of a BIM where the software is used to generate different views-
plans, sections, elevations, databases; and it is used for analysis and visualization.

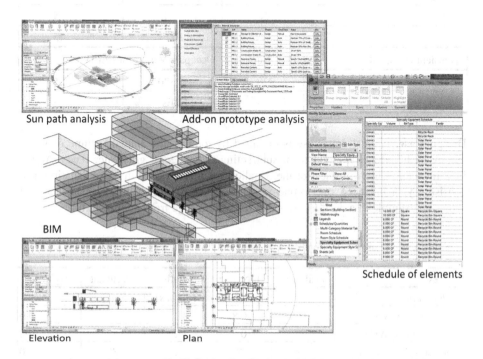

Sun path analysis   Add-on prototype analysis

BIM

Schedule of elements

Elevation   Plan

Fig. 3. Example of Revit as a BIM

3.1   Water Use Calculations

Water use calculations principally follow the LEED 2.2 method, which is outlined
below. Water use reduction for a building/project corresponds to the difference
between the *design* case and a *baseline* case.

In this methodology water use is calculated by estimating occupant usage and
fixture flow rates. Occupants are determined by calculating full time equivalent (FTE)
occupancy of a building. This is based on a standard 8-hour occupancy period,
resulting in a value based on the hours per day divided by 8. In the case of transient
building populations such as students, visitors, or customers, hours are estimated for a
representative daily average. Table 3 illustrates the calculations for determining FTE
occupancy.

Table 3. Sample Occupancy Calculation for a College Building

Occupant Type	Number	Person- hrs/day	Subtotal FTEs
Full Time Staff (assuming 8hr/day)	8	64	8
Full Time Faculty	6	48	6
Part Time Faculty (assuming 2hrs/day)	24	48	6
Part Time Researchers	20	40	5
		Total FTEs	25
Transient Occupant	Peak Number	Occupant Values for LEED	
	320	320	25
		Total FTEs	345

Design Case. Annual water use is obtained by totaling the annual volume of water use by each fixture type and then, subtracting rainwater or graywater reuse. Actual flow rates and flush volumes for the installed fixtures are used in the calculation. For consistency, a balanced one-to-one ratio of male and female is assumed. Table 4 shows an example of a design case study for water usage from interior fixtures.

Table 4. Water use calculation based on flush and flow fixtures from a sample case study

Fixtures	Daily use	Flowrate	Duration	Occupant	H_2O use
Flush Fixture		*GPF*	*(flushes)*	*(gal)*	
Ultra Low Flow WC (m)	0	0.8	1	80	0
Ultra Low Flow WC (f)	3	0.8	1	80	192
Composting Toilet (m)	1	0	1	80	0
Composting Toilet (f)	0	0	1	80	0
Waterless Urinal (m)	2	0	1	80	0
Waterless Urinal (f)	0	0	1	80	0
Flow Fixture		*GPM*	*(minutes)*		
Conventional Lavatory	3	2.5	0.20	160	240
Kitchen sink	1	2.5	0.2	160	80
Shower	0.1	2.5	5	160	200
				Total Volume (gal)	712
				Work days	260
				Annual volume	185120
				Rain water or graywater reuse	0
				Annual water use (gal)	185,120

Baseline Case. According to LEED methods, to create a baseline case the design case table is used to provide the number of male and female occupants, with fixture flush and flow rate values adjusted as per EPAct default specifications [9]. Table 5 shows the baseline case for the same design case study.

Table 5. Baseline calculations for the same case study

Fixtures	Daily use	Flowrate	Duration	Occupant	H_2O use
Flush Fixture		*GPF*	*(flushes)*	**(gal)**	
Conventional WC (m)	1	1.6	1	80	128
Conventional WC (f)	3	1.6	1	80	384
Conventional Urinal (m)	2	1	1	80	160
Conventional Urinal (f)	0	0	1	80	0
Flow Fixture		*GPM*	*(minutes)*		
Conventional Lavatory	3	2.5	0.25	160	300
Kitchen sink	1	2.5	0.25	160	100
Shower	0.1	2.5	5	160	200
				Total Volume (gal)	1272
				Work days	260
				Annual volume	330720
				Rain water or graywater reuse	0
				Annual water use (gal)	330,720

Water use calculations are straightforward. However, it can be problematical owing to missing data as a result of integrating requirements from a rating system with a particular building information model. As a model is only as complete as the information entered, designers must ensure that for water use calculations all pertinent information—occupant numbers, fixture costs and materials—are included within the model. There are always other required and pertinent information that are normally stored externally to any project for any building information model; these include rainfall data, plant water use data, etc. Such information is not expected to fall directly into a designer's purview, yet these factors have to be accounted for. Table 6 shows the objects required for calculating LEED NC 3.0 water related credits.

Water fixtures are components stored in the Revit library. As stored, when queried, only dimensions of instances are returned. Dimensions are incorporated into the object names; there is no other way of getting at object parameters, or other needed material properties from the objects, unless the information from manufactures specifications has been filled in.

Figure 4 shows a family of fixtures in Revit with essential information pertaining to water use calculation such as flow rate. By default, flow rate is not specified as an attribute of a fixture; instead it has to be added as a customized parameter. Likewise, occupant data has to be added to the project. In the this release, Revit Architecture 2010, there is no standard way of specifying independent male and female occupant numbers. These are treated as separate attributes that can be aggregated.

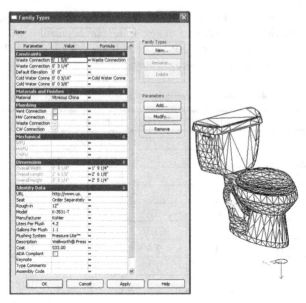

Fig. 4. Fixture information related to water use

To calculate Water Efficiency credits, we implemented external databases for fixtures and landscapes. In the prototype shown in Figure 5 there are two tabs under the Water Efficiency category. These contain the necessary tasks to be fulfilled when evaluating water efficiency credits.

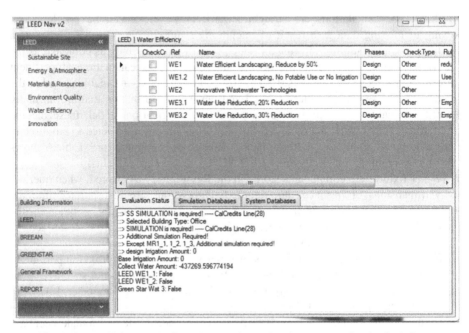

Fig. 5. Water efficiency tabs for rating credits, and various water related calculations

Table 6. LEED credit requirements for water efficiency calculations

Credit Name	Description	Existing objects in Revit™	Required Properties	New objects and required properties	Associated info	External info
WE pre	Water use reduction	Plumbing fixtures	Low flow fixtures, male and female; Kitchen, sink, shower		Number of male and female users	
WE 1.1	Water Efficient Landscaping Reduce by 50%	Plant	1. Species factor 2. Density factor 3. Landscape coefficient 4. Irrigation efficiency	Site area covered by specific plant		
WE 1.2	Water Efficient Landscaping No potable water use or no irrigation	Plant	1. Species factor 2. Density factor 3. Landscape coefficient 4. Irrigation efficiency	Site area covered by specific plan	Water harvested	ET rate database; CE value
WE 2	Innovative Wastewater Technologies	Plumbing fixtures	Water usage properties: flow rate, frequency used	Water treatment facilities and properties	Number of male and female users	
WE 3.1	Water Use Reduction 20% Reduction	Plumbing fixtures	Low flow fixtures, male and female; Kitchen, sink, shower		Number of male and female users	
WE 3.2	Water Use Reduction 30% Reduction	Plumbing fixtures	Low flow fixtures, male and female; Kitchen, sink, shower		Number of male and female users	

The overall workflow for wastewater management, firstly, retrieves information about the numbers of male and female occupants, which are specified in the building information section of the Revit building information model. Differences between the baseline and design cases are then compared to determine the number of credits that are earned at this stage. The comparison between the baseline and design case yields a percentage reduction of water use.

Most building information modelers usually offer the facility to calculate the areas covered by buildings, for example, site area. On the other hand, certain site-specific information such as ground cover type typically has to be manually specified. Additional materials and object parameters such as material porosity and fixture flow rates are also needed. Fixture cost values from manufacturers databases are used in the comparison for water use and for the ultimate savings in costs.

The prototype was implemented as an add-on to Revit Architecture 2010. It collects information such as flow rates from the fixtures placed in the model and calculates credits according to methods set out by LEED and the other standards. The application has the potential to be extended to accumulate information from multiple buildings and aggregate total water use. This approach, however, would work only when all pertinent information (number of occupants and fixtures allocated in all the buildings) are available.

4   Modeling Urban Water Use

In one sense, extending the water use model from the scale of a single building to the urban scale is straightforward; we simply aggregate single unit water use to multiple units. At the urban scale, we face the challenge of propagating results from one building to many, especially when each buildings' occupants and fixture type has to be specified by modeling. In this study we assume that the buildings are commercial office buildings.

Note that we have made assumptions. Firstly, the urban environment comprises many single unit buildings of the same type. Each building holds similar information on occupants and fixtures.

By using a building information model we can embed, store and query different kinds of information. In this case we are interested in information required for carrying out water use evaluation. We have already seen in section 3 that models only carry certain default values with their objects.

Assumptions and Challenges. In modeling for water use on a larger scale, we have far less information. Here, we adopt a slightly different approach, and employ a combination of different commercial software. The parameters that affect water use are similar to those seen in Tables 4 and 5. At this stage, graywater quantity and rainwater harvesting is not accounted for in the calculation.

As there are many buildings, assigning users to each individual building is difficult owing to lack of information; in this case, we have adopted the method of assigning occupant numbers used by Green Star's approach to space allocation [21]. In Green Star, the number of occupants in a building is allocated as a percentage of the net floor area. In contrast, there is no direct method in LEED to calculate occupants for a given area. As we have the floor area of all the buildings in the sample case study, we are able to allocate occupant number as a function of floor area.

Urban Case Study. The sample case study covers a total area of 17346.85 m^2, of which 11706.56 m^2 covers the building footprint. The remainder comprises roads, pavements and parking areas, which are assumed to have an impervious ground cover. There are also open spaces, which have potential for planning for rainwater catchments and water management. The model is generated from a 2D CAD drawing, and converted into a mass model for the purpose of calculating the total floor areas of buildings. Figure 6 shows the CAD drawing of a portion of the urban area modeled.

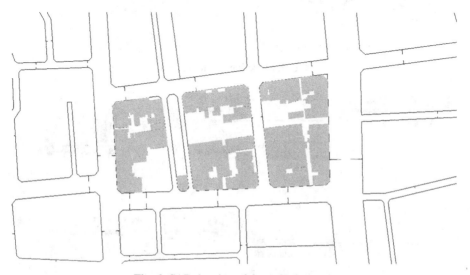

Fig. 6. CAD drawing of the test urban area

In order to estimate water use on a larger scale we used Rhinoceros® (Rhino) [22] with Grasshopper™ [23] to generate the three dimensional model. Rhino is a commercial NURBS-based 3-D modeling tool. Grasshopper is a graphical constraint propagation editor and is mainly used for parametric generation. Rhino with Grasshopper offer a quick flexible way to visualize information from databases, which includes such building information as building footprints, heights, occupants, fixtures and parameters for calculating water use on a larger scale. Both Rhino and Revit are built on top of the .NET framework [24], thereby making communication of specific information between the softwares fairly straightforward. Figure 7 shows the mass model generated in Rhino. A CAD model of the site plan which included building footprints were imported into Rhino, each building footprint was identified by a unique number and corresponding height to generate the 3D massing. The Grasshopper definition file in Figure 8 shows the connection between the model geometry and the external databases that contain fixture information to generate the water use model for the urban area.

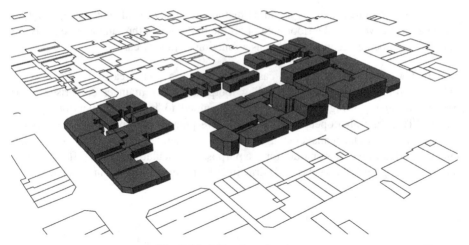

Fig. 7. Modeling the urban area

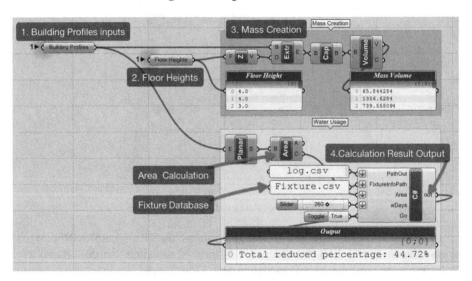

Fig. 8. Grasshopper definition file for water use model generation

As the scale changes from building to urban, we begin to notice that water use reduction is only a piece of the overall water management scheme. The model reveals potential spaces for artful rainwater catchment areas [25]. Rainwater management, collection and reuse in buildings, and for community activities, rely not only on individual buildings and their storm water collection strategies, but also become part of urban planning, as this is not always cost effective to do so for smaller projects. Information for groundcover type, vegetation, rainfall data for the area are critical to calculating rainwater runoff and collection potential. This is information that is not originally part of the building information model; however, such data needs to be supplied whether calculations are done either in Revit or Rhino, or some other combination of commercial building/urban information models.

5   Analysis

Our sample model for urban water use considered a total building area of 52439m^2 and 3516 occupants. By changing design cases we were able to see explore variations in water use reduction rates. Tables 7 and 8 depict a portion of the sample urban area. For both design cases the number of uses of the fixtures was the same and distribution of male and female were evenly balanced at a ratio of 1:1.

Table 7. Water use reduction: design case 1

Building No.	Case 1	Area (m^2)	Occupant	Water Use
Building_000	BASE	1174.0848	79	617247.540
Building_000	DESIGN	1174.0848	79	340844.868
Building_001	BASE	1356.6284	91	711006.660
Building_001	DESIGN	1356.6284	91	392618.772
Building_002	BASE	153.9494	11	85945.860
Building_002	DESIGN	153.9494	11	47459.412
Building_003	BASE	1001.68	67	523488.420
Building_003	DESIGN	1001.68	67	289070.964
Building_004	BASE	739.5551	50	390663.000
Building_004	DESIGN	739.5551	50	215724.600
Building_005	BASE	65.8443	5	39066.300
Building_005	DESIGN	65.8443	5	21572.460
			Total reduced percentage	44.78%

Table 8. Water use reduction: design case 2

Building No.	Case 1	Area (m^2)	Occupant	Water Use
Building_000	BASE	1174.0848	79	617247.54
Building_000	DESIGN	1174.0848	79	298918.62
Building_001	BASE	1356.6284	91	711006.66
Building_001	DESIGN	1356.6284	91	344323.98
Building_002	BASE	153.9494	11	85945.86
Building_002	DESIGN	153.9494	11	41621.58
Building_003	BASE	1001.68	67	523488.42
Building_003	DESIGN	1001.68	67	253513.26
Building_004	BASE	739.5551	50	390663
Building_004	DESIGN	739.5551	50	189189
Building_005	BASE	65.8443	5	39066.3
Building_005	DESIGN	65.8443	5	18918.9
			Total reduced percentage	51.57%

With the tool it is possible to vary the number and type of fixtures, change the ratio of male and female occupants, and also allocate different design cases to different parts of the urban area in order to parametrically model various scenarios for water use. The two design cases shown have different fixture flow rates; the resulting water reduction savings for design case 1 is 44.78%, and 51.57% for design case 2. Case 1 also has a savings of 12.3 million liters of potable water annually.

6   Conclusions

We have hinted at a fraction of the possible calculations that stem from combining a rating system requirement (in this case, LEED) with capabilities provided by a specific commercial building information modeler (in this case, Revit). We have also given an alternate approach, based on a combination of commercial software, that is, Grasshopper and Rhino, external databases and rating system requirements, to illustrate how information (in this case, for modeling water use) can be gathered and processed on a larger scale. These methods can be used to both pre-certify a building for sustainability, and on a larger scale, to project the effects on environmental resources. Through the use of different parameters, generally simple calculations, and by augmenting extant databases of materials and objects, we show how current commercial tools can be used to model environmental resources at both the building and urban scales.

There is also no technical reason to suppose that the approach will not work with other green rating system requirements, other commercial building information models and software, or for other environmental resource related calculations. The process used for modeling urban water use, prepares the groundwork for implementing other water resource management tools, for example, for graywater and rainwater collection, design of green roofs and water runoff calculation from different surfaces. The prototype described in this chapter was developed primarily for research purposes. It was implemented as a plug-in module on top of Revit. Currently, it is based on a simple water use model. It would require a more sophisticated water use modeling before it can be employed for non-research use.

The findings described in this chapter lead to the conclusion that strategies, which focus on water use reduction from the scope of the individual building to the urban scale, are among the components required for water management that have to be cohesively integrated to create a 'Green Urbanism' [26].

Acknowledgments. This work reported in this chapter is an extension of a project on integrating building information models and rating systems funded by Autodesk®, which aims to bringing sustainability principles closer to design. However, any opinions, findings, conclusions or recommendations presented in this chapter are those of the authors and do not necessarily reflect the views of Autodesk®. We would like to thank the facilities department at Carnegie Mellon University for their assistance in providing us data and insights on strategies used for achieving credits in the water reduction category though the LEED rating system.

References

1. UNEP.: Cities and Green Buildings (2009)
2. US Department of Transportion,
   http://www.fhwa.dot.gov/planning/census/cps2k.htm
3. US Geological Survey, http://pubs.usgs.gov/circ/1344/
4. EPA, http://www.epa.gov/owm/gapreport.pdf
5. Xing, W., Akinci, B., Davidson, C.I.: Modeling Graywater on Residences. J. of Green Building. 2(2), 111–120 (2007)
6. Ezel, C.: http://www.globalwarmingisreal.com/blog/2009/06/23/water-use-in-commerical-buildings-where-does-it-all-go/
7. McGraw Hill Construction, http://construction.ecnext.com/coms2/summary_0249307522_ITM_analytics
8. Vickers, A.: Handbook of Water Use and Conservation. Waterplow Press, Amherst (2001)
9. USGBC.: New Construction and Major Rennovation Reference Guide. USGBC, Washington, DC (2006)
10. Mayer, P.W., DeOreo, W.B., Optiz, E.M., Kiefer, J.C., Davis, W.Y., Dziegielewski, B., Nelson, O.J.: Residential End Users of Water. AWWA Research Foundation and American Water Works Association, Denver, CO (1999)
11. Dziegielewski, B.: Commercial and Institutional End Users of Water. AWWA Research Foundation and American Water Works Association, Denver, CO (1999)
12. Fowler, K.R.: Sustainable Building Rating Systems Summary. Pacific Northwest National Laboratory, Department of Energy (2007)
13. Autodesk, http://www.autodesk.com/revitarchitecture
14. Muller, P., Wonka, P., Haegler, S., Ulmer, A., Gool, L.V.: Procedural Modeling of Cities. In: International Conference on Computer Graphics and Interactive Techniques, pp. 301–308. ACM, New York (2001)
15. Congressional Budget Office,
    http://www.cbo.gov/publications/bysubject.cfm?cat=19
16. Leatherman, P.: Burton School Rain Water Harvesting System-An Educational Tool with Sustainable Benefits. J. Green Building 4(4), 19–28 (2009)
17. Reed, T.J., Clouston, P.L., Hoque, S., Fiestte, P.R.: An Analysis of LEED and BREEAM Assessment Methods for Educational Intitutions. J. Green Building 5(1), 132–154 (2010)
18. BREEAM, http://www.breeam.org/page.jsp?id=117
19. USGBC, http://www.usgbc.org/LEED/Project/CertifiedProjectList.aspx?CMSPageID=247
20. Eastman, C., Teicholz, P., Sacks, R., Liston, K.: BIM Handbook A Guide to Building Information Modeling. John Wiley & Sons, NJ (2008)
21. Green Building Council Australia,
    http://www.gbca.org.au/green-star/rating-tools/green-star-office-design-v3-green-star-office-as-built-v3/1710.htm
22. Rhinoceros, http://www.rhino3d.com/
23. Grasshopper, http://www.grasshopper3d.com/
24. Microsoft, http://www.microsoft.com/NET/
25. Echols, S.: Artful Rainwater Design in the Urban Landscape. J. Green Building 2(4), 151–170 (2007)
26. Lehmann, S.: Sustainability on the Urban Scale:'Green Urbanism'-Mark II. Journal of Green Building 2(3), 61–78 (2007)

Part III

Behavior Modeling and Simulation

Simulation Heuristics for Urban Design

Christian Derix[1], Åsmund Gamlesæter[1], Pablo Miranda[1],
Lucy Helme[1], and Karl Kropf[2]

[1] AedaslR&D, Hardwick Street 5-8, London EC1R 4RG, United Kingdom
{christian.derix,a.gamlesaeter,pablo.miranda,
lucy.helme}@aedas.com
[2] Studio I REAL Ltd, 59-63 High Street, Kidlington OX5 2DN, United Kingdom
kkropf@studioreal.co.uk

Abstract. Designing simulations for urban design not only requires explicit performance criteria of planning standards but a synthesis of implicit design objectives, that we will call 'purpose rules', with computational approaches. The former would at most lead to automation of the existing planning processes for speed and evaluation, the latter to an understanding of perceived urban qualities and their effect on the planning of cities.

In order to transform purpose rules into encoded principles we argue that the focus should not be on defining parametric constraints and quantities, but on aligning the perceptual properties of the simulations with the strategies of the stakeholders (planner/ urban designer/ architect/ developer/ community).

Using projects from the Computational Design and Research group at Aedas [CDR] as examples, this chapter will discuss how an open framework of lightweight applications with simple functionality can be integrated into the design and planning process by using computational simulations as urban design heuristics.

Keywords: urban design, design heuristics, meta-heuristics, simulation, algorithm visualization.

1   Spatial Strategies

Reviewing urban design and planning publications such as *By Design: Urban Design in the Planning System* [1] or the *Urban Design Compendium 1 & 2* [2] and Urban Task Force's *Towards an Urban Renaissance* [3], it becomes clear that the key requirements for creating sustainable communities rest largely on design aspects of the public realm. While some of these aspects can be quantified and standardized, most appear based on an inherent understanding of 'first principles' of good urban structures, spatial and social conditions.

The proliferation of urban design guidance in the 1990s followed in the wake of a weariness and discontent with city planning and design methodologies from the 50s to the 80s based on statistical or formal rules. As stated in *By Design*, "An aim of this guide is to encourage a move away from the negative reliance on standards towards a

S. Müller Arisona et al. (Eds.): DUMS, CCIS 242, pp. 159–180, 2012.

more positive emphasis on performance criteria. Standards specify precisely how a development is to be designed (by setting out minimum distances between buildings, for example). Performance criteria are the means of assessing the extent to which a development fulfils a specific planning requirement (such as maintaining privacy). Imaginative designers can respond to performance criteria with a variety of design solutions." [1]

Further: "Good urban design is rarely brought about by a local authority prescribing physical solutions, or by setting rigid empirical design standards but by approaches which emphasise design objectives or principles." [1]

Performance criteria and design objectives are clearly defined as means of assessing results that can partially be specified through quantitative constraints but often rely on implicit knowledge of the nature of such objectives. The objectives are based on the above mentioned 'first principles' and include aspects that are difficult to generate explicitly or measure numerically, such as

- Character (local patterns of development, landscape and culture)
- Continuity and Enclosure (clearly defined private and public areas)
- Quality of Public Realm (attractive, safe and accessible public spaces)
- Ease of Movement (accessibility and permeability)
- Legibility (image and way-finding)

Each objective refers to 'place making' and the perception of the citizen inside those places rather than a regional or building perspective, emphasizing public space, i.e. space between buildings. Such aspects are difficult to encode as cost functions for performance assessment but rely on learned experiences in generating spatial and social conditions during the design process (in other words: it is good to have assessment criteria but how do you get there?). To be able to approximate the desired assessment criteria, the emphasis of simulation should lie on the design strategies that best achieve urban conditions. Strategies that organize the design search are called heuristics. Can the equivalents from computing science – meta-heuristics – be successfully applied to align with urban design heuristics and create new strategies that don't rely on standards and assessment performances only?

1.1   Scales and Objectives

Early computational urban models from the 60s to the 90s were almost exclusively developed for urban planning, not design, to simulate regional land-use and transport patterns for regulation and policy compliance. In academia, models were developed for research into growth dynamics. These models almost exclusively used discrete representations for geographic locations or demographic units where spatial properties hardly featured at all (other than say distances).

Extending this approach, some current developments in urban simulations are moving towards the idea of 'behavioural modelling' where the behavioural choices implemented reflect socio-economic statistical probabilities on regional scales rather than design choices [4, 5]. While such models combining urban growth simulation with geometry generation are very sophisticated, they are more valuable to regional planning (economic, demographic or transport), academics (historic growth etc) or gaming (fast procedural geometry generation imitating urban patterns). Too many spatial and temporal scales and too many design objectives are integrated simultaneously into the simulation, producing a closed product that polarizes human/computer interaction, much in the tradition of scientific simulations of the 60-80s: humans feed and evaluate data - the computer generates output. The design objectives of more recent design and planning publications are located at intermediate scales between the regional and the architectural and must allow designers to collaborate spatially with the simulation.

Even though all design disciplines agree that cities – or even individual buildings for that matter – are complex because they have a structure of multiple, interconnected scales, urban design simulation has yet to effectively interrupt processing of an urban structure at the different intermediate levels between regional planning policy and the lamp post.

The original development of Space Syntax by Hillier *et a.* set out to generate spatial structures that include behavioural (social) rules [6]. Their approach was one of the first (apart from Negroponte's URBAN 5 [7]) to attempt to generate global form from local processes computationally, not the other way around. Despite Space Syntax having transformed into an analytical approach, it might be speculated that due to its local spatial perspective, it has consequently developed into the only computational design tool consistently used by urban designers in the 90s and 00s.

The original Space Syntax, URBAN 5 and other such local spatial generative simulations were built on the premise that design assumptions could be modelled. Typically, the assumptions have been treated as an intended 'performance' but it is important to distinguish between different kinds of performance. The term *performance* is commonly associated with measurable output and generally tends to be reduced to regulatory quantities. This kind of performance is explicit and tends to be expressed as a 'constraint rule'. Performance as used by CABE in *By Design* refers instead to qualitative properties generated during a design process. These, more tacit performances are better seen as 'purpose rules'. The most important difference is that 'purpose rules' can apply to different specific design scales and require interpretation at each scale to identify the appropriate solution to achieve the desired performance. In contrast, 'constraint rules' are valid across all scales and can produce automated urban structures without the designer's interaction.[1]

In professional urban design workflows, continuous simulations that integrate many scales and temporal stages alienate the designer and his or her heuristic tools. In effect, the simulation only operates as a black box not as a collaborative design instrument. Through trials on live projects at Aedas and with other partners, monolithic academic simulations were abandoned in favour of a modular system of discrete simulation units for distinct urban morphological aspects and their phenomena. While phenomena are often clearly cross-scale, it appears that a preferred

---

[1] Imagine constraint rules to be like 'distances' or 'ratios' that apply 'objectively' and can be automated. Purpose rules on the other hand instil design intentions that have to be evaluated at each scale and can't be coded as generally applicable without adaptation, like 'permeability'.

mode of working depends on the ability to assemble simulation units into bespoke workflows negotiated by the urban designer. The units or applets need to be functionally limited with clear visible behaviours that the user can interact with in order to participate in the search for potential solutions. The designer needs to be able to comprehend the search mechanism of the simulation in order to identify with proposed model states. That means that processes cannot encompass too many scales as phenomena become too complex to visually grasp and important aspects or elements are lost (that is, the machine chunking of the simulation does not correspond to the human designer's learned psychological chunking). Using an approach that explicitly incorporates scale and morphological phenomena avoids the simulation framework getting stuck with specific performance criteria and parametric standards.

1.2   Master Planning and Regeneration

While continuous simulations can be effective for evaluating site loading scenarios of large master plans of 'blank slate' developments, it is more difficult to apply them to situations that require active incorporation of existing features such as regeneration sites and area plans. Site loading scenarios visualizing development quanta and densities require only a small amount of regulatory properties and are generated before the design process begins.

Regeneration and area plans on the other hand rely on more sensitive processes where planners and designers demand illustrations of spatial consideration such as context, character and legibility. The distinction into non-spatial development scenarios and spatial regeneration scenarios also hints at their geographic application. Commercially, it has made less sense so far to develop simulations for smaller area plans for regeneration sites in historical environments than for large green-field developments.

1.3   Cities Are Not Buildings

Architects draw visual sketches of their buildings before designing them. And if architects play urban designer (like Le Corbusier), they also draw sketches of whole cities (more recently, Will Alsop famously said that urban design is 'big architecture'). If simulation produces quick sketches of whole cities down to the curb, then the complexity of a city has not been grasped. We cannot expect cities to be susceptible to modelling like buildings via Building Information Modelling (BIM). Cities are not designed as 'absolutes' or fully specified objects. They are designed essentially as configurations of objects and voids (or flow spaces as Hillier would say) at a number of different scales. And the nature and characteristics of the objects and voids at the different scales are not the same.[2]

The notion of BIM for buildings represents the old modernist paradigm of 'engineering' a solution by crunching numbers. The problem can be solved if enough data is available. Current urban simulations transfer that model from buildings to

---

[2] Thanks to Katja Stille of Tibbalds Urban Design for the discussion about 'absolutes'.

cities with the aim of engineering cities with as much information as possible. But cities and especially parts of cities subject to regeneration are not defined by finite sets of information amenable to linear solution-processes. As Rittel described it, planning already made the mistake in the Modernist period of seeing itself as 'applied science' [8].

2   Implicit Performance Criteria

Urban morphology represents a balance between public (void) and private (mostly solid) spaces. As Negroponte puts it, there are two classes of problems: under-constrained and over-constrained. By the measure of explicit performance criteria and parameters, public spaces tend to be under-constrained. By implicit performance criteria, public spaces might well be over-constrained to the extent that urban designers are seeking to achieve a number of different purposes and so apply a range of assumptions and heuristics. The solutions are thus likely to contain redundancy for adaptation to long term as well as ephemeral phenomena.

Producing holistic simulations for under-constrained aspects of design is a well known problem in architectural computation. Five decades of development on a perceived obvious design problem like space allocation modelling or layout generation has not produced any generally applicable simulation. As Liggett states, facility layout automation in practise is an ill-defined problem that requires a significant amount of knowledge from the designer to be integrated into the simulation via interaction or taking turns within a run of the simulation [9], i.e. not just running the simulation and then analysing the results.

Through developing Aedas in-house space allocation simulations and trialling other developments such as Elezkurtaj's evolutionary layout model [10], it became apparent that the problems with application and generalization of simulations do not necessarily lie with the algorithms but with an ignorance of the 'purpose rules' used by the architects, that is, an ontological representation of the design space, or 'what else' constitutes circulation design. Architects do not have many explicit constraints for circulation other than conditions of emergency egress or operationally optimal performance like hospital routes. From demonstrations and tests of in-house simulations it became apparent that architects do not want holistic simulations that override their spontaneous and heuristic purpose rules (tacit knowledge)[3]. Simulation needs to allow for greater flexibility in horizontal organization instead of continuous (vertical) organization. In order for designers to apply their heuristics to ill-defined problems like circulation they need to apply varying interpretations of a spatial

---

[3] As in Liggett's displayed examples and Elezkurtaj's demonstration, the layouts tend to always be tightly packed according to topological constraints. A tight-packing of shapes in area polygons is the last step in the process, the result from a long search that includes other aspects of search. Architects felt that this limits their flexibility and forbids them to introduced 'intuitive' changes, mainly by arrangement around and of 'formless' circulation and semi-public areas.

property which in turn requires many short simulations concerning different aspects of the same design phenomenon,.

Cost or objective functions need to be spread across various simulation units and not bundled into a single equation. Some meta-heuristics approximate trade-offs such as the Pareto multi-criteria optimization that is not limited to statistical functions but ideally designers negotiate the 'trading'. Similarly, taking account of the full range of urban morphological characteristics requires modularized limited interactive simulations of distinct spatial phenomena where an urban designer – or for that matter a planning officer, developer or architect – can insert himself and potentially align the simulations to his heuristics. Negroponte described the desirable aim of computer aided design as an evolutionary dialogue between machine and human (even though he also wished for an all-knowing intelligent adaptable machine that would integrate analogue as well as digital performances) [7].

3   Assemblies of Heuristics

In 2007 a first series of tests were run for the Smart Solutions for Spatial Planning (SSSP), a model that intended to create a digital chain from GIS and census data surveys down to the scale of block massing and plot sizes [11]. The project's aim was to break up the standard academic vertical and holistic model to align with the core principles of urban design objectives as identified in section 1.

Two series of workshops were conducted with a team including the project's regeneration planners from the London Borough of Newham and Tower Hamlets and urban designers from Urban Initiatives and the Alternative Urbanism at University of East London. The first series aimed to extract urban planning standards like quantitative criteria such as street-aspect ratios, block depths, proximity matrices etc as well as to investigate the implicit heuristics of both the planners and designers regarding the process of spatial design in the urban environment and their performance indicators. The aim of the second series was to demonstrate, validate and steer the development on the basis that synthesized heuristics cannot be 'measured' explicitly for performance but must be validated 'by process inspection' or 'visual narrative'.

A key revelation during the development of SSSP came from the second series of workshops: the validation could not properly be performed when too many parameters and heuristic indicators, i.e. 'purpose rules', were integrated to generate a morphological aspect. This meant that besides a vertical break-up, a horizontal break-up into individual elements of a morphological phenomenon was required to generate multiple representations separately rather than overlaying many perspectives simultaneously. In this context, 'validation' refers to the visual comprehension of the results by the planners, regeneration officers and urban designers.

The example in question dealt with the generation of urban block massing but did not include the outlines of development blocks at the higher scale or plot boundaries at the lower scale. Massing was generated parametrically by association of the following calculated criteria:

- Centrality values of the street network
- Resulting street-aspect ratio
- Block-depth criteria (for offset from street and block types)
- Character indicators derived from density requirements (neighbourhood definition by block types and sizes)
- Access levels

Each listed aspect was generated in accordance with textual and geometric input like access points, context circulation, development quantum, street type definitions and envelops of urban blocks derived from UK planning regulations. The generated outcomes read much like a static sketch of the actual geometry of a place. Hence, attention was drawn to the solids not the voids. Our partners quickly dismissed the solid formations as inadequate even though they were derived from 'their own' regulatory specifications and quantities. The salient criticism voiced concerned the representation of the result by geometric envelopes that did not convey the complexity of principles, and rules that formed them. In over-complex simulations, stakeholders can either accept the outcome blindly or question everything because they cannot perceive the process of formation.

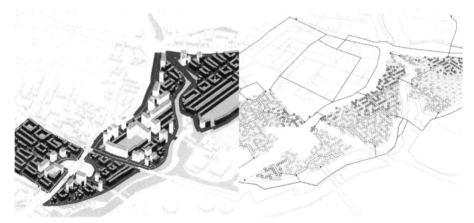

Fig. 1. The early massing simulation of SSSP integrated many morphological aspects like centrality of network, accessibility levels, scale and street character ratios, producing an opaque representation of place (left). The following redesign was based only adjacencies land-use units, proximity to site conditions and accessibility. The units were abstracted to diagrammatic place-holders as circles (right).

It became apparent that the morphological aspects for massing that were initially integrated into the simulation relied on disparate parameters and processes that apply across different design stages in an urban design workflow and are bound into other associations that had not been included. Two options to fix the conflict emerged: to include as many peripheral associated parameters as possible (following the current trend to rely on technology to fix the problem) or to reduce the complexity of the model to a core of clearly perceptible parameters and processes – the concept of parsimony.

To understand which parameters need to be included in a simulation, the question must be asked: what type of process is meant to be simulated? For urban design as with any design discipline, the processes should depend on the search space and heuristic employed by the designer. While the analogue heuristic is not meant to be mimicked, the search mechanism of the heuristic can give clues as to what types of computational techniques might fit the process best. Having established a link between a design heuristic and a computational approach to simulate a design search, the parameters can be pruned to a minimum by firstly aligning them with design drivers or performance indicators and secondly according to the 'purpose rules' or intentions.

Consequently, the massing model had to be broken down into processes that align with topological searches like land-use allocations and geometric generation such as the envelope based on criteria including street-aspect ratios, itself based on centrality measures etc.[4] The massing model was redesigned as a mixed-use and density simulation as well as a block definition simulation, dealing with the geometry of the block. The 'mix & density' simulation is based on levels of accessibility, development quantum, site conditions and the proximity matrix for uses. The search process was adjusted so that the dynamics of single decision steps can be visualized and the land-use units are abstracted to circles on an urban grid. The planners and urban designers could immediately understand the computational logic, because they could identify their 'design search behaviour' or heuristic with that of the simulation. The effect was a wholehearted 'urban design' conversation about the character of the place rather than quantities and technology.

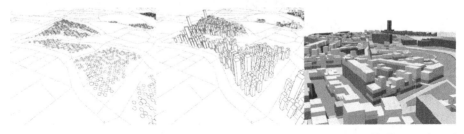

Fig. 2. The massing simulation split into two: Left: the search for the Mix. Middle: a scale and height (Density) approximation can be visualized during the land-use mix search. Right: a Massing simulation introduced at later design stages based on Pareto optimization.

While it appears that the simulation modules align more closely with traditional design stages, they open up possibilities to create new design workflows. For example, the traditional design stage of 'zoning' can be subverted. The zoning stage helps to tackle the complexity of the vast amount of data and constraints by pre-sorting into large areas of homogeneous functions. The second 'mix & density' simulation skips the zoning stage and instantly creates land-use mixes that afford

---

[4] Like the perceived problem in facility layout automation, design eventually synthesizes topological and geometric processes but design heuristics often follow the two strands distinctly to allow greater transparency and easier adaptation within the workflow.

immediate access to complex distributions with detailed impressions of places like demographic mix, safety requirements, density and scale indicators, amongst others.

As with the modularization of the initial massing simulation, assemblies of limited process-based simulations aligned with design heuristics help to include the designer, design team or stakeholders into the negotiation of 'constraint rules' and 'purpose rules'.

3.1   Diagrammatic I/O

The negotiation of lightweight simulations relies on the output being diagrammatic. Depicting results as 'realistic morphologies' tends to distract the viewer towards associated details that lie outside the search space. The diagrams produced from a simulation like the 'mix & density' are essentially temporary model-states in dynamic equilibrium, as the search process is still 'live' even after convergence (and waiting for new imbalances). It is the designers/ stakeholder's job to assemble the proposed diagrams into a whole and weigh each aspect in agreement with policies, context or concepts. From this consensus a visual may be constructed.

Equally important to the definition of the performance indicators and purpose rules are diagrammatic representations. As simulations are to capture processes that give rise to morphological phenomena, the process rules need to be represented through operational diagrams as input to the computational designers to create analogous simulation dynamics. Especially for urban design simulations, qualitative performances of public space are near impossible to sketch as an image (see cities are not buildings).

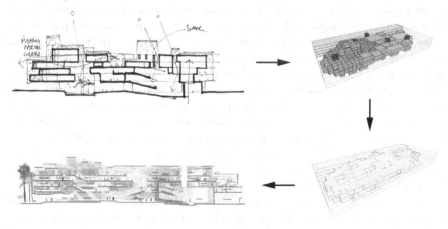

Fig. 3. Top: Initial diagram of solid/void composition for a building project. Right: Interactive simulation based on accommodation schedule including adjacencies, ceiling heights and envelope criteria. Bottom: final section from simulation diagrams.

This deconstruction of single models and sketches into modularized representations and diagrams is reminiscent of Christopher Alexander's pattern language [12]. Alexander's patterns however were not operational diagrams but direct descriptions of situations (unlike his system's diagrams in Notes on the Synthesis of Form). Nonetheless, it served as an analogy to software developers who extract principles of communication between modules that can be reused as templates that are called Design Patterns [13].

The complexity and depth (duration) of projects such as SSSP and the Ground Zero Memorial Museum created the basis for CDR to approach developments on the principles of the Agile software development methods. Agile advocates short development cycles that allow for small and lightweight codes to be extracted for further development and re-use. This modularization allows for flexibility and adaptability to changing scopes and briefs, avoiding monolithic long-term closed models. It is interesting to observe that the software community has adopted an analogy from design to organize and describe code templates for linking modules while the design community starts to adopt development principles from the software disciplines to organize (computational) design modules.

3.2   Computational Search

The original massing simulation was modularized into two computational search simulations: a simulated annealing model for the topological search and a Pareto optimization model for the geometric search. Both models belong to the class of meta-heuristic algorithms and approximate solutions within a complex design space. The field of meta-heuristics not only applies to difficult combinatorial optimization problem with no efficient solution mechanism (i.e., algorithm) but also to solution spaces where many alternatives can be equally valid. Urban Design is the ultimate ill-defined problem where the set of "reasonable" or "appropriate" solutions is huge. Urban design workshops, called charrettes, involve a participatory process for configuring block models where multiple users – designers, planners and other stakeholders – move abstracted volumetric blocks about, attempting to fit all units together as a site-wide development study or urban block capacity study. Results from charrettes are rarely optimal but produce series of alternatives until a good-enough or consensual solution has been found. This process of searching alternatives to satisfy both implicit and explicit constraints was called 'satisficing' by Herbert Simon who promoted artificial search for urban planning and design as early as 1969 [15].

Meta-heuristic algorithms are domain-based, meaning that the algorithm can't be generalized to the degree that it can be applied without adaptation to different design spaces. This is also an essential feature of design heuristics: while the general underlying 'rules of thumb' can be transferred to new situations (briefs/ sites) with similar conditions, the search strategy has to be adapted. In urban design terms, it can also be said that simulations should be tailored to scales and morphological aspects, and should not seek to span across many temporal and spatial scales because their conditions change. This property supports the modularization into horizontal assemblies of lightweight simulations with limited scope. It also aligns with the choice of search process as each scale and morphological aspect requires transparent search strategies based on an analogous search type. This in turn helps with diagrammatic specifications and output as well as the visualization of the dynamics of choice.

3.3   Visualizing Choices

Meta-heuristics can also be described as 'black box' processes due to the often hidden combinatorial nature of the transformation from state t to state $t+1$. But by that definition many simulations would be 'black boxes', especially when too many disparate aspects are being solved simultaneously. As already mentioned, it is important for users to be able to identify with the dynamics of simulations by visualizing the processes of choice or decisions. 'Seeing the struggle' to converge at a solution allows the designer to literally empathize with the computation, enabling her or him to interpret state transitions and equilibrium states without knowing the detailed workings of the algorithms. Barnes and Thagard describe empathy as a case of simulating someone or something else's intentions by creating an internal analogy unconsciously, meaning, without knowing the opposite's reasoning [16].

Behavioural simulation for us does not therefore reduce itself to statistical probabilities of fixed calculation units as in 'black boxes' but must extend to the visualization of decision-making processes creating affective responses from the user.

Another effect of the identification with simple and limited simulations is the ability of the user to single out moments at which to interfere with the simulation. All CDR simulations are interactive and allow for user manipulation. When the user perceives a deviation by the simulation from the expected reference heuristic (a reference heuristic is establish through the simulated internal analogy described by Barnes and Thagard), she/he can halt the process or change current conditions. The reasons for halting are most likely to be a deviation from the user's 'purpose rules' that are contained in her/his heuristics that the reference heuristics is analogous to.

The halting function of either a convergence towards a dynamic equilibrium or by user interference is akin to natural design searches and gets over the argument that meta-heuristics have no halting function. In fact, user interference and convergence in a design context with ill-defined cost functions seems to be an adequate mechanism to deal with implicit performance criteria.

One of the principal goals of the charrette as a design tool supports the arguments for identification with decision making processes, interference and limited scopes: the charrette is meant to evoke the sensation of 'joint ownership' of the results by all stakeholders, through equal inclusion in the decision making process and an ability to describe choices taken.

4   Approximating Urban Design Objectives

Urban Design objectives set out in *By Design* or the Urban Task Force are mostly of the ill-defined class with non-explicit performance evaluation criteria. These objectives describe properties of the public realm that cannot be generated in isolation from the heuristic of the designer[5] who guides the simulation and executes the halting function.

---

[5] A designer can apply at least two heuristics to generate a solution: 1) a professionally accepted heuristic that converged over time like the Urban Design and Planning Toolkit by CABE [1] to achieve the above mentioned Urban Design Objectives. Or 2) the designer's subjective heuristic consolidated by trial and error. It can now be argued that heuristics are subject to design paradigms, Zeitgeist and trends.

The following sections illustrate a selection of applications from the CDR Digital Master planning framework developed (or in development) with urban designers to help negotiate attributes of public space and apply 'purpose rules' without explicit cost functions. The selection is not reduced to meta-heuristics or simulations in a strict sense but also extends to 'semi-automatic' applications that overcome the traditional consultancy model where 'designers design' and 'consultants evaluate' (a kind of 'analytical divide') that even extents to the computational design discipline. As a collection they form a design search framework that can be assembled to align with many types of urban design briefs.

4.1   Movement and Legibility

Two of the objectives considered in detail are ease of movement in and legibility of urban spaces. In practice these two aspects are often considered simultaneously: how can legibility of the urban environment enhance the ease of movement?

A series of independent applications have been built corresponding to discrete aspects of the movement and legibility objectives that can be run in any order according to design priority and individual heuristic. Each application visualizes in real-time the investigated aspect and allows the designer to interfere with the simulation to avoid the 'analytical distance'. Currently, there are 6 simulations to investigate the objectives for path-finding, movement structure, permeability and legibility:

- Path network analysis with interactive improvement calculation via new link insertion
- Movement structure generation
- Catchment area and access levels
- Routes simulation
- People movement simulation
- Routes visibility simulation

The core of the currently emerging assembly that urban designers integrate into their workflow comprises the visualization of potential routes and the visual impact along those routes. This combination is not surprising as it illustrates most clearly the spatial design aspects currently absent from design processes when dealing with issues of accessibility.

For the routes simulation, a survey of pedestrian locations and quantities has to be conducted first as input to the simulation. The survey specifies departure points and quantities of people as an estimate for present or future scenarios. Equally, a set of possible destination points needs to be provided. The simulation generates three types of routes and the flow (footfall) along them. The routes are generated on the principles of 'motion-planning' [17], calculating a visibility graph to which the Dijkstra algorithm is applied to visualize

- Shortest distances (geometric)
- Least turns (topologic)
- Minimum deviation (angular)

The visualization shows the proposed path lines with thickness indicating flow rates and colour the user-defined distance gradients. When the designer adds, moves or erases a destination or departure location or changes pedestrian quantities, he can observe the updating network of paths and flow rates throughout the urban environment. This immediate feedback and visualized calculation along the visibility graph creates a feeling of transparency and control that does not require 'iteration'. The routes can be biased or can automatically select any destination point depending on survey and interviews. To mitigate incomplete survey data sets or add contextual noise, additional peripheral departure points or site-wide grid points with pedestrian quantities can be added live to investigate general flows or relax the sometimes too deterministic network. The simulation can also be used with topography and in multi-storey buildings.

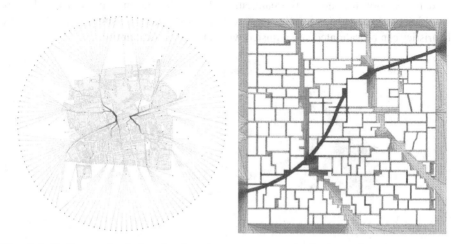

Fig. 4. Left: Routes simulation showing shortest routes to destination points from surveyed departure points and perimeter points that add contingency noise to site flows. Thickness of lines indicate footfall, colour indicates walking distances. Right: Catchment and Access levels visualization showing access levels by angular distance (minimum deviation to destination points). Vector grid shows direction towards nearest destination point.

While the simulation is not as elaborate as a full agent-based model or as exact as a Logit model, it appears to have achieved the right balance between abstraction (leanness of parameters and visual representation), speed and interactivity that is required to allow designers to use it instantly and simultaneously during their solution search. Agent-based (which the CDR has also created for more evaluative purposes), discrete or probabilistic models demand too much upfront preparation, duration of simulation or inappropriate formatting of results to allow designers intuitive access, let alone immediate feedback.

The routes simulation is often paired with the routes visibility simulation that generates a gradient map of surfaces seen while walking along the proposed routes. The previously generated routes are input to the simulation and a sampling sequence is set at which the routes produce a mapping of view-sheds. While the view-sheds produce an accumulative mapping of number of hits per surface, another simulation visualizes the dynamic (moving) views within the city in real-time. The gradient map is generated via ray-tracing and outputs a 3D colour map but the real-time visualization shows the live view sheds as they travel through the model. A hardware-accelerated stencil buffering algorithm is required for speed while the view-sheds are abstracted to grey-scales, the darker the more view-sheds overlap.

The designer can now observe the travelling views unfold from a global perspective to capture relationships between buildings and routes or descend onto street level to perceive 'other pedestrians seeing' as the simulation runs live.

Clients and stakeholders have caught onto the potentials of this approach to plug a gap in the design process, which is usually relegated to the evaluation stages. It has opened up a source of evidence that is currently post-produced. At the same time the evidence is not formatted as quantitative data only but intuitively accessible as graphic counterparts to objectives and 'search steps'. Design assumptions inherent in heuristics can be validated and adjusted without explicit descriptions.

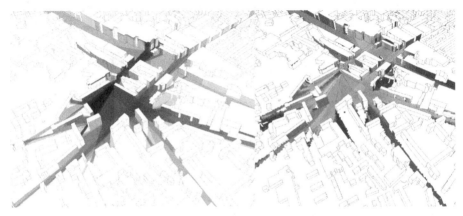

Fig. 5. Left: dynamic view-sheds moving along routes within site. Right: gradient mapping of resulting routes visibility.

The potentials for the movement & legibility simulation modules are being explored as they are still fairly new. Projects are moving fast from access and urban impact aspects to other public realm aspects like secure-by-design, landmark planning for path-finding, place making and identity via morphological hierarchies, all design objectives without explicit performance data or cost functions.

4.2   Mix and Density

This section introduces simulations that deal with plot outlines, mix and density. Currently, Digital Master planning comprises 6 simulations investigating these aspects

- Development plot outlines generation
- Block Scale Investigation (by Centrality)

- Mix & Density
- Block Capacity generation
- Overshadowing Envelope
- Visual Impact Analysis (by height)

Each simulation is built around a single process that aligns with a design heuristic, but more than one performance criterion is usually integrated to search the solution spaces. Three applications use meta-heuristics – development plot outlines, mix & density and block capacity while the others are designed with the same semi-automatic interactive real-time approach as described in the previous section.

As already illustrated in section 3, the original massing simulation during the development of SSSP was split into two applications so that the internal workings and the performance criteria could be made more transparent. The first of the two applications, mix & density, is complementary with the development plot outline (DPO) generation, which will now be briefly discussed.

The DPO originally represented the second application to support the generation of the movement structures – primary and secondary circulation. A first application investigates primary movement axes, access points like transport hubs and linkages to contextual roads, whereas the DPO application creates the secondary movement structure linking secondary access points like communal infrastructure into the primary circulation and generating as an output a subdivision of the site into development plot outlines. Creating the secondary circulation is an ill-defined problem with a few established heuristics to approach the search for a solution. One deals with 'cutting up' the site by elongating roads leading into the site, creating intersections and junctions where feasible. This works for relatively small and well-defined sites. Larger open sites are less constrained – unless for infrastructural conditions – and are often dealt with by working with a set urban grid that is tweaked to a selection of criteria. The DPO application represents a hybrid (as in reality do most analogue searches).

The DPO employs three visualizations of processes and states during its simulation:

- Intensity map of all tested paths accumulating over time
- Present circulation state updated at every calculation step t
- Best overall circulation state updated when improved circulation found

The intensity map expresses the search choices taken by an ant-colony optimization (ACO) algorithm that is driving a modified Steiner tree, which expresses the circulation state (meta-heuristics based on Blum & Blesa [18]). Any present tree that is better than the best overall circulation found so far replaces it as the new best overall circulation state. This triple visualization enables the designer to watch the simulation take instant choices, how they are built up and against what they are measured.

Fig. 6. The Development Plot Outline generation visualizes three states during simulation. Left: the ant-colony optimization approximates the shortest path network between access points on an urban grid and primary movement structure. Centre: a modified Steiner tree shows the current best interpretation of the ACO at time t (four consecutive solutions). Right: the overall best solution from the Steiner trees at any time t.

The ACO runs on a user-defined input grid derived from assumptions about character and standards of block sizes. The grid is populated with access points from GIS and manually placed data, and linked to the previously generated primary circulation (hence a composite between a polygonal, orthogonal and diagrid graph). Pheromone is used to inform the edges of the graph that form part of the shortest tree at each time t, increasing its chances to be picked again. The Steiner tree allows for interpolation of nodes within a graph and thus lends itself well in conjunction with an ACO to search an otherwise unwieldy solution space.

As with the original SSSP massing application, the circulation was initially thought to be generated as one, which turned out to be too complex to produce, interpret and interact with as a designer. Hence the search was split into primary circulation with less routes on a manually produced graph implementing a K-minimum spanning tree and the secondary circulation. This allows designers to apply heuristics more regularly and see the effects of their assumptions earlier. It can also be repeated as many times as necessary for more levels of network hierarchies. The resulting circulations can be separately specified via types of routes and access points while still being associated with each other. For urban design this helps with specifications of multi-modal transport networks, pedestrian routes, development plot outlines etc.

The mix & density application (MD) works in synergy with the DPO as it takes the development plot outlines and the development grid as two of its inputs (but doesn't have to – any given user-defined plot outlines and grid can be specified). As briefly described in section 3, the MD was developed for SSSP in order to study land-use distribution scenarios through varying the development quantum and adjacency definitions of each type of use. By incorporating adjacencies of land-uses, proximities to site conditions and accessibility, the simulation highlights the mutual implications of all three aspects on each other.

The MD simulation applies a Quantum Annealing meta-heuristic [19], which implements a technique called 'tunnelling' for finding good solutions in a noisy fitness landscape. The search is initialised by randomly placing the land-use units in the available grid and evaluating its fitness, i.e. how well the configuration corresponds to the ideal adjacencies specified by the user. The search attempts to improve the compliance of the configurations with the adjacency and development objectives. The tunnelling allows each configuration to search within a monotonously decreasing neighbourhood of configurations and hence enable the simulation to 'jump' local maxima to find new minima.

Fig. 7. The sequence from the Mix & Density shows from top left to bottom right the Quantum Annealing search for a good land-use mix by 'swapping' individual units within configurations until a satisfactory solution is reached.

To visualize this process, the notion of replacing complete configurations is replaced with 'swapping' individual land-use units within the present configuration. The number of swaps is determined by the time elapsed and represents the tunnelling neighbourhood. A large number of swaps are performed in the early stages when the solution is still immature, and decreases steadily while the fitness of the solution increasingly improves. The designer can watch the swaps taking place as if manually replacing the land-use units, knowing that complex performance criteria are simultaneously evaluating the search.

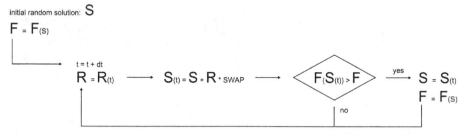

Fig. 8. Search diagram for the mix & density simulation implemented by the quantum annealing algorithm. S represents a Solution as a configuration of units of land-use, R represents the radius of the search as a function of time t and F represents the fitness or cost function of the search space.

The visualization for density in this simulation refers to an estimation of plot ratio and height according to plot ratios. Given the mix, plot ratios and height indication, further simulations investigate aspects of envelope and massing. The step from mix & density on previous development plot outlines to exact block outlines and plot capacity specification is a complex multi-scale problem that should not be generated in one continuous simulation as too many assumptions, intentions and performances inform each aspect. On the other hand, it was voiced by many urban design partners that the search for block types is often relatively quick by definition of 'character', which again relies on complex notions like 'experience' or 'intuition'.

4.3   Continuity and Enclosure

Eventually, three applications are briefly presented that deal with aspect of urban morphology, which are still in development but are intended to plug into urban design procedures from a spatial heuristic perspective.

If a movement structure has been agreed, there are many ways to look at the envelope and public realm – space between the buildings – before fixing the block boundaries. One such consideration is the street-aspect ratio for block envelopes that are associated with criteria such as character, access levels, density and mix. One application in development called Urban Block Editor (UBE) looks at block volumes on the basis of the integration measure of the street network, called centrality. Centrality refers to the analysis of integration within a network. UBE uses the 'betweeness centrality' to measure the number of shortest routes that pass through a location. From this measure a probability of flow can be inferred that is similar to density measures from accessibility analysis.

In order to be able to design the block volumes with simultaneous street network analysis, a polygonal mesh representation was used that implements the half-edge data structure where associative relations between vertices, edges and polygons allow for easy modification with live local updating. The edges and vertices form the base graph for the network analysis that implements the 'edge-betweeness' algorithm of Girvan- Newman [20].

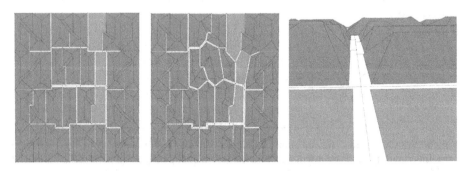

Fig. 9. The Urban Block Editor visualizing potential street widths, street-aspect ratios and associated volumes by evaluating the betweeness-centrality of the street network. As most simulations, the UBE can be used interactively in the design process and updates real-time any changes in evaluation as seen in the left and middle images.

The centrality values along the edges determine the street width and their related aspect ratios. The aspect ratios are currently not visualized as vertical elevations but as set-back volumes whose slopes depend on the adjacent street centrality. A polygon with multiple edges produces a maximum height depending on the surrounding street centralities and the resulting slopes. The indicative volume illustrates an approximate density and scale of the urban block. The designer can interact at will by adding, subtracting or modifying the polygons (within limits of rational block constraints). It is also possible to repeat the subdivisions of the plots between manual editing or change a block type from solid to void.

To speculate on the perceived proprietary areas, another interactive live application is being tested to visualize and design spatial partitioning. The application analyses geometrical boundaries of areas shared between building footprints. Each building edge is assumed to have a 'sphere of influence' that is determined by the proximity to other building edges. The equidistant limit between edges could be perceived as the most public area while the areas closest to building edges are more private.

To visualize these transitions between public and private spaces, a medial representation was used implementing a straight skeleton algorithm [21]. Essentially, the algorithm calculates equidistant points that form intermediate axes. The areas between the edges and axes constitute different gradients of perceived 'publicness', where different types of spatial occupations are likely to appear (for example in a square where areas towards edges often serve for stationary activities and central areas for movement). Similarly, it can be observed that configurations of buildings produce open spaces with a directionality as the axes form spines in the direction of the longest symmetrically opposing buildings. In other words, a 'transit value' and directions of transit can be illustrated [22]. Depending on the 'slope' or gradient between the central spines and building edges, it might be possible to attribute speed of transit as well. These speculations require validation but also extend into the exploration of spatial properties otherwise regarded as qualitative and ephemeral phenomena. We would agree with David Leatherbarrow's complaint that performances are nowadays all too often fixated on dry engineering quantities when spatial phenomena could also be approximated by computing [23]. Leatherbarrow reminds us that 'flows' are not only 'transits' but also represent different forms of occupation and experience. This last application attempts to open the discussion towards a phenomenological simulation of urban design.

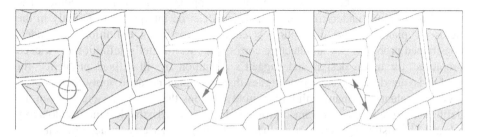

Fig. 10. The proprietary area visualization based on a medial axes representation indicates gradients of 'publicness' and can potentially reveal directionalities of spaces

5   Conclusion

While this paper has attempted to illustrate the use of computational simulation to produce new heuristics for urban design, it also acknowledges that the approach sits uncomfortably between two positions: designers and computational designers (or more likely software developers) There are many issues over which this fragile approach often breaks down and gets dragged into one of the two camps.

In many architecture schools (and practices) there is a perception that design with computers is solely applicable to problem-solving but not problem-worrying (to use Sanford Anderson's words [24]). Design is portrayed as a 'creative' and therefore under-constrained inductive search, while computation (programming) deals with over-constrained deductive problems. Surely part of the problem lies with the fact that very few designers have solid computer programming experience and vice versa, leading to barely any examples of successful computational design workflows or projects in either urban design or architecture.

Using simulation as a generative agency for spatial and occupational phenomena requires a change of perception of computation as optimization tools. While it could be tempting to perceive cities as ideal analogies for system theoretic and computational approaches, it is dangerous to represent cities – or the built environment in general – as an accumulation of simulation processes. This would lead to the automation (repeatability) and standardization of urban morphologies, creating spatial anonymity. Loosening of tolerances and greater redundancy must enter computational heuristics that are expressions of designers' purpose rules not mere statistical or stochastic deviations. The framework of applications described in this paper begins to achieve that aim. By developing them further there is the potential for computation and simulation to become regarded as equivalent to analogue design search approaches like charettes or sketching where the emphasis doesn't rest on the wooden blocks or pencils as tools but on the activity that allows purpose rules and assumptions to be explored. When Juhani Pallasmaa [25] argues against the computer as a 'spatial thinking' device, he laments this lack of intentional contingency.

Further, both disciplines – software developers as well as designers – are starting to borrow terminologies from each other. Definitions in either field carry different connotations that might contradict the intended approach (rather than outcome). The terms 'over-' and 'under-constrained' problems can be interpreted differently in the fields of planning and computing science. Negroponte's definition of 'under-constrained problems' for architecture corresponds with Rittel's definition of 'wicked problems' for urban design and Liggett's definition of 'ill-defined problems' for facility-layout design. Negroponte argues that a designer needs to apply 'intuition' in order to evaluate the many valid alternative solutions that can be generated from the definition of the under-constrained problem. In other words, the designer has to apply a learned heuristic to generate or evaluate solutions to under-constrained problems.

In computer science, meta-heuristics generally apply to 'over-constrained' problems where many known parameters create a vast solution space too complicated to search through without a short cut. This 'short-cut' is analogous to a designer's rule-of-thumb or heuristic.

At the same time, when taking into account the full range of purpose rules, many problems of urban design would appear to be over- rather than under-constrained. Too often competing or contradictory design objectives apply to a given problem. As important, the public nature of urban design and the desire for consensus adds to the problem with multiple interpretations of the various stakeholders. While the concepts of 'heuristic' as a learned rule-of-thumb to get to a satisfactory solution correspond in the two fields, their problem definitions appear to oppose each other.

As Liggett pointed out in his conclusions about spatial layout simulations [6], a balance between design and computing approaches still needs to be found to allow ill-defined problems to be meaningfully simulated through computation. We believe this balance will be achieved when computation is understood as more than just a set of tools or black boxes and designers start using computation as part of a design methodology that produces new heuristics.

References

1. Commission for Architecture & the Built Environment (CABE): By Design: Urban design in the planning system: towards better practice. Department for the Environment, Transport and the Regions (DETR), London (2000)
2. Baxter, A., Associates, Llewelyn-Davies ltd. (eds.): Urban Design Compendium. English Partnership, London (2000)
3. Rogers, R. (ed.): Towards an urban renaissance: final report of the Urban Task Force. E & FN Spon, London (1999)
4. Waddell, P., Ulfarsson, G.F.: Introduction to urban simulation: design and development of operation models. In: Hensher, D., Button, K., Haynes, K., Stopher, P. (eds.) Transport Geography and Spatial Systems, Handbook in Transport, vol. 5, Elsevier, Amsterdam (2004)
5. Vanegas, C., Aliaga, D., Benes, B., Waddell, P.: Interactive Design of Urban Spaces using Geometrical and Behavioral Modeling. ACM Transactions on Graphics (Proceedings SIGGRAPH Asia) 28(5) (2009)
6. Hillier, B., Leaman, A., Stansall, P., Bedford, M.: Space Syntax. Environment and Planning B 3, 147–185 (1976)
7. Negroponte, J.: The Architecture Machine. MIT Press, Cambridge (1980)
8. Rittel, H., Webber, M.: Dilemmas in General Theory of Planning. Policy Sciences 4, 155–169 (1973)
9. Liggett, R.: Automated Facility Layouts: past, present and future. Automation in Construction 9, 197–215 (2000)
10. Elezkurtaj, T., Frank, G.: Algorithmic Support of Creative Architectural Design. Umbau 19, 129–137 (2002)
11. Derix, C.: In-Between Architecture & Computation. International Journal for Architectural Computing 7(4), 565–586 (2009)
12. Alexander, C., Ishikawa, S., Silverstein, M., Jacobson, M., Fiksdahl-King, I., Angel, S.: A Pattern Language. Oxford University Press, New York (1977)
13. Gamma, E., Helm, R., Johnson, R., Vlissides, J.: Design Patterns. Addison-Wesley, Boston (1995)
14. Highsmith, J.: Adaptive Software Development: A Collaborative Approach to Managing Complex Systems. Dorset House Publications, New York (2000)

15. Simon, H.: The Sciences of the Artificial. MIT Press, Cambridge (1969)
16. Barnes, A., Thagard, P.: Empathy and Analogy,
    http://cogsci.uwaterloo.ca/Articles/Pages/Empathy/html
17. O'Rourke, J.: Computational Geometry in C. Cambridge University Press, Cambridge (1994)
18. Blum, C., Blesa, M.: New metaheuristic approaches for the edge-weighted K-cardinality tree problem. Computers & Operations Research (2004)
19. Das, A., Chakrabarti, B. (eds.): Quantum Annealing and Related Optimization Methods. Lecture Notes in Physics, vol. 679. Springer, Heidelberg (2005)
20. Girvan, M., Newman, M.: Community structure in social and biological networks. Proc. National Academy of Science of the USA 99, 7821–7826 (2002)
21. Aichholzer, O., Aurenhammer, F.: Straight Skeletons for General Polygonal Figures. In: Cai, J.-Y., Wong, C.K. (eds.) COCOON 1996. LNCS, vol. 1090, pp. 117–126. Springer, Heidelberg (1996)
22. Leymarie, F., Latham, W., Todd, S., Derix, C., Miranda, P., Coates, P., Calderon, C., Graves, F.: Medial Representations for Driving the Architectural Creative Process. In: International Architecture Symposium, Barcelona (2008)
23. Leatherbarrow, D.: Architecture Oriented Otherwise. Princeton Architectural Press, New York (2009)
24. Anderson, S.: Problem-Solving and Problem-Worrying. Architectural Association, London (1966)
25. Pallasmaa, J.: The Thinking Hand: Existential and Embodied Wisdom in Architecture. Architectural Design Primer. John Wiley and Sons, Chichester (2009)

Running Urban Microsimulations Consistently with Real-World Data

Gunnar Flötteröd and Michel Bierlaire

Transport and Mobility Laboratory
Ecole Polytechnique Fédérale de Lausanne
1015 Lausanne, Switzerland
{gunnar.floetteroed,michel.bierlaire}@epfl.ch
http://transp-or.epfl.ch/

Abstract. We present concepts and methods to cope with the enormous data needs of urban microsimulations. In the first part of the article, we adopt a process-oriented perspective on relocation, activity participation, and transportation and then refine this perspective in the microsimulation context. The second part of the article considers the parameter and state estimation problem. First, the different time scales of an urban system are identified and a rolling horizon framework for its continuous state estimation is developed. Second, the parameter estimation problem for an integrated urban microsimulation problem is investigated. The operational difficulty of jointly estimating all parameters of the urban model is met with two different approaches: the decoupling through estimated process interactions and the use of response surfaces and metamodels to mathematically approximate intractable, simulation-based processes.

Keywords: transportation and land use microsimulation, state estimation, parameter calibration.

1 Introduction

Microsimulation-based models of urban systems have proven to be powerful tools for prediction and scenario analysis, with a particular yet continuously expanding focus on transportation and land use. They bring along a high level of detail, but they also come at the cost of enormous data needs for their estimation. This article presents concepts and methods to cope with these challenges.

The text is structured in two parts. The first part, which consists of Sections 2 and 3, focuses on modeling and simulation: First, Section 2 defines the considered urban processes and casts them into a basic formal framework. Second, Section 3 adopts a microsimulation-based perspective on these processes.

The integration of real data into an urban microsimulation is the topic of the second part, which consists of Sections 4 through 6: First, Section 4 defines the respective terminology and indicates two important and new data sources. Second, Section 5 discusses the urban state estimation problem, with a focus on the different time scales on which an urban system unfolds. Third, Section 6

S. Müller Arisona et al. (Eds.): DUMS, CCIS 242, pp. 181–199, 2012.
© Springer-Verlag Berlin Heidelberg 2012

elaborates on the parameter estimation problem for urban models, with a focus on the advantages and difficulties of estimating interacting model components in an integrated manner. Finally, Section 7 summarizes the article.

2   Urban Systems

An urban system consists of several interacting components, which are outlined in the following. See Wegener (2004) for a more comprehensive introduction to integrated transportation and land used models and Ghauche (2010) for a recent review with an activity-based modeling focus (Bowman and Ben-Akiva; 1998). Three processes are crucial to a microsimulation-based urban modeling approach: relocation, activity participation, and transportation. Strongly related to these, one may account for energy consumption, the economy, environmental effects, and social interactions. The outline given below and depicted in Figure 1 focuses on the mutual interactions of the basic processes relocation, activity participation, and transportation.

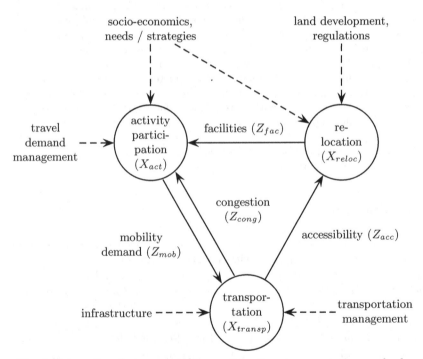

Fig. 1. Interactions between activity participation, transportation, and relocation

Relocation. The relocation model takes as exogenous inputs the socio-economics of households and firms, their long-term needs and strategies, the development of the building infrastructure, and possible regulations regarding its use. Its endogenous input are the accessibility measures Z_{acc}

obtained from a transportation model. The relocation model captures how households select their dwellings, how businesses select their offices, how land prices adapt in reaction to this (this may involve a separate economic model), and how these in turn affect the relocation decisions of all involved actors. We denote by X_{reloc} the allocation of all households and firms to all buildings in the system. The output of the relocation model are the facilities Z_{fac}, which provide activity opportunities to households and firms.

Activity Participation. The activity participation model takes as exogenous inputs the socio-economics of households and firms, their long-term needs and strategies, and possible travel demand management measures. Its endogenous input are the facilities Z_{fac} defined by the relocation model. Household members conduct activities in different places, including working, regular shopping, and spontaneous leisure activities, all of which may require them to travel to the respective facilities. Firms assemble production inputs such as raw materials or components into their products or provide services. We denote by X_{act} the activity and travel plans of all households and firms in the system. The output of the activity participation model(s) are sequences of (desired) trips through the transportation network for different modes (or mode combinations) and demand sectors, which we collectively refer to as the mobility demand Z_{mob}. The decision to make a trip also depends on the congestion state of the transportation network Z_{cong}.

Transportation. The transportation model takes as exogenous inputs the transportation infrastructure and possible transportation management measures. Its endogenous input is the mobility demand Z_{mob} from the activity participation model. The transportation model represents the physical world of mobility and describes how the mobility demand is served by the transportation infrastructure. The transportation model captures congestion, the temporary over-utilization of the system. We denote by X_{transp} the state of the transportation system, including all mobile entities (vehicles, buses, trains, ...), their occupations, and possibly the internal states of intelligent control mechanisms (such as adaptive traffic lights). The transportation model has two outputs: it feeds back congestion information Z_{cong} to the activity participation model, and it feeds back the resulting changes in location accessibility Z_{acc} to the relocation model.

Formally, we denote by $Z_{mob} = G_{mob}(X_{act})$ the mapping of activity participation on mobility demand, by $Z_{cong} = G_{cong}(X_{transp})$ and $Z_{acc} = G_{acc}(X_{transp})$ the mapping of the transportation system's state on congestion and accessibility, and by $Z_{fac} = G_{fac}(X_{reloc})$ the mapping of the building infrastructure's use on the availability of facilities. Collecting all $Z...$, $X...$, and $G...$, one obtains the **process interaction equations**

$$Z = G(X). \tag{1}$$

The activities $X_{act} = F_{act}(Z_{cong}, Z_{fac})$ are a function of congestion and available facilities. The transportation system's state $X_{transp} = F_{transp}(Z_{mob})$ evolves depending on the mobility demand. The building usage $X_{reloc} = F_{reloc}(Z_{acc})$ is a function of the accessibilities. Collecting all $F...$, this yields the **process state equations**

$$X = F(Z). \tag{2}$$

Combining (1) and (2), one obtains

$$X = F(G(X)), \tag{3}$$

which fully specifies the state X of the urban model in terms of a fixed-point relationship, which states that all processes evolve consistently with each other. We deliberately omit exogenous factors for notational simplicity and postpone the introduction of model parameters to Section 4.

An explicit introduction of the time dimension into this model is postponed to Section 5. For now, we observe that the presented notation allows for both a static equilibrium model or a dynamic (either equilibrium or out-of-equilibrium) model: One may think of X and Z as time-independent long-term average values and of F and G as likewise static functions. This turns (3) into an equilibrium model. One may also think of X and Z as time-dependent values $X = \{x(t)\}_t$ and $Z = \{z(t)\}_t$ with t being the time dimension. In this case, (3) does not necessarily call for an equilibrium but at least for the mutually consistent dynamic evolution of all processes.

3   Microsimulation

A large number of urban microsimulations has evolved in the last decades. To name a few, there are the transportation microsimulations DynaMIT (Ben-Akiva et al.; 1998) and MATSim (Raney and Nagel; 2006), the activity participation simulations TASHA (Miller and Roorda; 2004) and Albatross (Arentze and Timmermans; 2004), and the more comprehensive land use simulations UrbanSim (Waddell and Ulfarsson; 2004) and ILUTE (Salvini and Miller; 2005). The software platform OPUS is a recent effort to provide a technical framework for integrated urban microsimulations (Waddell et al.; 2005).

Microsimulation can be seen both as a modeling paradigm and a model solution technique, and both perspectives apply in the context of urban models.

Microscopic modeling. If the system under consideration consists of interacting entities, then a modeling approach that captures these entities individually is structurally consistent in that the real entities have distinct counterparts in the model. This holds in particular if the system is (i) coarse-grained in that a continuous-limit perspective that aggregates individual entities into real-valued quantities is not appropriate and/or (ii) heterogeneous in that the entities differ too much from each other to be represented by a limited number of homogeneous groups. If these properties do not apply then a macroscopic model may sometimes be preferable, for example in thermodynamics. In land use and transportation, however, there is broad agreement that both the coarse granularity of and the differences between the involved actors favor a microscopic modeling approach (Nagel and Axhausen; 2001). Last but not least, microscopic models deal with entities that have counterparts in the real world, which makes them more intuitive and easier to communicate than abstract systems of equations.

Microscopic simulation. Even if macroscopic modeling is feasible, it usually is uncertain and hence involves distributional assumptions about quantities that cannot exactly be determined. The solution of such models requires to solve possibly complicated integrals over these distributions. This mere computational problem can be solved by simulation in the numerical sense (Ross; 2006): instead of evaluating the integral directly, a number of random realizations is generated, the resulting indicators are calculated, and their average is used as an approximation of the integral. The substantial uncertainty clinging to land use and transportation models in combination with the impossibility to evaluate them in closed form motivates a simulation-based approach from this technical perspective as well. In particular, the uncertainty of microscopically modeled behavior calls for a probabilistic analysis, which for all but the most simple models can only be conducted through simulation.

The microscopic approach is essentially characterized by disaggregation. However, there may be different degrees of disaggregation. We make this observation formally concrete for the individually simulated actors in the system. These **agents** are indexed by $n = 1 \dots N$, where N is the size of the simulated population. Consistently with the framework of Section 2, the state X_n of agent n consists of its activity state $X_{act,n}$, its transportation state $X_{transp,n}$, and its relocation state $X_{reloc,n}$.

$X_{act,n}$ represents the activity and travel plan of the agent. $X_{transp,n}$ describes if, where, and how the agent is currently mobile in the transportation system. $X_{reloc,n}$ defines the dwelling of the agent (housing for a household and, e.g., office space for a firm). If the agent represents more than one individual (members of a household, employees of a firm), then the respective state variables represent all of these individuals. The process states X_{act}, X_{transp}, and X_{reloc} comprise the individual-level components for all members of the population but may contain additional information, depending on the scope of the whole simulation system.

The disaggregate activity participation, transportation, and relocation models for agent n are written in the following way:

$$X_{act,n} = F_{act,n}(Z_{cong}, Z_{fac}, Z_{transp,n}, Z_{reloc,n}) \tag{4}$$

$$X_{transp,n} = F_{transp,n}(Z_{cong}, Z_{act,n}) \tag{5}$$

$$X_{reloc,n} = F_{reloc,n}(Z_{fac}, Z_{acc}). \tag{6}$$

Equation (4) states that the activity and travel plans $X_{act,n}$ of an agent n depend on the congestion status Z_{cong} of the transportation network, the available facilities Z_{fac}, and the transportation and relocation state

$$Z_{transp,n} = G_{transp,n}(X_{transp}) \tag{7}$$

and

$$Z_{reloc,n} = G_{reloc,n}(X_{reloc}) \tag{8}$$

of this very agent. (An explanation of the $G_n(X)$ notation follows immediately. For now it may be read as $G_n(X) = X_n$.) Equation (5) expresses the transportation state $X_{transp,n}$ of agent n as a function of the congestion state Z_{cong} of the transportation system and its activity and travel plan

$$Z_{act,n} = G_{act,n}(X_{act}). \tag{9}$$

Finally, (6) expresses the relocation state $X_{reloc,n}$ of agent n as a function of the available facilities Z_{fac} for relocation and their accessibilities Z_{acc}. Recall that all of these models may be static or dynamic, as explained in the last paragraph of Section 2.

The degree of model disaggregation, which has important implications for the consistency of an individual agent's state variables, differs between mesoscopic and truly microscopic models.

Mesoscopic models. In the mesoscopic approach, disaggregation takes place within the processes, but the interactions between processes are still based on aggregate information. This disconnects individual entities in different processes in that the $G_n(X)$ functions in (7)-(9) anonymously sample/infer the state of an agent in one process when feeding it into another process:

- $G_{transp,n}(X_{transp})$ reconstructs what agent n experiences in the transportation system, but without reference to a particular entity in that system. Typically, this is done by following the agent's path based on aggregate travel time information.
- $G_{reloc,n}(X_{reloc})$ assigns a relocation state to agent n based on the population's distribution in the relocation model.
- $G_{act,n}(X_{act})$ infers agent n's activity and travel plan from the distribution of all plans in the activity participation process. This comprises the quite typical process of (i) breaking down the activity patterns into trip sequences (ii) aggregating these trips into origin/destination (OD) matrices (this would be Z_{mob} in the process-based perspective), and (iii) re-sampling individual trip-makers from these matrices.

Because of their aggregate process interactions, mesoscopic models can integrate macroscopic model components relatively naturally. Their major deficiency is their limited ability to relate individual-specific information obtained in one process to individuals in other processes.

Microscopic models. Microscopic models maintain the integrity of the simulated entities, both in the processes and their interactions. Here, the $G_n(X)$ functions in (7)-(9) are true identities: $G_{transp,n}(X_{transp})$, $G_{reloc,n}(X_{reloc})$, and $G_{act,n}(X_{act})$ extract those components of X_{transp}, X_{reloc}, and X_{act} that uniquely belong to agent n.

While the microscopic approach guarantees consistency between the agent representations in different processes, it does not keep disaggregate model components from interacting through macroscopic quantities. For example, the decision of a household to move into a certain region may be based on aggregate characteristics like shopping facility density and noise levels, the decision of a land developer to construct a new building may depend on the average propensity of the targeted household segment towards this type of dwelling, or the mobility behavior of an individual may depend on average travel times in the transportation network.

The use of $Z_{transp,n}$, $Z_{reloc,n}$, and $Z_{act,n}$ in (4)-(9) allows to treat mesoscopic and microscopic models within the same formal framework. Unless stated otherwise, the following discussion therefore applies to both model classes. Furthermore, all statements in terms of the process-based notation (1), (2) can be mapped on mesoscopic or microscopic models through appropriate composition of the state (interaction) variables X and Z.

4 Estimation

This section consists of two parts. First, Subsection 4.1 distinguishes the notions of parameter estimation and state estimation and introduces some basic notation. Second, Subsection 4.2 presents two emerging data sources of particular relevance for the estimation of urban microsimulations.

4.1 Formal Framework

We distinguish between the estimation of parameters and states. Parameters are by definition time-independent. The parameter estimation problem is to identify temporally stable system properties that identically apply in the future and for different scenarios. States, on the other hand, evolve over time. The state estimation problem is to identify a complete configuration of the system's endogenous variables. In either case, the estimation combines structural model information with observations from the real system.

Parameter estimation. The process model is now assumed to depend on the parameters β, i.e., (2) is augmented into

$$X = F(Z|\beta). \tag{10}$$

β comprises components β_{act}, β_{transp}, and β_{reloc} for the respective processes. The parameter estimation problem is to infer a β^* that is most consistent with the model structure and all available data Y. Denoting this estimator by $\mathcal{B}$, we write

$$\beta^* = \mathcal{B}(Y). \tag{11}$$

Typical methods implemented in $\mathcal{B}$ are Bayesian or Maximum Likelihood estimation (Greene; 2003). $\mathcal{B}$ also comprises all available information about the model structure, in particular the interplay of the state (interaction) variables X and Z through the process (interaction) functions F and G.

State estimation. Even if the model parameters are well calibrated, some uncertainty about the model state X remains. The measurements Y can be used to reduce this uncertainty. Denoting the respective state estimator by $\mathcal{X}$, we write

$$X^* = \mathcal{X}(Y|\beta) \tag{12}$$

for the estimated state X^*. Typical methods implemented in $\mathcal{X}$ are Kalman Filtering or Bayesian inference (Arulampalam et al.; 2002; Chui and Chen; 1999). Again, the estimator $\mathcal{X}$ comprises all available information about the model structure.

From (12), it is clear that the state estimation problem is solved conditionally on the parameter estimation problem. The converse setting, where the parameters are estimated conditionally on the estimated states, also has some practical relevance and is visited later in Subsection 6.2.

4.2 New Data Sources

The amount of data needed to calibrate a model depends on its granularity. Macroscopic models that function in terms of aggregate quantities can be estimated based on aggregate data alone. Microscopic models of individual behavior need to be estimated from disaggregate data. This turns urban microsimulations into data-hungry systems, and instruments for the affordable provision or substitution of such data are essential for their estimation. In the following, we indicate two emerging and particularly relevant data sources, smart phones and vehicle/traveler identification systems. Note, however, that all established data sources, ranging from postal surveys that query complete activity and travel patterns to inductive loops that merely count vehicles on roads, should be deployed in combination with these new technologies.

Smart phones. These devices collect a wealth of information about their users' environment, travel, and activities. This includes GPS (global positioning system) tracks and the MAC (media access control) addresses of nearby devices as well as all communications and running applications on the phone, and it can go as far as taking visual and acoustic samples of the environment. Methodological work is underway for the identification of the user's current travel and activity from smart phones, and it is reasonable to anticipate that the smart phones of selected individuals will soon serve as reliable travel and activity sensors in the urban system (Bierlaire et al.; 2010; Bohte and Maat; 2009; Hato; 2010; Hurtubia et al.; 2009; Raj et al.; 2008; Schüssler and Axhausen; 2009).

Vehicle/traveler identification systems. The identification of a vehicle or a traveler at one or several locations in the network reveals individual-level information about the chosen destination, route, and departure time of the traveler. Vehicle identification systems usually rely on cameras and/or transponder-based short range communications. These systems are crucial for electronic toll collection systems, and hence this data source can be accessed wherever such a system is installed. The estimation of travel demand from vehicle identification systems is an active field of research that has already resulted in the implementation of operational prototypes (Antoniou et al.; 2006; Vaze et al.; 2009; Zhou; 2004). The identification of travelers at different points in the network is also possible through electronic payment devices for public transport.

Both data sources continuously reveal individual-level behavior at a relatively low cost once the system is installed. This makes them attractive not only for the estimation of model parameters but also for real-time state estimation purposes. Note, however, that in the urban simulation context, the objective is to estimate disaggregate behavior without a one-to-one mapping from simulated to real actors. This differs from other applications of the same sensor technology that require person-specific estimates. For example, a smart phone may internally keep track of its user's activity preferences in order to provide customized, context specific information.

5   State Estimation

The continuous tracking of the urban state allows to manage the system more effectively in response to its most recent internal changes. An important problem in this context is that urban processes evolve at vastly different time scales. Based on an analysis of these time scales in Subsection 5.1, a rolling horizon state estimation framework is developed in Subsection 5.2.

5.1   Time Scales of an Urban Microsimulation

We distinguish short-, medium-, and long-term dynamics.

Short-term dynamics. This refers to dynamics within a day. The physical transportation system evolves on the time scale of minutes or even seconds. Its state on subsequent days may be considered as decoupled if congestion does not persist over night and vehicles are parked in the same location every night. Travel behavior and activity participation are, within limits, also variable within a single day, either in reaction to exogenous events or in reaction to variations in the transportation system's performance.

Medium-term dynamics. This refers to dynamics across a limited number of days. Many aspects of activity participation and the resulting travel behavior are linked across a number of days. Households and firms schedule their maintenance activities across weeks or even months. Travel behavior is based on anticipated network conditions, which are extrapolated from information collected during many previous days. Relocation is also relevant on medium-term time scales in that it continuously changes the facilities that are available for activity participation.

Long-term dynamics. This refers to dynamics in the order of years. It is the time scale of the relocation model. However, even if individual relocations are unlikely to take place more than once per year, population relocation is a continuous process that affects activity and travel behavior also on medium time scales. The accessibility feedback from the transportation system on relocation, however, occurs with such an inertia that the relocation model can be considered as decoupled from the transportation system on short and medium time scales.

This classification leaves out all but the three central processes identified in Section 2. Apart from transportation and short-term activity participation, communication is another important short-term process. This comprises centralized information distribution systems (radio, Internet) as well as direct communications along the edges of social networks. Energy consumption is to a large extent derived from activity participation and hence occurs on short time scales as well. Ecological and economical processes and the evolution of social networks, however, may safely be constrained to medium and long time scales.

Most of the existing literature on state estimation in the urban context focuses on the tracking of the physical transportation system's state (e.g., Chrobok et al.; 2003; Tampere and Immers; 2007; Wang and Papageorgiou; 2005). The real-time tracking of the behavioral states is mainly constrained to limited aspects of the derived travel patterns such as OD matrices or path flows (Ben-Akiva et al.; 1998; Bell et al.; 1997; Zhou and Mahmassani; 2007). A mentionable exception is Flötteröd (2008); Flötteröd et al. (2010), where full-day activity and travel plans are estimated from traffic counts and supplementary model information. The relocation state may be considered as completely measurable based on sufficient data access rights and enough time to process it.

5.2 Rolling Horizon Framework

The simulation-based nature of an urban microsimulation model renders the application of computationally and mathematically convenient recursive filtering techniques infeasible. We therefore opt for a rolling horizon framework. Here, it is advantageous to consider transportation, activity participation, and relocation separately.

Estimation of X_{transp}. An estimation of the transportation system's state requires, on the most disaggregate level, to track individually simulated (yet anonymous) transportation units (vehicles, pedestrians, ...). This requires to account for high-resolution dynamics in the order of seconds or minutes. A reasonable length of the estimation time horizon is typically between 30 and 60 minutes. Formally, the transportation system state estimator is written as

$$X^*_{transp} = \mathcal{X}_{transp}(Y_{transp}|Z_{mob}; \beta_{transp}) \tag{13}$$

where Y_{transp} comprises all sensor data that is relevant for the transportation state estimation problem. The estimator depends on the mobility demand Z_{mob} and the parameters β_{transp} of the transportation system.

Estimation of X_{act}. Activity and travel scheduling happen both within-day and day-to-day. However, it is not advisable to estimate daily activity schedules during a limited time window within a day because activity scheduling is not a temporally linear process. The complex internal logic of daily activity schedules, including their various constraints, require to schedule and estimate a day as a whole (Bowman and Ben-Akiva; 1998). Formally, the activity state estimator is written as

$$X^*_{act} = \mathcal{X}_{act}(Y_{act}|Z_{cong}, Z_{fac}; \beta_{act}) \tag{14}$$

where Y_{act} comprises all sensor data that is relevant for the activity estimation problem. The estimator may be conditional on the activity participations of previous days and depends on the congestion Z_{cong}, the available facilities Z_{fac} for activity participation, and the parameters β_{act}. (The activity and travel participations of firms may be more difficult to observe than those of individual volunteers for reasons of market competition, although they are likely to be more structured and better documented.)

Estimation of X_{reloc}. It is reasonable to assume that, given enough time and access to the necessary data bases, the relocation state of the urban system is directly measurable. However, this is possible only with a lag, and a real-time tracking of urban relocations appears infeasible. We may assume that relocations are measurable in yearly intervals and that the relocations of the upcoming year have been planned with such a lag that that they are not affected by the events within that year. This allows to simulate all upcoming relocations at once at the beginning of the year, to derive a day-by-day relocation sequence from this, and to feed the resulting facility information Z_{fac} exogenously into the mid- and short-term state estimation processes. Directly observable facility changes such as openings of shopping malls can also be exogenously incorporated.

These considerations suggest to estimate the urban system state on a daily basis, where the transportation system's state is tracked with a rolling horizon within the day and the activity and travel behavior is estimated without a rolling horizon for the day as a whole, possibly conditional on the activities of previous days. Figure 2 gives an overview.

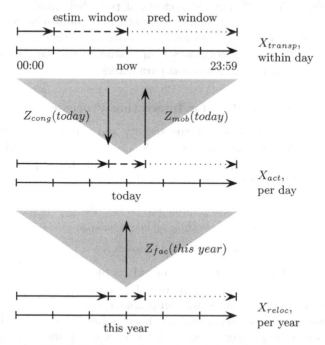

Fig. 2. Rolling horizon urban state estimation

The physical transportation system and the activity and travel behavior need to be estimated in mutual dependency; they are coupled through the mobility demand and the congestion information. The coupling between the relocations and the activity and travel behavior estimator is unidirectional in that relocation events are predicted infrequently and then disaggregated across the time line in order to allow for a continuous evolution of the boundary conditions for the activity and travel behavior.

We close this section with the observation that a microsimulation-based state estimator is unlikely to represent distributional information differently but through samples. Considering that a single sample represents an entire urban state, we are facing a computationally enormous problem. Unless randomness is artificially reduced, this is likely to require (loosely coupled) parallel computing efforts where a number of computers calculates one realization of the urban state each. The sample-based approach connects the urban state estimator to particle filtering techniques (Arulampalam et al.; 2002), however, on a vastly increased scale of computational complexity.

6   Parameter Estimation

We now consider the problem of how to calibrate the structural model parameters β from some data set Y. As stated in Section 4.1, one may assume a comprehensive estimator $\mathcal{B}$ to be given that estimates all parameters β jointly from all available data Y. This, however, is a rather extreme case, and it is more likely to assume that different components of the whole model are estimated separately and possibly conditional on each other. In Subsection 6.1, we clarify this observation for the process-based decomposition of Section 2. Subsections 6.2 and 6.3 then discuss two techniques to approximately account for the process interactions when estimating submodel parameters.

6.1   Parameter Estimation for Interacting Processes

In a process-based decomposition, the activity and travel participation, transportation, and relocation parameters β_{act}, β_{transp}, and β_{reloc} are estimated from subsets Y_{act}, Y_{transp}, and Y_{reloc} of Y that are relevant to the respective processes, and the process boundaries Z are considered as given:

$$\beta_{act}^* = \mathcal{B}_{act}(Y_{act}|Z_{cong}, Z_{fac}) \tag{15}$$

$$\beta_{transp}^* = \mathcal{B}_{transp}(Y_{transp}|Z_{mob}) \tag{16}$$

$$\beta_{reloc}^* = \mathcal{B}_{reloc}(Y_{reloc}|Z_{acc}). \tag{17}$$

Since the boundaries of each process depend on the states of all adjacent processes, which in turn depend on the respective parameters, one does not face three independent parameter estimation problems but one large, coupled problem. The least one can do to account for this coupling is to repeatedly solve the individual estimation problems conditional on each other until a state of mutual consistency is attained.

Since we are dealing with a microsimulation, the estimation of behavioral models from individual-level data sources deserves particular attention. Denoting by $m = 1 \ldots M$ the observed individuals in reality, a typical parameter estimation approach is to define $\mathcal{B}$ as a maximum likelihood estimator

$$\mathcal{B}(Y) = \arg\max_{\beta} \mathcal{L}(\beta) \tag{18}$$

with the log-likelihood function

$$\mathcal{L}(\beta) = \sum_{m=1}^{M} \ln p(Y_m|\beta) \tag{19}$$

where $p(Y_m|\beta)$ is the probability of measurements Y_m being generated given the parameters β. Again, this estimator can be decomposed by process. Assuming that the individual-level observations Y_m are related to the parameters β only through the individual-level state X_m, (4)-(6) yield

$$\mathcal{L}(\beta_{act}) = \sum_{m=1}^{M} \ln p(Y_{act,m}|Z_{cong}, Z_{fac}, Z_{transp,m}, Z_{reloc,m}; \beta_{act}) \tag{20}$$

$$\mathcal{L}(\beta_{transp}) = \sum_{m=1}^{M} \ln p(Y_{transp,m}|Z_{cong}, Z_{act,m}; \beta_{transp}) \tag{21}$$

$$\mathcal{L}(\beta_{reloc}) = \sum_{m=1}^{M} \ln p(Y_{reloc,m}|Z_{fac}, Z_{acc}; \beta_{reloc}). \tag{22}$$

In the context of choice models, the individual-level boundary conditions Z_m can be considered as person-specific attributes and choice set information, whereas the aggregate boundary conditions Z define further attributes of the alternatives. Together, they define the choice context of the observed individual.

The possibility to measure the choice context from smart phones or vehicle identification systems, in particular in terms of non chosen alternatives and perceived attributes of the alternatives, is limited. It depends on unobservable information the individual has gathered through experience in the urban environment and, due to the anticipatory nature of decision making, on attributes that are spatially and temporally remote and hence not accessible to the sensor. Since this information is crucial to the estimation of behavioral models (Ben-Akiva and Lerman; 1985; Train; 2003), it appears plausible to impute the context information within the urban simulation. This requires to estimate behavioral models conditional on their simulated environment – which in turn is defined through the estimated behavior.

Some previous research was conducted in this context. Balakrishna (2006) reports on the joint calibration of travel demand and traffic flow parameters in the DynaMIT traffic microsimulator. Sevcikova et al. (2007) calibrate the UrbanSim land use simulator, which comprises, amongst other components, a relocation model and an external transportation model. Methodologically, these efforts are constrained to the application of black box calibration techniques, which by definition exploit no problem structure. Also, they are limited to the time scales of their respective processes: DynaMIT operates in the order of days, whereas UrbanSim runs from year to year.

The remainder of this section discusses two integrated parameter estimation approaches that account for system structure and different time scales. First, Section 6.2 describes a combined state and parameter estimator that loosens the process interactions based on data. Second, Section 6.3 proposes response surfaces and metamodels as means to improve the tractability of integrated parameter estimation approaches.

6.2 Decoupling of Submodels through State Estimation

Any set of decoupled parameter estimators can be written as

$$\beta^* = \mathcal{B}(Y|Z^*) \tag{23}$$

where Z^* comprises the true yet unknown boundary conditions between the respective processes.

An integrated parameter estimation is enabled if the boundary conditions are computed conditional on the parameters, i.e., if (23) is solved jointly with

$$Z^* = G(X^*) \tag{24}$$
$$X^* = F(Z^*|\beta^*). \tag{25}$$

The main difficulty of solving the integrated estimation problem is that the mathematical intractabilities of simulation-based components (such as a traffic flow microsimulation) also enter other, themselves well-behaved estimation problems (such as the maximization of a log-likelihood function for a behavioral model).

Essentially, an estimation of the true process interactions Z^* in (24) results from a plausible combination of structural model information and the data Y. Observing that a very similar problem is solved by the urban state estimator (12), one may approximate the calibrated process states X^* in (24) by that estimator:

$$Z^* = G(X^*) \approx G(\mathcal{X}(Y|\beta^0)) \tag{26}$$

where β^0 is an initial guess of the process parameters used during the state estimation. The advantage of this approximation is that, given sufficient data Y, the state estimation computes process interactions Z that are close to those interactions that would result from a simulation based on the estimated parameters. Hence, these interactions need no adjustment during the parameter estimation, which decouples the respective processes.

An operational implementation of this combined state and parameter estimation approach is outlined in Figure 3. The urban state estimator is deployed continuously based on given parameters. In regular intervals (e.g., monthly) these parameters are re-estimated based on all data collected so far. All process inter-actions up to the present point in time are approximately known from the state estimator. (Very old data may be discarded, which results in a rolling-horizon parameter estimator.) After the parameter estimation, the urban state estima-tion is further deployed based on the updated parameters. This approach iterates between parameter and state estimation, where the iterations take place along the time line. It can be expected to result in increasingly consistent parameter and state estimates as time progresses.

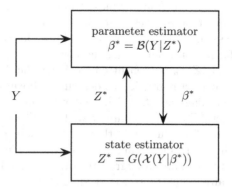

Fig. 3. Integrated parameter and state estimation

A complete decoupling of all model components may not be desirable. In particular, if the initial parameter estimates during an early application of the combined estimation system are far from their true values, some of the interac-tions should be accounted for, but in a mathematically tractable setting. This is the topic of the following subsection.

6.3 Response Surfaces and Metamodels

Response surfaces and metamodels were developed in the context of simulation-based optimization (e.g., Osorio; 2010).

Response surfaces. A response surface is typically a linear or quadratic poly-nomial that is fitted to the input/output signal of a complex simulation. Data availability is only limited by the computational effort to simulate it. However, a polynomial captures little to no structure about the simulation, and hence it may require a relatively large number of coefficients to reflect the simulation's relevant behavior.

Metamodels. Here, the polynomial is replaced by a mathematical model that structurally resembles the simulation. Metamodels can be expected to re-quire less parameters than response surfaces for the same measurement fit because they contain more structural information. A drawback is that they are likely to lose the convenient linear-in-parameters form of polynomial models.

Both techniques can be used to approximately capture some interactions/processes in the integrated simulation when estimating its parameters. We exemplify this through a response surface and a metamodel for a vehicular traffic flow simulation. Assume that the mobility demand $Z_{mob} = (z_t^{od})$ consists of the number of vehicles z_t^{od} that want to travel between each OD pair in each time period t. The traffic flow simulation takes Z_{mob} as input and outputs the congestion information $Z_{cong} = (z_{at})$ where z_{at} is the number of vehicles entering link a in time period t.

To obtain a response surface approximation, a matrix A is introduced that maps the OD flows Z_{mob} on *desired* link entrance flows $D = (d_{at}) = AZ_{mob}$ where d_{at} is the number of vehicles that plan to enter network link a during period t. A combines route choice information from the travel demand model with travel time information from the traffic flow model. A linear response surface $Z_{cong} = BD = BAZ_{mob}$ is then fitted to the traffic flow simulator, where the matrix B results from a regression as described above. An efficient approximation is to choose a diagonal B, which relates the flow across a link only to those vehicles that actually want to enter that link. The estimation of B from simulated data accounts for spillback in that some vehicle may be kept from entering their desired links in time because of congestion. This approach has been successfully applied to estimate disaggregate travel demand from traffic counts (Flötteröd and Bierlaire; 2009; Flötteröd et al.; 2010).

The same problem can also be tackled based on the nonlinear metamodel described by Osorio and Bierlaire (2009a). This model goes structurally beyond a linear approximation in that it operates based on closed-form link state distributions and correctly accounts for spillback effects across network nodes. Its relative tractability is owed to the fact that it captures stationary conditions only, which may be a drawback in highly dynamic conditions. Recently, a dynamic version of this model has been proposed by Osorio et al. (2010). The flexibility of a response-surface approach and the structural power of a nonlinear metamodel can also be combined, which is demonstrated in Osorio and Bierlaire (2009b).

7   Summary

We presented concepts and methods to cope with the enormous data needs of urban microsimulations. In the first part of the article, we adopted a process-oriented perspective on relocation, activity participation, and transportation and then refined this perspective in the microsimulation context. The second part of the article considered the parameter and state estimation problem. First, the different time scales of an urban system were identified and a rolling horizon framework for its continuous state estimation was developed. Second, the parameter estimation problem for an integrated urban microsimulation problem was investigated. The operational difficulty of jointly estimating all parameters of the urban model was met with two different approaches: the decoupling through estimated process interactions and the use of response surfaces and metamodels to mathematically approximate intractable, simulation-based processes.

While this presentation was largely at the conceptual level, first experiences with a partial implementation of this approach were recently obtained. In that work, the activity-based multi-agent transport microsimulation MATSim (Raney and Nagel; 2006; Nagel et al.; accessed 2011) is combined with the estimation code Cadyts ("Calibration of dynamic traffic simulations", Flötteröd; 2009, accessed 2011) to estimate a fully disaggregate travel demand for the city of Zurich (Flötteröd et al.; 2009). Both the involved softwares and the Zurich application are subject to ongoing developments.

References

Antoniou, C., Ben-Akiva, M., Koutsopoulos, H.N.: Dynamic traffic demand prediction using conventional and emerging data sources. IEE Proceedings Intelligent Transport Systems 153(1), 97–104 (2006)

Arentze, T., Timmermans, H.: A learning-based transportation oriented simulation system. Transportation Research Part B 38(7), 613–633 (2004)

Arulampalam, S., Maskell, S., Gordon, N., Clapp, T.: A tutorial on particle filters for on-line non-linear/non-Gaussian Bayesian tracking. IEEE Transactions on Signal Processing 50(2), 174–188 (2002)

Balakrishna, R.: Off-line calibration of dynamic traffic assignment models, PhD thesis, Massachusetts Institute of Technology (2006)

Bell, M., Shield, C., Busch, F., Kruse, G.: A stochastic user equilibrium path flow estimator. Transportation Research Part C 5(3/4), 197–210 (1997)

Ben-Akiva, M., Bierlaire, M., Koutsopoulos, H., Mishalani, R.: DynaMIT: a simulation-based system for traffic prediction. In: Proceedings of the DACCORD Short Term Forecasting Workshop, Delft, The Netherlands (1998)

Ben-Akiva, M., Lerman, S.: Discrete Choice Analysis. MIT Press series in transportation studies. The MIT Press (1985)

Bierlaire, M., Chen, J., Newman, J.: Using location observations to observe routing for choice models. In: Proceedings of the 89. Annual Meeting of the Transportation Research Board, Washington, DC, USA (2010)

Bohte, W., Maat, K.: Deriving and validating trip purposes and travel models for multi-day GPS-based travel surveys: a large-scale application in the Netherlands. Transportation Research Part C 17(3), 285–297 (2009)

Bowman, J., Ben-Akiva, M.: Activity based travel demand model systems. In: Marcotte, P., Nguyen, S. (eds.) Equilibrium and Advanced Transportation Modelling, pp. 27–46. Kluwer (1998)

Chrobok, R., Pottmeier, A., Wahle, J., Schreckenberg, M.: Traffic forecast using a combination of on-line simulation and traffic data. In: Fukui, M., Sugiyama, Y., Schreckenberg, M., Wolf, D. (eds.) Traffic and Granular Flow 2001, pp. 345–350. Springer, Heidelberg (2003)

Chui, C., Chen, G.: Kalman Filtering with Real-Time Applications. Springer Series in Information Sciences. Springer, Heidelberg (1999)

Flötteröd, G.: Traffic State Estimation with Multi-Agent Simulations, PhD thesis, Berlin Institute of Technology, Berlin, Germany (2008)

Flötteröd, G.: Cadyts – a free calibration tool for dynamic traffic simulations. In: Proceedings of the 9th Swiss Transport Research Conference, Monte Verita/Ascona, Switzerland (2009)

Flötteröd, G.: Cadyts, http://transp-or2.epfl.ch/cadyts (accessed 2010)

Flötteröd, G., Bierlaire, M.: Improved estimation of travel demand from traffic counts by a new linearization of the network loading map. In: Proceedings of the European Transport Conference, Noordwijkerhout, The Netherlands (2009)

Flötteröd, G., Bierlaire, M., Nagel, K.: Bayesian demand calibration for dynamic traffic simulations, Technical Report TRANSP-OR 100105, Ecole Polytechnique Fédérale de Lausanne & Berlin Institute of Technology (2010)

Flötteröd, G., Chen, Y., Rieser, M., Nagel, K.: Behavioral calibration of a large-scale travel behavior microsimulation. In: Proceedings of 12th International Conference on Travel Behaviour Research, Jaipur, India (2010)

Ghauche, A.: Integrated transportation and energy activity-based model, Master thesis, Massachusetts Institute of Technology (2010)

Greene, W.: Econometric Analysis, 5th edn. Prentice-Hall (2003)

Hato, E.: Development of behavioral context addressable loggers in the shell for travel-activity analysis. Transportation Research Part C 18(1), 55–67 (2010)

Hurtubia, R., Flötteröd, G., Bierlaire, M.: Inferring the activities of smartphone users from context measurements using Bayesian inference and random utility models. In: Proceedings of the European Transport Conference, Noordwijkerhout, The Netherlands (2009)

Miller, E., Roorda, M.: Prototype model of household activity-travel scheduling. Transportation Research Record 1831, 114–121 (2004)

Nagel, K., Axhausen, K.: Microsimulation. In: Hensher, D., King, J. (eds.) The Leading Edge of Travel Behavior Research, pp. 239–246. Pergamon (2001)

Nagel, K., et al.: MATSim, http://www.matsim.org (accessed 2010)

Osorio, C.: Mitigating network congestion: analytical models, optimization methods and their applications, PhD thesis, Ecole Polytechnique Fédérale de Lausanne. EPFL thesis 4615 (2010)

Osorio, C., Bierlaire, M.: An analytic finite capacity queuing network model capturing the propagation of congestion and blocking. European Journal of Operational Research 196(3), 996–1007 (2009a)

Osorio, C., Bierlaire, M.: A multi-model algorithm for the optimization of congested networks. In: Proceedings of the European Transport Conference, Noordwijkerhout, Netherlands (2009b)

Osorio, C., Flötteröd, G., Bierlaire, M.: Dynamic network loading: a differentiable model that derives link state distributions, Technical Report TRANSP-OR 100815, Transport and Mobility Laboratory, Ecole Polytechnique Fédérale de Lausanne (2010)

Raj, A., Subramanya, A., Fox, D., Bilmes, J.: Rao-Blackwellized particle filers for recognizing activities and spatial context from wearable sensors. In: Siciliano, B., Khatib, O., Groen, F. (eds.) Experimental Robotics, pp. 211–221. Springer, Heidelberg (2008)

Raney, B., Nagel, K.: An improved framework for large-scale multiagent simulations of travel behavior. In: Rietveld, P., Jourquin, B., Westin, K. (eds.) Towards Better Performing European Transportation Systems, pp. 305–347. Routledge (2006)

Ross, S.: Simulation, 4th edn. Elsevier (2006)

Salvini, P., Miller, E.: ILUTE: an operational prototype of a comprehensive microsimulation model of urban systems. Networks and Spatial Economics 5(2), 217–234 (2005)

Schüssler, N., Axhausen, K.: Processing raw data from global positioning systems without additional information. Transportation Research Record 2105, 28–36 (2009)

Sevcikova, H., Raftery, A., Waddell, P.: Assessing uncertainty in urban simulations using Bayesian melding. Transportation Research Part B 41(6), 652–669 (2007)

Tampere, C., Immers, L.: An extended Kalman filter application for traffic state estimation using CTM with implicit mode switching and dynamic parameters. In: Proceedings of the 10th IEEE Intelligent Transportation Systems Conference, Seattle, USA, pp. 209–216 (2007)

Train, K.: Discrete Choice Methods with Simulation. Cambridge University Press (2003)

Vaze, V., Antoniou, C., Wen, Y., Ben-Akiva, M.: Calibration of dynamic traffic assignment models with point-to-point traffic surveillance. Transportation Research Record 2090, 1–9 (2009)

Waddell, P., Sevcikova, H., Socha, D., Miller, E., Nagel, K.: Opus: an open platform for urban simulation. In: Proceedings of the Computers in Urban Planning and Urban Management Conference, London, UK (2005)

Waddell, P., Ulfarsson, G.: Introduction to urban simulation: design and development of operational models. In: Hensher, D., Button, K. (eds.) Transport Geography and Spatial Systems. Handbook 5 of the Handbook in Transport, pp. 203–236. Pergamon/Elsevier Science (2004)

Wang, Y., Papageorgiou, M.: Real-time freeway traffic state estimation based on extended Kalman filter: a general approach. Transportation Research Part B 39(2), 141–167 (2005)

Wegener, M.: Overview of land-use transport models. In: Hensher, D., Button, K. (eds.) Transport Geography and Spatial Systems. Handbook 5 of the Handbook in Transport, pp. 127–146. Pergamon/Elsevier Science (2004)

Zhou, X.: Dynamic Origin-Destination Demand Estimation and Prediction for Off-Line and On-Line Dynamic Traffic Assignment Operation, PhD thesis, University of Maryland, College Park (2004)

Zhou, X., Mahmassani, H.: A structural state space model for realtime traffic origin-destination demand estimation and prediction in a day-today learning framework. Transportation Research Part B 41(8), 823–840 (2007)

Urban Energy Flow Modelling:
A Data-Aware Approach

Diane Perez and Darren Robinson

ÉCOLE POLYTECHNIQUE FÉDÉRALE DE LAUSANNE (EPFL),
School of Architecture, Civil and Environmental Engineering (ENAC),
Solar Energy and Building Physics Laboratory (LESO-PB)
{diane.perez,darren.robinson}@epfl.ch

Abstract. The estimation of building's energy use at the urban scale
is an increasingly popular and necessary approach to minimise the primary energy use and GHG emissions. However, this activity involves
the collection and management of a huge amount of data, which is often not organised in a (re)usable way by neither collectivities nor researchers. This chapter details the difficulties related to the collection of
data from multiple sources, regarding incompatibilities and incomplete-
ness in particular, and introduces the advantages of a data management
using well-structured databases or GIS instead of spreadsheets or specific
input files. Some research fields of interest for this matter, such as GIS,
spatio-temporal databases and ontologies are introduced, and a complete
approach to create a solid data management solution is proposed. The
methodology described leads to a sound basis for advanced simulation
and analysis of energy flow in urban zones.

Keywords: Urban energy modelling, energy demand simulation, data
availability, data management, quality assessment, spatio-temporal database.

1 Introduction

Owing to increasingly stringent inter-governmental commitments to minimise
the adverse consequences of climate change, coupled with increasing rates of ur-
banisation, there is a growing interest in studying and improving upon the energy
performance of urban settlements. To this end a range of modelling techniques
has been developed in recent years.

At one extreme are macro-simulation approaches, in which a city is abstractly
represented as aggregate stocks (e.g. housing, fossil fuels, and the ambient environment as a source of renewable energy) and flows of resources between these
stocks. At the other extreme are micro-simulation approaches, in which for example individual houses are physically represented in their true spatial context.

The appropriate approach (micro, macro or somewhere in between) depends
upon the objectives of the task in hand, but also on the availability of both data
and time to prepare the model and subsequently to test alternative hypotheses

S. Müller Arisona et al. (Eds.): DUMS, CCIS 242, pp. 200–220, 2012.

for improving upon the energy performance of the case study site under investigation. Clearly these resource demands (data and time) increase with the scale of our case study in the case of micro-simulation. But this is contrasted with greater utility, as locale-specific decision support is provided. We postulate thus that there is a dichotomy between the desire for detailed and context-specific modelling results and the resources required by such models; a dichotomy which increases with the scale of the urban settlement.

Fortunately however, several municipalities and private organisations already systematically acquire a considerable amount of data which can be of use to the urban energy modeller. Such data includes cadastral maps, building registers, inhabitants' census, meteorological data and energy consumption data. However, these data tend neither to be centralised nor to be readily compatible.

There is thus a need to centralise and to harmonise disparate data sources, if these are to be compatible with the needs of urban micro-simulation tools; and where there are errors or gaps in available data, to use well adapted solutions. This is an ambitious task, but if it is addressed efficiently, the benefits may be shared between complementary simulation programs, and the model may in principle be transferred to municipalities to maintain and perform studies of their own. Thus the greater need in data and time of such a model can be balanced by its longevity and its various uses.

To this end, this chapter proposes a different approach to urban energy modelling, thought of as a mid- or long-term collaboration with municipalities or other third-parties, and with a focus on data importation, management and use. It addresses the constraints of data models in this domain and the ways their creation can be optimised. After introducing the role of data, relative domains of interest are briefly reviewed. We then discuss approaches for the management of data, and go on to put forward a possible solution to data importation and matching problems. Finally, after considering ways of using incomplete or uncertain data, we close this chapter with a summary of our discussions and some indications of where further developments are necessary.

1.1   The Role of Data in Urban Energy Modelling

With some partial exceptions [11] [21], the subject of input data quality in the literature relating to urban energy micro- and macro-simulation research tends to be little discussed or even overlooked entirely. For some simulation models, the simulation (i.e. the hypotheses and simplifications made within) may be regarded as the most important source of uncertainty. For others, such as well tested physically-based simulation models, the input data itself, its limited degree of detail and the use of default data can instead be the main source of uncertainty. When results corresponding to the real-world are expected, the model of the reality used as input thus becomes as important as the simulation tool, if not more important: low quality input will produce unreliable results. In such a case, studying and improving the results actually means studying and improving the input, with corresponding improvements to the reliability of the output. It thus becomes necessary to question which data are used as input, and how. Or, if the base case model has been improved, which data were used for a previous simulation, to understand better the difference with the new results.

And yet, data often seems to be treated as a side question; a simple, if difficult to obtain, input to a central modelling tool. Whilst data sources are often mentioned, the process of creating the data model and / or the input files for a simulation project is usually not touched upon in articles about energy flow simulation of existing urban zones, particularly with respect to the problems encountered, the workload involved and the quality of the data sources.

Based on what seems to be current practise in several research groups at EPFL, this input data preparation process seems often to be rather haphazard. Consider the extreme case of an isolated student project to study alternatives to improve the energy performance of an urban zone by changing the energy systems or improving the buildings' envelope. Such a project requires first that a model of the zone's buildings and energy systems be created. The most straightforward way to do this is to collect all useful data (cadastre data, 3D data, buildings register, inhabitant census, local knowledge about energy systems, meteorological data, energy consumption data, ...), inevitably involving files of diverse format (Microsoft Office's .xls, .xlsx, .mdb or .accdb; varying .txt, .csv or .xml formats; ArcGIS' .shp, .shx, .dbf, ... ; AutoCAD's .dwg; .xyz raster files; etc.). Depending on the time and infrastructure available, default or statistical data may be used, either because more detail is not available, or because collecting it is too time-consuming. To create a coherent and complete data file, part of the data of each file is then copied to a main file, solving case by case the incompatibilities between the sources: conflicting values (the buildings register records that a building is heated with a boiler, but the energy provider gives a district heating consumption), incompatible units (one cadastre building corresponds to several entries in the buildings register or in the consumption data file), etc. Finally, this input file is completed with default values, and possibly modified or updated again, to create a unified and comprehensive scene description. Some potentially useful data items might also be dropped for their lack of reliability or because it is too time-consuming to transform them into a compatible format.

Whilst the above gives a rather extreme and pessimistic picture of the process of input preparation for urban energy modelling, similar difficulties are likely to arise with any project in this domain. Depending on how these difficulties are handled, one will obtain a model that can be used as a basis for simulation and analysis, but whose quality is hard to estimate, given the mixed origin of the data, the limited reliability of the sources and the multiple modifications added to make it coherent. This also makes the model very difficult to improve or update, given that modified or corrected data is mixed with low quality data. Whereas creating the input files was probably highly time-consuming, the data model created is likely to have a rather short life-time and may not use all available data efficiently.

Instead of this inefficient use of available input data, we would like to develop a more sustainable and holistic approach. Our main objectives are simple. They are to:

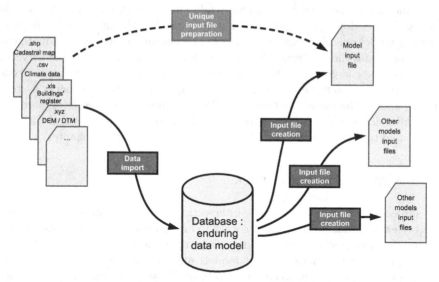

Fig. 1. Data for urban energy simulation : direct input file preparation (dotted line) versus the organised management of data discussed in this chapter (continuous lines)

- gain time in creating the model
- maximise the utilisation of available data
- increase the model's longevity

Other compatible objectives for the creation of our data model might be to:

- organise original and formatted data correctly,
- avoid repetitive actions,
- avoid the need for third-party software (GIS, spreadsheet, ...) and the associated learning time,
- limit arbitrary decisions by defining clear rules,
- automate a first check of data validity (range checking and other simple rules),
- distribute the effort of acquiring and entering data,
- allow for collaboration on data verification,
- increase the share of available data that is actually and efficiently used,
- allow simulation even when the model is incomplete, with effective use of default data,
- make sure the data can be updated,
- provide feedback on incomplete or out-of-date data to the third-party sources (if desirable),
- keep track of data model modifications and / or simulation scenarios.

This work is undertaken as part of a project on the Management of Energy in the Urban environment (MEU, meu.epfl.ch) in partnership with four swiss cities (Lausanne, Neuchâtel, La Chaux-de-Fonds and Martigny).

In parallel with analysing specific case-study sites in each city, the goal of this project is to develop a platform to ultimately be used by the cities' energy departments to model neighbourhoods or districts (eventually cities) and evaluate energy scenarios for them. The platform is to be based on the modelling tool CitySim to simulate the energy demands and performances of buildings (although real energy use data is also to be used when available), on a database of energy system models, and on the modelling tool EnerGIS to optimise advanced integrated energy conversion system use. The ongoing work on the MEU project and CitySim will be used to illustrate the concepts discussed throughout this chapter.

2   Review of Related Work

The subjects treated here are at the intersection of various domains of research. This review will first present relative work in urban energy use modelling, with a view to identifying what could be improved with a more "data-aware" and long term approach, and where different models might be efficiently used together. We then introduce quickly some research in database management systems and in ontologies, as they suggest interesting approaches which should be considered when developing a flexible data framework for urban energy modelling. We also present a brief overview of the availability and management of data related to our domain in Switzerland.

2.1   Urban Energy Flow Simulation

As mentioned in section 1 above, we may conceptually think of urban energy simulation methodologies as being macro-simulation, micro-simulation or some hybrid of the two. We may also differentiate modelling research focusing on energy demand from that focusing on energy supply, or on a composite of both.

Macro-simulation approaches tend to abstract a whole system as a set of interrelated stocks, flows and feedback mechanisms of resources between these stocks. In this way, using system dynamics modelling [5] we may simulate a city (our system) as an aggregation of housing, fossil fuels or indeed the ambient environment as a source of renewable energy (stocks) between which we simulate the flows of resource (energy, materials, etc.) and associated feedback mechanisms. Examples of these approaches include models of the energy use of the housing stock of the city of Basel [4] and of the energy demand of the housing stock of Norway [18]. These models are usually based on available aggregated or statistical data and provide valuable information at a large scale, but are rather limited when more specific knowledge is required (for the refurbishment of specific buildings or the design of local energy systems for example).

At the other extreme are micro-simulation approaches, in which for example individual houses are physically represented in their true spatial context. Such approaches could in principle make use of very detailed simulation programs which have been designed for modelling individual buildings, such as EnergyPlus (apps1.eere.energy.gov/buildings/energyplus) or ESP-r (www.esru.strath.ac.uk). But in this case, a unique scene description would need to be prepared for each building to be simulated, the radiation models do not faithfully represent the effects of adjacent occlusions on surface radiation exchanges and district energy centres cannot be modelled. To address these and other issues rather more comprehensive simulation programs such as SUNtool [16] and its more recent successor CitySim [17][15] have been developed, which are expressly designed for modelling ensembles of buildings and the supply of energy to them. But these tools, designed for urban energy demand prediction, require a significant amount of data. As such they have thus far tended to be used for relatively small scale (neighbourhood) problems or applied in conjunction with a large proportion of statistical default data.

In between these two extremes are techniques in which representative buildings from different classes of building typology may be simulated and the results extrapolated to the built area or volume of each typology. Such is the approach of the Energy and Environmental Prediction programme (EEP) [11] and the model of Shimoda [20]. There is also a range of rather less comprehensive micro-simulation programs, designed for simulating specific sectors of a city's built stock, such as SEP for residential buildings and solar energy systems [6] and the model of Yamaguchi et al [23] for commercial buildings and associated district heating systems. (For a more comprehensive review of urban-scale energy modelling techniques, we refer the reader to [15]).

On the energy supply side, recent research has tended to focus on renewable energy technologies and energy efficiency improvements, producing models to optimise the design of such energy systems given the energy demand. Energy efficiency analysis, together with pinch analysis [12] and exergy analysis [1] [13] has led to significant developments regarding the design of heating systems, combined heat and power production systems and district heating and cooling networks. Several models, such as the pinch-analysis based EnerGIS [7] consider how complementary energy conversion systems might be efficiently combined to meet the heating demand of a district (see also [22]). When no measurements are available, these supply-side models usually use simplified demand-side models to predict the temporal distribution of energy or heating demand. Such approaches may be well adapted when most measurements are available, but may also lead to unsafe conclusion regarding the optimal energy supply technology(ies) in other situations. Thus these models could potentially benefit greatly from a coupling with more sophisticated energy demand prediction models, which consider in detail the buildings' dynamics.

In summary, urban energy flow models are confronted by a compromise between the data demands for a detailed model and the limitations of statistical models. However, energy modelling studies do not usually consider a long-term approach and thus do not try to handle the problem in a concerted way: there is little effort made to ensure that the data can be updated, or to adapt the models to the available registers, census or other data sources, which are normally maintained up-to-date by a third-party. Most of these models thus tend to be short-lived, and considering the limited return on investment of the model, the investment granted to create it is usually also limited.

For the purposes of the MEU project we wish to model buildings and energy systems in a spatially explicit way, so that detailed hypotheses, organised in "scenarios", may be tested for improving upon overall energy performance. These scenarios might consist of modifications to specific buildings' attributes, to energy conversion systems or to related energy supply networks, which will modify in turn the primary energy demand of our urban scene. It is also our intention to develop a flexible and enduring platform which can, in the future, be extended to other types of simulation program. A spatially explicit representation of buildings in their urban context lends itself well to such extensibility. We have thus selected a micro-simulation approach. To capitalise on recent advances in both energy demand and supply modelling, CitySim has been chosen for its detailed and comprehensive models of buildings' energy demands and EnerGIS will be used to optimise the integration of energy conversion systems. These tools will utilise an extensible database of technology models, including the most recent technologies. Our ambition is that the greater need for data of this disaggregated approach be compensated by the longevity of the model and well adapted handling of data.

2.2 Spatial and Temporal Databases

Database management systems (DBMS) have been around for almost fifty years, and are now extensively used to store and manage data. However, some functionalities are more recent: advanced spatial DBMS started to emerge at the beginning of the 1990's to meet the demand for geographical data storage [9], leading to the definition of the standard Simple Feature by the Open Geospatial Consortium (www.opengeospatial.org). This standard defines new data types (points, linestrings, polygons, etc.) and functions to create, access, manipulate or combine them. Most leading DBMS now offer these standard spatial types and functions or have implemented them as a complementary spatial module, and have optimised the methods to handle the queries on them.

Temporality is another domain of current research: multiple applications require the temporal dimension to be taken into account. If the storage of time or date data types has long since been common, the coherent handling of the continuous nature of time remains the focus of development effort [10]. An increasingly common approach is that of bi-temporal databases, which store for each entry its valid time, i.e. the time period during which the data is valid in the modelled reality, and its transaction time, i.e. the time period when the data is valid in the database. Support for these temporalities is still limited; in particular, it is currently extremely complicated to write constraints related to the temporal validity of data.[1]

---

[1] In temporal databases, the same object can be described for various periods of time, and thus correspond to several entries. However, a typical constraint is that there should not exist two versions of the same object at the same valid time and at the same transaction time. This is currently difficult to express in constraints, with the exception of the new exclusion constraints in PostgreSQL 9.0. Even with this advance, the verification of references' validity becomes quickly perilous. [2].

Finally, research is also exploring the unification of time and geography in spatio-temporal databases [14]. However, the full range of these functions has yet to be implemented in most available DBMS.

2.3   Data Availability and Management

Even with the current capabilities of DBMS, there is little technical limitation in data management functionality; rather, the difficulties lie in the collection, sanitation and harmonisation of data, in the setting up of its actual management and in its updating. As previously noted, for urban energy modelling our data tends to be derived from third-party sources, such as official cadastral maps, building registers, inhabitants' census, energy use measurements from energy providers, etc., as well as on direct observations to possibly complete the available data. However, energy providers' data are not always accessible and direct surveys are very time-consuming. On the other hand, public databases and registers are continually evolving: whether at the national or regional level, the trend is to digitize the data, to unify the registers, and to improve their management. Finally, access to most of this data tends to be restricted for privacy or marketing reasons; and when it is provided, it is often under the proviso that a confidentiality agreement is signed, thus limiting the possible uses and/or publication of the data. Close collaboration with a municipality can thus yield advantages for the collection of data.

In Switzerland, the register of buildings identifies all residential buildings at the national level and stores a short description of each, based on the varying quality data that the municipalities must supply. It includes information about the construction date or period, the kind of building and its use, the surface area, number of floors, and optionally the type of heating system(s). The inhabitants' census contains data regarding people and households, and although not performed at the national level, this is also unified to ensure the collection of the same data in the same format everywhere. The cadastre is managed individually by each municipality, usually including data describing buildings' footprints and energy networks, as well as other spatial data of interest to the municipalities and possibly to modellers. Depending on the domain of study and the local administration and organisations, other useful data sources[2] might be available, but these registers are often scattered amongst departments and not used or managed together and are consequently incompatible. Some cities have undertaken to remedy this problem: in Geneva for example, the format of numerous territorial information registers has been adapted to allow

---

[2] Less usual but potentially useful data sources range from chimney sweep data (which in some places contains the kind and possibly the efficiency of individual heating systems) to official firm census (containing very sensitive data about all firms in a district such as the kind of activity and the number of employes), through natural resource maps or construction policy.

access through a single unified website, without actually centralising the data (etat.geneve.ch/sitg/accueil.html).

Although a high quality and compatibility of data is still the exception, third-party registers are likely to be regularly updated, and the current tendency is towards further improvement of registers in the future. These data sources are thus of great interest for the research and development of data models, which suffer from lack of longevity. The data used for research and simulation should thus be based on these third-party registers in such a way that the models can be easily updated when the third-party sources are completed, corrected or updated.

2.4 Data Accessibility and Ontologies

Following the rapid development of the internet, there has also been a growing interest in means for sharing data over the web and to automatically use that data. Most database management systems (DBMS) include web services for remote access. More recently, geographical information systems (GIS) have also developed solutions (based on DBMS) for data sharing and network accessibility. GIS impose specific model limitations for their databases but also offer advanced access tools, geometrical functionalities and visualisation possibilities.

The prospect of exploiting the richness of data available on the Internet in a wide range of formats led to the development of the semantic web and the use of ontologies for structuring the data [19]. The goal is to make the data understandable by programs and thus automate its accessibility. This implies that formal metadata be attached to the data to describe it, or going further, that a complete description of elements and relationships be provided. An example of a simple ontology used on the web is the Dublin Core standard for describing and cataloguing resources (www.dublincore.org). Feigenbaum et al. [3] introduce numerous examples of semantic web applications, including the Friend-of-a-friend project (www.foaf-project.org) and the public health problem detection system SAPPHIRE.

But what is an ontology ? According to Gruber [8] it is a formal description of a given knowledge domain, including precise definitions of entities in the domain and logical explanations of their relationships. Its use on the internet has thus far been limited to specific domains where an agreement on the ontology could be achieved, or for private firms' networks. It is also used to define a shared vocabulary and structure in some domains, to support the development of more general-purpose and more compatible software. In our domain, an ontology would define precisely what an "energy resource", an "energy conversion system" and a "building" are, grouping those under a more general concept of "energy flow node". Each instance of these classes has several attributes and can be linked to others classes, for instance through "energy connections" to other instances of "energy flow node", or through their geographical position to an "urban zone" instance. A "building" object is also linked to several "surface" objects ("facade","roof" or "floor") describing its 3D physical representation in a formalised way. A complete ontology would also include full definitions of each class and of the kinds of relation it can have with other classes.

An important example is CityGML (`www.citygml.org`), an ontology meant to become a standard for urban scene descriptions. It defines a common structured XML language to describe 3D buildings and other urban objects, originally focusing on the visual characteristics required to support visualisation of the scenes described. Although it does not presently include any energy system or energy network information, nor sufficient physical attributes to support energy simulation (it is not yet sufficiently semantically enriched), it does define classes and relations for the main objects in city models, including spatial, visual and semantical information and thus provides a shared basis for data exchange.

3   Organising the Management of Data

3.1   Storage: The Advantages of Databases

Ironically, the antithesis of sustainable data management is probably still common practise: using files of various format (.xls, .txt, .shp, .dwg, .csv,), without structure and for which modifications cannot be traced.

One usually has little influence over the format of the data provided by third-party sources, and online access to compatible third-party databases is still far from being a common reality. However, it is possible to organize better the data obtained in order to maximise its utility.

Thus our solution must allow for the *structured* storage of *all* the data considered, which might be a constraint when dealing with geographical, temporal or raster data. It should place no limits on size, and the import of data and the connection or export for modelling tools must be convenient. More to the point, it should allow for automatic retrieval by means of another program. It should also allow the user to track modifications or to create a mechanism to do so. Finally, a server system allowing for several people to work on the same data would be very beneficial.

Most currently available database management systems (DBMS) fulfil these expectations, with PostgreSQL/PostGIS (open-source) and Oracle (commercial) being amongst the most advanced spatial databases. Almost all DBMS follow the SQL (Structured Query Language) standards for the input and retrieval of data, provide API to access the database through self-made programs and offer server functionalities for remote access. But to benefit from these functionalities, some form of data model must be defined.

At a higher, perhaps more user-friendly level, Geographical Information Systems (GIS) such as ArcGIS and Manifold (both commercial), provide a more visual way to store and use data, with a strong emphasis on geographical data, analysis and presentation. Apart from their graphical interfaces and visualisation tools, a large part of their functionalities are similar to those of databases. These programs can also be used in combination with a DBMS for the storage of data, but they impose limitations in terms of data model compatibility and accessibility through third party software. They can also be used to a certain extent to access the contents of a third-party database, but with limited editing functionalities. The use of a GIS thus depends on the users' needs and preferences, but their limitations can be problematic in a research and development context.

Whereas most DBMS do not offer a complete temporal data management solution (with the exception of Oracle's "Workspace Manager"), basic temporal functionalities of DBMS can be used to create a structure to keep track of modifications. PostgreSQL for example offers an extension called "Timetravel" which can be used to keep the original version of the data when it is modified. It does so by adding to each table additional fields to save the transaction time, i.e. to define the period of time when the data was valid in the database, so that the state of the database at any point in time can be retrieved through a filter on these fields, without saving new versions of a file each time it is modified. A versioning control mechanism — saving the original version of the data and keeping track of the successive modifications to be able to reconstruct any version — is out of the scope of standard DBMS and thus usually not implemented. However, such a system is used for the versioning functionality of ArcGIS[3], and could also be built again on a database, although it might greatly limit the efficiency of SQL queries.

Using SQL queries, the data needed for simulation can be retrieved with precise queries either to text files, by a small program directly creating a specific input file, or by the simulation program itself, if it is adapted to use the database, for input as well as output. The database can also be stored on a server to be accessed and modified remotely by multiple users working on the same project.

The tendency not to use a formal database for short-term energy modelling projects is arguably related to a lack of knowledge about DBMS and to the investment in time it requires. However, the numerous advantages of databases mentioned above will clearly compensate for the workload of creating the database; in particular if the same kind of data is used regularly for similar studies. This does however require that a complete data model be defined for the domain of interest, usually in the form of a relational model.

3.2   Data Model

Before being able to use the database efficiently, one must first create a structure of tables that fits the data considered, i.e. to decide which data must be saved in what table, in which format and with what relations with other tables.

The registers and census have their own implicit or explicit data model, consisting firstly of the choice, naming and format of the data, and possibly of more precise definitions of the data. However, these are usually quite different from the simulation programs' data model, potentially using different codes and units. In general, the sources' data models cannot be used as such, as they

---

[3] In ArcEditor and ArcInfo, using ArcSDE geodatabases.

are numerous and usually not compatible and not adapted to the simulation tools. For instance, neither a standard cadastral data model, nor a buildings' register model alone are sufficient to simulate energy demand with a tool such as CitySim: the data must be combined in a global data model. On the other hand, the input data models are not appropriate either, as they are specific to one program and thus limited: they may not include all relevant data for other energy-related purposes. A tool specialised in energy demand simulation usually focuses on the modelling of buildings and does not consider all the parameters needed for detailed energy system models or energy system integration models, and vice-versa. Thus, the data model defined for the database can be a helpful bridge between these multiple data models, as it can be correctly adapted to the domain studied but less specific than a simulation program's input data model. It must be built taking into account what data is available, what data is needed and what data constitutes a sensible model of the domain.

In the case of the simulation tool CitySim, the data used to create a 3D physical model of the buildings comes from cadastral maps, digital terrain and surface models (DTM & DSM), the buildings' register, etc, and the input for the simulation consists of an xml file describing the site context as well as each building, its construction materials, occupants and energy systems. In order to create a basic input file, the average height of each building in the cadastre can for instance be extracted from the DTM and DSM by straightforward geometrical functions (see figure 2). Default typical construction parameters may be associated with these buildings based on the age of the building as registered with a code in the buildings register, once the corresponding "building" entry in the register has been defined.

Most of the steps involved in the creation of the input file can be automated, once the various sources are combined into one consistent data model. The other tasks relate to matching the data sources to create this consistent data model, which should be stored in the database. An optimal data model is the closest to the data sources that would allow an automated creation of input files for the simulation, without extensibility restrictions.

Thus the data model can be quite close to an ontology of the domain (in our example: the urban context with a focus on energy flow), whether the ontology itself is constructed as such or not. The main tables must correspond to the obvious entities (building, wall, city, energy system, ...), which must be sufficiently well defined so that the link with the data sources is as clear as possible and the creation of an input file is straightforward.

Databases also allow one to define constraints on the data, or on the valid values of each field, to enforce uniqueness for a field[4] or to enforce relationships between tables. A relationship can then prescribe that each entry in the table "building" must correspond to an entry in the table "city" (the city where it belongs), or that each entry of the table "wall" must reference the corresponding

---

[4] For instance, a constraint can be used to make sure that a building id remains unique, i.e. that two entries in the table "building" will never have the same id.

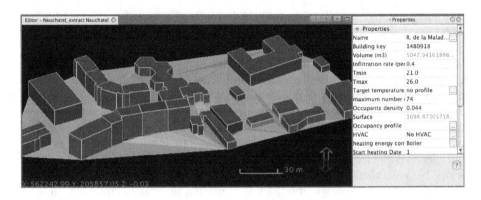

Fig. 2. Example of a 2.5D model and a building's attributes in CitySim

entry in the table "building". These constraints ensure that the database will not be corrupted with incoherent data, by adding intelligence to the model.

Adding constraints to the data model brings it one step closer to the definition of an ontology, which would define the same table (objects), field (properties) and constraints (relationships and rules), but with the all-important addition of their formal meaning and/or description. Thus the effort required for the creation of the data model for the database can easily be completed or coupled with the definition of a formal representation of the knowledge of the domain, primarily as documentation, and possibly as a basis for studying compatibility in the case of data exchanges.

Finally, the model can accommodate methods for defining "scenarios", i.e. variations of the base case model. In our domain a scenario might involve the insulation of all old buildings or the change of one energy system for another technology or fuel, etc. This can be done for instance by copying modified entries in the database and by tagging each of them with an identifier of the scenario. Furthermore this process can be optimised so that only modified data are registered as part of a scenario, the inventory being the base case scenario. The complete scenario scene model can then be retrieved through simple SQL queries.

Whereas modifying slightly the data model by adding tables or columns is straightforward, the underlying structure must be well thought through before implementation. Choosing different elementary entities or altering the structure of references between tables without corrupting the data is more hazardous, while introducing scenario or time management afterwards might prove impossible without redefining completely the model. However, even in this case, the structured data in the previous model will be easier to import in a new model than the original third-party data. On the other hand, any adjustment made on the database model (other than additions which are not to be accessed) will require modifications of the tools using that database.

The MEU project database is planned to take into account all the features mentioned above. Based on a standard representation of the energy domain, it will use "building", "energy system" (equally building-embedded or district-wide) and "resources" entities, seen as nodes linked with energy connections describing the networks. These fundamental units will then refer to all kinds of other data, including cities, zones, energy technologies, surfaces (walls, roofs and floors), official regulations, etc. It will also handle scenarios and both valid time and transaction time temporalities.

3.3 Database Access and Integration

Once a database comprised of a coherent data model has been built, it should be straightforward to create a small utility or to modify a simulation program to connect to the database, retrieve the relevant information, and use it to create an input file or to directly launch a simulation. Similarly, one can interface with various third-party simulation tools that use the same data (or some different subset of the data in the database), provided that the corresponding bridge utility is coded. Database management systems also offer server tools, allowing one to remotely access it over a network. Thus the database and the simulation program(s) need not reside on the same computer and both may be accessed remotely, creating a distributed architecture based on web services.

This is the case for the future MEU platform architecture. The database will reside on one server and be accessed both directly through the website interface, for visualisation and modification, and through the MEU web service dedicated to the management of data, which will also act as a bridge for the simulation tools. These will reside on dedicated servers and be called as web services by the central MEU web service (Fig. 3).

As we will discuss in the next section, database functionalities will also prove useful in managing potential problems arising from data import.

4 Data Import and Matching

We have argued that a good data model implemented in a database should prove to be a solid basis for a long-term urban energy modelling project. Unfortunately however, the population of the database with source data is deceptively complex. As mentioned earlier, aside from the variety of file formats that need to be handled, the reliability of the source data can be highly variable, and data sources are also often incompatible.

4.1 Matching Incompatible Sources

When importing data, the main challenge relates to incompatibilities between the sources, making this step a very time-consuming one (whether using an appropriate database model or not). To create an (energy-oriented) urban model, the main difficulties can be summarised as follows:

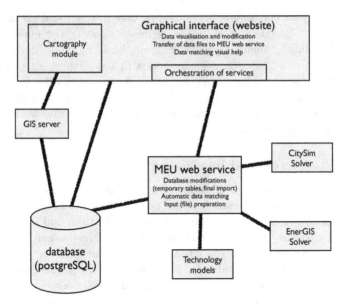

Fig. 3. Planned MEU platform architecture. Each box represent an independent web service: the interface will call the MEU web service to process data or use the solvers. The MEU web service will prepare the input, call the solvers' individual web services and manage their output.

- The elements or units considered in each source databases are different. In our case, the main obvious units are buildings and energy systems. However, a building in the official cadastre can correspond to several or no entries in the buildings' register; no entries can correspond to a lack of information or to incorrect identifying values, whereas multiple entries can be duplicates as well as clearly distinct entities. Similar but different problems arise when matching energy use data from the energy providers: the energy use values are sometimes connected simply to the address where the bill is sent instead of the address where the gas, oil, water or heat is delivered.

- The identifiers are different. When addresses are available, varying formats and spelling might be used; where geolocation is used, this might not be provided for all entries; when numerical id's are provided, these might be locale-specific and not correspond to those used in other data sources.

- Data is missing or incorrect. Furthermore, when very limited data is available describing a given entity, we may question if that entity exists as such, so requiring a decision as to whether it should be considered or not.

These problems are frequent and cannot be solved systematically without undermining confidence in the result. But if a user must consider each problem individually, there are ways to optimise the work involved and thus to significantly decrease the time needed for it. This first requires that the primary data source fixing the entities of interest be chosen[5]. The other sources can then be matched to these entities, to complete their description. The next step is to automatically detect the problematic cases and to provide a simple intuitive graphical user interface presenting these cases and possible actions to resolve them.

Such an import help tool is under development as part of the MEU project, and is planned to be much more complete. Given the chosen architecture for the project, it will consist of several web services which will access the database, and which will themselves be accessible through the MEU platform website. This structure has the great advantage that various users will be able to work on the same data, including civil servants.

This tool will first offer to load data files of certain specified formats, which can then quite easily be imported in the form of a temporary table in the database. The user will then have to identify the columns containing the pertinent identifiers and data for each source and to give an estimate of the quality of that data. Once a cadastral file has been loaded to define the building entities, other data sources will be matched to these, based on common identifiers (including addresses) or on geo-localisation, to be eventually imported into our data model. This task is clearly simplified by the choice of using a database management system, allowing the use of powerful SQL queries for selection, research, update and joining of data.

Unsolved cases will then be accessible through the interface, visually presented on a map to help with its interpretation, in particular for persons familiar with the location in question. For each case, the following potential actions will be proposed: erase the entity, modify it, choose, when there is a multiple match, which entry from the available sources must be retained, select a corresponding entry if none has been automatically found, or fill in manually the missing data.

Automatic checks will also be run to detect unexpected attribute values (unusually high figures, invalid codes, etc). These cases will also be presented to the user for verification and modification. The correctly matched and corrected data will finally be imported into the main database (and tagged with adequate metadata, see below), possibly after a complete visual verification to correct or complete the entries, depending on the user's choice.

4.2   Data Update

Data reliability is not as such a problem, provided that data is used with appropriate care and associated with an uncertainty assessment. More complex is to

---

[5] This is actually an important decision. Having such a basis will secure a systematic entity definition and limit the number of decisions to be taken, and thus gain time. However it might also be a limitation: when other sources are more detailed, some information will have to be dropped. In our case, the footprints of the buildings contained in the cadastre have been chosen to define the building entities, as this is one of the most official, reliable and up-to-date data sources. Still, one footprint sometimes corresponds to several distinct buildings register's entries, and representative attributes must be chosen amongst those available.

keep track of the quality of data when various sources are used and corrections are introduced. It is also difficult to know what data should be modified when importing from a new source: is the data already present of better or worse quality ? An older data source might be considered of lowest worth, but it is probably not the case if that data has been manually corrected. This question is especially relevant for the more important object attributes, i.e. those to which simulation results are highly sensitive and where effort should be invested to limit the uncertainty.

The best way to handle this issue for a long term project is to attach metadata to each significant attribute, that stores a simple estimation of quality and the kind of the source. A new value is then accepted only if its estimated quality is higher, or if it is similar but of a type that has higher priority. For instance, it can be decided that a manually entered value has priority over all other types of source (registers, cadastre, ...). Such a modus operandi demands some additional work, but it ensures a more rational management of data and offers the opportunity to correctly assess the results of a simulation based on the quality of the input.

As discussed earlier, it is also possible to build the database in such a way as to track modifications and thus to be able to retrieve any previous version of the data. Some database management systems already incorporate utilities to do this (such as timetravel for PostgreSQL), but it is possible to add this functionality manually, based on two date fields (valid_from and valid_until, for instance) or an equivalent period field and triggers. Using such a mechanism, updated or deleted rows will not actually disappear: their "valid_until" date will simply be set to the time when they became invalid. For the update action, a new row will be created, with a corresponding "valid_from" value. The current state of the database can be retrieved by selecting only the entries valid at the current time, but any previous state can also be obtained by choosing another date of validity.

To further support modelling longevity, several other functionalities might be of use; one would be to provide feedback to the data providers regarding which data were incompatible or have been corrected. Once the operation of matching data sources has been structured, this can easily be achieved with a simple text file containing a summary of each decision made. Another function would be to keep track of how problems were solved, to be able to apply the same rules if the same source is used to update the database in the future. This can be achieved with the help of a matching table, where a specific identifier of a data source is linked with the identifier of an entity in the main database.

5   Dealing with Incomplete Data

One of our key goals is to make sure that missing data will not prevent us from simulating a scene and obtaining results. However, another key goal is to ensure that a minimum of available useful data is dropped because of time constraints or homogeneous default data use. We believe that the structure developed above provides a sound basis for achieving this.

When modelling several hundred individual buildings and energy systems, one cannot expect to be able to acquire all the data needed for explicit attribution for micro-simulation modelling: it is necessary to use statistically derived default data. However, it is possible to use default data only where needed and as long as no better information is available. There does nevertheless exist a certain minimum level of information that is required to be able to consider an entity, which depends on the aggregation scale and the precision that is expected for the results.

For instance, to simulate the energy demand of a building with a tool such as CitySim, it must at the very least be associated with a footprint, number of floors and period of construction so that its approximate geometry and some default construction properties can be deduced. A simple 2.5D model of the envelope can be built based on the footprint and approximate height, whilst the walls' composition, the glazing ratio and physical properties of windows, etc, can be attributed as defaults based on the period of construction and possibly the location.

To be able to improve the model when new data is available, it is sufficient to record where original data or default data has been used. One way to do this is to keep only real data in the database, and complement this with default data when it is retrieved to provide the input for a simulation tool. Alternatively, to keep track of how results were obtained and to be consistent, it might be preferable to include the default data in the data model, appropriately tagged with metadata describing it as default. All potential simulation programs using the data model will thus consider the same data and be able to assess to what degree its input consists of default values. In the same way, data updates will systematically replace default (and thus of low estimated quality) data.

A coherent and flexible data framework thus ensures that the best use is made of all available data, limiting the use of default values without loosing our capacity to evaluate or improve the model.

6   Conclusion

As mentioned in the introduction, the goal of the MEU project is to provide a modelling and simulation platform for more effective urban energy management in cities. A crucial issue in developing such a tool is to maximise its scope of applicability as well as its longevity. From this perspective, the effective management of data is of primary importance, as data retrieval, import, matching, correction, management and updating is arguably the most time-consuming task involved in urban scale energy flow modelling.

The goal of this chapter was thus to present techniques and tools that can be employed to help with data management for urban energy modelling, and to propose approaches that may be adapted to similar applications, where a decrease of the time dedicated to preparing input data and an increase of input data model longevity is clearly desirable. To this end we have suggested that a structured organisation of information with a database management system (or a similar tool) is a profitable investment at multiple levels: it can help track the origin of the data, support the more efficient organisation of data from various sources, allow the quality of input data to simulation programs to be assessed, simplify model updating and increase its value by increasing its longevity, accessibility and reusability.

In parallel with improving upon data management practices, a further goal is to simplify the use of simulation programs by using data flexibly. Although the use of statistical or default data pays dividends in terms of model preparation time, such data should not be overexploited, particularly when disaggregated results are required. A compromise is thus needed: we should use real data where feasible and especially for variables to which simulation results are sensitive, and use default data elsewhere, without impairing the data model or its ability to be updated. Again, the proposed structure, including the monitoring of data origin and quality through metadata, allows for an optimal utilisation of data, whatever the level of detail available, by using default data attribution in a systematic and reversible way.

We believe that the key to more effective future energy management in cities lies in a better knowledge of the current situation and the use of robust energy modelling tools to support decision making by the municipalities' energy departments. But we are some way off from achieving this aim, both in terms of modelling tools' maturity and in the availability, compatibility and accuracy of corresponding data sources.

Regarding the latter issue, this chapter has highlighted the current limitations on the path towards a solid data framework for urban energy flow modelling. As well as the continuous improvement of data quality and reliability (which mostly concern third-party sources), both Geneva's example and research related to the semantic web show that the grouping of data and its unified access has become an acknowledged priority. However, achieving this still requires some considerable effort in practice.

Further developments of database management systems are also needed, in particular regarding temporal databases. Even though the data types and functions available presently allow for the manual creation of bi-temporal databases, the support provided for handling temporality remains too limited. It is now necessary to implement the results of theoretical research in this field, and to provide easy and efficient temporal database management systems.

In the short term however, we have seen that it is possible to bridge the gaps between data and modelling tools and to create a sound basis for study with existing sources and database management systems. The goal of the MEU project is to provide municipalities with a platform for urban energy management which will benefit from recent advances in the related modelling domains. It is also our hope that such collaboration will in turn encourage a better management of the key data sources by cities.

But the goal of this project is also to promote future exchanges: the development of this platform will continue through a consortium of municipalities and academic partners. As well as consolidating the data foundations of the platform, the middle- to long-term ambition is to take further advantage of this foundation and to extend its scope to provide for decision making support in domains such as water management, waste management (and possible feedback to energy management), transport, etc. The concerted use of a common and structured spatial database for multiple ends will allow for economies of scale. This will hopefully lead the way to more enlightened and efficient actions to implement sustainable urban development policies.

References

1. Ahern, J.: Exergy method of energy systems analysis (1980)
2. Date, C.J., Darwen, H., Lorentzos, N.A.: Temporal Data and the Relational Model. Morgan Kaufmann Publishers, USA (2003)
3. Feigenbaum, L., Herman, I., Hongsermeier, T., Neumann, E., Stephens, S.: The semantic web in action. Scientific American Magazine 297(6), 90–97 (2007)
4. Filchakova, N., Robinson, D., Thalmann, P.: A model of whole-city housing stock and its temporal evolution. In: Proc. Building Simulation, Glasgow, UK (2009)
5. Forrester, J.: Urban dynamics. MIT Press (1969)
6. Gadsden, S., Rylatt, M., Lomas, K., Robinson, D.: Predicting the urban solar fraction: a methodology for energy advisers and planners based on GIS. Energy & Buildings 35(1), 37–48 (2003)
7. Girardin, L., Marechal, F., Dubuis, M., Calame-Darbellay, N., Favrat, D.: EnerGis: A geographical information based system for the evaluation of integrated energy conversion systems in urban areas. Energy (2009)
8. Gruber, T., et al.: Toward principles for the design of ontologies used for knowledge sharing. International Journal of Human Computer Studies 43(5), 907–928 (1995)
9. Güting, R.: An introduction to spatial database systems. The VLDB Journal 3(4), 357–399 (1994)
10. Jensen, C., Snodgrass, R.: Temporal data management. IEEE Transactions on Knowledge and Data Engineering 11(1), 36–44 (2002)
11. Jones, P., Patterson, J., Lannon, S.: Modelling the built environment at an urban scale—Energy and health impacts in relation to housing. Landscape and Urban Planning 83(1), 39–49 (2007)
12. Linnhoff, B.: Pinch analysis: a state-of-the-art overview: Techno-economic analysis. Chemical Engineering Research & Design 71(5), 503–522 (1993)
13. Lior, N.: Thoughts about future power generation systems and the role of exergy analysis in their development. Energy Conversion and Management 43(9-12), 1187–1198 (2002)
14. Pelekis, N., Theodoulidis, B., Kopanakis, I., Theodoridis, Y.: Literature review of spatio-temporal database models. The Knowledge Engineering Review 19(03), 235–274 (2004)
15. Robinson, D. (ed.): Computer modelling for sustainable urban design. Earthscan Press, London (2011)
16. Robinson, D., Campbell, N., Gaiser, W., Kabel, K., Le-Mouel, A., Morel, N., Page, J., Stankovic, S., Stone, A.: SUNtool–a new modelling paradigm for simulating and optimising urban sustainability. Solar Energy 81(9), 1196–1211 (2007)

17. Robinson, D., Haldi, F., Kämpf, J., Leroux, P., Perez, D., Rasheed, A., Wilke, U.: CitySim: Comprehensive micro-simulation of resource flows for sustainable urban planning. In: Proc. Building Simulation (2009)
18. Sartori, I., Wachenfeldt, B., Hestnes, A.: Energy demand in the Norwegian building stock: Scenarios on potential reduction. Energy Policy 37(5), 1614–1627 (2009)
19. Shadbolt, N., Hall, W., Berners-Lee, T.: The semantic web revisited. IEEE Intelligent Systems 21(3), 96–101 (2006)
20. Shimoda, Y., Fujii, T., Morikawa, T., Mizuno, M.: Development of residential energy end-use simulation model at city scale. In: Proc. Building Simulation (2003)
21. Shorrock, L., Dunster, J.: The physically-based model BREHOMES and its use in deriving scenarios for the energy use and carbon dioxide emissions of the UK housing stock. Energy Policy 25(12), 1027–1037 (1997)
22. Sugihara, H., Komoto, J., Tsuji, K.: A multi-objective optimization model for determining urban energy systems under integrated energy service in a specific area. Electrical Engineering in Japan 147(3), 20–31 (2004)
23. Yamaguchi, Y., Shimoda, Y., Mizuno, M.: Development of district energy system simulation model based on detailed energy demand model. In: Proceeding of Eighth International IBPSA Conference, pp. 1443–1450 (2003)

Interactive Large-Scale Crowd Simulation

Dinesh Manocha and Ming C. Lin

Department of Computer Science
University of North Carolina
Chapel Hill, NC, U.S.A.
{dm,lin}@cs.unc.edu
http://gamma.cs.unc.edu

Abstract. We survey some recent work on interactive modeling, simulation, and control of large-scale crowds. Our primary focus is on interactive algorithms that can handle a large number of autonomous agents. This includes techniques for automatically computing collision-free trajectories for each agent as well as generating emergent crowd behaviors including lane formation, edge effects, vortices, congestion avoidance, swirling and modeling varying crowd density. Some of these methods map well to current multi-core and many-core processors and we highlight their performance in different urban scenarios.

1 Introduction

Crowds are ubiquitous in the real world and are an important component of any digital urban modeling or simulation system. The problem of simulating large number of agents or crowds has been studied in different fields including computer graphics, robotics, architecture, physics, psychology, social sciences, and civil and traffic engineering. In particular, crowds are regarded as complex systems that exhibit distinct characteristics, such as emergent behaviors, self-organization, and pattern formation due to multi-scale interactions among individuals and groups of individuals.

The problem of simulating the flow or movement of pedestrians in large urban environments is getting more important as the populations of our cities grow. This is especially true in Asia, Africa and other densely populated parts of the world, which seem to be undergoing the largest wave of urban growth. In 2007, for the first time, more than half of the world's population were living in cities. Many studies related to pedestrian flows in urban settings have been undertaken over the last few decades. However, our knowledge about the flow of crowds is rather inadequate as compared to other transport modes [26]. Besides pedestrian flows, there are many other sources of crowd modeling including transport systems, holy sites or religious events, political demonstrations, evacuation planning, etc. In each of these cases, the crowd behavior tends to vary and needs to be modeled accordingly.

One of the main challenges is to simulate large-scale crowds with tens or hundreds of thousands of agents. Such large crowds are becoming increasingly common in urban simulation systems. Furthermore, some applications such as games

S. Müller Arisona et al. (Eds.): DUMS, CCIS 242, pp. 221–235, 2012.
© Springer-Verlag Berlin Heidelberg 2012

or virtual environments need interactive simulation capabilities, i.e. simulating at 30 fps or more on current desktop systems. In addition to the overall performance, another major challenge is generating realistic crowd behaviors. Despite decades of observation and studies, collective behaviors are particularly not well understood for groups with *non-uniform spatial distribution* and *heterogeneous behavior characteristics*. Such scenarios are common including pedestrian movement, evacuation flows in complex structures, and coupled human-natural systems.

In this paper, we survey some recent works on addressing the problem of modeling, simulating, and directing the large-scale individual agents in complex dynamic environments. These components are needed to compute crowd trajectories, and eventually generate emergent behaviors. While these techniques have been studied for more than two decades, we limit our coverage to recent methods that are used to simulate the motion of large number of agents at interactive rates. We give a brief overview of prior work on multi-agent and crowd simulation, and give a broad classification of prior methods into various categories (see Section 2). Next, we describe many recent approaches for local collision avoidance between multiple agents and global navigation that have been designed by our team at the University of North Carolina at Chapel Hill. These include (a) a new local collision avoidance algorithm between multiple agents [8] (see Section 3); (b) a novel formulation to model aggregate dynamics of dense crowds [21] (see Section 4); (c) an effective approach to direct and control virtual crowds using guidance or navigational fields [22] (see Section 5); (d) a least-effort approach that can generate energy-efficient trajectories and emergent behaviors [9] (see Section 6).

Many of these methods can be combined together to generate crowd behaviors that are frequently observed in urban environments. Furthermore, we use the computational capabilities of commodity multi-core and many-core processors and exploit the parallelism to achieve interactive performance for tens of thousands of agents.. We also demonstrate their application to simulating pedestrian crossings, motion of thousands of pilgrims at a mosque, trade shows, etc.

2   Multi-agent and Crowd Simulation

In this section, we give a brief overview of prior work related to multi-agent navigation and interactive crowd simulation. This includes work on computing collision-free motion for robots or agents in robot motion planning. There is also extensive work on crowd simulation and generating emergent behaviors in computer animation, virtual environments and social sciences.

2.1   Motion Planning for Multiple Entities

The goal of collision-free motion planning for multiple agents moving simultaneously in an environment is challenging. The problem is known to have exponential complexity in terms of number of agents or the degrees of freedom [20].

This problem has been extensively studied in robotics and related areas, where the main goal is to compute collision-free paths for one or more robots. At a broad level, prior work on motion planning can be classified into two kinds of approaches.

The *centralized* approaches [19,20] consider the sum of all the robots or agents and treat the resulting system as a single composite system. In these methods, the configuration spaces of individual robots are combined (using the Cartesian product) in a composite space, and the resulting algorithm searches for a solution in this combined configuration space. As the dimension of the composite space grows with the number of degrees of freedom added for each entity, the problem complexity becomes prohibitively high. As a result, the practical solutions are limited to low DOF robots.

By contrast, the *decoupled* planners proceed in a distributed manner and co-ordination is often handled by exploring a *coordination space*, which represents the parameters along each specific robot path. Decoupled approaches [33,41] are much faster than centralized methods, but may not be able to guarantee theoretical completeness.

Some of these robotics techniques have been applied to generate group behaviors for virtual agents [2,16] and real-time navigation of large numbers of agents [36,7].

2.2   Multi-agent and Crowd Simulation

There is extensive literature on simulating crowd movements and dynamics. We refer the reader to a recent survey [24]. Several techniques have been proposed to animate or simulate large groups of autonomous agents or crowds. Most of these methods use a rather simple representation for each agent - this could be a circular shape in a 2D plane or a cylindrical object in the 3D space, and compute a collision-free trajectory for each agent. After computing the trajectory using a simple representation, these techniques use either footstep planning or walking synthesis methods to compute a human-like motion for each agent along the given trajectory.

At a broad level, prior methods for computing crowd movements can be classified into the following six categories [9]:

- *Potential-based methods:* These algorithms focus on modeling agents as particles with potentials and forces[10].
- *Boid-like methods:* These approaches are based on the seminal work of Reynolds which create simple rules for computing the velocities [27,28].
- *Geometric methods:* These algorithms compute collision-free paths using sampling in the velocity space [38] or by using optimization methods [8,5].
- *Field based methods:* These algorithms tend to compute fields for agents to follow [42,25,4,12], or generate navigation fields for different agents based on continuum theories of flows [37] or fluid models [21].
- *Least effort crowds:* Based on the classic principle of Least Effort proposed by Zipf [44], many researchers have used that formulation to model the paths

of crowds [35,18,30,15]. Recently, it has been combined with multi-agent collision avoidance algorithms [5] and used to efficiently and automatically generate emergent behaviors for a large number of agents [9].

In addition to these broad classifications, there are many other specific approaches designed to generate crowd behavior based on cognitive modeling and behavior [32,43] or sociological or psychological factors [23]. Other techniques include directing crowd behaviors using guidance field specified by the user or extracted from videos and computing smooth navigation fields [22].

2.3   Motion Synthesis

A key component of any crowd simulation system is synthesizing the motion of each agent. Human motions (including walking, etc.) can be modeled from motion captured from the real-world data [1,13] or by applying learning methods to pedestrian walking data extracted from videos [31]. Energy minimization techniques have also been used for character animation and synthesizing motions like walking, running etc. [17,14]. Gait generation algorithms have been applied to minimize the cost function of energy consumption for the agents [3,29].

2.4   Scene Representation

We assume that the scene consists of multiple heterogeneous agents, each of which is moving toward an independent goal. The goal position can change or some agents may only have intermediate goals. Furthermore, the scene consists of static and dynamic obstacles and it is important that each agent avoids collisions with other agents and all the obstacles. The behavior of each agent is governed by some extrinsic and intrinsic parameters and computed in a distributed manner for each agent independently. The overall simulation proceeds in discrete time steps and we update the state of each agent, including its position and velocity during each time step based on its goal position and the other agents or obstacles in the scene.

Our overall framework assumes that the agents are moving on a 2D plane, though our approach can be extended to handle agents moving in 3D space [34]. At any time instance, each agent has the information about the position and velocity of nearby agents. The proximity information in terms of nearby agents can be computed using a kD-tree. Moreover, the simplest representation of each agent corresponds to a circle or a convex polygon. In the rest of the paper, we describe algorithms for circular agents.

3   ClearPath

Guy et al. [8] present a highly parallel and robust collision avoidance approach, *ClearPath*, for multi-agent simulation. This formulation extends and generalizes the concept of *velocity obstacles* (VO) [6,39] for local collision avoidance among dynamic obstacles. The authors use an efficient velocity-obstacle based formulation that can be combined with any underlying multi-agent simulation. Moreover, it is shown that local collision avoidance computations can be reduced to solving a quadratic optimization problem that minimizes the change in underlying velocity of each agent subject to non-collision constraints.

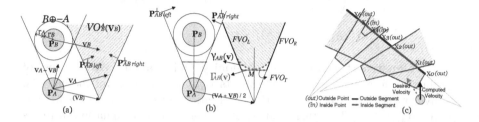

Fig. 1. (a) The Velocity Obstacle $VO_B^A(\mathbf{v}_B)$ of a disc-shaped obstacle B to a disc-shaped agent A. This VO represents the velocities that could result in a collision of A with B (i.e. potentially colliding region). (b) The Fast Velocity Obstacle $FVO_B^A(\mathbf{v}_B)$ of a disc-shaped obstacle B to a disc-shaped agent A. This formulation takes into account the time interval for local collision avoidance. (c) Classifying FVO boundary subsegments as Inside/Outside of the remaining FVO regions for multi-agent simulation. Our optimization algorithm performs these classification tests to compute a non-colliding velocity for each agent.

Guy et al. present a polynomial-time algorithm for each agent to compute collision-free, 2D motion in a distributed manner. Given an agent A, let the symbols $\mathbf{p}_A$, $\mathbf{r}_A$, and $\mathbf{v}_A$ denote its position, radius and velocity, respectively. We assume that the underlying simulation algorithm tends to compute the desired velocity for each agent ($\mathbf{v}_A^{des}$) during the time step.

The local collision avoidance problem for N agents as a combinatorial optimization problem and extend the VO formulation by imposing additional constraints that can guarantee collision avoidance for each agent during the discrete interval. The resulting formulation, *Fast Velocity Obstacle (FVO)*, is defined using a total of four constraints. The *two* boundary cone constraints of the FVO are same as that of RVO [39,40]:

$$FVOL_B^A(\mathbf{v}) = \phi(\mathbf{v}, (\mathbf{v}_A + \mathbf{v}_B)/2, \mathbf{p}_{ABleft}^\perp) \geq 0$$
$$FVOR_B^A(\mathbf{v}) = \phi(\mathbf{v}, (\mathbf{v}_A + \mathbf{v}_B)/2, \mathbf{p}_{ABright}^\perp) \geq 0,$$

where $\mathbf{v}_A$ and $\mathbf{v}_B$ denote the velocities of two each agents, A and B. Moreover, $\mathbf{p}_{AB}^\perp$ represents the boundary of FVO.

In order to take into account, some of the characteristics of the simulation, the approach imposes *two* more types of constraints into this formulation:

Type-I Constraint - Finite Time Interval: In this case, the algorithm guarantees collision avoidance for the duration ΔT of the simulation (as the simulation proceeds in discrete time steps). The resulting approach computes a finite subset of the RVO cone that corresponds to the forbidden velocities that could lead to collisions in ΔT. Due to efficiency reasons, we replace $\gamma_{AB}(\mathbf{v})$ with a conservative linear approximation $\Gamma_{AB}(\mathbf{v})$. This additional constraint is represented as $\mathrm{FVO}_{TB}^A(\mathbf{v}) = \Gamma_{AB}(\mathbf{v}) = \lambda \left(M - \widehat{\mathbf{p}_{AB}^{\perp}} \times \eta, \, \mathbf{p}_{AB}^{\perp} \right)$, where

$$\eta = \tan \left(\sin^{-1} \frac{\mathbf{r}_A + \mathbf{r}_B}{|\mathbf{p}_{AB}|} \right) \times (|\mathbf{p}_{AB}| - (\mathbf{r}_A + \mathbf{r}_B)), \text{ and}$$

$$M = (|\mathbf{p}_{AB}| - (\mathbf{r}_A + \mathbf{r}_B)) \times \widehat{\mathbf{p}_{AB}} + \frac{\mathbf{v}_A + \mathbf{v}_B}{2}$$

Type-II Constraint - Consistent Velocity Orientation: Without loss of generality, we force each agent to choose its *right* side in terms of the half-line that divides the plane. We impose this orientation constraint as $\mathrm{FVO}_{CB}^A(\mathbf{v}) = (\phi(\mathbf{v}, \mathbf{p}_A, \mathbf{p}_{AB}^{\perp}) \leq 0$. This turns out to be a conservative formulation in terms of computing collision-free motion for each agent.

Any feasible solution to all of these constraints, which are separately formulated for each agent, will guarantee collision avoidance. This problem is formulated as a quadratic optimization function with non-convex linear constraints for each agent. It can be shown to be NP-Hard [8] for non-constant dimensions via reduction to quadratic integer programming. However, it has a polynomial time solution when the dimensionality of the constrains is constant – two in this case. In practice, ClearPath is more than one order of magnitude faster than prior velocity-obstacle based methods and presents an efficient and reliable approach that can handle a very high number of agents in a distributed manner.

P-ClearPath: Parallel Collision Avoidance: Guy et al. [8] further show that ClearPath is amenable to data-parallelism and thread-level parallelism on commodity processors and suggest a parallel extension. The resulting parallel extension, P-ClearPath, exploits the structure of our optimization algorithm and architectural capabilities such as gather/scatter and pack/unpack to provide improved data-parallel scalability. ClearPath operates on a per-agent basis in a distributed manner, finding each agent's nearest neighbors and computes a collision-free velocity with respect to those neighbors. There are *two* fundamental ways of exploring Data-Level parallelism (henceforth referred to as DLP).

Intra-agent Computation: Consider Fig. 2(a). For each agent, we explore DLP within the ClearPath computation. Since the agents operate in 2D, they can perform their X and Y coordinate updates in a SIMD fashion. This approach does not scale to wider SIMD widths, that are becoming increasingly common on current many-core processors.

Inter-agent Computation: This formulation operates on multiple agents at a time, with each agent occupying a slot in the SIMD computation. This approach is scalable to larger SIMD widths, but needs to address the following two issues:

1. Non-contiguous data access: In order to operate on multiple agents, ClearPath requires *gathering* their obstacle data structure into a contiguous location in memory. After computing the collision-free velocity, the

results need to be *scattered* back to their respective non-contiguous locations. Such data accesses become a performance bottleneck without efficient *gather/scatter* operations.

2. Incoherent branching: Multiple agents within a SIMD register may take divergent paths. This degrades SIMD performance, and is a big performance limiter during intersection computations and inside/outside tests. One or more of the agents may terminate early, while the remaining ones may still be performing comparisons.

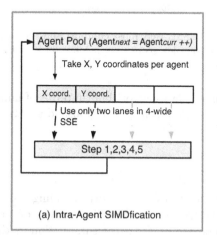 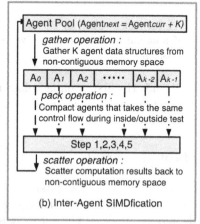

(a) Intra-Agent SIMDfication   (b) Inter-Agent SIMDfication

Fig. 2. Data-Parallel Computations: (a) Intra-Agent SIMDfication for SSE; (b) Inter-Agent SIMDfication for wide SIMD

Current SSE architectures on commodity CPUs do not have efficient instructions to resolve the above two problems. Hence, we used the intra-object SIMDfication approach and obtain only moderate speedups. P-ClearPath uses the Inter-agent approach, and performs computation on $\mathcal{K}$ agents together. Fig. 2(b) shows a detailed mapping of the various steps in ClearPath algorithm. For collision-free velocity computation, each agent A_i is given as input its neighboring velocity obstacles (truncated cones) and the desired velocity. For more detail, see [8].

Results: The performance is evaluated in various scenarios on different platforms, including current multi-core CPUs and a many-core processor code-named Larrabee. In practice, P-ClearPath demonstrates 8-15X speedup on a conventional quad-core processor over prior VO-based algorithms on similar platforms. When executed on a Larrabee simulator with 32-64 cores, P-ClearPath achieves additional speedup of up to 15X, resulting in up to 100-200X speedup over prior VO-based approaches.

Overall, for simple game-like scenarios with a few hundred agents, P-ClearPath takes about 2.5 milliseconds on a single Larrabee core, while a complex simulation with a few hundred thousand heterogeneous agents takes only 35 milliseconds on the simulated 64-core Larrabee processor. To the best of our knowledge,

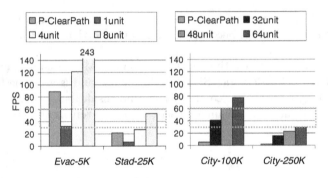

Fig. 3. Performance (FPS) of P-ClearPath on SSE (left most column) and Larrabee (with different units) architectures. Even on complex scenes, we achieve 30 − 60 FPS on many-core processors.

P-ClearPath is the first scalable collision avoidance algorithm (in terms of number of cores) for multi-agent simulations with a few hundred thousand agents at interactive rates.

4   Hybrid Crowds

Dense crowds exhibit a low interpersonal distance and a corresponding loss of individual freedom of motion. This observation suggests that the behavior of such crowds may be modeled efficiently at a coarse level, treating its motion as the flow of a single aggregate system. Based on such an abstraction, Narain et al. [21] develop a novel inter-agent avoidance model that decouples the computational cost of local planning from the number of agents, allowing very large-scale crowds consisting of hundreds of thousands of agents to be simulated at interactive rates. A key characteristic of large-scale crowds is not only the number of agents, but also the density of the agents in terms of number of agents per square meter. Whenever the density goes beyond 4 agents per square-meter, which is considered very high, the crowd is treated as a whole. This includes modeling the crowd as a fluid and a continuum that responds to local influences by assuming that the individuals in the continuum move so as to optimize their behavior to reach non-local objectives [11].

The overall method proposed by Narain et al. for very large-scale crowds combines a Lagrangian representation of individuals with a coarser Eulerian crowd model, thus capturing both the discrete motion of each agent and the macroscopic flow of the crowd. In dense crowds, the finite spatial extent occupied by humans becomes a significant factor. This effect introduces new challenges, as the flow varies from freely compressible when the density is low to incompressible when the agents are close together. This characteristic is shared by many other dynamical systems consisting of numerous objects of finite size, including granular materials, hair, and dense traffic. The authors propose a new mathematical formulation to model the dynamics of such aggregate systems in a principled manner, which is detailed in [21].

Fig. 4. Some examples of large, dense crowds simulated the hybrid algorithm of Narain et al. (a) 100,000 pilgrims moving through a campsite. (b) 80,000 people on a trade show floor. (c) 10,000 agents attempt to cross over to the opposite points of a circle and meet in the middle, before forming a vortex to resolve the deadlock. (d) 25,000 pilgrims with heterogeneous goals in a mosque.

Results: Fig. 4 shows some of the results for dense crowds of up to 100,000 agents closely packed in complex scenes simulated at interactive rates. The authors measured the performance of their algorithm on an Intel Core i7-965 machine at 3.2 GHz with 6 GB of RAM. Even with very large numbers of agents, they can achieve close to interactive performance. This method supports general scenarios with independent, heterogeneous agents and the number of unique goals has no effect on the performance of the system.

5   Directing Crowds Using Navigation Fields

Most existing agent-based systems assume that each agent is an independent decision making entity. Some of the methods also focus on group-level behaviors and complex rules for decision making. The problem with these approaches is that interactions of an agent with other agents or with the environment are often performed at a local level and can sometimes result in undesirable macroscopic behaviors. Due to the complex inter-agent interactions and multi-agent collision avoidance, it is often difficult to generate desired crowd movements or motion patterns that follow the local rules.

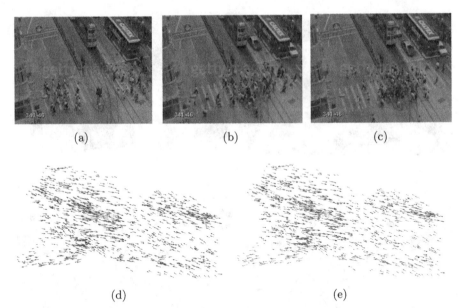

(a)   (b)   (c)

(d)   (e)

Fig. 5. Motion patterns detected in a video of a crosswalk in Hong Kong. (a,b,c) Frames from the original video; (d) Motion flow field; (e) Detected motion patterns.

In recent work, Patil et al. address the problem of directing the flow of agents in a simulation and interactively control the simulation at run time [22]. Their approach is mainly designed for goal-directed multi-agent systems, where each agent has knowledge of the environment and a desired goal position at each step of the simulation. The goal position for each agent can be computed from a higher-level objective and can also dynamically change during the simulation.

This approach for directing the crowds uses discretized *guidance fields* to direct the agents. These guidance fields correspond to a vector field, which are used to specify the motion direction of the agents. Based on these inputs, they compute a unified, goal-directed, smooth *navigation field* that avoids collisions with the obstacles in the environment. The guidance fields can be edited by a user to interactively control the trajectories of the agents in an ongoing simulation, while guaranteeing that their individual objectives are attained. The microscopic behaviors, such as local collision avoidance, personal space and communication between individual agents, are governed by the underlying agent-based simulation algorithm.

Results: This approach is general and applicable to a variety of existing agent-based methods. The usefulness of this approach is illustrated in the context of several simulation scenarios shown in Fig. 6. The user edits the simulation by specifying guidance fields, that are either drawn by the user or extracted from a video sequence (Fig. 5). The overall approach can be useful from both artistic and data-driven perspectives, as it allows the user to interactively model some macroscopic phenomena and group dynamics.

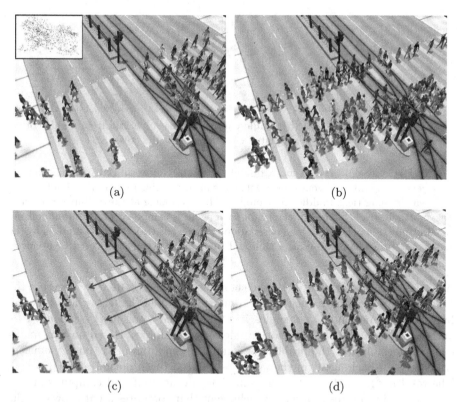

Fig. 6. Crosswalk Simulation: (a) Video-based motion patterns from Figure 5(e) used as guidance fields; (b) Agent motion generated by the navigation fields. (c) Sketch-based guidance fields to specify lane formation in the simulation; (d) Lane formation generated by goal-directed navigation fields.

6 Least-Effort Crowds

Many researchers in different fields have noticed that the human and crowd motion in real-world scenarios is governed by the *principle of least effort* (PLE). One of the earliest works in this area is Zipf's classic book on human behavior [44]. The basic essence of this principle is that humans tend to move through the environment to their goals using the least amount of effort, by minimizing the time, cost, congestion, or the change in velocity of their trajectory. The least-effort formulation has already influenced the design of some recent crowd modeling systems based on cellular automata [35,18,30]. However, it is hard to extend these methods to simulate large crowds with thousands of agents.

Recently, Guy et al. [9], present an optimization-based algorithm to generate energy-efficient trajectories for each agent. Their formulation tends to follow two principles in terms of computing the trajectories:

- Take the shortest available route to the destination.
- Attempt to move at the underlying preferred speed for each agent.

(a) Simulated crossing at (b) A different view of the (c) A still from a video of
Shibuya Station in Tokyo simulated crossing   the crossing

Fig. 7. The least-effort crowd simulation algorithm of Guy et al. (2010) can automatically generate many emergent crowd behaviors at interactive rates in the simulation of Shibuya Crossing (left, middle) that models a busy crossing at the Shibuya Station in Tokyo, Japan. (right). The trajectory for each agent is computed based on minimizing an effort function. There is a high correlation between the trajectories computed by the least-effort crowd simulation algorithm and the real trajectories captured by a video.

A key issue in this formulation is the choice of the function used to represent the "effort". Guy et al. [9] present a novel metric to model the least-effort function based on bio-mechanical principles in terms of the total energy expended by an individual during the locomotion, measured in Joules. Based on this mathematical formulation, the problem of computing an appropriate energy-efficient trajectory for each agent in the crowd is reduced to an optimization problem. The resulting algorithm takes this function into account and computes an appropriate collision-free motion for each agent that computes a path towards the goal. The performance of the overall algorithm has been tested in different scenarios and also compared with the trajectories computed by many of the prior crowd simulation methods. Furthermore, the resulting trajectories are compared with the prior data collected on real humans and the authors observed a close match. A key characteristic of this algorithm is that it is automatically able to generate many emerging behaviors in various simulations. These include:

- Jamming/Bottlenecks - congestion forms at narrow passages;
- Arching - arches form at exits;
- Lane formation - opposing flows pass through each other;
- Wake effect - not immediately filling in space after obstacles;
- Uneven densities - regions form with more or less people than the surrounding areas;
- Edge effects - agents move faster near the edges of crowds;
- Overtaking - faster individuals move past slower neighbors;
- Congestion avoidance - individuals tend to avoid overly dense regions if possible;
- Swirling - vortices can form in cross flows.

Furthermore, it is relatively simple to parallelize the algorithm on a multi-core processor and get almost linear speedup with the number of cores.

7   Discussion

In this paper, we have presented a brief survey of algorithms for real-time collision avoidance, modeling, simulation, and control of multiple virtual agents in dynamic scenes. We also highlighted their applications on interactive crowd simulation in urban simulations and virtual environments.

Among these methods, ClearPath is designed to take advantage of upcoming many-core architectures to achieve real-time collision avoidance of hundreds of thousands of discrete agents at interactive rates. In contrast, the hybrid approach for large-scale crowds is better suited for highly dense scenarios, capable of simulating up to millions of individual agents in nearly real time by exploiting their constrained movement.

The approach to direct and control crowds using navigation fields is general and versatile. It can use any low-level collision avoidance algorithm and is complimentary to most current methods that compute trajectories for the agents. The resulting system allows the user to specify the navigation fields by either sketching paths directly in the scene via an intuitive authoring interface or by importing motion flow fields extracted automatically from crowd video footage. This technique is complementary to other methods and most suitable for interactive editing and testing during interactive applications such as virtual environments.

Finally, the algorithm to simulate least-effort crowds can also be combined with other collision-free or navigation methods that use optimization techniques. In practice, this algorithm generates natural-looking trajectories for the agents as well as a high number of emergent crowd behaviors that we observe. It is relatively easy to parallelize on multi-core architectures. The overall approach is quite promising in terms of simulating a large-number of agents in urban environments and related applications.

Acknowledgments. We would like to thank all our students and collaborators, whose work is described in this survey. These include Jur van den Berg, Jatin Chuggani, Sean Curtis, Pradeep Dubey, Abhinav Golas, Stephen Guy, Rahul Narain and Sachin Patil. The research presented here is supported in part by Army Research Office, Intel, National Science Foundation, DARPA, and RDECOM.

References

1. Antonini, G., Venegas, S., Bierlaire, M., Thiran, J.-P.: Behavioral priors for detection and tracking of pedestrians in video sequences. International Journal of Computer Vision 69(2), 159–180 (2006)
2. Bayazit, O.B., Lien, J.-M., Amato, N.M.: Better group behaviors in complex environments with global roadmaps. In: Int. Conf. on the Sim. and Syn. of Living Sys. (Alife), pp. 362–370 (2002)
3. Channon, P.H., Hopkins, S.H., Phan, D.T.: Derivation of optimal walking motions for a biped walking robot (1992)
4. Chenney, S.: Flow tiles. In: Proc. 2004 ACM SIGGRAPH / Eurographics Symposium on Computer Animation (2004)

5. Van den Berg, J., Seawall, J., Lin, M.C., Manocha, D.: Virtualized traffic: Reconstructing traffic flows from discrete spatio-temporal data. In: Proc. of IEEE Virtual Reality Conference, pp. 183–190 (2009)

6. Fiorini, P., Shiller, Z.: Motion planning in dynamic environments using velocity obstacles. International Journal on Robotics Research 17(7), 760–772 (1998)

7. Gayle, R., Sud, A., Andersen, E., Guy, S., Lin, M., Manocha, D.: Real-time navigation of independent agents using adaptive roadmaps. IEEE Trans. on Visualization and Computer Graphics, 34–38 (January/February 2009)

8. Guy, S., Chhugani, J., Kim, C., Satish, N., Lin, M.C., Manocha, D., Dubey, P.: Clearpath: Highly parallel collision avoidance for multi-agent simulation. In: Proc. of ACM SIGGRAPH/Eurographics Symposium on Computer Animation, pp. 177–187 (2009)

9. Guy, S., Chuggani, J., Curtis, S., Dubey, P., Lin, M., Manocha, D.: Pledestrians: A least-effort approach to crowd simulation. In: Proc. of Eurographics/ACM SIGGRAPH Symposium on Computer Animation (2010)

10. Helbing, D., Molnar, P.: Social force model for pedestrian dynamics. Physical Review E 51, 4282 (1995); Copyright (C) 2008 The American Physical Society; Please report any problems to prola@aps.org

11. Hughes, R.L.: A continuum theory for the flow of pedestrians. Transportation Research Part B: Methodological 36, 507–535 (2002)

12. Jin, X., Xu, J., Wang, C.C.L., Huang, S., Zhang, J.: Interactive control of large crowd navigation in virtual environment using vector field. In: IEEE Computer Graphics and Application (2008)

13. Johansson, A., Helbing, D., Shukla, P.K.: Specification of the social force pedestrian model by evolutionary adjustment to video tracking data. Advances in Complex Systems 4(10), 271–288 (2007)

14. Juang, J.: Minimal energy control on trajectory generation. In: International Conference on Information Intelligence and Systems, p. 204 (1999)

15. Kagarlis, M.: Method and apparatus of simulating movement of an autonomous entity through an environment. United States Patent No. US 7,188,056 (September 2002)

16. Kamphuis, A., Overmars, M.: Finding paths for coherent groups using clearance. In: Proc. of ACM SIGGRAPH / Eurographics Symposium on Computer Animation, pp. 19–28 (2004)

17. Kang, Y., Park, S., Lee, E.: An efficient control over human running animation with extension of planar hopper model. In: Pacific Graphics, pp. 169–176 (1998)

18. Karamouzas, I., Heil, P., van Beek, P., Overmars, M.H.: A Predictive Collision Avoidance Model for Pedestrian Simulation. In: Egges, A., Geraerts, R., Overmars, M. (eds.) MIG 2009. LNCS, vol. 5884, pp. 41–52. Springer, Heidelberg (2009)

19. Latombe, J.C.: Robot Motion Planning. Kluwer Academic Publishers (1991)

20. LaValle, S.M.: Planning Algorithms. Cambridge University Press (2006), http://msl.cs.uiuc.edu/planning/

21. Narain, R., Golas, A., Curtis, S., Lin, M.C.: Aggregate dynamics for dense crowd simulation. In: ACM Transactions on Graphics (Proc. of ACM SIGGRAPH Asia) (2009)

22. Patil, S., van den Berg, J., Curtis, S., Lin, M.C., Manocha, D.: Directing crowd simulations using navigation fields. Technical report, Department of Computer Science, University of North Carolina (May 2009)

23. Pelechano, N., Allbeck, J.M., Badler, N.I.: Controlling individual agents in high-density crowd simulation. In: Proceedings of the 2007 ACM SIGGRAPH/Eurographics Symposium on Computer Animation, pp. 99–108 (2007)

24. Pelechano, N., Allbeck, J.M., Badler, N.I.: Virtual Crowds: Methods, Simulation and Control. Morgan and Claypool Publishers (2008)
25. Pettré, J., Ondřej, J., Olivier, A., Cretual, A., Donikian, S.: Experiment-based modeling, simulation and validation of interactions between virtual walkers. In: Symposium on Computer Animation, pp. 189–198. ACM (2009)
26. Wigan, M.R.: Why should we worry about pedestrians. In: 15th Conference of Australian Institutes of Transport Research, CAITR (1993)
27. Reynolds, C.W.: Flocks, herds and schools: A distributed behavioral model. ACM SIGGRAPH Computer Graphics 21, 25–34 (1987)
28. Reynolds, C.W.: Steering behaviors for autonomous characters. In: Game Developers Conference (1999)
29. Roussel, L., Canudas de Wit, C., Goswami, A.: Generation of energy optimal complete gait cycles for biped robots. IEEE Transactions on Robotics and Automation 16, 2036–2041 (1998)
30. Sarmady, S., Haron, F., Hj, A.Z.: Modeling groups of pedestrians in least effort crowd movements using cellular automata. In: Proc. of 3rd Asia International Conference on Modeling and Simulation, pp. 520–525 (2009)
31. Scovanner, P., Tappen, M.F.: Learning pedestrian dynamics from the realworld. In: ICCV (2009)
32. Shao, W., Terzopoulos, D.: Autonomous pedestrians. In: SCA 2005: Proceedings of the 2005 ACM SIGGRAPH/Eurographics Symposium on Computer Animation, pp. 19–28. ACM Press, New York (2005)
33. Simeon, T., Leroy, S., Laumond, J.: Path coordination for multiple mobile robots: a geometric algorithm. In: Proc. of IJCAI (1999)
34. Snape, J., Manocha, D.: Navigating multiple simple-airplanes in 3d workspace. In: Proceedings of the IEEE International Conference on Robotics and Automation, pp. 3974–3980 (2009)
35. Still, G.: Crowd Dynamics. PhD thesis, University of Warwick, UK (2000)
36. Sud, A., Andersen, E., Curtis, S., Lin, M., Manocha, D.: Real-time path planning for virtual agents in dynamic environments. In: Proc. of IEEE VR, pp. 91–98 (2007)
37. Treuille, A., Cooper, S., Popovic, Z.: Continuum crowds. In: Proc. of ACM SIGGRAPH, pp. 1160–1168 (2006)
38. van den Berg, J., Guy, S.J., Lin, M., Manocha, D.: Reciprocal n-Body Collision Avoidance. In: Pradalier, C., Siegwart, R., Hirzinger, G. (eds.) Robotics Research. STAR, vol. 70, pp. 3–19. Springer, Heidelberg (2011)
39. van den Berg, J., Lin, M.C., Manocha, D.: Reciprocal velocity obstacles for realtime multi-agent navigation. In: Proc. of IEEE Conference on Robotics and Automation, pp. 1928–1935 (2008)
40. van den Berg, J., Patil, S., Seawall, J., Manocha, D., Lin, M.C.: Interactive navigation of individual agents in crowded environments. In: Proc. of ACM Symposium on Interactive 3D Graphics and Games, pp. 139–147 (2008)
41. Warren, C.W.: Multiple path coordination using artificial potential fields. In: Proc. of IEEE Conf. on Robotics and Automation, pp. 500–505 (1990)
42. Yersin, B., Maim, J., Ciechomski, P., Schertenleib, S., Thalmann, D.: Steering a virtual crowd based on a semantically augmented navigation graph. In: VCROWDS (2005)
43. Yu, Q., Terzopoulos, D.: A decision network framework for the behavioral animation of virtual humans. In: Proceedings of the 2007 ACM SIGGRAPH/Eurographics Symposium on Computer Animation, pp. 119–128 (2007)
44. Zipf, G.K.: Human behavior and the principle of least effort. Addison-Wesley Press (1949)

An Information Theoretical Approach to Crowd Simulation

Cagatay Turkay[1], Emre Koc[2], and Selim Balcisoy[3]

[1] Cagatay Turkay, University of Bergen, Bergen Norway
Cagatay.Turkay@ii.uib.no
[2] Emre Koc, Sabanci University, Istanbul Turkey
emrekoc@su.sabanciuniv.edu
[3] Selim Balcisoy, Sabanci University, Istanbul Turkey
balcisoy@sabanciuniv.edu

Abstract. In this study, an information theory based framework to automatically construct analytical maps of crowd's locomotion, called *behavior maps*, is presented. For these behavior maps, two distinct use cases in crowd simulation domain are introduced; i) automatic camera control ii) behavioral modeling.

The first use case for behavior maps is an automatic camera control technique to display interest points which represent either characteristic behavior of the crowd or novel events occurring in the scene.

As the second use case, a behavioral model to control agents' behavior with agent-crowd interaction formulations is introduced. This model can be integrated into a crowd simulator to enhance its behavioral complexity and realism.

1   Introduction

Crowd constitutes a critical component in many virtual environment and entertainment applications. Today it is common to have crowded virtual environments in massive multiplayer online games, crowd simulations and movie pre-visualizations. In order to increase the feeling of presence in a virtual environment, the environment should contain virtual crowds which must be simulated realistically and believably. In this work, we propose methods to solve two distinct issues in crowd simulation domain. First of these issues is the automatic camera control methods and second one is the adaptive behavioral modeling for crowd simulations.

The core element of our methods is a framework which uses information theoretical concepts to automatically construct analytical maps of crowd's locomotion. The framework includes a probabilistic model developed in order to use information theory quantities, and the framework includes structures to produce analytical maps representing crowd's locomotion, which are called *behavior maps*.

Efficient camera control is essential to perform navigation and monitoring tasks in a virtual environment, therefore camera control has always been an interesting problem for the graphics community. A recent survey by Christie and Olivier (2006) provides a comprehensive taxonomy of motivations and methods in camera control. Traditional camera control techniques based on user input, character follow-up or scripts do not provide camera control suitable for complex scenes with hundreds of animated characters. Hence, we need a tool which monitors the entire virtual environment, explores

S. Müller Arisona et al. (Eds.): DUMS, CCIS 242, pp. 236–261, 2012.
© Springer-Verlag Berlin Heidelberg 2012

interest points and toggles the camera between them to improve user experience while exploring a crowded virtual environment. To aid users through navigational tasks in a crowded scene, an automated camera should build a cognitive model on where the user *would like to look at*. Such an automated camera should provide sufficient information and insight about the scene being monitored. Our motivation is to find quantitative measures to determine where a user draws her attention in an animated crowded scene.

In order to improve a virtual environment's realism, crowds must be simulated believable in terms of their appearance and behavior. Recent advances in graphics hardware address the issue of photo-realistic rendering of crowds. However, due to the complex nature of human behavior, realistic behavior of agents in crowd simulations is still a challenging problem. Previous approaches either propose i) global solutions with high level formulations (Treuille et al., 2006) - which can simulate large numbers of agents however not suitable for creating complexity in the crowd or ii) low-level scripted, complex agent-based methods - which are computationally expensive and requiring expertise and effort in the production phase (Musse and Thalmann, 2001). In this study, we are proposing an analytical agent-based behavioral model that integrates global knowledge about crowd formation into local, agent-based behavior control. Principal elements of our behavioral model are;

- Analytical representations of crowd's activities, which are built by using a statistical model based on information theory.
- An agent definition responsive to behavior map values.
- Agent-crowd interaction formulations in order to control agents locally by using analytic crowd representation.

When integrated into an existing crowd simulator, we believe that our model creates a simulation with agents behaving in realistic, variable and complex manners, without the need for low-level scripting.

Our methods and models developed for crowd simulations can be integrated into existing applications which involve virtual crowds and they can provide valuable solutions to enhance virtual environment applications. Our methods can make critical contributions in urban visualizations and urban design tools. In addition, they can be integrated into massive multiplayer games to increase the reality of the environment and to enhance user experience by providing automatic navigation tools.

The rest of the chapter is organized as follows: in Section 2, we review the related literature. In Chapter 3, our crowd analysis framework is explained in detail. Automatic camera control technique based on interest points selected from behavior maps to aid navigation in a large crowded environment are covered in Section 4. In Section 5, we present our behavioral model based on behavior maps for agent-based crowd simulations. Section 6 presents the results obtained from both of the studies. To conclude, final remarks are made at the conclusion section.

2 Related Work

Both of automatic camera control and behavior modeling for crowds fields involve extensive literatures. Therefore, we will review these fields separately.

2.1   Automatic Camera Control

Several aspects of camera control paradigm have been studied in the literature, we will try to review studies in which the expressiveness of the camera is investigated. There have been notable studies in manipulating the camera with respect to different user preferences. Blinn introduced an algebraic approach (Blinn, 1988) to place certain objects at specified locations in the scene. Gleicher and Witkin (1992) proposed *through the lens* camera control, in which the user chooses feature points and their desired locations as seen from the lens of the camera. Due to the difficulty of the problem, there were attempts to put some constraints and perform higher level camera control. *The Virtual Cinematographer* by He et al. (1996) proposed film idioms, each of which decodes cinematographic expertise and responsible for particular scene organizations. They organize these idioms in finite state machines to compose shots and transitions. All of these techniques require expert users or predefined constraints and not suitable for dynamic and crowded scenes.

A different group of researchers are interested in finding measures to evaluate the visual quality of the view and manipulate camera parameters to provide the best available shot (Kamada and Kawai, 1988; Arbel and Ferrie, 1999; Lee et al., 2005). Most of these algorithms focus on viewing a single object and aim to find the best view on a sphere around this object. Although the best view on a sphere is not directly applicable, the idea of finding a good view is relevant to our problem. In some of these studies, information theory based metrics have proven to be successful. The most notable metric in this category is called *viewpoint entropy* proposed by Vázquez et al. (2001) which expresses the amount of information in a selected view. They define their metric as the ratio of the projected area of each surface to the total area of all the surfaces projected to the view sphere. An extension of this work for time varying volumes is done by Ji and Shen (2006). They find best views of a volume data in each frame by enhancing viewpoint entropy measure and do a smooth transition between good views as time evolves. A recent and interesting study by Kwon et al. (2008) determines camera parameters for a single animated character. They proposed *motion area* which is the total area swept by the joints of the character projected onto the view plane. By maximizing this motion area, they achieve to display the motion of a single animated character effectively. One application where the camera is manipulated automatically to capture some events is done by Stoev and Straßer (2002). They developed an automatic camera control mechanism for visualizing historical data where the timing and location of events are pre-defined. They maximize both the projected area and the normalized depth of the scene to select a good view as camera moves between pre-defined locations.

2.2   Behavioral Modeling for Crowds

An overall idea of the challenges and improvements in crowd simulation can be obtained in (Thalmann and Raupp Musse, 2007). There are several behavioral models proposed in the literature and a survey by Kasap and Magnenat-Thalmann (2008) covers most of these studies. There have been many studies on agent-based crowd models to create human-like behaviors. Seminal works of Reynolds used behavioral models considering local rules (Reynolds, 1999) and create emergent flocking (Reynolds, 1987) behaviors. There is considerable work on agent-based crowd simulators incorporating psychological models and sociological factors. Luo et al. (2008) model social group and crowd related behaviors. Their main focus is a layered framework to reflect the natural pattern of human-like decision making process. Rymill and Dodgson (2005) tried to improve the quality of agent behavior by adding theories from psychology. In their work, they tried to produce more realistic collision avoidance responses. Musse and Thalmann (2001) developed virtual human agents with intentions, beliefs, knowledge and perception to create a realistic crowd behavior. Pelechano et al. (2005) assigned psychological roles and communication skills to agents to produce diverse and realistic behaviors. In a more recent work, Pelechano et al. (2007) created an improved model by using psychological and geometrical rules with a social and physical forces model. Hu (2006) proposed an adaptive crowd behavior simulation, where he defines a static behavior context layer. When the behavior context is altered with a predefined event, the new context adaptively inhibits certain behavior in agents. However, this scheme is not suitable for dynamic environments. There are studies which model the virtual environment as maps to guide agents' behaviors. In (Shao and Terzopoulos, 2007), Shao et al. modeled the environment with topological, perception and path maps to generate autonomous agents. Gayle et al. (2009) used adaptive roadmaps, which evolve with the dynamic nature of the environment. In (Sung et al., 2004), Sung et al. assign situations and behaviors directly to environment rather than the agents themselves. The concept of behavior maps have been used in robotics and vision field. Dornhege and Kleiner (2007) defined behavior maps as encoding context information of the environment, and use these maps to autonomously navigate a robot on rough terrain. Berclaz et al. (2008) used behavior maps to encode probabilities of moving in a certain direction on a specified location and used these maps to track trajectories of people and to detect anomalies in people's behaviors. In their study, they used expectation maximization algorithms to detect anomalies.

We integrated theories from behavioral modeling and borrowed ideas from studies representing the environment with guidance maps. To compute these maps, we employed quantities from information theory. Information theory have been introduced into computer graphics field by Feixas et al. (1999) which proposes a framework to measure scene complexity by using information theory quantities. In a recent study, Turkay et al. (2009a) used information theory based formulations to automatically control the virtual camera in a crowded environment. In (Turkay et al., 2009b), they extended their information theory based model to control how agents behave in a crowd simulation. We improve the behavioral model proposed in (Turkay et al., 2009b) and develop concrete formulations and methods to use this behavioral model to extend any crowd simulator's variability and realism.

3   Information Theory Based Crowd Analysis

In this section we will introduce the information theory framework which constitutes the core of our automatic camera control and behavioral modeling methods. We will begin by introducing the information theory quantities we have utilized in this framework, we will continue with proposing the probabilistic model developed in order to use information theory quantities, and finally, we will explain how the proposed structures are used to produce analytical maps representing crowd's activities, which are called *behavior maps*. Information theory framework can be seen in Fig. 1.

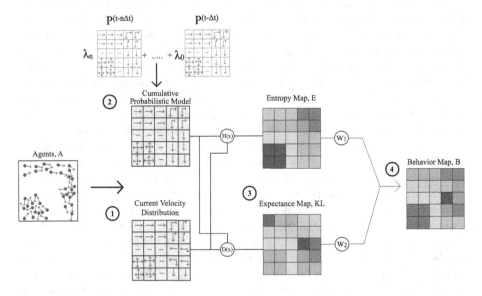

Fig. 1. Behavior map construction. 1) Current distribution of crowd locomotion 2) Older distributions are merged with a temporal filter 3) *Entropy* and *expectance maps* are calculated 4) Behavior map is constructed with convex combination using user-defined weights

3.1 Information Theory Quantities

Information theory deals with quantification of information. It has been used in a wide range of areas such as computer science, physics, biology and natural language processing. The key measure in information theory, *information entropy*, which defines our current understanding of information, is proposed by Shannon (Shannon, 1948). Let X be discrete random variable which takes values from set χ with probability distribution $p(x) = Pr[X = x], x \in \chi$. Entropy, $H(x)$ of random variable X can be defined by:

$$H(x) = -\sum_{x \in \chi} p(x) \log p(x) \tag{1}$$

Entropy is a measure of uncertainty of a random variable. It provides us with an insight about how likely a system produces diverse outcomes. Namely, a system with low entropy tends to yield same outcomes in successive tries.

Another critical concept for our measurements is $Kullback - Leibler\ divergence$ (KL) (Kullback, 1997). Take two probability mass functions (*pmf*) $p(x)$ and $q(x)$, divergence between *pmf*'s $p(x)$ and $q(x)$ is given by:

$$D(p\|q) = -\sum_{x \in \chi} p(x) \log \frac{p(x)}{q(x)} \tag{2}$$

which is a non-symmetric metric expressing the difference between two probability distributions. Given the *true distribution* $p(x)$ of data, KL measures the loss of information if we use $q(x)$ instead of $p(x)$ while coding a sample. For further reading on information theory, please refer to (Cover and Thomas, 1991).

3.2 Probabilistic Model

Let $A = \{a_1, a_2, ..., a_n\}$ be the set of agents present in a simulation, where a_i represents a single agent. Physical properties of an agent can be described as $a_i = \{u, v : u, v \in \mathbb{R}^2\}$ where u defines the position and v defines the velocity of agent a_i. All the agents' movements are projected onto the same plane and the calculations are done on a 2D map, so both of these vectors are in $\mathbb{R}^2$. We classify the activity of an agent by: the location the agent is on, the direction of the agent's movement and the speed the agent is moving with. Different *pmf* structures are used to capture these characteristics. *Pmf*'s for direction and speed values and how this values are mapped into the corresponding *pmf*'s are explained below ;

- $P_{\hat{x}}(x) = \Pr(X = x), x \in \{0, 1, .., n\}$
  Values of random variable X in this *pmf* is found by quantizing the normalized velocity vector $\hat{v}$ (belonging to an agent a) into one of n categories. $\hat{v}$ is categorized by function;

$$q_1(v) = \{\lfloor \hat{v} \angle \langle 1, 0 \rangle / (2\pi/n) \rfloor : n \in \mathbb{N}, 0 < n \leq 2\pi\} \tag{3}$$

  which finds the angle between $\hat{v}$ and $\langle 1, 0 \rangle$ in a 2D Cartesian coordinate system and finding which interval this angle is in. The value of n effects the quantization resolution.

- $P_{\|x\|}(x) = \Pr(X = x), x \in \{0, 1, .., n\}$
  Assuming that $\| v \|$ is in the range $[a, b]$, i.e. the agents move with a speed in $[a, b]$, function

$$q_2(v) = \begin{cases} 0 \text{ if } \| v \| < a \\ \lfloor \| v \| / m \rfloor \text{ if } a \leq \| v \| < b \\ n \text{ if } b \leq \| v \| \end{cases} \tag{4}$$

  calculates which value will the random variable X will take depending on the magnitude of velocity vector. The n value in the above definition is dependent on the values of a, b and m. If the range $[a, b]$ is large, n can be made lower by quantizing this range with m.

The above *pmf*s are illustrated in Fig. 2. We merge these two *pmf*s into a single *pmf*, P_v, with a user defined constant α, which distributes importance to direction or speed distributions, as:

$$P_v = \alpha P_{\hat{v}} + (1 - \alpha) P_{\|v\|} \tag{5}$$

This combination provides the user with a degree of flexibility to choose which of these distributions to put emphasis on. As P_v is taking samples over a period of time, a Gaussian shaped filter is applied to control the importance given to temporally cumulated

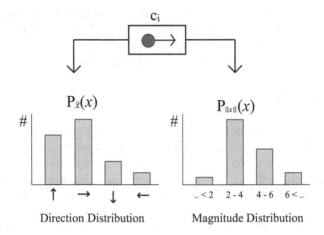

Fig. 2. Two types of *pmfs* used in our model. Notice that $n = 4$ for both of the distributions.

distributions. Let t_1 and t_2 be two time steps where $t_2 - t_1 = n\Delta t$ and $n \in \mathbb{N}^*$, temporal filter is applied as;

$$P_v^{t_1 \to t_2} = \lambda_0 P_v^{t_2} + \lambda_1 P_v^{t_2 - \Delta t} + \ldots + \lambda_n P_v^{t_2 - n\Delta t} \tag{6}$$

$$\lambda_n = \frac{1}{\sigma\sqrt{2\pi}} e^{\frac{-(n-\mu)^2}{\sigma^2}}, \; \mu = 0 \tag{7}$$

where, n is defined as *historical depth* defining the maximum *age* to consider, while *age* meaning the time passed from the moment the distribution have occurred. Δt defines the time interval between two adjacent frames. The λ constants are aging coefficients and they are calculated by using Gaussian distribution function (7) with $\mu = 0$. These values can be interpreted as a Gaussian filter applied in temporal domain. By changing the variance of the distribution function (i.e. by changing σ^2), importance given to older distributions are manipulated. Choosing a lower variance gives less importance to older distribution, making the model highly adaptable to current changes but leaving it more prune to noise. On the other hand, a higher variance creates a model that slowly evolves over time; i.e. only large changes have effect on the model immediately.

Having this temporal probabilistic model in hand, we need to extend our model to cover the spatial characteristics of activities. To accomplish this, a 2D grid G is placed on the scene. G contains w rows and h columns, where each cell is a square with side length l. The grid is adjusted to cover all the extent of the scene, so that every activity on the scene takes place inside this sampling grid. We combine the temporal model we have developed with this grid to end-up with a 2D map carrying temporal dimension. We define the state of the grid G at time t as,

$$G^t = \{g_{i,j}^t \; ; \; 0 \le i < w, \; 0 \le j < h\}$$
$$g_{i,j}^t = \{(P_v^{(t-n\Delta t) \to (t-\Delta t)})_{i,j}, \; (P_v^t)_{i,j},\} \tag{8}$$

Every cell, $g_{i,j}^t$ in grid G contains two *pmfs*; one extending back n time steps from time $t - 1$, and the other characterizing the distribution at time t. With this definition, we categorize activities depending on their spatial characteristics. The spatial catego-rization process works by assigning the agent to the corresponding $g_{i,j}$. This spatial categorization finalizes our probabilistic model which takes both the spatial and tem-poral properties of activities into consideration. At each time step, each agent, a_i is assigned to a cell in grid G and agent's v_{vel} is transformed by q_1, q_2 given in (3) and (4), to be included as samples in probability distributions associated with $g_{i,j}$.

3.3   Behavior Maps

Behavior maps are analytical representations of crowd's activities which span over the whole virtual environment and monitor agents' locomotion during the simulation. A behavior map, B, is a 2D grid, consisting of w rows and h columns, where each cell is associated with the corresponding cell in G to access to the *pmf*s in this cell.

The information theory quantities, probability distribution functions and the tempo-ral filter mechanism are utilized to construct the behavior map components, we called as *entropy* and *expectance map*. A behavior map is constructed as a convex combination of these two information theory based maps. In (Turkay et al., 2009a), these maps have proven to represent the temporal and spatial dynamics of crowd's locomotion.

Entropy Map. Entropy measures the uncertainty of a random variable. If locomotion of an agent is considered as a random variable, entropy values represent the magni-tude of predictability of crowd's movements. Entropy values denote whether agents move independently or in a group. Locations with smaller entropy values denote where agents move with similar velocities. Conversely, locations with higher entropy values represent disorder in agents' locomotion. To build an entropy map, E, we begin by con-sidering a random variable, $X_{i,j}$ (i,j indicating location on E), drawn according to *pmf* $(P_v^{(t-n\Delta t)\to t})_{i,j}$. Then, E can be defined as

$$E^t = \{H(X_{i,j}) \ : \ 0 \le i < w, \ 0 \le j < h\} \qquad (9)$$

where $H(X_{i,j})$ is the entropy of $X_{i,j}$ as defined in (1). Fig. 3 illustrates how agents' locomotion determine entropy map values. Notice that entropy values are lower in zones where crowd has similar locomotion.

Expectance Map. Probability distribution of crowd's activities defines the characteris-tics of locomotion that are likely to occur at specific locations. We define the distribution of crowd's locomotion from time $(t - n\Delta t)$ to $(t - \Delta t)$ by *pmf* $P_v^{(t-n\Delta t)\to(t-\Delta t)}$ in-troduced in (6) and the current distribution of crowd's locomotion at time t by P_v^t. We use these two *pmf*s in (2) to calculate KL divergence values. These values constitute the second type of behavior map called *expectance map*. Expectance map KL is defined as

$$KL^t = \{(D(P_v^{(t-n\Delta t)\to(t-\Delta t)}\|P_v^t))_{i,j} \ : \ 0 \le i < w, \ 0 \le j < h\} \qquad (10)$$

KL values indicate the difference between the current distribution and the cumulative distribution of crowd's locomotion. Use of KL divergence values to indicate *surprise* is proposed in (Itti and Baldi, 2005), where they use KL divergence values to discover

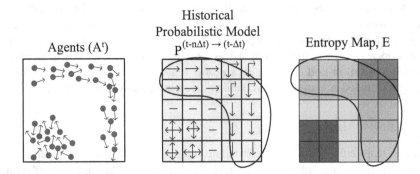

Fig. 3. Crowd's movement and corresponding entropy map values. Selected zone indicates lower entropy values.

surprising events in video. They employed a principled approach to prove that KL is a powerful measure to represent *surprise*. We use KL values to indicate unexpected, surprising crowd formations. In an expectance map, cells with high KL values denote *surprising* activities taking place at those locations. At cells with lower KL values the state of the crowd remain as *expected*. Figure 4 displays that expectance values are high at locations where the current distribution is not "similar" to historical distribution.

Both of these maps address different aspects in the locomotion of crowd and each map has certain effects on agent's behavior. Therefore, a behavior map, B, is the convex combination of the values of *entropy* and *expectance* maps. This map can be formulated by;

$$B^t = \{w_1 e^t_{i,j} + w_2 k l^t_{i,j} : 0 \leq w_n < 1, w_1 + w_2 = 1, 0 \leq i < w, 0 \leq j < h\}, \quad (11)$$

where each w_i represents user-defined weight values to determine the contribution of each map. These user-defined weights provides a mechanism to control how a behavior map is constructed according to the simulation scenario.

4   Automatic Camera Control

In this study, we propose a novel automated camera control technique for large and crowded virtual environments on top of the scene analysis framework introduced in Section 3. This framework can be included into game engines or any virtual environment system to automatically aid camera control by using the behavior maps we have developed. These behavior maps give us quantitative answers to questions *"What are the characteristic behaviors of the crowd?"* and *"Where are the novel events happening in the scene?"*. Utilizing the calculated *entropy map*, camera makes a tour over zones which display characteristic behaviors of the crowd. And, in case of a novel event, by analyzing the *expectance map* camera moves to the location of this novel event and capture the moment of surprise.

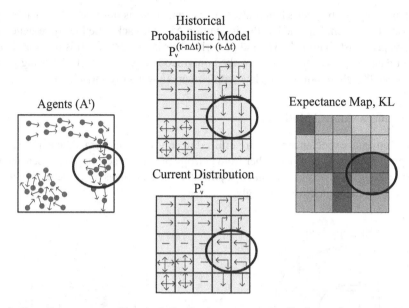

Fig. 4. Crowd's movement, historical distribution, current distribution and corresponding expectance map values. Selected zone indicates unexpected event, where there is high KL values.

4.1 Conceptual Foundations

The notion of *interest points* is very suitable for our camera control problem. We borrow the idea of interest point from computer vision domain. It is briefly "..any point in the image for which the signal changes two dimensionally." (Schmid et al., 2000). Our understanding of an interest point in this work have to be more extensive than this definition. Unlike a static image, a scene full of dynamic objects; or specifically, characters as in crowd simulation, carries both spatial and temporal characteristics. To define interest points in such a multi-dimensional domain, more comprehensive terms come into play, namely; *saliency, novelty* and *surprise*.

Saliency and novelty are essential terms to understand how we perceive information and guide our attention while we are viewing visual images. A salient feature can be briefly described as a spatial point standing out to be "different" then its surrounding (Wolfe, 1998). Salient features have been shown to attract human attention by studies in neurophysiology and vision (Itti et al., 1998). In other words, a salient point can be interpreted as, *where you would like to look at* in a visual image. But saliency alone is not adequate to answer this question on a temporally dynamic scene. Novelty complements saliency in temporal dimension and defines an event which have never occurred or occurs seldom as *novel* (Singh and Markou, 2004). Novelty detection works as follows: a model of the system is formed as a basis by examining the behavior of the system over time. Having this base model in hand, current status of the system is evaluated and examined if any novel event is existent. Novelty detection can be interpreted as detecting salient features on temporal domain. Itti et.al combine these two complementary terms and come up with the notion of *surprise* (Itti and Baldi, 2005). They define surprise as the change in the observer's belief after the current status is observed. To calculate the surprise of a system modeled with distribution M, Kullback - Leibler divergence (2) between prior distribution $P(M)$ and posterior distribution $P(M|D)$ is measured after current data D is presented. They worked on video images to detect surprising points and proved that these points correlate with human viewer's eye movements.

4.2 Camera Control Methods

The entropy and expectance maps are utilized to control the camera. At each time step, an interest point is determined either from entropy or expectance map is chosen and the camera is toggled to display this interest point. Figure 5 displays how interest points are selected to update camera accordingly.

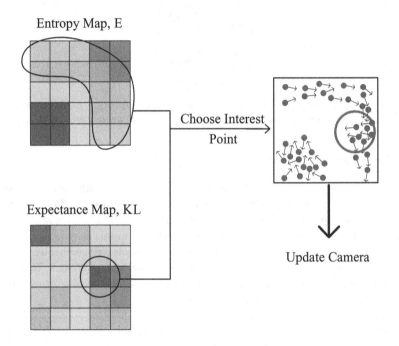

Fig. 5. Interest point selection for camera control

Capturing unexpected events: In the first phase of the algorithm, τ_{kl}^t threshold value which is an adaptive threshold, is calculated. It is found by storing n last kl_{max} values, where n is the *historical depth* value we have mentioned before. Let μ_{kl}^t be the mean of these kl_{max} values, and σ_{kl}^t be the standard deviation, τ_{kl}^t is calculated by $\tau_{kl}^t = \mu_{kl}^t - \sigma_{kl}^t$. The maximum expectance value, kl_{max} is selected and compared with τ_{kl}^t. If the selected value is larger than this threshold, it is marked as an interest point, which can be interpreted as a *salient* location where there is a *novel* event.

Displaying characteristic behaviors of crowd: If there is no kl value marked as an *interest point*, attention can be drawn to locations where the characters moves more *together*, i.e. cells with lower entropy values. Under these conditions, camera makes a tour over low entropy zones, until some *novel* event occurs. To have a continuous tour over low entropy points, our method keeps track of the already visited points. At the beginning of the entropy tour, cell with the lowest entropy value is chosen and in each step of the entropy tour, camera starts to search unvisited zones in its neighborhood beginning with the direction of crowd movement. And entropy values are checked against the adaptive threshold value τ_e^t, which is also an adaptive threshold, calculated the same way as μ_{kl}^t, using $e_{i,j}$ values. Visited nodes are kept in a stack, in order to not to visit same zones again. Whenever a point from expectance map is chosen, the visited node stack is cleared to make camera ready for a new tour.

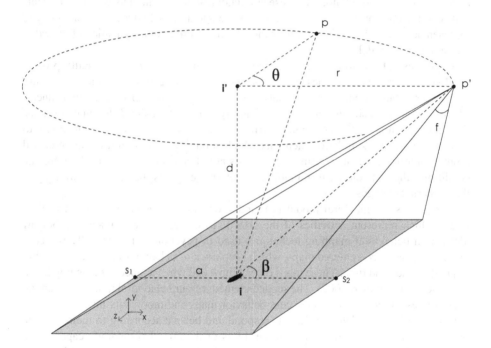

Fig. 6. Given a fixed field of view f and viewing angle β, the camera should be placed appropriately to cover a square zone with sides $2a$ targeted at point i. First p' is recovered by finding d and r geometrically. Final position p is found by incorporating pre-calculated θ angle.

Camera placement: After one point of interest is computed, a good view to this point have to be calculated. We use a three-parameter camera model which represents the camera with its position p, aim direction l and up-vector u where $p, l, u \in \mathbb{R}^3$. The camera placement problem is shown in Fig. 6. After p' is found , θ angle is calculated to make the camera look in the direction which is found to be most frequent direction of crowd movement in the underlying grid. Final position of the camera p is computed by rotating p' with θ degrees on the calculated circle. The second parameter of our camera, l, is determined by using i and P. Finally, camera's up vector, u, is adjusted properly that the camera never turns upside down through its interpolation. Using l and the current aim vector of the camera a quaternion q is built to interpolate the camera rotation using SLERP, proposed by Shoemake in (Shoemake, 1985). While the camera is rotating, it moves from its current position to the calculated position p following a quadratic Bezier curve for smooth translation.

5   Behavioral Model for Crowd Simulations

Interactions with a crowd are important psychological factors which determine how humans behave (Bell, 2001), however "agent-crowd" interactions are not considered by agent-based crowd simulators. In these simulators, an agent interacts with other agents and with the environment. In order to formulate agent-crowd interactions, an analytic representation which displays both of the spatial and temporal dynamics of crowd is required in our model.

Agent-based behavioral models use rule sets to mimic certain personality properties like aggressiveness, shyness etc. As stated in (Shoda, 2007), personality structure can be static but its behavioral output changes greatly under specific circumstances. Therefore, an agent should reflect its personality differently under different conditions. Such a representation should contain intrinsic properties that are altered in response to dynamic and static simulation elements which should also contain a dynamic crowd representation. As agents' intrinsic properties are altered in response to the dynamic conditions, there should be formulations to determine agents' behavior accordingly to these internal changes.

Our proposed behavioral model is founded on *behavior maps* introduced in Section 3 which represent activities of the crowd. To utilize behavior maps, we borrow ideas from behavioral mapping techniques used in psychology research. These techniques involve place-centered maps, which keep track of behavior of individuals within a specific space and time. These maps display how and when a place is being populated (Sommer and Sommer, 2002). The second element of our behavioral model is a generic agent representation which can access behavior maps and modify its intrinsic properties. We finally formulate how agents respond and behave according to their intrinsic properties and behavior maps within the limits of the crowd simulator's capabilities. Consequently, we achieve agents behaving adaptive to current simulation conditions.

Beneath all this high level structure, we utilize a multi-agent navigation system to solve agent-agent and agent-environment interactions through collision detection and path planning algorithms. Our model can extend any existing agent-based crowd simulator.

Our model provides global knowledge on crowd's activities and enables the crowd simulator to incorporate agent-crowd interactions to modify agents' behavior. Behavior maps constitute the foundation of our model. They record and analytically represent crowd's activities. Second element of our model is a generic agent representation to access behavior maps. The final element in our model is a set of formulations to link the underlying crowd simulator with behavior maps. We customize the agent representation to fit into the current crowd simulator's features before developing these formulations.

Prior to performing tests and using our model in crowd simulation scenarios, we define certain analogies between analytical maps, agent representation and agent-crowd interaction formulations. Figure 7 illustrates the overall structure of our model.

5.1 Agent Representation

Agent based crowd simulators have access to several motion engines and animation sets which define behavioral output types. These types can range from basic behaviors like changing direction, to complex behaviors like spreading shoulders to clear its path. The feature set of the crowd simulator and the underlying agent model define the complexity of agent behavior. In our behavioral model, we need a generic agent representation to fit into any type of agent based crowd engine. Our agent representation includes two properties, i) *behavior state* which enables interaction between agents and behavior maps and ii) *behavior constants* to determine agents' behaviors in combination with behavior state.

Behavior state, β, is the behavior map cell value assigned to an agent. Agents on the same cell of the map share the same behavior state. As behavior map values are altered temporally and spatially, these values are used in agent-crowd interaction formulations to adaptively control agents' behavior. Behavior constants, f, are agent specific values which are evaluated as personality attributes. Each feature of an agent which we want to control adaptively is paired with a behavior constant. By assigning an f value, behavioral complexity of an agent is extended and by varying f values, responses of agents to behavior map values are varied. Behavior constants can be regarded as a mechanism to create complexity and variation in crowd. To wrap up these concepts with an example, assume a crowd simulator where agents have the feature of sweating, which we denote as p_0. In our representation, a behavior constant, f_0, defines how easy an agent sweats. And β values adaptively control when and where an agent will sweat. The agent representation is extended to include these properties, in addition to physical properties, which are position, u, and velocity, v:

$$a_i = \{u, v, \beta, \langle f_0, p_0 \rangle, .., \langle f_n, p_n \rangle : \beta, f_n \in [0, 1] \forall\, n\} \tag{12}$$

p_n is a symbolic representation to indicate a feature associated with a_i. A single $\langle f_n, p_n \rangle$ pair represents p_n is controlled by f_n. Notice that for each $\langle f_n, p_n \rangle$ pair, a formulation should be developed to define how β and f_n values control p_n.

5.2 Extending a Crowd Simulator

Any crowd simulator can be extended with our behavioral model. Our model introduces agent-crowd interactions into agent based crowd simulators. In order to integrate our model, we first need to customize the agent definition given in (12) according to the capabilities of the crowd simulator. This representation is then accompanied with formulations to define how agents handle behavior map values.

In this study, we use Reciprocal Velocity Obstacles (RVO) multi-agent navigation system introduced in (van den Berg et al., 2008). We extended this system by implementing *composite agents* proposed in (Hengchin et al., 2008). A composite agent, a_i,

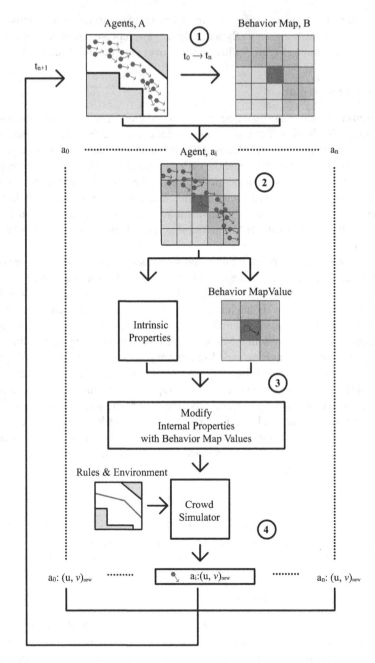

Fig. 7. Overall structure of the behavioral model. 1) Behavior map is constructed 2) Agents are assigned a specific cell value 3) Agent's intrinsic properties are modified with behavior map value 4) Agents' locomotion is determined by simulator

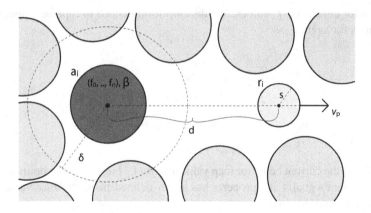

Fig. 8. A composite agent a_i, its associated proxy agent r_i and certain features of agent representation

is a special agent equipped with a proxy agent, r_i, to model a number of emergent behaviors realistically. A proxy agent is a virtual agent, which is visible to all agents in the simulation except its parent a_i. r_i moves according to a_i's preferences. For example, if a_i wants to move in a certain direction, r_i is placed in that direction to clear a_i's path. With this mechanism a_i can display particular behaviors. The features, p_n, of the underlying simulation system (i.e. RVO) can be listed as;

- d : Distance between proxy agent's position, $r_i[u]$, and a_i's position u. The longer the distance, the further a_i can proceed with less collisions.
- s : Radius of the circular area r_i occupies. The larger the area, the easier a_i can move.
- v_p: This is the *preferred velocity* of an agent a_i. It is the optimal velocity that would bring the agent to its goal. We modify v_p's direction with a normalized velocity vector, v_b, which is calculated with respect to behavior map values. v_b is calculated as a vector leading to lower value zones found as a result of a local search.
- m : Indicates agent speed.
- δ : Indicates safety factor which is the range considered by an agent while calculating possible future collisions. With a high safety factor, an agent considers a higher number of possible collisions and behaves more careful to make less collisions.

The agent representation proposed in (12) is customized with respect to the features of the underlying simulator:

$$a_i = \{type, u, \boldsymbol{v}, r_i, \beta, \langle f_0, d \rangle, \langle f_1, s \rangle, \langle f_2, \boldsymbol{v}_p \rangle,$$
$$\langle f_3, m \rangle, \langle f_4, \delta \rangle : \boldsymbol{v}_p \in \mathbb{R}^2; f_n, \beta, d, s \in \mathbb{R}\} \tag{13}$$

where *type* indicates whether the agent is a composite or proxy agent. Each f value with their associated feature is given as pairs. Definition of customized agent is illustrated in Fig. 8. The next step is developing the formulations to include behavior state, β, and behavior constants, f, values. We develop formulations to represent agent-crowd interactions for agent a_i as:

$$\beta = B_{i,j}$$
$$d = \sqrt{f_0\beta}\, d_{max} + d_{min}$$
$$s = \sqrt{f_1\beta}\, s_{max} + s_{min} \tag{14}$$
$$v_p = (v_p^o + \widehat{\sqrt{f_2\beta}\, v_b})(\sqrt{f_3\beta}\, m_{max} + m_{min})$$
$$\delta = \sqrt{f_4\beta}\, \delta_{max} + \delta_{min}$$

where $B_{i,j}$ is the current behavior map value at cell $\{i,j\}$ and v_p^o is the optimal velocity leading to agent's goal. Each property has a user-defined min and max value to keep the values in a certain range.

5.3   Analogies for Extending a Crowd Simulator

We define analogies between the interpretations of analytical maps with f values in order to produce realistic crowd simulations. We interpret the analytical maps of our model as seen in Table 1.

Table 1. Analytical maps and their interpretation

Analytical Map	Behavioral Interpretation
Entropy	Predictability
Expectance	Surprise

In the test environment, agents can have aggressiveness and/or carefulness properties. To create certain agents which are aggressive and careful, we relate features of agents and formulations with f and β values. In Table 2, these behavior types with their related features and f values are listed.

The interpretations of behavior maps are used to define how agents respond to them. In areas with high entropy, where agents' locomotions are diverse, agents become more careful to avoid collisions, and they become more aggressive to get through these regions as quickly as possible. As the expectance map indicates the level of *surprise* in a specific location, aggressive agents do not panic and behave more goal-oriented by preserving their optimal velocity, v_p^o, and enlarge s, d and m values in order to display their aggressiveness. On the other hand, high KL values make an agent less careful. Notice that, while carefulness is proportional to entropy values, it is inversely proportional to expectance values.

Figure 9 illustrates how agents respond to expectance map ($w_1 = 0; w_2 = 1$ in (11)) at micro level. In this figure, a_1 is an aggressive agent and a_2 is a calm agent. In time interval t_1, a_1 and a_2 behave identical. In t_2, they enter a high KL zone. a_1 responds by enlarging s and d values to keep its v_p as close as possible to optimal. However, a_2 mimics a panicking behavior and behaves in an unexpected manner. At t_3, agents return to their initial state. Notice that at the end of t_3, a_1 proceeds further.

Table 2. Behavior types, related features and f values associated with these features

Behavior Type	Feature	f
Carefulness	δ	f_4
Aggressiveness	d, s, v_p, m	f_0, f_1, f_2, f_3

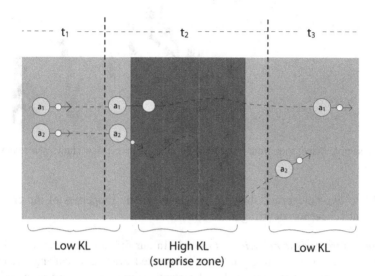

Fig. 9. Responses of agents to expectance map

6   Results

We run a number of tests to demonstrate our model's performance on a system with Intel QuadCore 2.8 GHz and Nvidia GeForce GTX-280. We run two different sets of tests for evaluating the performance of automatic camera control and behavioral model for crowd simulations. We begin with the tests for automatic camera control, followed by the set of tests to evaluate our behavioral modeling system. We implemented two different rendering platforms to visualize our results. One platform works on OpenGL with simple models and environment to provide easily observable results. The other platform works on DirectX and it provides a virtual environment with detailed models and a complex environment. This module enables us to evaluate our methods in a state of the art crowd rendering system.

6.1   Tests for Automatic Camera Control

We tested the effectiveness of the developed automatic camera control techniques on a number of different scenarios. We implemented a real-time crowd simulation environment using a modified version of OpenSteer library (Reynolds, 2004). Our tests are

Fig. 10. A sample screenshot from our test environment. Screenshot shows selected viewing angle.

grouped into two categories; showing the characteristic properties of the crowd and displaying novel events occurring in the simulation.

Displaying characteristic behaviors of crowd: In our first test scenario, crowd movement forms patterns over time while no unexpected event is occurring. Hence, expectance map contains low values below the adaptive threshold and our method chooses interest points among low values from the entropy map. Storing visited zones in a stack enables the camera to make a complete tour over the low entropy zones. It is seen in Fig. 11-(1) that camera follows a path over low entropy zones which corresponds to locations where the crowd moves in an apparent pattern. The thresholding mechanism prevents the camera from considering vague patterns in the scene, thus visits to false positive zones are avoided.

Table 3. Expectance map values of a cell where a scripted unexpected event occurs at t_1. Value of σ^2 modifies temporal filter.

	t_1	t_2	t_3
$\sigma^2 = 0,1$	0,292	0,046	0,021
$\sigma^2 = 1,0$	0,314	0,164	0,06
$\sigma^2 = 5,0$	0,306	0,245	0,167

Capturing unexpected events: As it can be seen in Fig. 11-(2), whenever there is a high value in expectance map, camera moves to that location immediately and retains its position until a new unexpected event occurs or the current interest point loses its importance over time. The duration, attention span, for the same event to remain interesting (to illustrate, duration between t_7–t_8 in Fig. 11) is dependent on the temporal

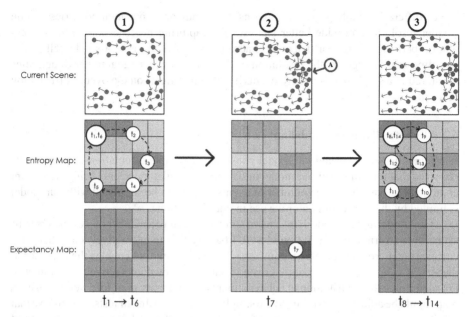

Fig. 11. Example of moving camera with accompanying analysis maps from time t_1 to t_{14}. The circles represent visited points at the indicated time steps. 1) There is no unexpected event. Camera makes a tour over low entropy zones and after all the low entropy zones are visited, restarts the tour. This tour displays characteristic behaviors of the crowd. 2) At time t_7 number of characters enter the scene from point A and this is interpreted as an unexpected event and the camera immediately goes to the location of the event. 3) Between time steps t_7 and t_8 characters keep entering from A and this activity becomes a pattern in the scene, so the point is not interpreted as a surprising event anymore. The camera continues its tour over low entropy zones with an updated entropy map.

filter parameters we are applying in our model. If we set the temporal filter to give higher importance to past distributions, the attention span is longer as the unexpected event effects the underlying model slowly. In Table 3 we investigate KL values of the same interest point over a period of time for different σ^2 values of the temporal filter. Higher variance values creates a filter which also takes older distributions into account. The results show that with increasing variance, the corresponding KL values decrease more slowly. The variance of the temporal filter can be modified to suit the needs of the application. Figure 11-(3) displays how the camera behaves after an unexpected event vanishes. As the stack for visited nodes is cleared at this instant, camera moves to the location with lowest entropy value to start a new tour.

Camera placement: To view the computed point properly, camera is placed to cover the entire area of interest. The direction of most dominant crowd motion at the inspected location is chosen as the view angle. In Fig. 10, the selected viewing setting can be observed. The camera looks in the direction of character movement to give more insight about how the crowd behaves. This view selection mechanism can be accompanied with other metrics which can be user defined entities based on cinematographic concepts.

For different sampling grid resolutions, the behavior of our method varies. While smaller resolutions provide better analyses for capturing micro events, a higher resolution performs better for detecting macro events. If the size of a single cell of the sampling grid is large i.e. the resolution of the grid is low, a large number of activities are stored in a single cell, so micro events have minor effects on the overall distribution of a cell.

6.2   Tests for Behavior Modeling

Formulations in our behavioral model constitute of simple calculations, therefore we observed that integration of our model into a crowd simulator does not bring significant computational overload. The number of agents which can be simulated with our model is limited by the crowd simulator we use in our simulations.

Our model and the underlying crowd simulator require a number of parameters to be set before performing a test. We build a GUI-based editor to interactively enter behavior constants and crowd simulator parameters. This authoring tool enables the designer to disperse f values over the agents to create variation in crowd interactively. w_n values in (11) determine the contribution of behavior map's components, therefore weights of each map should be adjusted according to the simulation scenario. In our tests, we observe that equal w_n ($w_1 = 0.5; w_2 = 0.5$) values for each map performed successfully in most of the scenarios. A screenshot from our test environment can be seen in Fig. 12.

Fig. 12. Screenshot from the test environment, red diamonds indicate aggressive agents

Test - 1. We perform a test to prove the validity of our approach by a comparison with a real world scenario. We used room evacuation videos and data produced in Research Center Jülich, Germany and made available in (Ped-Net, 2009). These videos measure the flow of 60 students while evacuating a room with a variable exit width. We measure the flow of our agents with the formula $J = \Delta N/\Delta t$, where N is the number of agents and Δt is calculated as the difference between the evacuation times of the first and the last agent. As the video incorporates students evacuating the room calmly, we set low aggressiveness to our agents. We observe that our results are consistent with the real world case (Fig. 13). We made further studies with this scenario setting and instead of adding calm agents, we add aggressive agents into the room. Agents are competing more to get out quickly in this case, as a result clogging occurred through the exit (Fig. 13).

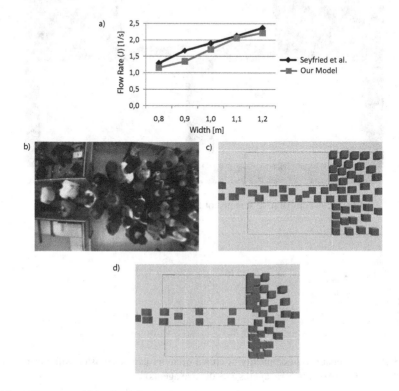

Fig. 13. a) Flow vs. width of exit b) Real-world scenario c) Our test environment with less aggressive agents d) Clogging occurs when agents are more aggressive.

Test - 2. We made comparison tests with two agent-based crowd simulators. The first one is the flocking model developed by Reynolds (Reynolds, 2004) and the second is the RVO library (van den Berg et al., 2008), which we also used as the underlying navigation library in this paper. These comparative tests incorporate a scenario where four groups of agents walk through at a piazza. Throughout these test, we create a crowd with varied f values in our crowd simulator and this creates diversity in crowd's behaviors. In other models, agents do not respond to the dynamics of the crowd and behave identically; the result of this test is illustrated in Fig. 14.

Test - 3. We run the same scenario from Test - 2 incorporating a crowd consisting of i) only calm (not aggressive) agents ii) 10% aggressive agents and iii) agents with various f values. Figure 15 displays the results of these tests. We see that only by varying the

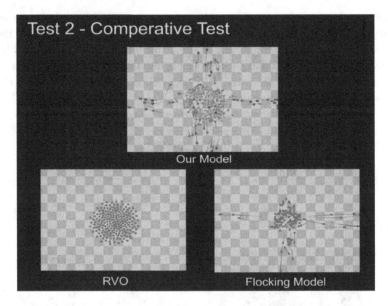

Fig. 14. A comparative screenshot for RVO, Reynolds and our model

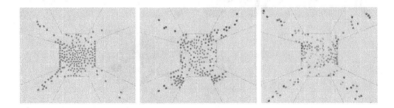

Fig. 15. Agent diversity and complexity of crowd behavior can be adjusted with our model (left to right: uniform, 20% calm 80% aggressive, diverse agents)

dispersion of f values, our model is capable of creating diverse and realistic results without requiring any additional scripting or editing effort.

Test - 4. We adopt a scenario where two groups of agents move towards each other. This scenario highlights the function of entropy maps ($w_1 = 1$; $w_2 = 0$ in (11)). Before these groups meet, they do not display aggressive behavior as they produce a behavior map zone with low entropies. However, when these groups meet, there is a high level of disorder and entropy values increase. This variance in crowd formation adaptively modifies agents' responses and they start behaving aggressive.

7   Conclusion

In this study, we proposed an automatic camera control approach and an adaptive behavioral modeling method for crowd simulations. As the core of these solutions, we developed a set of analytical maps, called behavior maps, which are produced by monitoring and analyzing the locomotion of agents in a virtual crowd. In order to build these maps, we first developed a probabilistic model to handle agent's locomotion as a random variable and use this random variable to construct analysis maps which keeps track of the crowd temporally and spatially. This probabilistic model is then utilized in the calculations based on information theory quantities namely, information entropy and Kullback - Leibler Divergence. As a result of these calculations, a set of behavior maps are constructed. These maps were then utilized in our methods for automatic camera control and behavioral modeling for crowd simulations.

As the first part of our studies, we have presented a novel automatic camera control technique for crowded scenes which monitors the entire scene and improves user experience. Our automatic camera control approach provides user two different tools: i) A tour over the crowded scene in which the characteristic behaviors of the crowd are displayed. ii) Monitoring of activities in the scene and capturing a location at the moment a novel event occurs. We tested our method in a crowd simulation environment to evaluate its performance under different scenarios.

Our method can easily be integrated into existent camera control modules in computer games, crowd simulations and movie pre-visualization applications. It provides some parameters like the resolution of the grid and the span of the temporal filter; which can be modified to adapt to the needs of the application into which our method is integrated. As a future work, we will integrate certain cinematographic constraints into our automatic camera control approach to create a camera providing more visually pleasing results. However, due to their subjectiveness, cinematographic constraints are harder to model analytically.

As the second phase of our studies, we presented a novel analytical behavioral model which automatically builds behavior maps to control agents' behavior adaptively with agent-crowd interaction formulations. The presented behavioral model can be integrated into existing agent-based crowd simulators and improve the complexity of resulting crowd behavior. In most of the crowd simulators, low-level scripts are developed to drive complex agent behaviors. The analytical maps produced in our model are utilized to control these behaviors automatically. An important advantage of the proposed model lies in reducing the time spent on creating agents displaying diverse behaviors.

We did a comparative analyses of the presented behavior model with measured crowd data and two agent-based crowd simulators. We also run several well-known test scenarios to demonstrate the performance of our model.

References

Arbel, T., Ferrie, F.P.: Viewpoint selection by navigation through entropy maps. In: IEEE International Conference on Computer Vision, vol. 1, p. 248 (1999)

Bell, P.A.: Environmental Psychology. Wadsworth Pub. Co. (2001)

Berclaz, J., Fleuret, F., Fua, P.: Multi-camera Tracking and Atypical Motion Detection with Behavioral Maps. In: Forsyth, D., Torr, P., Zisserman, A. (eds.) ECCV 2008, Part III. LNCS, vol. 5304, pp. 112–125. Springer, Heidelberg (2008), doi: http://dx.doi.org/10.1007/978-3-540-88690-7_9, ISBN 978-3-540-88689-1

Blinn, J.: Where am i? what am i looking at? IEEE Computer Graphics and Applications 8(4), 76–81 (1988)

Christie, M., Olivier, P.: Camera control in computer graphics. In: Eurographics 2006 State of The Art Report (2006)

Cover, T.M., Thomas, J.A.: Elements of information theory. Wiley-Interscience, New York (1991)

Dornhege, C., Kleiner, A.: Behavior maps for online planning of obstacle negotiation and climbing on rough terrain. In: IEEE/RSJ International Conference on Intelligent Robots and Systems, IROS 2007, pp. 3005–3011 (2007)

Feixas, M., del Acebo, E., Bekaert, P., Sbert, M.: An information theory framework for the analysis of scene complexity. Computer Graphics Forum 18, 95–106 (1999)

Gayle, R., Sud, A., Andersen, E., Guy, S.J., Lin, M.C., Manocha, D.: Interactive Navigation of Heterogeneous Agents Using Adaptive Roadmaps. IEEE Transactions on Visualization and Computer Graphics 15(1), 34–48 (2009)

Gleicher, M., Witkin, A.: Through-the-lens camera control. In: Computer Graphics (Proc. SIGGRAPH 1992), vol. 26 (1992); Proc. Siggraph 1992

He, L.-W., Cohen, M.F., Salesin, D.H.: The virtual cinematographer: a paradigm for automatic real-time camera control and directing. In: SIGGRAPH 1996: Proceedings of the 23rd Annual Conference on Computer Graphics and Interactive Techniques, pp. 217–224. ACM, New York (1996)

Hengchin, Y., Sean, C., Sachin, P., van den Jur, B., Dinesh, M., Ming, L.: Composite agents. In: Symposium on Computer Animation - SCA 2008 (2008)

Hu, X.: Context-Dependent Adaptability in Crowd Behavior Simulation. In: 2006 IEEE International Conference on Information Reuse and Integration, pp. 214–219 (2006)

Itti, L., Baldi, P.: A principled approach to detecting surprising events in video. In: IEEE Computer Society Conference on Computer Vision and Pattern Recognition, pp. 631–637. IEEE Computer Society (2005)

Itti, L., Koch, C., Niebur, E.: A model of saliency-based visual attention for rapid scene analysis. IEEE Trans. Pattern Anal. Mach. Intell. 20(11), 1254–1259 (1998)

Ji, G., Shen, H.-W.: Dynamic view selection for time-varying volumes. IEEE Transactions on Visualization and Computer Graphics 12(5), 1109–1116 (2006)

Kamada, T., Kawai, S.: A simple method for computing general position in displaying three-dimensional objects. Comput. Vision Graph. Image Process. 41(1), 43–56 (1988)

Kasap, Z., Magnenat-Thalmann, N.: Intelligent Virtual Humans with Autonomy and Personality: State-of-the-Art. In: New Adv. Virt. Hum.: Arti. Intel. SCI, pp. 43–84. Springer, Heidelberg (2008)

Kullback, S.: Information Theory and Statistics (Dover Books on Mathematics). Dover Publications (July 1997) ISBN 0486696847

Kwon, J.-Y., Lee, I.-K.: Determination of camera parameters for character motions using motion area. The Visual Computer 24(7-9), 475–483 (2008) ISSN 0178-2789

Lee, C.H., Varshney, A., Jacobs, D.W.: Mesh saliency. In: SIGGRAPH 2005: ACM SIGGRAPH 2005 Papers, pp. 659–666. ACM, New York (2005)

Luo, L., Zhou, S., Cai, W., Low, M.Y.H., Tian, F., Wang, Y., Xiao, X., Chen, D.: Agent-based human behavior modeling for crowd simulation. Comput. Animat. Virtual Worlds 19(3-4), 271–281 (2008)

Musse, S.R., Thalmann, D.: Hierarchical model for real time simulation of virtual human crowds. IEEE Transactions on Visualization and Computer Graphics 7, 152–164 (2001)

Ped-Net (May 2009), http://ped-net.org/

Pelechano, N., OBrien, K., Silverman, B., Badler, N.: Crowd simulation incorporating agent psychological models, roles and communication. In: First International Workshop on Crowd Simulation (2005)

Pelechano, N., Allbeck, J.M., Badler, N.I.: Controlling individual agents in high-density crowd simulation. In: Proceedings of the 2007 ACM SIGGRAPH/Eurographics Symposium on Computer Animation, pp. 99–108. Eurographics Association (2007) ISBN 978-1-59593-624-4

Reynolds, C.: Opensteer, steering behaviors for autonomous characters (2004), http://opensteer.sourceforge.net/ (last visited: November 1, 2008)

Reynolds, C.W.: Flocks, herds and schools: A distributed behavioral model. In: Proceedings of the 14th Annual Conference on Computer Graphics and Interactive Techniques, pp. 25–34 (1987)

Reynolds, C.W.: Steering behaviors for autonomous characters. In: Game Developers Conference (1999)

Rymill, S.J., Dodgson, N.A.: A Psychologically-Based Simulation of Human Behaviour. In: Theory and Practice of Computer Graphics, pp. 35–42 (2005)

Schmid, C., Mohr, R., Bauckhage, C.: Evaluation of interest point detectors. Int. J. Comput. Vision 37(2), 151–172 (2000)

Shannon, C.E.: A mathematical theory of communication. Bell Systems Technical Journal 27, 623–656 (1948)

Shao, W., Terzopoulos, D.: Autonomous pedestrians. Graphical Models 69(5-6), 246–274 (2007)

Shoda, Y.: Computational modeling of personality as a dynamical system. In: Handbook of Research Methods in Personality Psychology, pp. 633–652 (2007)

Shoemake, K.: Animating rotation with quaternion curves. SIGGRAPH Comput. Graph. 19(3), 245–254 (1985)

Singh, S., Markou, M.: An approach to novelty detection applied to the classification of image regions. IEEE Transactions on Knowledge and Data Engineering 16(4), 396–407 (2004)

Sommer, R., Sommer, B.: A Practical Guide To Behavioral Research: Tools and Technique, 5th edn. Oxford University Press (2002)

Stoev, S.L., Straßer, W.: A case study on automatic camera placement and motion for visualizing historical data. In: VIS 2002: Proceedings of the Conference on Visualization 2002. IEEE Computer Society, Washington, DC (2002) ISBN 0-7803-7498-3

Sung, M., Gleicher, M., Chenney, S.: Scalable behaviors for crowd simulation. Computer Graphics Forum 23, 519–528 (2004)

Thalmann, D., Musse, S.R.: Crowd Simulation. Springer, Heidelberg (2007)

Treuille, A., Cooper, S., Popović, Z.: Continuum crowds. ACM Trans. Graph. 25(3), 1160–1168 (2006) ISSN 0730-0301

Turkay, C., Koc, E., Balcisoy, S.: An information theoretic approach to camera control for crowded scenes. The Visual Computer 25(5-7), 451–459 (2009a), doi: http://dx.doi.org/10.1007/s00371-009-0337-1, ISSN 0178-2789

Turkay, C., Koc, E., Yuksel, K., Balcisoy, S.: Adaptive behavioral modeling for crowd simulations. In: Proceedings of International Conference on Computer Animation and Social Agents (Short Papers), pp. 65–68 (2009b)

van den Berg, J., Lin, M., Manocha, D.: Reciprocal Velocity Obstacles for real-time multi-agent navigation. In: Robotics and Automation, 2008, pp. 1928–1935 (2008)

Vázquez, P.-P., Feixas, M., Sbert, M., Heidrich, W.: Viewpoint selection using viewpoint entropy. In: VMV 2001: Proceedings of the Vision Modeling and Visualization Conference 2001, Aka GmbH, pp. 273–280 (2001)

Wolfe, J.: Visual search. In: Pashler, H.E. (ed.) Attention, ch. 1, pp. 13–69. University College London Press, London (1998)

Integrating Urban Simulation and Visualization

Daniel G. Aliaga

Department of Computer Science, Purdue University
West Lafayette, IN - USA
aliaga@cs.purdue.edu

Abstract. Urban simulation and visualization are useful to a variety of applications, including content generation for entertainment, simulation, and training, and for regional planning agencies to evaluate alternative transportation investments, land use regulations, and environmental protection policies. In this chapter, we provide a brief overview of urban simulation models, an overview of visualization strategies applied to urban models, and how recent work has built upon a synergy of urban simulation, urban visualization, and computer graphics to produce new approaches that tightly integrate previously separate areas. This last aspect exploits a form of in-situ visualization enhancing the ability of both the simulations and the visualizations. The presented collections of works represent state-of-the-art methods that will educate the reader on the latest thoughts and approaches in the field.

Keywords: urban simulation, urban visualization, computer graphics, urban planning.

1   Introduction

Urban simulation and the visualization of the computed datasets are of large importance to a variety of stakeholders. For example, urban simulation and visualization is used to help regional planning agencies evaluate alternative transportation investments, land use regulations, and environmental protection policies. Emergency response agencies seek models to train emergency response personnel in current and speculative (future) urban environments. A variety of entertainment applications also seek to simulate and grow plausible cities for use in games and in movies.

Cities, however, are extremely complicated entities exhibiting a variety of phenomena including emergent behaviors. Warren Weaver's [41] historical address to the Rockefeller foundation provides a profound summary of science and complexity which is useful in understanding how to model cities. Weaver states that science can be classified into trying to solve (i) problems of simplicity, (ii) problems of disorganized complexity, and (iii) problems of organized complexity. The first category models phenomena using only a few fundamentally different categories of variables (e.g., differential equations) and such has been a popular target of many

S. Müller Arisona et al. (Eds.): DUMS, CCIS 242, pp. 262–276, 2012.

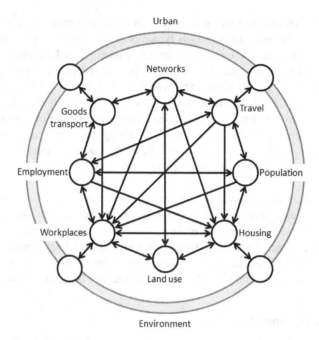

Fig. 1. Urban Simulation Framework. An outline of the typical interdependencies between components of an urban simulation (based on [43]).

visualization methods. The second category addresses problems of such a large number of variables that statistical methods are applied and only general information about the observed phenomenon is modeled (e.g., average number of collisions per unit volume). The third category is the one of most relevance to urban simulation for it involves highly-complex problems of a large number of variables with both a local and a global organization. As Batty [6] points out, cities are great examples of problems of organized complexity. Behaviors in problems of this third category are not helter-skelter but rather organized, interrelated in a complicated way, and exhibiting emergent behaviors. As computational abilities increase, problems of this third category are being addressed with increasing frequency.

The desire to model urban environments has been propelled by the need to plan and to forecast the development of today's large, ever-growing, and ever-changing cities. While hundreds of years ago, cities could be organized and planned by a small committee and built as per the specifications, today the entanglement of urban growth, complex economic dependencies of cities, large interconnected transportation systems, and centralization of the population from farmland to the cities necessitates evaluating many "what if" scenarios. Thus, understanding urban environments is of clear importance to society and, more generally, being able to model large problems of organized complexity is of clear importance to science.

Urban simulation systems attempt to model the underlying large problems of organized complexity and to provide predictions of real estate development, prices, and location choices of households and firms at fine-grained levels of geography such as grid cells or parcels, over entire metropolitan areas, and over planning horizons of several decades. The simulation models typically output massive spatially-distributed data about several variables, including number of inhabitants, land prices, and traffic. This is in addition to the input data which itself is very large. For example, the raw image and street data for the United States will easily reach and exceed peta-byte size image databases (e.g., the United States' 10M km^2 at 6-inch per pixel resolution already amounts to peta-byte size databases). Thus, the amount of data generated by such a microscopic model over a long forecasting horizon and a large scale is overwhelming for users to easily interpret. Thus, visualization techniques are essential to be able to render useful information from the mass of data generated by such simulations.

In this chapter, we will provide an overview of three bodies of work. We will discuss urban simulations modeling the behavioral and spatial patterns of agents within a city. In addition, we will review several visualization methods that pursue intuitively conveying information about urban spaces and interdependencies within them. Finally, we will also provide a summary of recent methods that tightly integrate visualization and simulation, yielding an improvement in both dimensions.

2   Urban Simulation

Urban simulation refers to the use of behavioral or process modeling of the spatial patterns of urban economic agents and objects such as jobs, population, housing, and land use. Figure 1 presents a generalized framework for describing the behaviors that urban simulation models attempt to represent in varying degrees of comprehensiveness and with differing approaches to temporal abstraction and detail of agents and location [43]. It highlights the interaction among household and business agents that are locating in housing and nonresidential buildings, and on the differing time scales of the evolution of buildings, transportation networks, urban form, and travel that connects the agents within the urban system. Urban simulation models consider part or all of the shown dependencies and can be loosely divided into three dominant paradigms.

2.1   Cellular Automata

Early models attempting to represent emergent dynamics adopted cellular automata (CA) as the modeling framework [31]. The essential principles of CA include the following four concepts:

- cells - the object space (e.g., city) is divided into a discrete set of cells often arranged in a grid; with each cell, a variety of data fields or variable values (e.g., job counts, population, housing details, etc.) can be stored,
- state - each cell can take on exactly one state selected from a predetermined set of possible states (e.g., land, water, dense urban, suburban, forest, etc.),
- neighborhood - given a set of cells, we can easily establish a spatially compact set of adjacent and/or proximate cells, and

- transition rules - for a given CA, we can define a set of transition rules that given a current state of a cell and its neighbors, we can alter the state of the cell. Typically, the rules are uniformly tested for applicability to all cells.

One of the most widely known CA methods is the Urban Growth Model [9]. A CA-based method, using approximately 500x700 cells, was calibrated using historical digital maps of an urban area. Then, it was applied to two very different urban areas (i.e., San Francisco and Washington/Baltimore, both in the United States) and produced reasonable predictions as compared to other methods. In other work, it has been applied to long-term changes in land cover patterns classified from remote sensing data [2]. Unfortunately, the CA modeling approach only simulates the conversion of land use based on the characteristics of cells and their immediate spatial context. Hence there is no action generated at a distance. This limitation of a CA method prohibits modeling the effect of changes to the built environment or its occupants based on more global entities, such as travel networks and large-scale economic dependencies.

2.2   Agent-Based Models

Agent-based models (ABM) have extended the CA framework to include mobile and interacting agents in a spatially large urban context. Agent-based models mainly differ from cellular automata in that the used agents are objects without a fixed location. Agents can interact with each other as well as the environment in a very flexible manner and are usually regarded as acting autonomously. Succinctly, an ABM has the following characteristics:

- agents are explicitly designed to represent a particular mobile object (e.g., a perso); there may be more than one agent type in a single simulation thus the agents are implicitly distributed throughout the environment, and
- agents can sense and act within their environment in one of several ways; their behavior can be reactive (e.g., they behave based solely on their surroundings) or deliberative (e.g., they have their own agenda or goal which drives their behavior); clearly, the design of the agents sensing and acting is critical to a simulation.

Altogether, agents exhibit a form of autonomous behavior and thus lend themselves to a variety of simulated behaviors including emergent patterns. Within urban simulation, many works have focused on examining cities as self-organizing complex systems, and solutions have been designed to explore the emergent properties of agents with relatively simple behavioral rules embedded by the modeler [23]. However, relatively little attention has been paid to issues of validating models using observed data or trends, and, as with CA models, traditional ABM urban simulations have behaviors influenced only by a localized context.

2.3   Urban-Economic Discrete-Choice Models

An approach to urban simulation has emerged from a combination of urban economic analysis with statistical modeling of choices made by agents in the urban environment, such as households choosing residential locations. This work integrates agent-based models with the pioneering work of McFadden on Random Utility Theory [17] and the development of discrete choice models, for which he recently won the year 2000 Nobel Prize in Economics. In the classical continuous modeling, calculus methods are used to determine an optimum configuration of a model (e.g., regression analysis). In contrast, discrete choice models use statistical procedures to describe choices (e.g., as made by people) among a finite set of alternatives and thus is more amenable to simulation urban environments. Research using this approach diverges on the

- level of aggregation - aggregate (discrete choice) models represent agents by grouping them based on types and by grouping large zones based on locations; microsimulation models represent individual agents, such as households and jobs, and objects, such as buildings and parcels, and
- time representation - there are contrasting approaches to the representation of time, with earlier research focusing on equilibrium in a set of equations of locating agents and buildings, and later work exploiting a dynamic representation that uses explicit chronological time and incorporates path-dependence; examples of the aggregate and equilibrium approach to urban simulation include spatial interaction models [24] and equilibrium discrete choice models [3, 16].

2.4   UrbanSim

An example of more recent work in this area using a dynamic microsimulation approach is UrbanSim [11, 38, 39], which simulates the choices of individual households, businesses, and parcel landowners and developers interacting in urban real estate markets. This approach works with individual agents as is done in the ABM, with very small cells as in the CA approach, or with buildings and parcels. But it differs from these approaches by integrating discrete choice methods [32], an explicit representation of real estate markets, and statistical methods to estimate model parameters and to calibrate uncertainty in the model system [28].

The core of UrbanSim consists of a series of models that run in a specified order once per a simulated year, using individual agents and entities, as a microsimulation. A simulation is usually performed for a period of several years---up to 30 years for long-term project evaluation. Data for the model systems are derived from large datasets obtained from a variety of sources, including local tax assessor files of parcels and buildings, employment data from unemployment insurance records or other administrative sources, census data, household surveys, spatial data on streets, terrain and other environmental features, and land use and transportation plans. Parameters of the price models are obtained by using the hedonic regression framework [27, 37], estimated using observed real estate data and estimated by Ordinary Least Squares, or alternatively Maximum Likelihood Estimation (MLE) [13]. Parameters of the location choice models are obtained by using observed data and MLE of Multinomial Logit Models based on a Random Utility Maximization framework [17, 18, 19, 32]. Most of the models are stochastic, and involve Monte

Carlo sampling of choice outcomes conditional on a probability generated from a Multinomial Logit Model.

a)   b)

Fig. 2. Traditional Urban Visualization. a) A typical indicator based visualization system (in this case from [29]). b) A typical choroplethic map used to visualize a simulation variable using color coding

The robustness of the UrbanSim system to date has been assessed in several ways. One measure of success is its increasingly widespread adoption by public agencies responsible for regional planning of multi-billion dollar transportation plans for which robust models are essential. UrbanSim has been the subject of a favorable peer review process to assist in resolving a lawsuit over the environmental impacts of a highway project in Salt Lake City [40]. The accuracy of the model has been validated by simulating relatively long periods for which observed data were available, and the model system was found capable of reproducing key spatial dynamics in households and jobs [38]. Finally, methods compatible with UrbanSim have been developed to calibrate the uncertainty in the model system in order to be able to make principled inferences about the uncertainty embedded in the model predictions [28].

3   Urban Visualization

Urban visualization approaches generally make use of techniques including choroplethic (colored) maps generated by exporting simulation results, summarized by a zonal geography, to a Geographical Information System (GIS) for rendering (e.g., see Figure 2); other variants include animations generated by rendering a series of such 2D maps in a loop, viewing different time slices or quantities, and 3D renderings of simulation results by extrusion of polygonal forms to indicate density, or by spatial smoothing in the form of contour or terrain maps with the elevation representing some quantity of interest. Several groups of population with different levels of expertise in handling urban simulation data are normally interested in these results, including urban planners, policy makers, the public, or even the modelers running the simulation. On the one hand, traditional information visualization techniques have focused in handling large urban simulation data sets and making their analysis more intuitive to urban planners. Simulation systems have been relatively limited in their scope of visualization, in spite of providing a sophisticated economic and behavioral simulation engine to model the location and travel choices of millions of agents in the system. A typical scenario is that manual post-processing of simulation results must be done by a model user to extract summary indicators from the results, export them from the simulation environment into a GIS system, establish relational joins of the indicators to existing GIS layers, and then manually rendering thematic or choroplethic maps to render the spatial variation in the resulting indicators. On the other hand, recent research works have proposed an interdisciplinary collaboration between visualization, computer graphics, and urban modeling to produce new visualization techniques of urban simulation data sets. These techniques aim to facilitate the presentation and increase the impact of urban simulation data to different population sectors. It is in this arena that significant growth is expected.

Batty [4] first introduced various approaches that relate urban modeling, GIS, and computer graphics. The same author later described the impact of virtual reality and 3D visualization to GIS and he has demonstrated this on a variety of examples [5]. More recently, Batty [6] presents models demonstrating how complexity theory can embrace a myriad of processes and elements that combine into large nearly organic entities. He argues that bottom-up processes can be combined with new forms of geometry to describe highly complex systems such as cities.

Simulation systems, such as UrbanSim, have been relatively limited in their scope of visualization. A typical visualization task consists of drawing one or more sets of indicators. In urban planning, example indicators include population count, job count, land price, miles traveled per year, or greenhouse gas emissions. Values can be produced for a user-selected region either small or large in size. In addition, values can be computed for one instant in time or over a multi-year scenario. The final values are then displayed as tables, charts or maps. For example, the work of Schwartzman and Borning [29] developed a web-based indicator system and evaluated design techniques, including Value Sensitive Design, paper prototyping, and frequent user testing, in order to arrive at a well-tuned and highly useful system for the urban planning community (Figure 2).

While there has been a large amount of work on GIS, very little research has been done evaluating the usefulness of various types of visualizations for this domain. A study by Pinnel et al. [22] examines various visualization types and attempts to find appropriate visual representations for urban modeling tasks. The types of visualizations considered include graphs, pie chart, 2D and 3D maps, symbol charts, and bubble charts. They cross reference each of these types with the encodings that can be effectively utilized (e.g., color intensity, bars, area/height, marker size, marker shape). Their study concludes that for urban planning and analysis, map type visualizations provide the necessary geographical information, while for quantitative tasks (e.g., communicating population growth, distribution of jobs per economic sector, etc.) bar charts and summaries better present the needed information.

A widely used urban visualization technique is cartograms which use map shape warping to visualize relationships and values of urban and geospatial datasets. The core idea behind cartograms is to distort a map by resizing its regions according to a statistical parameter, but in a way that keeps the map recognizable. Cartogram-style approaches have been proposed long before computing devices. Dent [10] provides a short historical overview. In general, it has been shown that computing the necessary map warp even in simple cases may be unsolvable. Because the feasible variants are NP-complete, heuristics are needed to solve the problem. Often, solutions suffer yield low-quality (i.e., high-distorted) solutions. For a cartogram to be recognizable, it is important to preserve the global shape or outline of the input map, a requirement that is often overlooked. One recent approach by Keim et al. [14] proposes an objective function including both global and local shape preservation. To measure the degree of shape preservation, they use a shape similarity function based on a Fourier transformation of a polygons' curvatures. Their method is efficient, founded on medial-axis theory, and lends itself to interactive and high-quality solutions.

Chang et al. [7] propose a novel aggregation method that combines buildings and city blocks into legible clusters. Their work addresses the question of how do people think about a city. By combining visualization, theories of city design and spatial structure, and Kevin Lynch's theory of urban legibility they determine what geometry-based and information-based elements of a city are necessary to clearly interact with an observer. Urban geometry is communicated via hierarchical building clustering. Information is expressed using a matrix view and parallel coordinates to show relationships between dimensions. View dependence is then used to change the location of focus and degree of focus of the geometry and information. For example, in their demonstrated system, the 3D model view and the data view are tightly integrated so that relationships between the geometry of the urban model and related urban data (e.g., census, employment, etc.) can be intuitively identified. While the user-study that they conducted showed that some features introduced by their system enhanced the user's ability to better understand an urban model, they also noted that creating legible cities for users of all backgrounds is not a trivial task and would require knowledge of the user's perspective of the city prior to creating the clusters.

Dykes and Brunsdon [12] introduced geographically weighted (gw) interactive graphics to explore spatial relationships between geographic processes. These techniques include standard color maps, maps of gw-means, gw-residual maps, and a localized version of the box-and-whisker plot. These techniques concurrently reveal information about geographically weighted statistics at several scales.

Roman et al. [26] branch out from computer vision and computer graphics to present an interactive system for constructing multi-perspective images from sideways-looking video captured from a moving vehicle and use it to visualize urban areas. The input to their system is a set of video frames with known camera pose. Their system automatically computes an additional cross-slits camera between every pair of adjacent user-specified cameras leading to a smooth interpolation of viewpoint in the final multi-perspective image. Multi-perspective image of a whole city block can be created in a few minutes. The goal of this work is to simultaneously view real-world urban scenes that cannot be captured in a single photograph, rather than to visualize the simulation data of an urban space. New techniques could be explored that combine such a multi-perspective approach with other forms of data visualization.

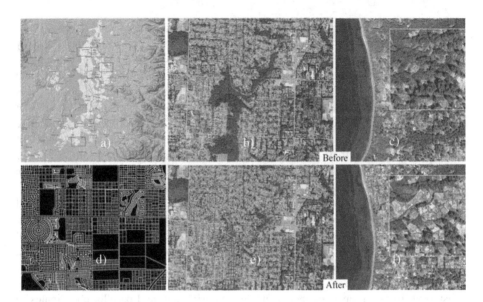

Fig. 3. Time-based Urban Simulations. a) An overview of a simulated region (Puget Sound, Washington State, USA). b-c) Two example regions that will be simulated over a 30 year time period. d) Close-up example of streets and parcels generated during a simulation run (new geometry drawn in cyan). e-f) Corresponding regions to (b-c) but after the simulation. Images c and f also contain a close up where new developments are predicted.

4   Integrating Visualization and Simulation

The processes of simulation and visualization face many challenges, even when handled in isolation. Although in-situ visualization has been defined by recent large visualization centers, it still does not dominate in the scientific process. Hence, often too little visualization is done in practice. This leads to a diminished ability of being able to analyze and diagnose simulation results. This, in turn, can delay the ability to produce a correct simulation and can compound the uncertainty of knowing whether an observed anomaly is the consequence of the simulation or of the visualization. A solution which is being recently explored by several groups is to tightly combine simulation and visualization with the hope of leading to a more accurate and robust understanding of cities and urban environments.

4.1   Time-Based Urban Simulations in Computer Graphics

Two recent works have combined urban simulation with the creation of detailed 2D or 3D geometric models. Vanegas et al. [35] uses and creates 2D urban layouts for the visualization of urban simulation results. This work builds upon existing visualization techniques of urban simulations and extends them by automatically inferring new urban layouts for any time step of the simulation sequence, by considering both the values of the state variables of the simulation model (i.e., UrbanSim [38]), and the

Fig. 4. Interactive Geometric Simulation of 4D Cities. Two time series are shown in the columns based on the work of Weber et al. 2009. a) Shows the transition from low density to high density in the city center. b) Shows a transition of a city based on sustainable development with sufficient green areas.

original street network, parcels, and aerial imagery of the simulated city (Figure 3). Their approach exploits that users are comfortable with understanding and gathering intuition from aerial views of the urban landscape, whether from viewing aerial photographs or satellite images, or from observing the cities they have flown over. Aerial views are holistic representations that allow the viewer to perceive various aspects of a place in a coherent way. Even without inspecting up close and in detail, the overall pattern of streets, size of yards, amount of vegetation, mixture of non-residential buildings, amount of open space all contribute to an intuition about the nature of the place. Similarly, parcel and street maps convey a sense of concreteness about an urban landscape and the nature of the development. By generating streets, parcels, and aerial imagery, their work offers a substantial step forward in building integrated visualization and behavioral simulation systems for use in community visioning, planning, and policy analysis.

The aforementioned method selects important urban simulation variables and then uses them to produce visualizations. The input variables to the urban simulation include values for the number of buildings, number of households per parcel, population within zones, etc. The algorithms exploit the typical organization of an urban layout into streets, blocks, and parcels. These units are clustered and partitioned according to the uniqueness of their simulation parameter values. Then, as the simulation progresses, the method appropriately extends or reuses a portion of the original urban layout producing both plausible street and parcel network and plausible aerial images of the city. The effectiveness of this approach is improved as the size of the urban layout and its simulation grows (both spatially and tem-porally). Altogether, this approach allows for traditional visualizations as well as that of new content. It has been applied to visualize over 16,000 km^2 of urban space including 200 GB of data including high-resolution aerial imagery, per-year simulation data, and GIS data defining more than 1.4 million parcels.

Another approach is that of Weber et al. [42] who describe a system to combine procedural modeling techniques with urban simulation to obtain 3D models that change over time (Figure 4). Although much simpler than full-featured urban simulators, the simulation is interactive and the user can make modifications during the simulation, such as controlling the major growth areas, editing road segments, editing land use, and changing parameters used to control the simulation. The goal of their work is to provide a generic framework that can be configured for different types of land use categories.

The input to their system consists of (1) the environment (i.e. the topography given as a height map, a water map, and a forest map), (2) an initial urban layout configuration ranging from a single street up to a larger (potentially already existing) city, (3) land use type definitions, and (4) user input data that can change over time to interactively control the simulation. The system itself includes a street simulator, land-use simulator, and a building lot and building construction algorithm. The street simulation process accounts for expansion demands based on population, employment, and a simple traffic flow model. The land-use simulator takes into consideration local and global criteria in order to optimize a land use value function. Finally, given a street network and land-use assignments, their system estimates building lots and plausible 3D building geometries. Altogether, they present an urban simulation system which includes geometric rules for the generation of streets, lots, and land use on a small scale. Their work was applied to several cities and high-quality visual output was clearly demonstrated.

4.2   Hybrid Behavioral and Geometrical Simulations

An alternative approach which has been recently proposed is to tightly close the loop between behavioral modeling and geometrical modeling of urban spaces [36]. They model the design and editing process as a dynamical system using a set of functions that describe the change to the variable values. This is in spirit similar to that performed for large crowd modeling (e.g., [30, 33]) and for flocking and animal behavior modeling (e.g., [25, 34]). Using a dynamical system, the approach continually alters the model being interactively designed so as to conform to plausible urban behavior and urban geometry, enabling the production of large models in just a few seconds (Figure 5), and being useful for a variety of applications ranging from games and movies to urban planning and emergency management.

Previous research in urban modeling can be divided into the areas of geometrical modeling and behavioral modeling: the first is purely computer graphics oriented (e.g., [1, 8, 15, 20, 21, 44]), and the second is primarily intended for decision-making regarding urban policies in current and future urban areas (e.g., [2, 38]). However, geometrical and behavioral modeling, when applied in isolation on the same underlying urban space, yields a functional disconnection between the two resulting models. This is because behavioral modeling is not concerned with generating the geometry of the urban space and because geometrical modeling usually does not consider behavioral properties of real-world cities. This disconnection is particularly disadvantageous during the computer graphics design and editing process of 3D geometric urban models. Real-world urban spaces exhibit relationships between variables such as terrain, road networks, building shapes, distribution of population, jobs, and transportation routes. Existing geometrical modeling systems can be used to perform the changes to the 3D model that are implied by altering these variables, but the designer would have to be aware of the subtle interdependencies between the variables. Ignoring these interdependencies may result in models that do not resemble real-world urban spaces such as tall buildings on top of mountains, cities with only skyscrapers and no residential areas, or an imbalance between road networks and buildings.

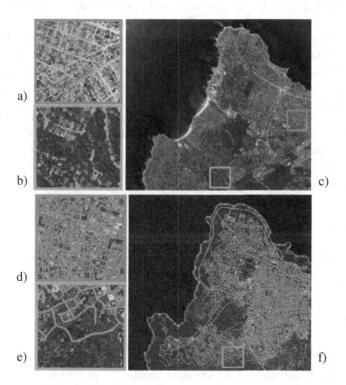

Fig. 5. Hybrid Geometrical and Behavioral Urban Modeling. Using the work of Vanegas et al. [36], a complete 3D city model is generated using only sparse geometric and behavioral data resulting in a model that resembles a real-world city. In this case, a user is given a satellite view (c) of Pacific Grove, California, and is asked to draw the terrain and highways, click on a downtown location and highlight the parks. The system generates the geometry of the roads and buildings (f) (colors are manually adjusted for comparison). Zoomed areas of the original (a, b) and synthetic (d, e) cities show how the density and style of the real city are reproduced at different locations, including high-density (a,d) and low-density (b, e) neighborhoods.

The key inspiration of the approach of Vanegas et al. [36] is to maintain a state of static equilibrium between the variables of an urban space by using differential equations. Traditional urban behavioral modeling simulates the temporal evolution of an urban space. The behaviors are the attempts to reach a state of dynamic equilibrium; i.e., a status of internal consistency between the demands of the population, job market, transportation routes, and building structures. They exploit the understood concepts in urban planning and simulation to create a behavior that is internally consistent with the current geometry of the urban model and, vice versa, they use adaptive geometric algorithms to generate geometry that satisfies behavioral demands. Their system consists of urban space design variables with spatially-varying values defined over an urban area. The variables control the distribution of population and jobs, land values, road network, parcel shape, and building geometry. Editing the variables is performed intuitively and visually using a graphical user interface combined with a paint-brush style tool. Any variable can be globally or locally increased, decreased, or constrained. The ability to constrain variables is crucial to support incremental design and editing at various scales. Moreover, the designer can constrain several distinct parts of an existing model and let the system complete the rest of the model. The changes in the values of the state variables are articulated via differential equations. These equations also express the (nonlinear) interdependencies between the variables. After an edit operation, the system attempts to bring the urban model back into equilibrium (Figure 2). Their system has been used to interactively create large models of urban environments containing up to 50,000 buildings, 3,000 km of roads, and 200 km^2 of area. The total interactive design process time, including several iterations of variable changes and modeling alterations, is just a few minutes on a standard desktop computer.

References

1. Aliaga, D., Vanegas, C., Beneš, B.: Interactive example-based urban layout synthesis. ACM Transactions on Graphics 27(5), 160 (2008)
2. Alkheder, S., Wang, J., Shan, J.: Fuzzy inference guided cellular automata urban-growth modeling using multi-temporal satellite images. International Journal of Geographical Information Science 22(11-12), 1271–1293 (2008)
3. Anas, A., Kim, I.: General equilibrium models of polycentric urban land use with endogenous congestion and job agglomeration. Journal of Urban Economics 40(2), 232–256 (1996)
4. Batty, M.: Urban modeling in computer-graphic and geographic information system environments. Environment and Planning B: Planning and Design 19(6), 663–688 (1992)
5. Batty, M., Cole, S.: Time and space: Geographic perspectives on the future. Futures 29(4-5), 277–289 (1997)
6. Batty, M.: Cities and Complexity: Understanding Cities with Cellular Automata, Agent-based Models, and Fractals. MIT Press, Cambridge (2007)
7. Chang, R., Wessel, G., Kosara, R., Sauda, E., Ribarsky, W.: Legible cities: Focus-dependent multi-resolution visualization of urban relationships. IEEE Transactions on Visualization and Computer Graphics 13(6), 1169–1175 (2007)

8. Chen, G., Esch, G., Wonka, P., Mueller, P., Zhang, E.: Interactive Procedural Street Modeling. ACM Transactions on Graphics 27(3), 1–10 (2008)
9. Clarke, K.C., Gaydos, L.J.: Loose-coupling a cellular automaton model and GIS: long-term urban growth prediction for San Francisco and Washington/Baltimore. International Journal of Geographical Information Science 12(7), 699–714 (1998)
10. Dent, B.D.: Cartography: Thematic Map Design, ch. 10, 4th edn. William C. Brown, Dubuque (1996)
11. De Palma, A., Picard, N., Waddell, P.: Discrete choice models with capacity constraints: An empirical analysis of the housing market of the greater Paris region. Journal of Urban Economics 62(2), 204–230 (2007)
12. Dykes, J., Brunsdon, C.: Geographically weighted visualization: Interactive graphics for scalevarying exploratory analysis. IEEE Transactions on Visualization and Computer Graphics 13(6), 1161–1168 (2007)
13. Greene, W.: Econometric Analysis, 5th edn. Pearson Education (2002)
14. Keim, D.A., North, S.C., Panse, C.: Cartodraw: a fast algorithm for generating contiguous cartograms. IEEE Transactions on Visualization and Computer Graphics 10(1), 95–110 (2004)
15. Lipp, M., Wonka, P., Wimmer, M.: Interactive visual editing of grammars for procedural architecture. ACM Transactions on Graphics 27(3), 102 (2008)
16. Martinez, F.: Mussa: A land-use model for Santiago city. Transportation Research Record 1552, 126–134 (1996)
17. McFadden, D.: Conditional logic analysis of qualitative choice behavior. In: Frontiers in Econometrics. Academic Press, New York (1973)
18. McFadden, D.: Modeling the choice of residential location. In: Karlqvist, A., Lundqvist, L., Snickars, F., Wiebull, J.W. (eds.) Spatial Interaction Theory and Planning Models, pp. 75–96. North Holland, Amsterdam (1978)
19. McFadden, D.: Econometric models of probabilistic choice. In: Manski, C.F., McFadden, D. (eds.) Structural Analysis of Discrete Data with Econometric Applications, pp. 198–272. MIT Press, Cambridge (1981)
20. Mueller, P., Wonka, P., Haegler, S., Ulmer, A., Van Gool, L.: Procedural modeling of buildings. ACM Transactions on Graphics 25(3), 614–623 (2006)
21. Parish, Y.I., Mueller, P.: Procedural modeling of cities. In: Proceedings of ACM SIGGRAPH 2001, pp. 301–308 (2001)
22. Pinnel, L.D., Dockrey, M., Brush, A.J.B., Borning, A.: Design of visualizations for urban modeling. In: VisSym: Joint Eurographics and IEEE TCVC Symposium on Visualization (2000)
23. Portugali, J.: Self-organization and the city. Springer, Heidelberg (2000)
24. Putman, S.: Integrated Urban Models 2 - New Research and Applications of Optimization and Dynamics. Pion, London (1991)
25. Reynolds, C.W.: Flocks, herds, and schools: A distributed behavioral model. In: Computer Graphics (Proceedings of ACM SIGGRAPH), pp. 25–34 (1987)
26. Roman, A., Garg, G., Levoy, M.: Interactive design of multi-perspective images for visualizing urban landscapes. In: Proceedings of IEEE Visualization, pp. 537–544 (2004)
27. Rosen, K.: Hedonic prices and implicit markets: Product differentiation in pure competition. Journal of Political Economy 82, 34–55 (1974)
28. Ševčíková, H., Raftery, A., Waddell, P.: Assessing uncertainty in urban simulations using Bayesian melding. Transportation Research B 41, 652–669 (2007)

29. Schwartzman, Y., Borning, A.: The indicator browser: A web-based interface for visualizing UrbanSim simulation results. In: Hawaii International Conference on System Sciences, p. 92a (2007)

30. Sung, M., Gleicher, M., Cheney, S.: Scalable behaviors for crowd simulation. Computer Graphics Forum 23(3), 519–528 (2004)

31. Torrens, P., O'Sullivan, D.: Cellular automata and urban simulation: where do we go from here? Environment & Planning B: Planning and Design 28(2), 163–168 (2001)

32. Train, K.: Discrete Choice Methods with Simulation, 2nd edn. Cambridge University Press (2009)

33. Treuille, A., Cooper, S., Popović, Z.: Continuum Crowds. ACM Transactions on Graphics 25(3), 1160–1168 (2006)

34. Tu, X., Terzopouolos, D.: Artificial fishes: Physics, locomotion, perception, behavior. In: Proceedings of ACM SIGGRAPH, pp. 43–50 (1994)

35. Vanegas, C., Aliaga, D., Beneš, B., Waddell, P.: Visualization of Simulated Urban Spaces: Inferring Parameterized Generation of Streets, Parcels, and Aerial Imagery. IEEE Transactions on Visualization and Computer Graphics 15(3), 424–435 (2009)

36. Vanegas, C., Aliaga, D., Beneš, B., Waddell, P.: Interactive Design of Urban Spaces using Geometrical and Behavioral Modeling. ACM Transactions on Graphics 28(5), 10 (2009)

37. Waddell, P., Berry, B., Hoch, I.: Residential property values in a multinodal urban area: New evidence on the implicit price of location. Journal of Real Estate Finance and Economics 7, 117–141 (1993)

38. Waddell, P.: UrbanSim: Modeling Urban Development for Land Use, Transportation and Environmental Planning. Journal of the American Planning Association 68(3), 297–314 (2002)

39. Waddell, P., Ulfarsson, F.: Introduction to Urban Simulation: Design and Development of Operational Models. In: Handbook in Transport. Transport Geography and Spatial Systems, vol. 5, pp. 203–236. Pergamon Press (2004)

40. Waddell, P., Ulfarsson, G., Franklin, J., Lobb, J.: Incorporating land use in metropolitan transportation planning. Transportation Research Part A: Policy and Practice 41, 382–410 (2007)

41. Weaver, W.: Science and Complexity. American Scientist 36, 536–541 (1948)

42. Weber, B., Muller, P., Wonka, P., Gross, M.: Interactive Geometric Simulation of 4D Cities. Computer Graphics Forum (Eurographics) 28(2), 481–492 (2009)

43. Wegener, M.: Operational urban models state of the art. Journal of the American Planning Association 60, 17–29 (1994)

44. Wonka, P., Wimmer, M., Sillion, F., Ribarsky, W.: Instant architecture. ACM Transactions on Graphics 22(3), 669–677 (2003)

Part IV

Visualization, Collaboration and Interaction

Visualization and Decision Support Tools in Urban Planning

Antje Kunze[1], Remo Burkhard[1], Serge Gebhardt[1], and Bige Tuncer[1,2]

[1] Chair for Information Architecture, ETH Zurich, Switzerland
{kunze,burkhard,gebhardt,tuncer}@arch.ethz.ch
[2] Design Informatics, Delft University of Technology
e.b.tuncer@tudelft.nl

Abstract. Cities are rapidly growing. There is an assumption that 90% of global population growth will be in cities between now and 2030. Therefore, infrastructures and the environment have to be adapted to the changing demands. Moreover, new urban development strategies have to be elaborated. In 2007, the first international Visualization Summit of more than 100 international researchers and practitioners stated a jointly developed research goal for the year 2010, namely 'Visualizing Future Cities'. Therefore in this chapter we provide an overview about visualization methods, decision support tools in architecture, urban and regional planning, stakeholder participation and collaborative environments. Also, new decision support tools for the visualization of future cities will be introduced.

Keywords: Visualization, future cities, decision support tools, stakeholder participation, collaborative environments, sustainable urban planning.

1   Introduction

In this chapter, we investigate visualization methods for the development of future cities, discuss new decision support tools, and propose how the support tools can become the foundation of a new visual design process for developing sustainable future cities. The importance of such tasks was made clear, for example, at the first international Visualization Summit in 2007. In this summit, more than 100 international researchers and practitioners defined and assessed nine original and important research goals in the context of Visualization Science, and proposed methods for achieving these goals in the near future. The synthesis of the whole event was presented in the 10th research goal, namely 'Visualizing Future Cities' [12].

Visualizing future cities is inherently a multi-disciplinary and multi-stakeholder objective. The term 'Future Cities' refers to emerging cities and mega-cities expressed as dynamic systems and networks. The term 'Visualizing' implies using methods from computer-aided design decision research fields such as urban modeling and visualization, geospatial information systems (GIS), as well as computer-based research fields such as urban planning, communication science, and film industry. Together these methods produce either analogue or digital, static or dynamic visual

S. Müller Arisona et al. (Eds.): DUMS, CCIS 242, pp. 279–298, 2012.

representations for analysis, planning, and decision-making. Visualizations can significantly supplement the design and realization of sustainable future cities: visual representations efficiently map different mental worlds among diverse stakeholders (e.g., individual urban planners, national planning authorities, investors, the general public, local neighborhoods).

A key challenge for planning and designing 'Future Cities' is tactfully integrating all notions of urban systems into resilient urban forms that provide a high quality of life. Traditionally, each sector uses its own visual representations for analysis, design, planning, management, surveillance, or maintenance. Future cities need to overcome classical sectoral planning boundaries. Compelling visual communication may help to establish a mutual understanding of the bigger picture and to establish a cross-sectoral understanding among the diverse groups of stakeholders.

With the goal of addressing the aforementioned challenge, we will provide a summary of related work as well as tentative new research directions that are appearing in the literature. First, we will describe a motivation for visualizing future cities and for using decision support tools in urban planning. Then, we will provide an overview about related work in visualization methods, decision support tools in architecture, urban and regional planning, stakeholder participation, and collaborative environments. Subsequently, we will introduce three decision support tools for the visualization of future cities. Finally, we will present two case studies for a novel participatory planning method used in (a) the design of the eco-city "Swiss Village Abu Dhabi" (SVA) located within Masdar [52] and (b) in the World Cup 2014 'Urban Scenarios' workshop in Porto Alegre, Brazil.

1.1 Motivation

Global Situation. Sustainable urban planning of cities involves many aspects besides urban structure. According to UN-Habitat [58], such planning approaches have to be strategic rather than comprehensive. As opposed to current master planning, they also should be flexible and not end-state oriented and fixed. Further, an important element of sustainable urban planning is the mind-set for action and implementation through links to budgets, projects and citywide and regional infrastructure. Some approaches describe the city as a dynamic system, represented by stocks of resources and flows of interrelated networks. The stocks and flows are modeled as behavioral urban systems. Resources may correspond to people, material, energy, water, waste, space, and information. Angélil and Hebel [2] address a "paradigm shift to a circular understanding of urban metabolisms". They established an Urban Design Laboratory in Addis Ababa, Ethiopia, having the research target of identifying strategies to transform existing unsustainable conditions into sustainable ones.

Future cities can be interpreted as networks that encompass dynamic properties and attributes operating at different spatial scales. These systems create and receive constant stimuli and measures on social, cultural, and economic dimensions, among others, and integrate urban and suburban structures with rural areas. Infrastructures and the environment have to be continually adapted in response to the rapid and massive growth rate of mega cities such as Shanghai. New sustainable urban development strategies need to be elaborated in order to ensure long-term quality of life in mega cities. Planners, designers, officials, and even the public are needed to understand, plan, and communicate the effects of persistently increasing consumption of unsustainable energy sources and natural resources as well as high demands on transportation and communication infrastructures. Because of the inherent complexity involved in city planning and the dynamism of the involved processes, it is often very hard to perceive, represent, and communicate intricate issues, proposals, or solutions. The large interdisciplinary scope of the involved processes requires combining many different skills. Therefore, it is crucial for large-scale planning projects to enable organized communication between experts among each other and laymen. Some of the actors in a process to plan future cities belong to the following disciplines or groups: computer science, environmental studies, sociology, design, communication, urban planning, strategic management, architecture, aesthetics, and the general public.

Participatory Urban Planning. The goal of a participatory urban planning process is to improve urban quality. As has been demonstrated by many modern cities, urban structures of cities have not been very successful in coping with rapid environmental, social, and economic changes. "Master planning has been subject to major critique, and in some parts of the world it has been replaced by processes and plans that are more participatory, flexible, strategic and action oriented" [58, pp. 11]. A reason for the challenge urban planning has encountered may be the failure to acknowledge that modern cities need to be comprehended as dynamic systems that bridge many scales, contain many dimensions, and interconnect research results from many disciplines and opinions of (future) occupants in order to establish a common vision and understanding for the design and planning of the cities [31]. One of the strongest characteristics of successful sustainable urban planning is the participation of stakeholders. The quality and effectiveness of a plan can be greatly enhanced through the integration of multidisciplinary and multi-actor insights, intelligence and perspectives that are usually not considered within the formal planning process. Stakeholders are an incredibly helpful stock when it comes to the evaluation of the effectiveness of a plan, and to weigh and rate various plan alternatives by judging a plan's performance. In this context it is important to encourage and enable the use of participatory approaches for urban planning during the conception and production of sketches, plans, maps, and 3D models. Thus, sustainable development benefits significantly from using participatory planning to organize and to manage the continuous demand for efficient stocks and flows and for considering the needs of future generations [38].

2   Related Work

2.1   Visualization Methods

Urban planning must take a lot of information and knowledge into account that are of various types: physical, social, numerical, graphical, etc. In order to support participatory urban planning, this information must be somehow visualized.

Visualizing the various stocks and flows and networks that are involved in urban planning will enhance and in many cases enable participatory urban planning. Information and knowledge visualization are scientific fields that are used in various disciplines. This section introduces knowledge visualization and scientific visualization in order to foster participatory urban planning processes.

Knowledge Visualization. Knowledge visualization research [11] can be split into five major interests: (1) identifying related fields that leverage visual methods to transfer or to create knowledge, (2) designing theoretical frameworks, (3) mediating between isolated fields, (4) bridging the transfer between scientific work and business, and (5) – most importantly – finding novel visualization techniques.

A shared understanding between involved partners is important to create a compelling "big picture" – especially in cooperative planning. Visual representations are important to foment and to coordinate processes for transferring and creating knowledge [20]. Static visual representations of strategic maps or road maps can significantly support those processes (Fig. 1) [13]. For example, a static map created by an individual is not adopted by the intended community as easily as a map created in a participatory process. Such participatory exchange of visual representations (e.g., sketches, diagrams, images, objects, interactive visualizations, information visualization applications, and imaginary visualizations, as in stories) can amplify proactive knowledge transfer between groups of two or more people [10].

Fig. 1. Static strategy maps help to create a mutual understanding between stakeholders by creating a "big picture" visually capturing the relationships between them [13]

Scientific Visualization. Scientific visualization is a growing interdisciplinary field to communicate ideas across several disciplines. New approaches are constantly evolving to enrich processes with information previously not visualized. A good example is the recent achievements in urban simulation. Traditional visualizations of urban spatial models have been rather abstract and not easy to read – they consist mostly of information associated with 2D maps. Recent methods, such as Vanegas et al. [60], provide clearer visualizations by including interactivity and 3D models. Large-scale interactive 3D urban models are increasing in importance and are becoming an irreplaceable component of interdisciplinary developments. Interestingly, mapping applications (e.g., Google Maps/Earth) are steadily augmenting data sets with detailed real-world information such as 3D models. The challenge is to bring all that information together in a meaningful way. The integration of the temporal scale along with 3D rendering could provide a very powerful and even more meaningful exploration of urban models.

3D procedural modeling is a promising grammar-based technique used in the urban planning field. Integrating shape grammars into the urban planning process offers unprecedented opportunities to understand and encode urban patterns [3] and to generate and visually assess urban design variations. Thus, the integration of shape grammars facilitates creating more sustainable urban designs [31]. Müller et al. [40] introduced an attributed shape grammar, called CGA shape grammar, suitable for architectural design – it is the basis for the CityEngine System [44]. CityEngine can rapidly produce and visualize 3D urban environments of any size. Ulmer et al. [57] and Halatsch et al. [29] later extended the system with urban planning and landscape rule sets. The combination of hierarchical organization and geometric configurations enables the introduction of design patterns expressed in a CGA shape grammar. Patterns can represent a facade design of an epoch or a given style. Patterns can also describe relational proportions of an object on a defined scope. For example, avenues consisting of street and edging vegetation can be easily set up as well as parks or other geometric configurations consisting of nested rules or geometry objects [57]. Beirão et al. [6] introduced a shape grammar based support tool for urban design, which integrates an urban pattern formulation model, a design generation model, and an evaluation model.

2.2   Decision Support Tools in Architecture, Urban and Regional Planning

Design research can be divided into three areas: describing design, providing design tools, and automating design generation. Erhan [21] stated that design support research concentrates on (a) how computers can assist designers, and in what area, (b) how design problems can be represented in a form suitable for computational support, (c) how computers can generate solutions using these representations, and (d) how computers can help to evaluate the quality of the generated solutions. Oxman and Gero [41] considered two approaches for the application of support systems in the design process: (a) design synthesis (e.g., to generate new designs) and (b) design diagnosis (e.g., to evaluate design critics).

One tool for design diagnosis in early phases of architectural design is the method 'Architectural programming (AP)'. It supports participatory processes and is used for visualizing stakeholder needs and requirements. It involves the gathering, compiling, weighting, and evaluating of information in terms of planning the needs of a facility and its physical, functional, and organizational requirements [21]. In the late seventies 'AP' was initially introduced by Pena [42]. Robinson and Weeks [46] integrated architectural programming in the design process. Later on, Henn [32] developed this method further as a quality control instrument for daily use in architectural offices. The use of an 'AP' method in urban planning [37] is a new application area currently being developed.

A number of implementations of design support have been realized in the field of building design to assist designers in early phases of design [23, 34, 43]. In Tunçer and Sariyildiz [55] present a framework consisting of a method and a computational model, which supports designers to communicate and collaborate using design information and knowledge.

In urban planning there are several strategies for the development of sustainable urban morphologies. A toolbox with interdisciplinary, digital and analogue instruments for creating sustainable conditions in urban areas was developed for a case study in Switzerland by Angélil, et. al [1]. Further scenarios, based on the input data of several case studies, were developed as a decision support method. On the urban and regional scale 'Urban Data Mining' [5] describes a methodological approach to visualize and extract knowledge from spatial data. Logical or mathematical and partly complex descriptions of urban assemblies and regularities are discovered from the data set.

First efforts in the development of decision support tools for urban simulation models are implemented in regional planning [62, 8, 24, 61]. The generated visualizations are used to assist regional planning agencies to evaluate alternative land use regulations, transportation investments and environmental protection policies. Integrated simulation models can help government agencies and citizens in the decision-making process. A further development is the interactive design of urban spaces [60]. Establishing a the link between behavioral and geometrical city modeling enables easy editing of urban design variables as well as visualization and simulation of urban scenarios concerning highways, accessibility, population, and planned employment.

In landscape planning there are several approaches for public participation. Wissen, et. al [64] represent landscape indicators in 3D visualizations, and their application for decision support in public participation processes. Further, participation in landscape planning and virtual landscapes for participatory planning are discussed in Wissen [65] and Schroth [48].

2.3   Stakeholder Participation

Stakeholder participation is considered a must-criteria for sustainable urban planning [58]. Fiorino [22] described three different arguments for public/stakeholder participation in societal decision making processes: i) the substantive argument means that lay people's knowledge may be as valuable as those of experts; ii) the normative argument is grounded in the contemporary theory of democracy, which legitimizes people to take part in decisions affecting them, and; iii) the instrumental argument assumes that participation provides more legitimacy, may decrease conflicts, increases acceptability, and fosters trust in administrative bodies.

Participation of stakeholders can be categorized into different types of interactions [4, 18, 63]. Although the need for stakeholder participation is widely acknowledged, it does not guarantee a successful planning process that considers comprehensive and robust design and development strategies [16, 33, 50]. It is essential that each step of the project being planned has a specific and adequate form of collaboration [36, 51].

For this purpose, the values, perceptions, and preferences of stakeholders with internal, external, or intermediate views should be taken into account [39, 49]. Similar to the "communicative action" of Habermas [27], the stakeholder participation has to be open, undistorted, and non-manipulative on matters of public importance. The conventional top-down distribution of information by institutional actors may result in a systematic manipulation of information, which Habermas calls "concealed strategic action". Planners also deal with social problems: "Planning Problems are inherently wicked" [45]. Such problems are different from the problems that scientist and engineers deal with. There are no optimal, definitive, or objective solutions to social problems. In this context, participatory methods can help to acquire a broad-based understanding and acceptance of final planning decisions.

2.4   Collaborative Environments

Collaborative Environments have been developed in order to enable stakeholders to sit in a single room and collaboratively solve conflicts during planning, construction or operation. Such rooms, or CAVEs, are typically designed with complex multimedia settings to enable participants to visualize the project model. Traditional human-computer interaction devices (e.g. mouse, keyboard) are typically focused to fulfill single user requirements, and are not adapted to work with the multiplicity of participants and the multi-dimensionality (as well as multiplicity) of the data sets representing large projects. Solutions have however been proposed to improve interactivity. A multi-screen setup can drastically enhance collaboration and participatory processes by simultaneously displaying various information to all attendees, and such a setup is commonly used in information caves [26, 35]. Additionally, (multi-) touch screens are since recently commonly available as more intuitive multi-user human-computer interaction devices. However, despite their definite advantages for interactions with multiple users, particularly in table settings, multi-touch screens remain inadequate for use in rooms with physically spread-out sets of screens, as they require the users to constantly move from one screen to another.

Schmitt [47] introduced the term Information Architecture, which links analysis and design in the context of information systems and collaborative environments. The paradigms and ideas behind the term Information Architecture have strongly influenced the final design of the ETH Value Lab [14, 28, 30].

ETH Value Lab: A Collaboration Platform: The ETH Value Lab (Fig. 2) is designed as a collaboration platform to visualize and assess various planning scenarios regarding optimization of urban environments and to increase the urban quality [28, 30]. Van den Bergh et. al [59] presents an approach to enable multiple users to interact with multiple screens from any location in an collaborative environment.

The Value Lab consists of a physical space with state-of-the art hardware, software (e.g. urban simulation and CAD/BIM/GIS data visualization packages) and intuitive human-computer interaction devices. The interface consists of several high-resolution large area displays including:

1. **Five large screens** with a total of 16 mega pixels and equipped with touch interface capabilities; and

2. **Three Full HD projectors:** Two projectors form a concatenated high-resolution projection display with 4 Megapixel in resolution. That particular configuration is used for instance for real-time landscape visualization. The third projector delivers associated views for videoconferencing, presentation and screen sharing.

The Value Lab combines hardware, software and interaction to further visual insights from experts and urban planners to stakeholders in a human-friendly computer environment [25].

Fig. 2. The Value Lab represents the interface to advanced city simulation techniques and acts as the front-end of the ETH Simulation Platform

3   Decision Support Tools

The motivation for using decision-support tools in urban planning is saving costs and time, enabling the creation of a mutual vision, supporting a broad understanding and acceptance of final planning decisions. We present three decision support tools for visualizing future cities: (a) a 'Visual Manager', which is a collaborative method to identify and manage risks, (b) an 'Architectural Information Map (ArcIMap)' - a collective framework - for gathering and collecting relevant information for the urban design and (c) a participatory method, 'Architectural Programming', for gathering needs and requirements from stakeholders and for translating them to design guidelines for a later 3D visualization.

3.1   Visual Manager: Towards a Visual Management of Strategies and Risks

In urban planning the assessment of risks has been mostly neglected so far, despite the strong negative consequences of bad risk management. A risk is inherently linked to many other risks. This complex inter-linking makes it essential to receive broad acceptance and agreement among the numerous stakeholders involved in order to find a way to reduce the overall risk. We have therefore devised an exemplary approach and tool (Fig. 3).

Our goal is a collaborative method to identify and manage risks by bringing stakeholders around a multi-touch table and allow for a playful tackling of this task in the context of a workshop. The tool-supported process is based on a method developed by Burkhard and Merz [15] as follows:

1. **prepare** a survey for stakeholders in order to gather the risks as perceived by them,
2. **identify** of the main risks (up to a hundred) among the stakeholders' survey replies and grouping into related categories,
3. **assess** during the workshop using a multi-touch table: perform an interactive rating of each risk by positioning it on a map in respect to likelihood (x-axis) and impact (y-axis),
4. **prioritize** during the workshop using a multi-touch table: interactively define the top ten risks in mutual agreement among all stakeholders,
5. **react** during the workshop using a multi-touch table: define actions and scenarios for each risk, assign a person to be in charge of adjusting deadlines and resources,
6. **disseminate** risks and actions to other related persons through tool-generated, individual reports and posters,
7. **control and iteratively re-assess** the risks through periodical workshops. In addition each group of similar stakeholders is encouraged to hold focused follow-up workshops in order to further expand on related risks.

Fig. 3. "Visual Manager" application (Copyright: R. Burkhard, vasp datatecture GmbH, vasp.ch)

A project jointly funded by CTI, Swiss Commission for Technology and Innovation [19], ETH Zurich and vasp datatecture GmbH further developed the approach into a multi-touch framework for other areas, such as strategy management, project management, and urban planning. Well-known industry partners successfully held productive workshops in the ETH Value Lab using this application as central tool [14]. We believe the project to be a stepping stone for a paradigm shift towards visual management of information.

3.2   Architectural Information Map (ArcIMap): 'Intelligent' Urban Design

At the beginning of a design project, design teams usually gather and collect relevant information in order to familiarize themselves with the project context, to set up the problem framework, and to define the design issues. This information is, implicitly or explicitly, organized around a number of design aspects. Designers already have individual notions and ideas on various design aspects even before the information collection activity. However, the collected information, without doubt, helps provide an improved cognitive framework of the design problems, entities, and their relationships and assists in better solving encountered design problems.

Such a cognitive framework has been developed as part of a participatory information gathering and structuring activity during an educational experiment of an M.Sc. elective course at TU Delft [53]. The elective course pursued implementing a design aid for urban designers in order to make informed design decisions. For this educational experiment, a methodology was followed that involves the collective creation of a knowledge model, and the use of this model for making informed design decisions in the final urban design. In a number of exercises, the students studied an urban design situation by collecting and processing information for a knowledge model, and then applying this model. The case study for the course was an urban design transformation of the Wijnhaven Island area in downtown Rotterdam into a high-rise residential urban area [17].

In the first exercise of the course, the students familiarized themselves with the site and the related considerations in order to then define a project description and program brief. The students collected relevant information from the current situation and collectively shared and managed this information using Architectural Information Map (ArcIMap) as a digital collaborative environment and as a participatory design method [54]. Students concentrated on information gathering and analysis of the site using a number of urban aspects including accessibility, functionality, views and daylight issues. Then, a collective framework was formed describing the important aspects that play a role in the preliminary design stage for this specific site, and the relationships between these aspects. First, a tree structure emerged. Then, students started defining more associations between various branches of the tree. This defined the final visual structure of concepts and relationships defined as a concept map. The students stated that some of these aspects and relationships came up from their previous knowledge as designers, and some they learned by searching for and collecting information. In any case, the resulting structure represented their collective cognitive framework for problem setting for a design for a specific site. The students then translated this map to the ArcIMap digital environment and refined it collectively over time, adopting it as the organizational backbone of the collected information and generated knowledge, and relied on this collection during the rest of the design process. Figure 4 presents the complex information structure as the result of the activities of the students using ArcIMap.

In the later exercises of the course, students worked with a list of aspects, which are mainly based on the Birmingham planning policy framework for tall buildings [7]. These aspects, grouped under the headings context, program criteria, impact on surroundings, architectural design, and on site accessibility, were collected in a data collection form. The students went to the site, interviewed people, read articles and did research about the site in relation to these aspects, and each student filled out at least 6 data collection forms. Each aspect in the form was marked by selecting one of 5 slots, ranging from 'strongly agree' to 'strongly disagree' as a reaction to the statement made. These marks were later normalized to a value between 0 and 1 and all the values from all the sheets were merged together to form a data matrix to train the knowledge model. These also served as the variables in the knowledge model. The knowledge model used a number of computational intelligence techniques: fuzzy logic, neural networks and genetic algorithms. Once the knowledge model was established, the design exercise aimed to obtain a certain design guide providing a quality of life, which is desirably high. This definition of quality of life was left up to each student, and achieved by creating a weighted combination of selected aspects. In order to fulfill these constraints, the selected aspects were taken to be at the output of the knowledge model where the rest of the variables were at the input. Having established the knowledge model as such, the pattern of the input variables, which yields the satisfaction of the quality of life criterion, was searched by means of a genetic algorithm. The definition of quality of life acted as the fitness function of the genetic algorithm. The knowledge model was presented to the students as an easy to use application. The use of the knowledge model clarified the relations between different aspects and allowed the user to infer urban design principles from it. The students used these relations and principles in their own design for the area, up to the level of massing studies, and for the specification of functional entities.

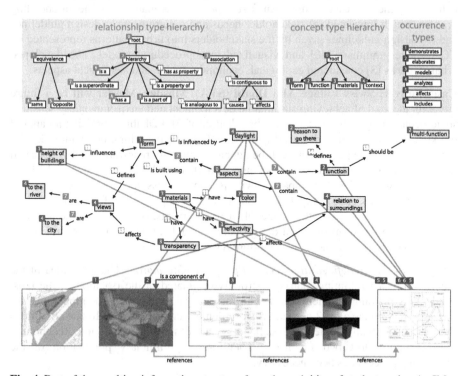

Fig. 4. Part of the resulting information structure from the activities of students using ArcIMap in an educational participatory design process

3.3   Architectural Programming: Method for Participatory Planning

'Architectural programming', a participatory method, is acknowledged as a decision support tool in the early stage of architectural and urban design. Architectural programming was used and evaluated for the gathering of needs and requirements of stakeholders [37, 42]. It was implemented (a) within a student course to develop urban patterns for the new eco-city "Swiss Village Abu Dhabi" in Masdar [52] and (b) within the World Cup 2014 'Urban Scenarios' workshop in Porto Alegre, Brazil.

The workshop was documented and annotated through the creation of cards that contained a phrase and an illustration. These cards were created by a group of researchers as the discussion was taking place among the stakeholders. Each card referred to a requirement expressed by a stakeholder during the discussion. Cards were categorized either as a 'fact card' – for analysis – or as a 'design concept card' – for a proposed reaction on an existing condition that was discovered during the briefing, and were hung on the wall, visible to everyone. An architectural programming matrix was composed from these cards expressed as requirements. The resulting matrix, which was visible to all participants, was evaluated and the requirements weighted against each other by the stakeholders. This then led to individual discussions. In an iterative process, the architectural programming matrix was interactively modified through the stakeholders' weighting of the requirements.

The collected needs and requirements were formulated in another step into urban patterns for the two case studies. An first approach was made to define an encoding process, which translated (a) stakeholder needs and requirements to design guidelines and (b) design guidelines given by the stakeholders into urban patterns represented by CGA shape grammars [40] and visualized in a procedural model. The developed urban patterns [3] considered ecological, economic, social, and aesthetical aspects.

Case Study 1: Swiss Village Abu Dhabi (SVA), Masdar. Masdar will be a future city with the goal of achieving sustainable development and environmentally sensitive socio-economic growth. It is a new urban district of Abu Dhabi comprising an area of 6.5 km^2. This future city, designed from scratch, will have a high population density (approx. 135 people per ha) and will be dependent on only renewable energy. Located in the core zone of Masdar, Swiss Village Abu Dhabi (SVA) with a size of 12 ha is planned in which Swiss companies will promote Swiss technology, design, and quality [52]. This case study [37] exemplifies the application of the participatory planning approach to (a) gather stakeholder requirements, (b) formulate the resulting information in the form of urban design patterns, and (c) define a procedural multi-dimensional procedural model of the future SVA.

Structure of the predefined architectural programming matrix. The main idea of the architectural programming matrix is strongly originated in the isolation of the most challenging planning problems during the very early design phase. The global goal for the SVA is to create a CO2 neutral urban settlement under extreme climate conditions that is additionally able to operate as a technology hub and technology implementation test bed for itself. Therefore a preliminary preparation of the monitoring process has been necessary.

Architectural programming workshop. The workshops were divided into two themes: sustainable aspects and passive design. Architectural and clean tech strategies with 60 students from architecture and environmental sciences and experts from SVA, architecture and clean tech domain joined the workshops. The main topics were transportation, supply system (e.g. energy, water, food), environment, passive design strategies (e.g. shadings, air ventilation), clean tech guidelines and building guidelines. The idea behind an architectural programming workshop (Fig. 5a) is to provide stakeholders with an integrated view on the planning facts and concepts and to incorporate personal and expert knowledge. Moderators used the structure of the matrix to steer the monitoring process. The gathered opinions have been collaboratively rated and weighted in their particular importance by the stakeholders. Furthermore, these opinions have been translated into figurative expressions – so called programming cards (Fig. 5b). Each cardboard describes one particular aspect represented by a simplified sketch or diagram, which is accompanied by textual and numerical attributes. The results are (a) single cards representing a detection of a planning problem (fact) or a definition of a potential solution (concept) and (b) a structured card matrix that represents the overall planning task definitions in a weighted and jointly agreed representation.

Fig. 5. (a) Architectural programming workshop and (b) programming cards, which were composed straightly in the workshop, showing concepts of sustainable aspects

Defining design rules concerning sustainability impacts. The architectural programming matrix is finally used to define sustainable design rules. The SVA design rules derived from the matrix concern performance criteria and measures for energy efficient settlements as well as for urban qualities such as pedestrian climate comfort. As a guideline, the system approach by Bossel [9] has been used to validate the selected sustainability criteria.

Defining urban patterns. Each sustainability criteria has been translated into a measure in the form of guidelines. A measure defines a required value – such as targeted air ventilation or heat distribution. Alternatively, a measure may result in a parametric definition of a geometric configuration that provides a particular performance – such as the shading of a facade. These guidelines are validated in a participatory process and translated and described as urban design patterns. The paradigm of an urban design pattern (Fig, 6a) is used as an interface for the implementation of the procedural model.

Implementing urban patterns into a procedural model. A procedural urban model offers several advantages compared to 3D analog models or digital urban model representations (Fig. 6b). A procedural model can provide a necessary level of detail for each element according to the need. Design measures can be communicated to participants already during the workshop. Jointly identified problems can be addressed and iterated immediately. Furthermore, a frozen model geometry can be evaluated in simulation software packages (e.g., to detect urban heat islands) or given to a model maker for public presentation. It can be used to report the fulfillment of key attributes and even to evaluate more intellectual goals such as architectural aesthetics.

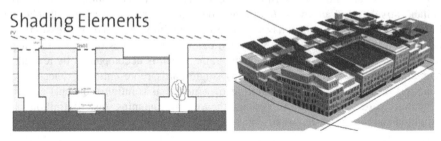

Fig. 6. (a) Urban Pattern and (b) an interactive procedural model for a specified parcel within Swiss Village Abu Dhabi (SVA)

Case Study 2: World Cup 2014 'Urban Scenarios' Workshop Porto Alegre, Brazil. The goal of this workshop, World Cup 2014 'Urban Scenarios' at Universidade Federal do Rio Grande do Sul (UFRGS), was to develop sustainable urban scenarios for the years 2014, 2025, 2050 by the use of several participatory methods. One of the challenges was to gather interdisciplinary planning knowledge from a diverse team of stakeholders (e.g. architects, urban and traffic planners, municipality, and public community) (Fig. 7).

Fig. 7. Architectural programming workshop with experts, urban planners, architectural students and public

The methodology used at the workshop "World Cup 2014 Urban Scenarios" is a collaborative modeling platform that allows iterative modification of an urban model through a set of participatory meetings. The methodology aims at devising sustainable development guidelines for Porto Alegre incorporating views of different stakeholders on requirements expressed in the form of design briefing for urban design patterns. The participation of a multi-disciplinary group of stakeholders is of great importance to strengthen the design process. The diverse group suggested key variables of Porto Alegre and analyzed different areas using their experience and knowledge about local problems and potential solutions. This process may lead to a sustainable development of the urban system as it brings modern planning techniques to local urban awareness (Fig. 8).

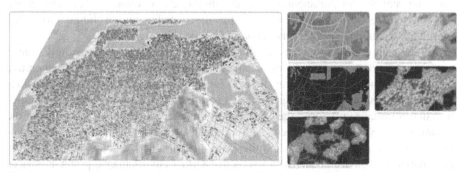

Fig. 8. Interactive visualization based on the method from Vanegas, et. al [60] of the scenario of Porto Alegre in 2025 with the simulated highways, accessibility, population, and planned employment

A tool chain was applied during the collaborative modeling process. We started with the 'AP' method for the formulation of stakeholder requirements into urban patterns for the procedural modeling of Porto Alegre. Then a system for interactive design of urban spaces using geometrical and behavioral modeling was used [60]. 'CityZoom' [56] was used for the performance of the urban model in order to to align the model with urban planning regulations. The developed models include building construction potential, solar radiation impact, pollution dispersion, and building interior illumination impact of neighboring buildings (luminance and illuminance). For the final 3D visualization, CityEngine [44] was used. A procedural model and final photo-realistic renderings of the different proposed scenarios were developed for further assessment with the stakeholders (Fig. 9).

Fig. 9. Final photo-realistic rendering of the proposed scenario for 2025 for one of the case study areas in Porto Alegre, Brazil

4   Conclusions

In this chapter, we have discussed the motivation and target for "Visualizing Future Cities" and have demonstrated some insights of the use of decision support tools for the development of sustainable future cities. The chapter also provided an overview of visualization methods, decision support tools in architecture, urban, and regional planning, stakeholder participation, and collaborative environments. Furthermore we presented three decision support tools for the visualization of future cities and presented two case studies for a novel participatory planning method.

Revitalizing cities and increasing urban qualities will become increasingly crucial goals for planners in the coming decades. We envision the use of collaborative environments and decision support tools to forge ahead in planning agencies of cities and regional institutions. Such agencies and institutions will adopt dedicated facilities in order to visualize proposed scenarios for all involved stakeholders and enhance the planning of sustainable future cities. Additionally, expert tools for simulation will become increasingly interactive and therefore more usable for non-experts. The link of collaborative environments with interactive virtual environments, portable devices and social networks will support these goals.

Acknowledgements. We would like to thank Jan Halatsch, Daniel Aliaga, Carlos Vanegas, Matthias Bühler, Martina Jacobi, Benamy Turkienicz, Christine Meixner, Yuliya Schlegel and Aiste Plentaite for their continuing support and for many helpful discussions as well as our students from 2009 and 2010, who participated in the courses 'Envisioning the Swiss Village Abu Dhabi' and 'New methods in urban simulations' at the ETH Zurich. This work was supported by the SNF Grant 130578 of the National Research Program NRP 65 'Sustainable Urban Patterns (SUPat)' and the Swiss Commission for Technology and Innovation Grant 10381.2 PFES-ES. Also, we are very grateful to the reviewers for their valuable comments.

References

1. Angélil, M., Martin, M., Cabane, P., Kueng, L., Maisano, P., Matter, M., Theiler, B.: Werkzeuge urbaner Morphogenese: Strategien zur Entwicklung zeitgenössischer urbaner Territorien, Schweizerischer Nationalfonds: Nationales Forschungsprogramm 54, Nachhaltige Siedlungs- und Infrastrukturentwicklung, Zürich, ETH Eidgenössische Technische Hochschule Zürich (2008)
2. Angélil, M., Hebel, D.: Addis Ababa by design. In: Urbanization. Investing in new cities. Global Investor 2.10, Oktober 2010, Expert know-how for Credit Suisse investment clients (2010)
3. Alexander, C., Ishikawa, S., Silverstein, M.: A Pattern Language: Towns, Buildings, Construction. Oxford University Press, New York (1977)
4. Arnstein, S.R.: A ladder of citizen participation. Journal of the American Institute of Planners 35(4), 216–224 (1969)
5. Behnisch, M.: Urban Data Mining, Universitätsverlag, Karlsruhe (2009)

6. Beirão, J. Duarte, J., Stouffs, R.: Structuring a Generative Model for Urban Design: Linking GIS to Shape Grammars. In: 26th eCAADe Conference Proceedings of Architecture in Computro, Antwerpen, Belgium, pp. 929—938 (2008)
7. Birmingham City Council. High Places, a planning policy framework for tall buildings, http://www.birmingham.gov.uk/cs/Satellite/highplaces?packeda rgs=website%3D4&rendermode=live+
8. Borning, A., Waddell, P., Forster, R.: UrbanSim: Using Simulation to Inform Public Deliberation and Decision-Making. In: Chen, H., Brandt, L., Dawes, S., Gregg, V., Hovy, E., Macintosh, A., Traunmuller, R., Larson, C.A. (eds.) Digital Government: Advanced Research and Case Studies, pp. 439–463. Springer, Heidelberg (2008)
9. Bossel, H.: Indicators for Sustainable Development: Theory, Method, Applications. International Institute for Sustainable Development, Winnipeg (1999)
10. Burkhard, R., Meier, M.: Tube Map Visualization: Evaluation of a Novel Knowledge Visualization Application for the Transfer of Knowledge in Long-Term Projects. Journal of Universal Computer Science 11(4), 473–494 (2005)
11. Burkhard, R.: Learning from Architects: Complementary Concept Mapping Approaches. Information Visualization Journal 5, 225–234 (2006)
12. Burkhard, R.A., Andrienko, G., Andrienko, N., Dykes, J., Koutamanis, A., Kienreich, W., Phaal, R., Blackwell, A., Eppler, M., Huang, J., Meagher, M., Grün, A., Lang, S., Perrin, D., Weber, W., VandeMoere, A., Herr, B., Börner, K., Fekete, J.D., Brodbeck, D.: Visualization summit 2007: ten research goals for 2010. Information Visualization 6(3), 169–188 (2007)
13. Burkhard, R.A.: Visualize Desires, not Cities. In: Thierstein, A., Förster, A. (eds.) The image and the region, pp. 169–180. Lars Müller Publishers, Baden (2008)
14. Burkhard, R., Meier, M., Schneider, C.: The ETH Value Lab and Two Software Tools for Knowledge Creation in Teams. In: 13th International Information Visualisation Conference, Barcelona (2009)
15. Burkhard, R.A., Merz, T.: A Visually Supported Interactive Risk Assessment Approach for Group Meetings. In: Proceedings of I-KNOW 2009 and I-SEMANTICS 2009, Graz, Austria, September 2-4, pp. 62–70 (2009)
16. Coaffee, J., Healey, P.: My Voice: My Place: Tracking Transformations in Urban Governance. Urban Studies 40(10), 1979–1999 (2003)
17. Christiaanse, K., van den Born, H.: Stedebouwkundig plan Wijnhaveneiland. Nova Terra 2(2), 24–28 (2002)
18. Cornwall, A.: Unpacking participation: Models, meanings and practices. Community Development Journal 43(3), 269–283 (2008)
19. Commission for Technology and Innovation, CTI, http://www.bbt.admin.ch/kti/index.html?lang=en
20. Eppler, M., Burkhard, R.: Knowledge Visualization. In: Schwartz (ed.) Encyclopedia of Knowledge Management. Idea Press, New York (2005)
21. Erhan, H.I.: Interactive support for modeling and generating building design requirements. Doctoral Thesis. School of Architecture, Carnegie Mellon University, Pittsburgh, PA (2003)
22. Fiorino, D.J.: Citizen participation and environmental risk: A survey of institutional mechanisms. Science, Technology, & Human Values 15(2), 226–243 (1990)
23. Flemming, U., Woodbury, R.: Software Environment to Support Early Phases in Building Design (SEED): Overview. Journal of Architectural Engineering 1(4), 147–152 (1995)
24. Förster, R.: Overcoming implementation barriers of scientific simulation models in regional development the functions of participatory modeling, ETH Zurich (2009)

25. Fox, A., Johanson, B., Hanrahan, P., Winograd, T.: Integrating information appliances into an interactive workspace. IEEE Computer Graphics & Applications 20(3), 54–65 (2000)
26. Gross, M., Würmlin, S., Naef, M., Lamboray, E., Spagno, C., Kunz, A., Koller-Meier, E., Svoboda, T., Van Gool, L., Lang, S., Strehlke, K., Moere, A.V., Staadt, O.: Blue-c: a spatially immersive display and 3D video portal for telepresence. In: ACM SIGGRAPH 2003 Papers, San Diego (2003)
27. Habermas, J.: The Theory of Communicative Action. Reason and the Rationalization of Society, vol. 1. Beacon Press, Boston (1985)
28. Halatsch, J., Kunze, A.: Value Lab: Collaboration in Space. In: Proceedings of 11th International Information Visualisation Conference, Zurich, pp. 376–381 (2007)
29. Halatsch, J., Kunze, A., Schmitt, G.: Using Shape Grammars for Master Planning. In: Gero, J.S. (ed.) Design Computing and Cognition DCC 2008, pp. 655–673. Springer, Heidelberg (2008)
30. Halatsch, J., Kunze, A., Schmitt, G.: Value Lab: A collaborative environment for the planning of Future Cities. In: Proceedings of eCAADe 2009, Istanbul (2009)
31. Halatsch, J., Kunze, A., Burkhard, R., Schmitt, G.: ETH Future Cities Simulation Platform: A Framework for the Participative Management of Large-Scale Urban Environments. In: Konsorski-Lang, S., Hampe, M. (eds.) The Design of Material, Organism, and Minds. X. Media. Publishing, Springer, Heidelberg (2010)
32. Henn, G.: Programming; Projekte effizient und effektiv entwickeln. In: Schurer, O., Brandner, G. (eds.) Architektur: Consulting. Kompetenzen, Synergien, Schnittstellen. Birkhauser, Basel (2004)
33. Healey, P.: The Communicative Turn in Planning Theory and its Implications for Spatial Strategy Formation. In: Campbell, S., Fainstein, S. (eds.) Readings in Planning Theory, 2nd edn., pp. 1237–1255. Blackwell, Malden (2003)
34. Keel, P.E.: EWall: A visual analytics environment for collaborative sense-making. In: Information Visualization, vol. 6, pp. 48–63 (2007)
35. König, W.A., Bieg, H.-J., Schmidt, T., Reiterer, H.: Position-independent interaction for large highresolution displays. In: IHCI 2007: IADIS International Conference on Interfaces and Human Computer Interaction 2007, pp. 117–125. IADIS Press (2007)
36. Krütli, P., Stauffacher, M., Flüeler, T., Scholz, R.W.: Functional-dynamic public participation in technological decision-making: Site selection processes of nuclear waste repositories. Journal of Risk Research (2010)
37. Kunze, A., Schmitt, G.: A Conceptual Framework for the Formulation of Stakeholder Requirements. In: 28th eCAADe Conference Proceedings of Future Cities, ETH Zurich, Switzerland, pp. 697–705 (2010)
38. Laws, D., Scholz, R.W., Shiroyama, H., Susskind, L., Suzuki, T., Weber, O.: Expert Views on Sustainability and Technology Implementation. International Journal of Sustainable Development and World Ecology 11(3), 247–261 (2004)
39. Luz, F.: Participatory landscape ecology: A basis for acceptance and implementation. Landscape and Urban Planning 50, 157–166 (2000)
40. Müller, P., Wonka, P., Haegler, S., Ulmer, A., Van Gool, L.: Procedural Modelling of Buildings. In: Proceedings of ACM SIGGRAPH 2006/ ACM Transactions on Graphics (TOG), vol. 25(3), pp. 614–623. ACM Press (2006)
41. Oxman, R., Gero, J.: Using an expert system for design diagnosis and design synthesis. Expert Systems 4(1) (February 1987)
42. Pena, W.M.: Problem Seeking: An Architectural Programming Primer. CBI publishing Company, Boston (1977)

43. Pinson, S.D., Louca, J.A., Moraitis, P.: A distributed decision support system for strategic planning. Decision Support Systems 20(1), 35–51 (1997)
44. Procedural Inc., http://www.procedural.com/
45. Rittel, H., Webber, M.: Dilemmas in a General Theory of Planning. In: Policy Sciences, vol. 4, pp. 155–169. Elsevier Scientific Publishing Company, Inc., Amsterdam (1973); Reprinted in: Cross, N. (ed.), Developments in Design Methodology, pp. 135–144 . J. Wiley & Sons, Chichester (1984)
46. Robinson, J.W., Weeks, J.S.: Programming as Design. JAE 37(2), 5–11 (1983)
47. Schmitt, G.: Information Architecture; Basis and Future of CAAD. Birkhäuser, Basel (1999)
48. Schroth, O.: From information to participation. interactive landscape visualization as a tool for collaborative planning. ETH Zurich (2007)
49. Selman, P.: Community Participation in the Planning and Management of Cultural Landscapes. Journal of Environmental Planning and Management 47(3), 365–392 (2004)
50. Selle, K.: The End of Public Participation? Stories of the Transformation of an Old Notion. In: Buhmann, E., Paar, P., Bishop, I., Lange, E. (eds.) Trends in Real-Time Landscape Visualization and Participation, Proceedings at Anhalt University of Applied Sciences 2005, Wichmann, Heidelberg, pp. 31–46 (2005)
51. Stauffacher, M., Flüeler, T., Krütli, P., Scholz, R.W.: Analytic and dynamic approach to collaborative planning: a transdisciplinary case study on sustainable landscape development in a Swiss pre-alpine region. Systemic Practice and Action Research 21(6), 409–422 (2008)
52. SVA, Swiss Village Abu Dhabi Association, Swiss Village in Masdar. The green business hub for Swiss companies. Swiss Village Association Brochure, http://www.swiss-village.com
53. Tunçer, B., Ciftcioglu, Ö., Sariyildiz, S., Cumming, M.: Intelligent design support. In: Bhatt, A. (ed.) Caadria 2005 (Proceedings of the 10th International Conference on Computer Aided Architectural Design Research in Asia), TVB School of Habitat Studies, New Delhi, India, pp. 436–446 (2005)
54. Tunçer, B.: The Architectural Information Map: Semantic modeling in conceptual architectural design, Ph.D. dissertation, Delft University of Technology, Delft, The Netherlands (2009)
55. Tuncer, B. Sariyildiz, S.: Facilitating Architectural Communities of Practice. In: 28th eCAADe Conference Proceedings of Future Cities, ETH Zurich, Switzerland, pp. 707–716 (2010)
56. Turkienicz, B., Goncalves, B.B., Grazziotin, P.: CityZoom: A Visualization Tool for the Assessment of Planning Regulations. International Journal of Architectural Computing 6(1), 79–95 (2008)
57. Ulmer, A., Halatsch, J., Kunze, A., Müller, P., Van Gool, L.: Procedural Design of Urban Open Spaces. In: Proceedings of eCAADe 25, Frankfurt, pp. 351–358 (2007)
58. UN-Habitat, Planning sustainable cities: global report on human settlements (2009), http://www.unhabitat.org/downloads/docs/GRHS2009/GRHS.2009.pdf
59. Van den Bergh, M., Halatsch, J., Kunze, A., Bosché, F., Van Gool, L., Schmitt, G.: A Novel Camera-based System for Collaborative Interaction with Multi-dimensional Data Models. In: CONVR Conference Proceedings, University of Sydney (2009)
60. Vanegas, C.A., Aliaga, D.G., Benes, B., Waddell, P.: Interactive Design of Urban Spaces using Geometrical and Behavioral Modeling. ACM Transactions on Graphics (also in Proceedings SIGGRAPH Asia) 28(5), 10 (2009)

61. Vanegas, C., Aliaga, D., Benes, B., Waddell, P.: Visualization of simulated urban spaces: Inferring parameterized generation of streets, parcels, and aerial imagery. IEEE Transactions on Visualization and Computer Graphics, 424–435 (2009)
62. Waddell, P.: Modeling urban development for land use, transportation, and environmental planning. Journal of the American Planning Association 68, 297–314 (2002)
63. White, S.: Depoliticising development: The uses and abuses of participation. Development in Practice 6(1), 6–15 (1996)
64. Wissen, U., Schroth, O., Lange, E., Schmid, W.A.: Approaches to integrating indicators into 3D landscape visualisations and their benefits for participative planning situations. Journal of Environmental Management 89, 184–196 (2008)
65. Wissen, U.: Virtuelle Landschaften zur partizipativen Planung - Optimierung von 3D Landschaftsvisualisierungen zur Informationsvermittlung. Vdf Hochschulverlag AG, Zürich (2009)

Spatiotemporal Visualisation: A Survey and Outlook

Chen Zhong, Tao Wang, Wei Zeng, and Stefan Müller Arisona

Future Cities Laboratory Singapore
ETH Zurich
{zhong,wang,zeng,arisona}@arch.ethz.ch

Abstract. Visualisation as a means of communication helps represent massive data sets, exchange knowledge and obtain better understanding of information. Spatiotemporal visualisation concerns changes of information in space and time. It has a natural advantage of revealing overall tendencies and movement patterns. Compared to traditional visual representations, it makes the notion of time accessible to non-expert users, and thus constitutes an important instrument in terms of decision-making that has been used in many application scenarios. As an interdisciplinary approach, substantial progress has been made in different domains, such as geographic information science, visualisation, or visual analytics, but there remains a lot of room for further advancements. In view of this, this paper presents a review of significant research in spatiotemporal visualisation, highlights a general workflow of data acquisition, information modelling and visualisation. Existing work from different domains are introduced, linked to the workflow, and possible integration strategies are given. Inspired by this summary, we also propose future work aiming at improving current spatiotemporal visualisation by integrating visualisation and interaction techniques more tightly.

Keywords: Spatiotemporal visualisation, spatiotemporal modelling, GIS.

1 Introduction

"To occur is to take *place*. In other words, to exist is to have being within both *space* and *time*. This entanglement of thing, space and time adds to the difficulty of analyzing these concepts" (Peuquet, 2002). This chapter looks at this entanglement from a viewpoint of how to visualise data that exists both within space and time, so-called spatiotemporal data.

A spatiotemporal model is defined as a data model used to efficiently organise and manage temporal geographic data sets that are associated with additional attributes and with spatial and temporal semantics (Zhang and Qin, 2004). In order to make use of such data sets, which are typically available in terms of sampled points, and to make them visually readable, spatiotemporal visualisation has been developed. This visualisation technique acts as a powerful tool to extract implicit knowledge and loosely related information. A significant advantage of spatiotemporal visualisation is that it provides a global view of activities or progress, from which evolutions and overall tendencies can be detected. Thus, it is widely used as an instrument for depicting processes, for demonstrating spatial and temporal analysis results, and for decision-making. The range of applications is diverse and includes dispersion of infectious diseases, flood

S. Müller Arisona et al. (Eds.): DUMS, CCIS 242, pp. 299–317, 2012.

management, land cover change, landscape simulation, land use simulation, or transportation simulation. The situation of today's environmental issues and the need for sustainable development increase the importance of spatiotemporal visualisation, which transforms dynamic modelling of multidimensional data into visual representations and consequently makes such data more accessible to experts as well as non-expert users.

The challenges of successfully applying spatiotemporal visualisation arise from various aspects. First, current data acquisition techniques have promised the acquisition of large spatiotemporal data sets, which could be used to reconstruct details and reflect changes. However, the size of such data sets demands considerable computing capacity for data management, and requires new algorithms and representations in order to extract new knowledge. Second, the form of data representation aims at providing sense of reality and immersion, as well as comprehensive knowledge. It evolves from traditional 2D map representations to 3D layered models, to ultimately four-dimensional spatiotemporal models. Such representations require a deep understanding of how information and knowledge can be extracted from raw data and how cognitive principles can be applied. Finally, models and methods originating from different disciplines are often complementary but not well combined. This is a common problem addressed by existing literature dealing with interdisciplinary work. For instance, in order to improve the readability of views and to enhance corresponding interactive operations, previous work included techniques from cartography, geographic information science, visualisation, and visual analytics (Kraak, 2006).

This paper looks at these challenges starting from the perspective of Geographic Information Systems (GIS), and reflects on how to fill the gap between GIS, urban simulation as well as other related topics. Literature and previous works are reviewed to summarise the topics on spatiotemporal information modelling and visualisation. Research in different domains from the perspective of visualisation and interactive operations is linked and potential future directions are proposed. However, we focus on urban spatiotemporal information and most of the visualisations we refer to are map-based, concerning urban information and originating from GIS applications.

2 Overview and Existing Work

As mentioned, spatiotemporal visualisation involves methodologies and techniques from different domains. From the perspective of GIS, it originated from GIS 2D maps and 3D layered representations, evolving towards 4D temporal GIS (3D GIS plus time). From the perspective of computer science, it has strong links to information models, computer graphics and visualisation, including elements from information visualisation and time-based visualisation. Moreover, it is used in urban simulation to illustrate changes over time.

2.1 Basic Concepts

The following sections provide a brief introduction in terms of these different backgrounds. First, we highlight specific characteristics to each domain and then highlight advantages and extract common points that exist despite the different usage both in terms of terminology as well as applications in each domain.

Computer Science. Spatiotemporal visualisation includes elements from computer science mainly from two areas: Visualisation and human computer interaction (HCI). More specifically, visualisation is applied to extract and transform complex raw data into an easily readable and understandable format. Depending on different data types and objectives, visualisation has developed into different branches, such as geo-visualisation referring to cartographic data, information visualisation referring to abstract data, or visual analysis referring to knowledge extraction. Various representations are designed to reflect information in terms of time series or multiple dimensions, while caring less about spatiotemporal relationships. In addition, HCI attempts to make data exploration more effective. For instance, today's rapid development of tangible interfaces is used to implement new means of navigation in large data sets, and current work also focusses on realising interaction with such data, e.g. by providing interactive selection and filtering operations. In addition, other areas such as data mining, or database management are involved.

Geographic Information System (GIS). A temporal GIS, is based on a 2D or 3D GIS that additionally stores temporal information, has the goal to answer questions such as where and when changes occur, what induced change patterns may be observed, and what may be the underlying causes of such changes. Langran and Chrisman (1988) explored the idea of temporal GIS to outline a framework for conceptual design and implementation of incorporating temporal information in GIS. They defined four representational models, which are space-time cubes; sequence snapshots; base state with amendments; and space-time composites, and resulted in four major temporal GIS models Zhang and Qin (2004). Many concrete applications are within this domain, since GIS has a strong foundation in geography and offers significant advantages for spatial analysis. In particular, companies and government organisations in many countries recently started and will continue to transform their databases towards 3D GIS and will move towards integration of temporal data, especially for decision-making.

Urban Simulation. Urban simulation models and the visualisation of their results are increasingly used to assess important urban aspects such as land use regulations or alternative transportation schemes. According to Waddell and Ulfarsson (2004), when designing an urban simulation system, different choices should be considered to reflect the real world as a fused, dynamic environment. The choices include the level of behavioral aggregation, the level of determinism, the temporal representation, and the resolution of space and time. Many concrete applications like crowd simulation include the analysis of change of an urban environment. In addition, temporal representations are designed to highlight long-term equilibriums. Spatiotemporal visualisation, which embeds temporal information, has a natural advantage to support these applications. It should also be noted that there are ongoing efforts of filling the gaps between behavioral urban simulation and visualisation, e.g. (Vanegas et al., 2009). With the advancement of such approaches, the inclusion of temporal characteristics will become an even more important topic.

These three fields can be subdivided into even more detailed domains, and all have a close relationship with spatiotemporal visualisation. Computer science contributes with very advanced visualisation techniques and interactive operations but deals less with geographic information. GIS, which evolved with a strong geographic background, now advertises itself to be a popular spatial analysis tool, but is still mainly used for data management and layer-based static visualisation. Urban simulation has the capability the realistically model temporal behaviour of urban state, but its results are often inadequately visualised. However, GIS and urban simulation already share common concepts in terms of urban information modelling. Thus, when we view these fields (and potentially others) together, the increasing importance of dynamic behaviour and the notion of time is clearly visible, and it is natural that their advantages should be combined.

2.2   Previous Reviews

Former reviews have been made from different perspectives. From the perspective of GIS, temporal GIS have become one of the main pillars of recent developments. Originally, Langran and Chrisman (1988) examined four representational models for spatiotemporality, which were (1) space-time cubes, (2) sequential snapshots, (3) base state with amendments and (4) space-time composites. The space-time cube (STC) is based on original definitions of the space-time-path and space-time-prisms (Hägerstrand, 1970), which nowadays are considered highly important methods of spatiotemporal visualisation. Kraak (1988) conducted a series of interactive operations on the space-time cube, and revised the progress of the advanced space-time cubes from the perspective of time geographic and revisualisation. Vasiliev (1997) proposed a framework for representing spatiotemporal information on static maps based on symbolisation in cartography. More recently, time series have been added to commercial geospatial software, such as in ArcMap (Goodall et al., 2004). Time series are used to show dynamic events, such as weather changes, water condition, and pollution desperation. From the perspective of the visual analyst, Andrienko et al. (2003) reviews visualisation methods by including the aspects of exploration technologies. Interactive operations are introduced for different data types and tasks.

In contrast to previous reviews, we summarise classical spatiotemporal visualisation techniques as well as related ones. The examples and illustrations in this chapter are not limited to a single research field. Thus, the main objective of the chapter is to provide an overview of basic ideas and recent trends in order to inspire future visualisation methods of comprehensive knowledge.

2.3   Workflow of Spatiotemporal Visualisation

Visualisation can be regarded as a translation from unstructured raw data to structured data representations. According to Spence (2007), "to visualise is to form a mental model or mental image of something." The relevant definitions of *model* in the Oxford Dictionary are given as "a thing used as an example to follow or imitate" and as "a simplified description, especially a mathematical one, of a system or a process, to assist calculations and predictions."

This paper introduces and adheres to a workflow that starts with data acquisition, performs information modelling, and concludes with actual visualisation techniques as shown in figure 1. First, section 3 deals with 4D data acquisition, which makes the automatic generation of spatiotemporal data efficient due to significant recent improvements.

After data acquisition, the original spatial datasets effect the subsequent processes in the workflow; thus section 4 has a closer look at information modelling. As shown in figure 1, this step in the workflow involves different tasks related to data storage, filtering, clustering, analysis; and results in a conceptual model that is based on abstract data types (ADTs). In practise, these tasks are not always performed sequentially, but rather iteratively. For instance, semantic information is required for data queries, pattern detection, as well as for spatial analysis. Or, the abstract data types used for storage are largely determined by the expected results of spatial analysis.

Section 5 deals with visualisation techniques, considering both data representation and interactive operations. Typical methods that involve time are summarised in terms of dimensionality, i.e. 1D (symbols), 2D (image series), 3D (space-time cube), 4D (real-time rendering of dynamic 3D scenes). Inspired by that, possible future possibilities for spatiotemporal visualisation and associated interactive operations are proposed in section 6.

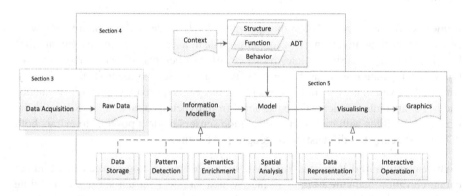

Fig. 1. Overall workflow to realise spatiotemporal visualisation

3   Spatiotemporal Data Acquisition

Spatial data acquisition has gone through revolutionary changes over the last fifty years. Evolving from labour-intensive and time-consuming points surveying, current technology involves high-precision and efficient satellite-based remote sensing techniques, as well as airborne and terrestrial methods supported by satellite-supported global positioning systems (GPS) (Longley et al., 2005). High-resolution and hyper-spectral imagery is now available at affordable cost, sometimes even for free, and includes data describing status and changes of natural phenomena and man-made artefacts, such as climate, water, land, vegetation, road and residential area development. Automatic methods to derive more detailed information or knowledge from image datasets have long attracted past and ongoing research efforts in photogrammetry, computer vision and geosciences. (Semi-)Automatic tools for 3D morphological reconstruction, such as terrain, vegetation, buildings, or infrastructure, have been implemented to support geospatial databases (Gruen, 2008). The following paragraphs provide a brief introduction of the most relevant data acquisition technologies and methods.

Global Navigation Satellite Systems (GNSS). were invented for military applications, but have in the meantime become available for civil applications. Current GNSS include the Global Positioning System (GPS) implemented by the United States, the GLObal NAvigation Satellite System (GLONASS) of Russia, the Compass Navigation System of China, and the Galileo Positioning System of European Union. The first two are providing global service while the latter two only provide regional service. As the most successful globally available system, the GPS is freely accessible by any user and has been the major choice for consumer usage in terms of positioning and navigation. In research and professional applications, the core functionality of GNSS is to survey 3D coordinates. The accuracy can yield 3 cm (horizontal) with the real-time or post differential processing supported by a terrestrial operating reference station. The availability of high-accuracy global positioning is highly relevant for many sensing and monitoring applications. With continuous data observation over a long period, dynamic visualisation in 3D of series of data can reveal the position and degree of changes of objects to be observed.

Remote Image Sensing (RS). is indispensable due to its capabilities of covering wide areas and for allowing continuous acquisition. The imagery can be acquired by satellite-based sensors or by aerial vehicles flying at different heights. Typically, there are two types of information that can be derived from remote sensing data: a) the geometry, which is derived mainly from high resolution images acquired by optical instruments, and b) the attributes, which can be extracted from hyper-spectral images. Recently, the launch of satellites with high spatial resolution sensors made it possible to extract both 2D and 3D geometric dimensions of geographic features.

Light Detection and Ranging (LiDAR). uses laser pulses to generate dense and accurate elevation maps of a target surface, which can be a terrain surface or building topology, or a combination thereof. The height or distance to a target surface is determined by the elapsed time between generation and return of each laser pulse. Combined with data from an inertial measuring unit and from GPS, the point clouds can be further correlated and processed resulting in a georeferenced dataset. When realised by a moving vehicle like an unmanned aerial vehicle (UAV), the density can be determined by flight speed, altitude and laser repetition rate. In order to fully employ the dense points clouds, classification and filtering algorithms are vital to the successful acquisition of precise surface features. Currently, there are open problems to accurately extract digital terrain elevation, especially in areas with vegetation cover or with abrupt changes such as in urban areas. In addition, the visualisation of LiDAR point clouds requires multi-scale preprocessing.

Volunteered Geographic Information. makes use of Web 2.0 technology, of crowd-sourcing techniques, and of the increasing popularity of portable computing devices: In contrast to traditional techniques, the users of maps and geographic information systems have become participants and producers of various geo-tagged information as well. Volunteered geographic information, or VGI, was coined as a new topic in geographic information science to research the integration, update and consistency considering professional datasets (Goodchild, 2007). In the meantime, the online community has produced huge amounts of imagery and videos at different locations and times, which bear more abundant information than that traditional geospatial database contains.

4 Information Modelling of Spatiotemporal Data

Generally, the workflow to realise data visualisation can be summarised in terms of four basic stages as follows (Ware, 2004):

1. Data collection and storage.
2. Data preprocessing designed to transform the data into understandable information.
3. Display hardware and rendering algorithms that produce one or multiple images on the screen.
4. Interpretation in the context of the human perceptual and cognitive system (the perceiver).

As a branch of visualisation in general, spatiotemporal visualisation fits into the above general pipeline. However, as one of the main challenges of spatiotemporal visualisation is not only making the raw data understandable, but also using it to depict dynamics, movements and activities, we suggest to further refine the overall process with additional steps as follows:

1. Data storage and query (Güting et al., 2000; Güting, 2008).
2. Data filtering and clustering, pattern detection (Nanni and Pedreschi, 2006; Palma et al., 2008).
3. Enriching data with semantics and knowledge (Baglioni et al., 2009).
4. Translation of data into object-oriented entities using a conceptual model (Brakatsoulas et al., 2004).
5. Spatial analysis according to actual concrete application tasks; formulation of moving patterns with mathematic models; and prediction of tendencies (Maguire et al., 2005).
6. Visualisation of the entities (Kraak, 2005; Eccles et al., 2008).

Except for the last step, which is treated in more detail in section 5, we consider these steps as the relevant steps for information modelling that precede the actual visualisation. In the following, we briefly introduce important elements that are part of the overall process.

Moving Objects Database. The database provides support for storing and querying time-dependent geometries and moving objects (Güting and Schneider, 2005). From the perspective of GIS, collected data can be divided into two categories: static and dynamic information. Static objects do not change within a given period of time; examples are roads, buildings, or land views. In contrast, dynamic data changes within a given time interval, either discretely or continuously; examples are urban expansion, spreading of infectious diseases, or people movements. Some dynamic phenomena are represented in terms of named moving objects, i.e., defined as specific objects that change position or extend continuously (Güting et al., 2000). Güting defined basic spatial data types as well as a corresponding query algebra. He emphasised the fact that the geometry may change continuously. Thus, in his research, the proposed database management system includes concepts for data models and data structures to represent moving objects (Güting, 2008) and to allow query and analysis of such objects.

Moving Patterns Detection. Since raw data sets can not be directly used for specific purposes, techniques are applied to detect patterns, trends, and relations for a given objective of investigation (Andrienko et al., 2003). In this context, the main goal is to filter and cluster the massive spatial data, and to allow for reasonable exploration of data sets. As shown in (Andrienko and Andrienko, 2011), clustering of trajectory data and transformation of the temporal structures for comparisons within and between clusters are proposed to improve the effectiveness of the space-time cube.

Semantic Enrichment. In order to transform the detected patterns into understandable knowledge, semantic analysis and enrichment is applied. A major class of the spatiotemporal data sets are records of human activities. They naturally contain social knowledge within a given context and can be described using semantics to allow for queries that can be well understood by normal users. An important concept is the identification of trajectories in space over time. Spaccapietra et al. (2008) provides a formal definition of trajectories in terms of stop and move states. The definitions serve as a standard approach to link numerical data with semantics and have been widely applied and extended in later visualisation methods. During analysis, the topology of geographic data (Shekhar and Chawla, 2003) and temporal relationships (like Allen relations) are considered and combined to detect and define patterns. Semantics based on ontologies (Baglioni et al., 2008) is added to enrich the data during all the above steps. A trajectory is then divided into a sequence of partial state, defined with function, behaviour and structure.

Conceptual Data Models. A conceptual model is built to formulate the moving information and to highlight the cause and effect in the dynamic phenomenon. Peuquet and Duan (1995) proposed a spatiotemporal GIS database framework. The *Event-based Spatiotemporal Data Model* (ESTDM) organises event changes in terms of an event list that comprises individual event entries. The representation of events in terms of a triple "when (time), what (attribute), and where (location)" contributed a substantially to the object-oriented representations of spatiotemporal data emerging later on. Based on these models, further researches mainly investigate the relationship between entities. In addition, and not limited to spatiotemporal data only, Bertin (1983) classified the related questions into three levels "elementary, intermediary and overall", which can be used to organise and analyse data at different scales.

Spatial Analysis. Many concrete applications incorporate spatial analysis methods that are applied to study entities using their spatial properties. Maguire et al. (2005) introduced the basic tools and techniques, and highlighted models that are available in GIS and modelling systems. In addition, they reviewed information models and applications in the context of urban simulation, such urban growth models, urban land-use and transportation models, and location planning applications. Due to the ubiquitous availability of GIS and the sinking costs of using it, the number of applications that employ data mapping techniques, powerful analysis methods, and user-friendly interfaces is growing.

Information modelling is a comprehensive process, and all involved processes deeply influence the data structures and the resulting visualisations. Through this step, the raw data sets are transformed into abstract data types (ADTs), which formulate the dynamic information. ADTs must be carefully designed so they can carry enough semantics and provide useful functionality. Typed entities, such as "people", "places", "events" and "time" are designed to describe moving objects. The first ADT for moving objects was proposed in (Erwig et al., 1999), in which data types and sets of operations are defined, and can be applied to perform uniform queries in various DBMS object algebras. For modelling the data, two main methods that had a strong influence on later research were proposed: event-based data models (Peuquet and Duan, 1995), and object-oriented data models (Worboys, 1992). ADTs play an important role as they determine how to link the objects with corresponding geometry that can be directly used for the next step: the actual visualisation techniques.

5   Visualisation Techniques for Spatiotemporal Data

The most widely applied method for representing interesting, geo-referenced phenomena are maps. Using maps, the geospatial characteristics, such as cluster patterns and associated rules, are generally more easily identified as opposed to data listed in a table. In order to efficiently communicate information encoded in a map to users, cartographers have set up many theories investigating linguistics and semiology to build a generic graphic language based on common understanding and perception. On analog maps, the symbols are usually decomposed into six visual variables besides of intrinsic location and geometry: shape, size, colour, orientation, hue, and texture. In digital maps, more variables can be introduced, such as appearance duration or flashing intervals to represent dynamic phenomena effectively (Slocum et al., 2009). Additional information visualisation techniques enhance the interactive ability of exploration; and visual analytics makes the patterns even more visible. The significant, rapid evolution of GIS, is enhancing traditional time-based visualisation with object-oriented visualisation methods. This section focuses on different forms of data representation, and summarises the most important methods, starting with static techniques and then moving towards dynamic and interactive methods.

Timestamps and Time Labels: Timestamps are series of events marked with date and time information and typically used in temporal GIS databases to include the dimension of time. Time labels are specific graphic variables and symbols used in maps indicating changes. The view is static. Minard's famous graphic of Napoleon's Russian campaign (figure 2) is often used to illustrate these types of representation, as it uses different variables in a temporal context: Line width indicates army size; horizontal and vertical position denote latitude and longitude, i.e., are used as location information; colour is applied to identify the direction of the march; and temperature is indicated in terms of a graph along the timeline.

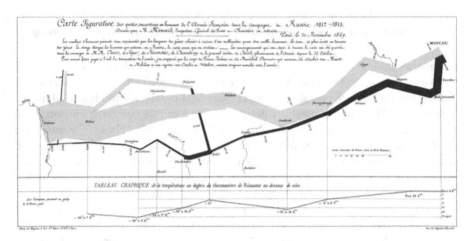

Fig. 2. Minard's graphic of Napoleon's Russian Campaign

Possible variables of graphic mapping have been summarised as shape, size, orientation, colour, texture, opacity, position and so on. Additional variables have been defined in the context of information visualisation, such as in (Spence, 2007). However, depending on the context, the specific symbols have to be carefully chosen, as they have to obey existing rules such as in cartography or urban planning.

Baselines. This technique uses arrows and lines, as well as charts and diagrams to indicate state changes, and frequently applies animation methods to represent the progress. It is widely used in 2D visualisations for both abstract and concrete information, such as for instance, a Gaussian distribution graphics to show demographic trends; an airline figure to show the entire flight plan (figure 3); or a vector field to show the movement directions (figure 4). While baselines can be used to provide an indication of time and dynamics, e.g. by using different arrow sizes for different speeds in a vector field, they cannot cover the absolute state of a model at a given point in time. Therefore baselines are not well suited for analysis of discrete events and relationships between events.

Image Series. As one class of dynamic representations, timelines are used as the basis for mapping events over time, and to dynamic information in terms of image series. When they are combined with a geographical map, they show the spatiotemporal patterns of those events (Hewagamage et al., 1999). Some basic timeline appearance types have been described by Kraak (2005), e.g., straight lines representing linear time like years; circular shapes to denote seasons in one year; spirals to indicate skewed time in geology. In map making, sequences of maps depict the changes of data in a region of interest. When a cursor moves along the timeline, maps change accordingly. The simplest animation type displays a small set of changing maps only, in terms of static pictures that change. An example is shown in figure 5, which gives a series of four remote sensing images indicating change over time. If the sets of changing images get larger, they can be shown in terms of animated video sequences. This technique can be applied in many cases for indicating continuous changes of the state of objects within a given

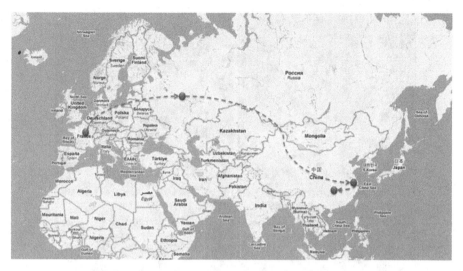

Fig. 3. Using a base line to indicate the flight path of a plane

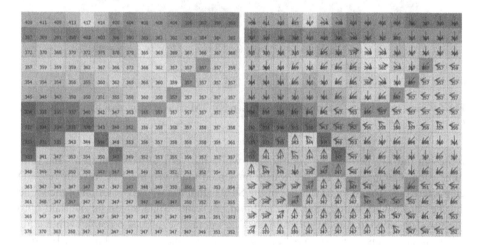

Fig. 4. Vector field used to indicate the direction of water flow

environment. For example, it is frequently used to visualise the output of mobility and transportation simulations, e.g., to depict activities and tendencies of movements over a period of time. A timeline animation can be enhanced with interactive operations, such as zoom in, zoom out, pan, or to focus on selected event types.

Space-Time Cube: In the early 70's, Hägerstrand (1970) developed a graphic view with time as an additional spatial dimension. He suggested a three-dimensional diagram, the so-called space-time cube (STC), to show life histories of people and how people interact in space and time. Two orthogonal horizontal axes were used to

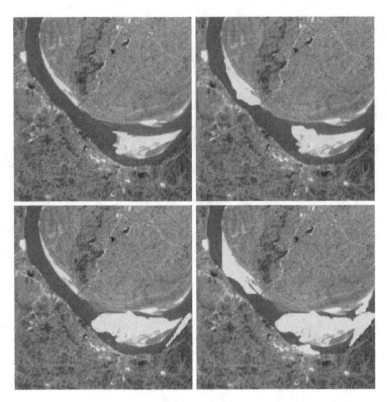

Fig. 5. Change detection: The multi-temporal Landsat TM change images of the famous Three Gorges

represent the x-y geographic coordinates, while the vertical axis represents the time dimension. Compared to the previously presented methods, the STC reveals real 3D characteristics. The main advantage of the STC is that the whole evolution of the scene can be shown within one image. In addition, more information can be overlaid onto the scene or individual events, thereby making interactive queries possible within a 3D environment. Thus, the STC has been extended with interactive techniques: In order to enhance the interactive manipulation and to reflect the detection of spatiotemporal clusters of events, based on the original space-time cube, Kraak (2005) presented an advanced version with operations of changing viewing perspective, temporal focusing, and dynamic linking of maps with corresponding symbols. Geotime (Eccles et al., 2008) as a mature commercial software supports many of these features. Today, many concrete applications using the STC have been realised (Kraak, 2006; ITC-2011, 2011). Three examples using space-time cube visualisation are shown in figure 6: the left image shows a visualisation of transportation simulation data; the top-right image shows trajectory data of people movements, and bottom-right shows the history of points of interest in a city. Gatalsky et al. (2004) compared baseline (2D) to space-time cube (3D) methods. They concluded that the space-time cube is comparably harder to understand for normal users, and interpretation errors can made. However, their evaluation showed that the users do benefit from space-time cube representations when analysing complex spatiotemporal patterns.

Real-Time Rendering of Dynamic 3D Scenes: One of the main limitations of the space-time cube is that usually movements along the vertical axis are lost (as this axis is used for time). This problem can be overcome to some extent by real-time animated 3D rendering techniques. For example, in urban simulation, timelines are used as an interface component to query instant changes. In contrast to the history timeline examples we mentioned above, for each frame, time is taken as one parameter input to simulate the current state of the model. In (Maguire et al., 2005), Batty and Goodchild introduce many concrete applications for urban simulation, including land use, transportation, or urban growth. In addition, Weber et al. (2009) presented a system that allows for interactive simulation of 4D cities, and lets the user change input parameters while the simulation runs. The system displays 3D models of an urban environment as the simulation evolves over time.

6   Potential Future Progress of Spatiotemporal Visualisation

In the report "space-time cube beyond time geography," Kraak (2006) reviewed different applications using space-time cube, and raised some open questions: Are there distinct strengths and weaknesses of the STC? Does the STC constitute a good alternative to other spatiotemporal visualisation techniques? Then, more specifically, can time and the third spatial dimension be used together along the same axis? When does a certain Space-Time-Path make sense?

   In the following we discussion, we shall address some of these questions, but also focus on the superordinate, more general question, whether users of STC applications understand what they see. The discussion is based on a concrete custom application that uses STC (figure 6, bottom-right). The application is a guidance system for tourism to help finding places of interests and for querying historical events of such points. In order to evaluate the users' understanding of the application, the following concrete questions were given:

1. Can users tell the meaning of the axes without any pre-instruction?
2. Can users tell the meaning of the results generated from the basic operations?
3. How much information can users obtain from the view?
4. What other interactive operations do users suggest?

It showed that nearly all the participators could quickly understand the basic functioning and meaning of the STC visualisation, as well as the basic operations like zoom, rotate, pan, select. However, many users found it hard to perceive precise information. In particular, when the amount of data was increased (i.e., adding more points of interest), the dense point sets made it hard select and isolate individual events. Some users were intrigued by the "cool-looking" 3D scene but questioned the usefulness of the representation (as opposed to more conservative, map-based approaches).

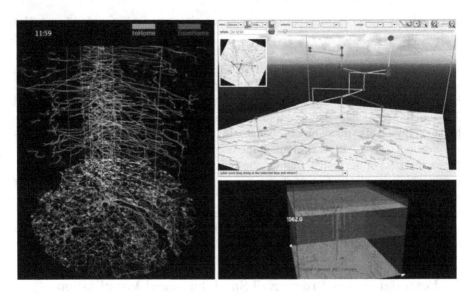

Fig. 6. Typical space-time cube applications: Spatiotemporal visualisation of transportation simulation data (left), visualisation of trajectories (top-right) and history visualisation of points of interest (bottom-right)

When it comes to question 4 (possible additional operations), the spectrum of answers was quite diverse, also reflecting different backgrounds of the users. Nontechnical users suggested to use two parallel views, 3D STC, as well as 2D traditional views to obtain a more focused view of specific data. Technically oriented users' feedback could mainly be categorised into two classes of extra operations: a) providing means of subdividing the cube and of clipping the cube using planes, and b) emphasise on data aggregation in order to provide a cleaner and less complex view.

Integrated 2D and 3D Visualisation. When comparing the visualisation techniques introduced in section 5, one obvious categorisation is by dimension, i.e. 2D vs. 3D views. Traditionally, 2D techniques have been most established and accepted in the GIS domain, a clear shift towards 3D (and 4D) also in these domains is recognisable, and today, high-performance 3D is available on consumer computers. Therefore we may ask what the most effective synergies between the two types might be, and how they could be combined. In GIS applications combined 2D and 3D views are commonly found – a prominent example is the combination of Google maps, street view, and Google Earth. Transfer the two representations can happen in both ways, e.g. extrude operations can generate 3D views from 2D base data, or dedicated projection operations may recreate 2D views from 3D geometry.

Based on this, we suggest a number of techniques that complement 2D and 3D STC views, as given in table 1. The images in the second column of the table were created from our research that focussed on semantic visualisation of trajectory data using STCs. It aimed at finding new visualisation methods to map defined semantics and to overlay additional information within the limited cube space while keeping the view at an

Table 1. Possible visualisation techniques that complement 3D and 2D views

Application	Space-Time Cube Visualisation	Information Visualisation
Multi-dimensional Data Visualisation		
Visualisation of Statistics Results		
Visualisation of Relationships Between Entities		

understandable level. The table presents three tasks that show the potential of integrating 2D and 3D visualisation:

1. Multi-dimensional data visualisation (first row). Here, we suggest the use of information visualisation techniques to make the interface more user friendly. Traditional interfaces use controls like combo-boxes to input query conditions (left image), which bloats the user interface and makes it confusing. Multi-dimensional visualisation techniques can be used to provide a cleaner view. In the right image, parallel coordinate are used to instead of combo-boxes, and a radar chart is used to evaluate the queried movements with multiple variables. An examples is found in (Forlines and Wittenburg, 2010): The 3D view is used to make an overall and direct understanding of the progress, while 2D view reflects details. In addition, animations and projections can be used to transform the 2D and 3D view between each other.

2. Visualisation of statistics results (second row). This visualisation has the goal of showing statistical data in real-time in order to make tendencies in a period of time understandable. The image on the left shows the result of a query, i.e. the number of visitors during a period of time. The image on the right enhances this view, and

Table 2. Possible operations that can be applied to space-time cube visualisation (images 2 and 3 in last row were recreated from Carpendale et al. (1996))

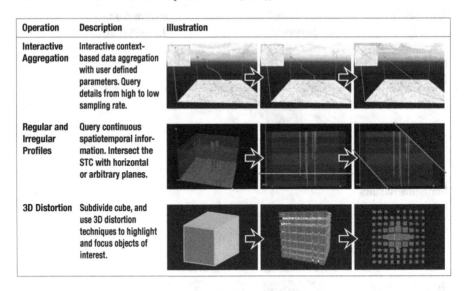

Operation	Description	Illustration
Interactive Aggregation	Interactive context-based data aggregation with user defined parameters. Query details from high to low sampling rate.	
Regular and Irregular Profiles	Query continuous spatiotemporal infor-mation. Intersect the STC with horizontal or arbitrary planes.	
3D Distortion	Subdivide cube, and use 3D distortion techniques to highlight and focus objects of interest.	

can provide additional degrees of freedom with peak values, area and gradients to denote different meanings. With this type of view, clusters can more easily be detected, as it has been shown in (Nanni and Pedreschi, 2006).

3. Visualisation of relationships between entities (last row). The example employs data mapping and aggregation of knowledge that includes geographic reference. It employs social network graphics, which have been widely used to reflect links between people. In spatiotemporal visualisation, one of the main objectives can be to find out the relationships and influences between people, activities and environment. With a time axis projection, the 3D view (left image) can be enhanced with a 2D network graphics (right image). Another example on visualising social elements was given in (Smith, 2009), where density maps demonstrated the mapping of social information like urban structure, employment structure with geographic reference, as well as data aggregation.

Interactive Operations. Today, 3D GIS platforms constitute an important communication platform for urban planners and decision makers. Successful commercial examples are ESRI ArcGIS or ERDAS VirtualGIS. Advanced spatial analysis operations such as time slice, oblique slice, or fence slice are designed to visualise features otherwise hidden. We believe that it is possible to transform and implement such operations into the context of space-time cube, so they can be used to query and highlight implicit spatiotemporal information, which in our view of point. We illustrate possible use cases in table 2, explained in more detail as follows:

1. Interactive aggregation (first row). As the size of data sets increases, massive amounts of points and lines make the view unreadable, and it becomes very hard to

carry out interactive selection of elements. We suggest two possible solutions; the first one filters data that is not related to the query, and the second that performs context-based aggregation. The latter provides varying level-of-detail according to different requirements (e.g. inspection versus selection). As in (Bertin, 1983), the three levels of information, "elementary, intermediary and overall" should be employed and generalised .

2. Regular and irregular profiles (second row). Indexing space-time data is a common querying operation, normally achieved by interacting with the timeline scrollbar. This corresponds to a "regular profile" (middle image), where a plane perpendicular to the time axis "cuts" through the STC. In contrast, an irregular profile lets the user define arbitrary planes or even surfaces to intersect with the STC (right image).

3. 3D shape distortion (last row). This operation suggests the separation of the whole space-time cube into smaller pieces with a dispersing transformation . Thus, each single sub-cube constitutes an independent spatiotemporal unit. User can easily interact with individual sub-cubes, focussing on information within a short period of time and within smaller area of interest. Additional operations would be navigation within a spatial structure of distorted cubes (Carpendale et al., 1996), or sorting operations among sub-cubes that could make relationships between them more explicit.

7   Summary and Conclusion

Spatiotemporal visualisation has been successfully applied in diverse domains. In this paper, we focussed on spatiotemporal visualisation related to urban models and data. We highlighted previous reviews, introduced a processing pipeline, that consists of data acquisition, information modelling, and the actual visualisation. For each of these steps we provided existing work, and established overall connections. Based on this, we proposed possible future progress, mainly dealing with closer integration of visualisation and interaction, and with enhancing the capabilities of interactive operations.

With wide-spread and increasingly available 3D and 4D urban data sets, spatiotemporal visualisation in the urban context also gains in importance. Our future work will focus on visualisation techniques for data stemming from urban simulations. Urban data, which includes both physical information from the environment as well as abstract information from social activities, constitutes an unique data set, and urban simulation attracts people from different domains to work together. Thus, many concrete applications can be proposed for urban simulation involving spatiotemporal issues. As the immediate step, we intend to realise the proposed future enhancements to spatiotemporal visualisations, so the resulting applications can contribute to better understanding dynamic phenomena that are ubiquitous in urban environments.

References

Andrienko, G., Andrienko, N.: Dynamic time transformations for visualizing multiple trajectories in interactive space-time cube. In: International Cartographic Conference, ICC 2011 (2011)

Andrienko, N., Andrienko, G., Gatalsky, P.: Exploratory spatio-temporal visualization: an analytical review. Journal of Visual Languages & Computing 14(6), 503–541 (2003) ISSN 1045-926X

Baglioni, M., Macedo, J., Renso, C., Wachowicz, M.: An Ontology-Based Approach for the Se-
   mantic Modelling and Reasoning on Trajectories. In: Song, I.-Y., Piattini, M., Chen, Y.-P.P.,
   Hartmann, S., Grandi, F., Trujillo, J., Opdahl, A.L., Ferri, F., Grifoni, P., Caschera, M.C.,
   Rolland, C., Woo, C., Salinesi, C., Zimányi, E., Claramunt, C., Frasincar, F., Houben, G.-J.,
   Thiran, P. (eds.) ER Workshops 2008. LNCS, vol. 5232, pp. 344–353. Springer, Heidelberg
   (2008)
Baglioni, M., Fernandes de Macêdo, J.A., Renso, C., Trasarti, R., Wachowicz, M.: Towards se-
   mantic interpretation of movement behavior. In: Advances in GIScience, pp. 271–288 (2009)
Bertin, J.: Semiology of graphics. University of Wisconsin Press (1983) ISBN 0299090604
Brakatsoulas, S., Pfoser, D., Tryfona, N.: Modeling, storing and mining moving object databases.
   In: Proceedings of International Database Engineering and Applications Symposium, IDEAS
   2004, pp. 68–77. IEEE (2004) ISBN 0769521681
Carpendale, M.S.T., Cowperthwaite, D.J., Fracchia, F.D.: Distortion viewing techniques for 3-
   dimensional data. In: Proceedings of IEEE Symposium on Information Visualization 1996,
   pp. 46–53 (1996)
Eccles, R., Kapler, T., Harper, R., Wright, W.: Stories in geotime. Information Visualization 7(1),
   3–17 (2008) ISSN 1473-8716
Erwig, M., Güting, R.H., Schneider, M., Vazirgiannis, M.: Spatio-temporal data types: An approach to modeling and querying moving objects in databases. GeoInformatica 3(3), 269–296
   (1999) ISSN 1384-6175
Forlines, C., Wittenburg, K.: Wakame: sense making of multi-dimensional spatial-temporal data.
   In: Proceedings of the International Conference on Advanced Visual Interfaces, pp. 33–40.
   ACM (2010)
Gatalsky, P., Andrienko, N., Andrienko, G.: Interactive analysis of event data using space-time
   cube. In: Proceedings of Eighth International Conference on Information Visualisation, IV
   2004, pp. 145–152. IEEE (2004) ISBN 0769521770
Goodall, J.L., Maidment, D.R., Sorenson, J.: Representation of spatial and temporal data in Ar-
   cGIS. In: GIS and Water Resources III, AWRA, Nashville, TN (2004)
Goodchild, M.F.: Citizens as sensors: web 2.0 and the volunteering of geographic information.
   GeoFocus (Editorial) 2, 24–32 (2007)
Gruen, A.: Building extraction from aerial imagery. Remote Sensing of Impervious Surfaces
   (2008)
Güting, R.H.: Moving object languages. In: Encyclopedia of Geographic Information Systems,
   pp. 732–740. Springer, Heidelberg (2008)
Güting, R.H., Schneider, M.: Moving objects databases. Morgan Kaufmann Pub. (2005)
Güting, R.H., Böhlen, M.H., Erwig, M., Jensen, C.S., Lorentzos, N.A., Schneider, M., Vazirgian-
   nis, M.: A foundation for representing and querying moving objects. ACM Transactions on
   Database Systems (TODS) 25(1), 42 (2000) ISSN 0362-5915
Hägerstrand, T.: What about people in regional science? Papers in Regional Science 24(1), 6–21
   (1970) ISSN 1056-8190
Hewagamage, K.P., Hirakawa, M., Ichikawa, T.: Interactive visualization of spatiotemporal pat-
   terns using spirals on a geographical map. In: vl, p. 296 (1999) ISSN 1049-2615
ITC-2011. What has ITC done with Minard's map (2011),
   http://www.itc.nl/personal/kraak/1812/minard-itc.htm   (accessed
   March 1, 2011)
Kraak, M.J.: The space-time cube revisited from a geovisualization perspective. In: Proceedings
   of the 21st International Cartographic Conference (1995/1988)
Kraak, M.J.: Timelines, temporal resolution, temporal zoom and time geography. In: Proceedings
   22nd International Cartographic Conference, A Coruna Spain (2005)
Kraak, M.J.: Visualization viewpoints: beyond geovisualization. IEEE Computer Graphics and
   Applications 26(4), 6–9 (2006) ISSN 0272-1716

Langran, G., Chrisman, N.R.: A framework for temporal geographic information. Cartographica: The International Journal for Geographic Information and Geovisualization 25(3), 1–14 (1988) ISSN 0317-7173

Longley, P., Goodchild, M.F., Maguire, D.J., Rhind, D.W.: Geographical information systems: principles, techniques, management, and applications. John Wiley & Sons (2005)

Maguire, D.J., Batty, M., Goodchild, M.F.: GIS, spatial analysis, and modeling. Esri Press (2005)

Nanni, M., Pedreschi, D.: Time-focused clustering of trajectories of moving objects. Journal of Intelligent Information Systems 27(3), 267–289 (2006) ISSN 0925-9902

Palma, A.T., Bogorny, V., Kuijpers, B., Alvares, L.: A clustering-based approach for discovering interesting places in trajectories. In: Proceedings of the 2008 ACM Symposium on Applied Computing, pp. 863–868. ACM (2008)

Peuquet, D.J.: Representations of space and time. The Guilford Press (2002) ISBN 1572307730

Peuquet, D.J., Duan, N.: An event-based spatiotemporal data model (ESTDM) for temporal analysis of geographical data. International Journal of Geographical Information Science 9(1), 7–24 (1995) ISSN 1365-8816

Shekhar, S., Chawla, S.: Spatial databases: a tour. Prentice Hall (2003) ISBN 0130174807

Slocum, T.A., McMaster, R.B., Kessler, F.C., Howard, H.H.: Thematic cartography and geovisualization. Pearson Prentice Hall, Upper Saddle River (2009)

Smith, D.: Mapping, analysing and visualising fine scale urban form and socio-economic datasets. In: Workshop on Geographic Information in a Web-based World, Centre for Advanced Spatial Analysis, University College London (2009)

Spaccapietra, S., Parent, C., Damiani, M.L., De Macedo, J.A., Porto, F., Vangenot, C.: A conceptual view on trajectories. Data & Knowledge Engineering 65(1), 126–146 (2008) ISSN 0169-023X

Spence, R.: Information Visualization: Design for Interaction. Prentice-Hall (2007) ISBN 0132065509

Vanegas, C.A., Aliaga, D.G., Wonka, P., Müller, P., Waddell, P., Watson, B.: Modeling the appearance and behavior of urban spaces. In: Proceedings of Eurographics, State of the Art Report, vol. 1-18, Eurographics Association (2009)

Vasiliev, I.R.: Mapping time. Cartographica: The International Journal for Geographic Information and Geovisualization 34(2), 1–51 (1997) ISSN 0317-7173

Waddell, P., Ulfarsson, G.F.: Introduction to urban simulation: design and development of operational models. Handbook in Transport 5, 203–236 (2004)

Ware, C.: Information visualization: perception for design. Morgan Kaufmann (2004) ISBN 1558608192

Weber, B., Müller, P., Wonka, P., Gross, M.: Interactive geometric simulation of 4d cities. Comput. Graph. Forum 28(2), 481–492 (2009) doi:http://dx.doi.org/10.1111/j.1467-8659.2009.01387.x

Worboys, M.F.: A model for spatio-temporal information. In: Proceedings of the 5th International Symposium on Spatial Data Handling, vol. 2, pp. 602–611 (1992)

Zhang, C.C., Qin, K.: GIS spatial analysis theory and methodology. Wuhan University Press (2004)

Multi-touch Wall Displays for Informational and Interactive Collaborative Space

Ian Vince McLoughlin, Li Ming Ang, and Wooi Boon Goh

Earth Observatory of Singapore
and School of Computer Engineering,
Nanyang Technological University,
Nanyang Avenue, Singapore 639798

Abstract. GeoTouch was envisaged as a multi-touch display and information portal for GIS data within the Earth Observatory of Singapore: specifically as a focal point for collaborative discussion and exploration. The original GeoTouch, built in 2008 used proprietary hardware and software, and pioneered various multi-touch interface methodologies within the centre. Since then, GeoTouch-II has been unveiled, based upon commercial hardware rather than the bulky projection-based systems of the original, although the underlying GIS information handling and interfaces continue to be developed in-house. This chapter discusses both systems, drawing conclusions based upon observation and survey of more than three years of use, revealing patterns related to hardware and software limitations, and reveals important information concerning correlation between placement and usefulness.

1 Introduction

GeoTouch was originally envisaged as a convenient showcase collaborative and display system for earth scientists and others within the Earth Observatory of Singapore (EOS) to convey ideas and share information. It leveraged upon technology developed within Nanyang Tecnological University to provide a rear-projection based multi-touch wall display interface located in the main entrance lobby of EOS.

The scientists of EOS required a means of quickly accessing accurate data in a showcase location for visitors, including dignitaries and members of the press, without resorting to a traditional wall projection system. In particular, a relatively natural multi-touch interface would allow users to move, rotate, expand and translate areas on the display at will to examine geographic and geological information.

Installed and built during 2008 and 2009, GeoTouch utilised a rear-projection display system, and a rear-mounted infra-red camera to detect light scattered from objects (fingers) entering the invisible sheet of infra-red illumination spaced a fraction of a millimetre away from the front of the display screen. Users would stand in front of a flat frosted glass screen, viewing images projected on the inner surface, and interact by touching fingers to the front surface. Single spots

S. Müller Arisona et al. (Eds.): DUMS, CCIS 242, pp. 318–338, 2012.

would be interpreted as single finger touches, and act as long or short duration single or double clicks. Two spots within a certain radius were detected as a two-finger interaction. Depending upon the motion used, this would map to rotation, expansion or translation of objects.

This chapter discusses the technology, interaction methodologies and utility of such displays, with particular emphasis on learning from almost two years experience of operating GeoTouch-I and GeoTouch-II in the Earth Observatory of Singapore at Nanyang Technological University.

2   Technology

Multi-touch technology, to be sure, is not something new. Researchers have worked in this field for much of the past 40 years, however the processing and software capabilities of computers, and of computer programmers, are arguably only now approaching the level at which natural multi-touch gesture input can be more widely exploited.

Today's computer users are moving from a desktop-based windows, icons, mouse and pointer (WIMP) experience, requiring a traditional keyboard, video and mouse (KVM), through to more esoteric input methods, largely fuelled by the move towards mobility. Trend-setting devices such as the iPod, iPhone and iPad have accelerated this change, assisted by a small but growing number of touchscreen desktop and netbook machines plus of course the ubiquitous Android powered mobile telephones. It is clear that the interface of choice for many modern computers, especially mobile machines, is the touchscreen. In particular, the term 'multi-touch' has appeared as an early feature discriminator among touchscreen products: the ability for the device to sense, and act upon, more than a single touch input at any time.

Touchscreen interfaces, despite their modern association with mobile devices, have actually been in common use for some time, in devices such as ATMs, information kiosks, transportation ticket machines, museum exhibits, and so on, which are far from mobile. In these situations, the advantage of not requiring a mouse or keyboard stems from their exposure to either unpredictable members of the public, or exposure to the elements. In fact, it was only during recent pandemic health scares, that potential disease transmission issues [16] began to limit the popularity of touchscreens for public systems. Today, the predominant use of touchscreens is in personal and mobile devices.

2.1   The History of Touchscreens and Multi-touch Systems

The technology for touchscreens has been under development for some time, beginning with television-based systems in the 1970s [23] through to generic touch-sensitive surfaces [31][18] with various types of user interaction supported [19]. Using the technology of the day (such as cameras, television screens and analogue electronics), these primitive efforts were bulky and inconvenient in use. Furthermore, the users had not been 'trained' in the operation of graphical user interfaces (since these did not exist), nor were the computers of the day able to effectively harness such interactions.

Moving forward in time, Matsushita et al. released the HoloWall [20] in 1997; a device in the form of a wall able to interact with finger, hand, body and other objects. A rear projector, displays onto the opposite side of the wall from the user (or users, since it is not limited to interacting with a single person), coated with translucent material. Located alongside the projector is an infrared illuminator and camera. Users touching the wall reflect back the infrared light to be detected by the camera and subsequently processed.

A much newer and more capable system is the Mitsubishi DiamondTouch, a multi-touch, multi-user table interface [6]. This electronic sensing system transmits a signal to a transmitter array embedded in its surface which, when a user touches the area of a transmitter, is received by a conductive pad embedded in the chair upon which the user sits. Up to four users (seated on separate chairs!) are able to use the system simultaneously. The DiamondTouch has a projector mounted above the table projecting downwards, and allows users to control applications with gestures [35]. Control software is able to detect gestures based on touch and even on the shape of the hand.

SmartSkin [26] is another multi-touch input device, consisting of copper wire electrodes arranged in a grid. A user's finger near a grid intersection will affect the capacitance between horizontal and vertical wires, and can be detected as a touch event when the grid is scanned. A top-mounted projector displays images onto the grid surface. It has been reported that a high density grid, allows the system to detect object shapes, and presumably gestures, in addition to single touch events.

reacTable, introduced in 2005 [17][15] is a collaborative electronic music instrument using a table top tangible multi-touch interface. This device is capable of tracking fiducial markers and their orientations, which allow users to add and control instruments to the table.

Adding and moving multiple markers, allows users to combined instruments to create unique sounds and music. Infrared light emitters illuminate the surface, and a camera detects reflections from markers. It has been reported that the device is also able to detect finger location and gestures [15].

Remaining with the music theme for a moment, JazzMutant Lemur was a standalone multi-touch device for audio and media applications, able to be interfaced to other devices via Ethernet. All controls (knobs and sliders) were virtual and multi-touch. The user could customise the interface as required using a host-side graphical design application. This pioneering commercial product advertised the fact that 'all ten fingers can be used for device control simultaneously' [14]. It has been superceded more recently by software such as TouchOSC for iOS and Android devices.

Touchlight, by Wilson et. al. [32] is a camera based input device allowing gesture based interaction over a vertical acrylic surface. Rear projection is onto translucent material (said to be more translucent than that of the HoloWall [1]). The system uses two cameras, allied to one infrared illuminator. The two camera, viewing the rear of the interaction screen from different angles, work to reduce noise, although now require geometric correction. A microphone is also used, to sense vibration of the screen and thus detect tapping inputs. The same group created the PlayAnywhere input device [33], a top mounted short-throw projector/camera based multi-touch system. In this arrangement, when a user interacts with the surface, the hands will become illuminated, and cast a shadow on the surface. Touch detection uses the contour of the fingertip compared with the detected shadow. A hover event would be where the fingertip shadow is located near to the fingertip, otherwise if no shadow is present near to the fingertip, the system detects a touch event. Despite being used with a flat surface, this system potentially allows almost any surface to transform into a multi-touch input system.

Seeking a more robust technique, Han [11][12] presented a low cost multi-touch system based upon the principle of Frustrated Total Internal Reflection (FTIR) in 2005. This involves trapping infrared light within a sheet of acrylic. Any touch to the sheet frustrates the effect of total internal refection, allowing trapped light to leak out, and thus be detected by a camera.

Perhaps the most revolutionary change to the world of multitouch systems came in 2007 when Apple released a new mobile phone: the Apple iPhone. Whereas other touch based mobile phones only supported single point interaction (irrespective of whether the hardware was capable of multitouch input or not), the iPhone embraced multi-touch technology to navigate the phones functions. The iPhone senses touch by using electrical fields [34], allowing the device to detect which part of the phone is being touched. The trackpad interface of Apple laptops also supported multi-touch input from a similar date.

By mid 2007 even Microsoft had developed a multi-touch table, the MS Surface [22], styled like a coffee table with an interactive surface and using a technique similar to that of the HoloWall (rear projection, illumination and cameras). The use of multiple cameras improved the achievable input resolution. Microsoft Research in Cambridge later demonstrated a multi-touch system attached to a notebook LCD panel, ThinSight [13]. This consists of a retro-reflective optosensor array placed behind the LCD panel. Each sensor contains an infrared light emitter and an infrared light detector. When an object touches the LCD panel, it will reflect infrared light which the detector can notice. Since this technique relies on reflecting infrared light, it allows interaction with fiducial markers, although its degree of resilience to ambient light is not known. Microsoft also unveiled two further touchscreen interfaces in the years following: the TouchWall [2][30], having a vertical orientation and larger screen area, and LaserTouch [9]. LaserTouch uses cheaper hardware to turn any display, LCD, plasma television or overheard projector into a multi-touch capable system. Both systems used a technique called laser light plane (LLP) in which several IR lasers, affixed at the edge of the touch surface, creates a thin sheet of invisible light fractionally above the display surface. Upon touching the surface, the user's finger interrupts the sheet of infrared light to cause scattering. The scattered infrared can be picked up by a rear-mounted camera and processed to determine the touch location.

Today, by far the largest use of touchscreens is on mobile phones running the Android operating system, which supports basic multi-touch input functionality [3]. Android also powers a new generation of tablet computer – competing with the Apple iPad and iPad2 devices. Meanwhile a plethora of companies are releasing larger multi-touch systems ranging from interactive whiteboards, public information terminals to corporate presentation devices, often inspired by scenes from the science fiction film Minority Report (2002).

In terms of larger scale multi-touch research, the emphasis has also shifted away from the mechanics of touchscreens themselves (since these are now available off-the-shelf) more towards how these are used and what information they display. This has led to consideration of information handling, display and collaborative efforts. The ETH Value Lab [10] is a prime example of multitouch in a research environment, in particular related to information architecture [27] of all forms: the lab consists physically of a large modern space capable of comfortably hosting several dozen people. The room is equipped with wall projectors, two large touch tables and three large rear-projection multi-touch screens (plus significant computing resource to handle these facilities). Floor-to-ceiling windows opposite the multi-touch screens allow maximum enjoyment of the weak Zürich sunshine, but make the job of the touchscreens to detect gestures, and to project with sufficient contrast, much more difficult. As a collaborative space, Value Lab is a shared resource at ETH Science City (Hönggerberg) campus that is extremely well used, and is probably the prime existing example of multi-touch systems in a multidisciplinary collaborative space.

2.2   Technology Overview

Fu et. al. [8] suggests that the following features differentiate multitouch systems from other displays:

1. Multitouch contact: able to simultaneously recognise multiple contact points and actions.
2. Direct integration: being able to 'grab' and manipulate objects in a realistic fashion.
3. Object recognition: single fingers, multiple fingers, hands and other objects could be used.
4. Multi-user experience: especially with large surfaces, many users could interact together.

From our survey of literature relating to multitouch systems, it is clear that several technology choices exist for display and interaction, supporting these features to different degrees, and having various cost, space, power and convenience implications. However we consider that two main scales of multitouch system exist: smaller mobile devices designed for single-handed use, and larger systems designed for multiple hand interfacing (from one or more users). Obviously overlaps will exist, but the technology, both hardware and software, needed for these two scales does differ.

This chapter will concentrate predominantly upon the larger scale wall- and table-sized multitouch systems designed for co-located collaborative use (rather than remote collaboration). Within those systems, the driving technologies can be classified into FTIR, diffused illumination and laser light plane (LLP) [1], with the more recent addition of large commercial capacitive touch screen systems (CT). A classification of these options is shown in Table 1, along with an evaluation of several of their features.

Table 1. Review of touch screen technologies for large interfaces

Item	FTIR	DI	LLP	CT
Construction complexity	High	Medium	Low	Low
Closed box required	No	Yes	No	No
Blob Contrast	Strong	Weak	Strong	Strong
Require extra image filters	No	Yes	No	No
Reliable finger tracking	No	Yes	Yes	Yes
Allows fiducial tracking	No	Yes	Yes	No
Influence of ambient light	Low	High	Average	Low
Specific touch surface	Yes(acrylic)	No	No	Yes
IR Illumination difficulty	Low	High	Low	Low
Requires compliant surface	Yes	No	No	Yes
Pressure capable (blob area)	Yes	Yes	Difficult	Difficult
IR Illumination Occlusion	No	No	Yes	No
Display contrast	Low	Low	Low	High

3 Interaction

As discussed in Section 2, the earliest multitouch devices predated the computer graphical user interfaces (GUI) which dominate our daily interactions with non-embedded computer systems today. So for those historic systems, custom human-computer interface methodologies had to be designed, implemented and taught. However today, an entire generation of computer users expect a WIMP-based method of interaction. These users know what happens when a button is pressed (clicked), or a scroll-bar is dragged.

This expectation of users provides an initial benefit to designers but also imposes limits based upon user expectations and comfort level when expectations are not met. The benefit that designers will experience is that as long as their hardware system can map touch gestures in a sensible way to common WIMP mouse events, then these events can be fed into the windowing system, and the software running on the system will respond in a predictable way: little modification will then be required for software to operate on the multitouch system. The limit is, of course, if other interaction types are to be used, they will be initially unfamiliar to users and may feel unnatural (at the very least will require learning).

Fu et. al. [8] also classifies interactions into direct and indirect gestures. The former allowing manipulation of on-screen objects that can have immediate effect (such as rotation, movement, deletion). The latter, indirect gestures, are used to represent abstract ideas (such as "display menu", or "exit application"). In fact, this is nothing new, the author himself was using mouse strokes on Mentor Graphics workstations in 1991, shapes that could be drawn with the mouse on the screen to trigger shortcut actions without having to move the mouse cursor to some area of the screen to press an action button – something that is a relatively time consuming proposition given the very high screen resolutions and slow mouse movements of those CAD workstations.

In terms of gestures, one and two-finger gestures are most common. A single finger can emulate a mouse click, or a mouse click-drag. The touch itself may be short or long, with many interaction systems being configured to raise a menu as a response to a long touch. Two-finger gestures may be a precursor to a zoom-in or zoom-out movement (dragging the fingertips closer together or further apart), a rotation (the fingertips rotate about an imaginary central point), or some kind of translation or scroll (both fingertips move together).

Some two-finger gestures are naturally ones that can be made with a single hand, whereas others are more likely to be made by the index finger of both hands [1]. The primary means of deciding whether it is a single handed or two handed two-finger gesture is through the physical distance between touch points. A further complication in a multi-user display is that two concurrent touch points could in fact signal a one-finger gesture by two users, rather than a two-finger gesture by one user. Again, distance between touch points should be the primary means of differentiating between these two possibilities. The basic one-finger and two-finger gestures are shown in Fig. 1.

Fig. 1. The three basic direct one-finger and two-finger multitouch gestures (from left): translate, rotate and scale

4   GeoTouch

The GeoTouch project was launched in 2008 to build a multitouch system for education, collaboration, public dissemination and private discussion within the Earth Observatory of Singapore (EOS), for the earth sciences community.

The original GeoTouch, installed in 2008, is a wall-mounted unit employing the LLP method. The 60-inch display includes a glass panel coated on the rear with a diffusing material. A rear mounted projector and camera are located in a wardrobe-sized box in the adjoining room, along with the PC used to drive the system. Five infrared lasers are located along the top edge of the screen, using prismatic couplers to produce fan-like sheets of light lying less than a millimetre above the surface of the display, and covering the entire display area. As with all LLP systems, the camera at the rear (in this case a standard digital camera, fitted with a custom infrared filter) picks up infrared light scattered from any object that occludes the light plane. A relatively low resolution of 400×300 is sufficient, but GeoTouch samples this fast (98 frames per second) to ensure smooth operation. The mechanical arrangement is shown in Fig. 2.

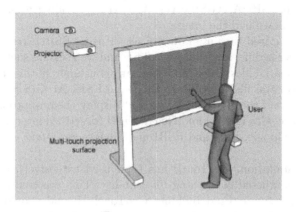

Fig. 2. GeoTouch mechanical system showing the opaque screen between the user and the camera/projector

To serve the earth science community, GeoTouch presents a camera view of the world, in much the same way as NASAs World Wind [24] or Google Earth. A large number of data sets are supported for viewing, including Google Earth image and map data, Microsoft Bing image and map data, open streetmaps, SRTM [28] and ESRI data. GeoTouch-II (see later) significantly increases the number of supported data sets.

The software, based upon TouchLib, and written primarily in Java, translates user gestures into both direct and indirect commands: translation, rotation and scaling. In addition a three-finger tilt gesture is supported. A custom interface has been developed, in consultation with earth scientists, that allows access to data, as well as tools such as freeform drawing, draggable image overlays and so on. For certain operations (such as freeform drawing), GeoTouch supports multiple users who can each have their own drawing control panel to change line colour, thickness, select line deletion and so on. Screen resolution is 1280×768 (WXGA).

After initial trials, the two-finger-hold gesture was removed to simplify interaction (with the current naïve audience), and up to the present time, no additional gestures other than the standard zoom and pan gestures have been supported.

Other datasets apart from the Google, Bing and ESRI tiled images are custom layers showing latest earthquakes (from USGS) and South-east Asian subduction zone maps.

The software was mainly developed using Microsoft .Net4 platform with libraries from ESRI ArcGIS Server Web API, Microsoft Surface Toolkit and many other helper libraries. Touch capability is achieved using native touch input messages from the operating system. Interfacing with Google, Bing and ESRI is done through ESRI ArcGIS Server Web API, providing a customized URL query string to download the images.

Local data is stored within an on-site server using ESRI ArcGIS Server software. This server is different from typical file and web servers such that it is able to publish Geospatial files. Once published, any consumer, in this case GeoTouch, using the Geospatial file's published URL, the ESRI ArcGIS Server Web API is able to download the Geospatial files and display them appropriately on the screen. Therefore, GeoTouch-I and GeoTouch-II (described later) share the same basic datasets. Google, Bing and ESRI map images are retrieved online via the Internet.

Since its installation, GeoTouch has been used extensively, and significant data has been gathered concerning its usability. This was analysed as part of the process of designing and building GeoTouch-II, and should reveal useful information for other builders of such systems. This data has been classified and analysed in the sections below:

4.1   Turn on Time

GeoTouch uses a rear-mounted projector display that, like most digital projectors, takes some time to turn on and 'warm up'. Even if the control PC is kept permanently turned on, a user confronted with a blank screen needs to wait for up to a minute to begin using the system after it has been turned on. The option of leaving the projector turned on continually was rejected due to the high cost of projector bulbs, as well as the waste of power that this would entail.

4.2   Turn on Method

With the control computer concealed in a cabinet in the adjoining wall, GeoTouch appears as a blank area of wall, with no visible controls. A method was required of waking up the system and turning the projector on. Eventually, it was determined that the control PC would remain powered most of the time (along with its camera and the LLP – both relatively low power). The PC can thus use its camera to detect screen gestures even when the projector is turned off. The system currently recognises a finger-drawn 'ON' or 'on', then responds by powering up the projector and launching the GeoTouch software. A small LED is placed in one corner of the screen to provide confidence that the PC is powered (after experiences of repeatedly and fruitlessly drawing the 'ON' shape on the blank screen when the PC was turned off). Turning the system off is accomplished through touching an 'off' icon located in a main menu (and responding to 'are you sure?').

4.3   Placement - Technical

The experience of EOS has noted two important categories of placement consequence: one is technical and the other is social. Technical issues include the problem of reflected sunlight confusing the infrared camera, effectively whiting out the infrared image. In the current location, infrared from the sun can be reflected off a nearby roof, enter the building through an office window and impinge directly on the GeoTouch screen. Even when there is little or no visible component in the light, the infrared component can be significant. Apart from moving the screen, the best solution is to coat the offending office window with reflected infrared film.

The viewing angle of GeoTouch is also limited, perhaps due to the diffusing layer coated on the inside of the unit, and it has been noted that GeoTouch appears to have very low contrast when reproduced on television (it was used in several news reports from 2008 to 2010). This contrast issue is also partly due to ceiling down-lighting installed near the screen.

The display should obviously be located close to power outlets, but should also be physically close to the control computer (USB typically limits connection distance to 7 m). This computer also requires power, and access to a high speed Internet connection.

4.4   Placement - Social

GeoTouch is located in the main entrance lobby of EOS. It can act as a draw, bringing curious passers-by into the building, and is ideally located where up to 100 people can gather and view it. However for most of the day it remains inactive; a blank screen. Thus it is not projecting a good image (literally) most of the time. Secondly, the entrance lobby is not a favourite gathering place of earth scientists. There is no comfortable seating or coffee nearby (we will contrast this to the experience with GeoTouch-II in a moment). Users and viewers are forced to stand, and to be in the public gaze, in an area that is not particularly comfortable. It is also a little out-of-the-way of scientists who are already at work, and with few potential users passing by, reduces the incidence of collaring a scientist as they pass and drawing them into a discussion.

In terms of placement, the height of GeoTouch is such that, at some areas of the screen, users trying to make a two-finger gesture, will naturally brush the knuckle of their third finger against the screen, resulting in a mistaken three-finger gesture.

It has also been noted that, perhaps because of the viewing angle, there is a 'sweet spot'. One user tends to stand in or near to this spot and dominate the activity on the screen. The software supports multi-user interaction, however it is generally a single user controlling the system, giving way after some time to a second user. Thus users naturally time-slice their activity. Is this due to their expectations grown from the use of computers having only one mouse? It is something to be explored further, especially as different multi-user multi-touch systems are developed in future, particularly ones with multiple display/touch interfaces.

4.5   GeoTouch Analysis

The first GeoTouch device thus achieves many, but not all of it's stated aims. It works well as an education tool, extremely well as a tool to interact with visiting media representatives, and (when it is turned on), works well as a 'high-technology' draw to attract attention to the research centre. It also provides good access to the static data sets provided.

However, the placement of the device and its turn-on latency, limits its usefulness for informal collaboration, or for use in shorter discussions. It also effectively functions most of the time as a single-user device. A secondary issue has been the difficulty of adding new data sets: this is a time-consuming manual process. It is therefore necessary to create a mechanism to enable scientists to self-publish their data sets onto the GeoTouch server.

With the benefit of having worked with this technology for several years in an application-driven environment (rather than as a research-driven project), GeoTouch-II was designed and constructed in 2010, coming online in January 2011.

5   GeoTouch-II

When the original GeoTouch was constructed, commercial touchscreens were not available (apart from some extremely expensive research devices), and thus it was sensible to embark upon extensive experimentation and eventually build a custom system. However in the intervening years, capacitative overlays have become available which can fit onto the front of even the largest LCD display panels. Referring to Table 1, a capacitive overlay is easy to procure, results in a slimline solution with minimal hardware difficulty. It is also of sufficient touch resolution, and yields a much higher display contrast ratio than back-projected solutions.

Thus, GeoTouch-II utilises a 32-point multi touch capacitive touch overlay, connected through USB to a control computer, overlaid onto a 55 inch Samsung flat panel LCD display. The main disadvantage of the solution (from PQ Labs) is that it does not support Linux, thus would be unsuitable for high-reliability applications. A list of supported touch sensitive overlays can be found in [7].

The GeoTouch-II software, again written completely in-house, builds upon the first release GeoTouch, to provide several additional features plus many additional data sets. A list of the main features would include the following:

- Spatially registered overlay visualisation with variable opacity.
- Surface profile mapping (draw a line across a map and pop up a surface profile window).
- Mark the latest volcanic activity.
- Tsunami simulation animation.
- Mark the latest earthquake activity.
- Email a screenshot.
- Search for location.
- Ink Canvas (freeform drawing).
- Image and Video gallery.

GeoTouch-II can be seen in use in Fig. 3, as an aid to explain geophysical events to visiting members of the media. Figures 4–6 show screen captures of GeoTouch-II capabilities (remember that one of its features is the ability to perform an arbitrary screenshot, and Email the resulting image to any recipient – a touch-screen keyboard pops up to allow the Email address to be entered). Fig. 4 shows the ink canvas freeform drawing capability (it was also partially visible in Fig. 3). Fig. 5 shows the Surface Profile tool and 6 shows two of the spatially registered overlay visualisation windows locked onto the display (named 'X-ray' in this system).

Fig. 3. A GeoTouch-II presentation session for local media in the aftermath of the 11th March 2011 earthquake and subsequent tsunami in Japan

Fig. 4. GeoTouch-II allows multiple users to simultaneously draw lines of different colours on a layer above the current map

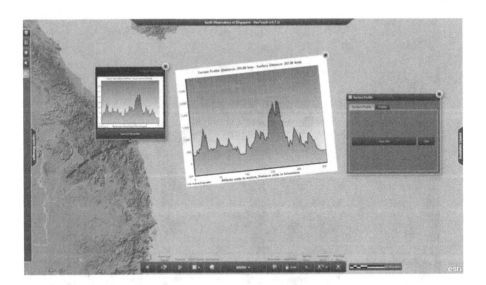

Fig. 5. The Surface Profile tool allows the elevation (height) information of the current terrain along any arbitrary line to be displayed. The height information is dervied from accurate SRTM data irrespective of the current map being displayed.

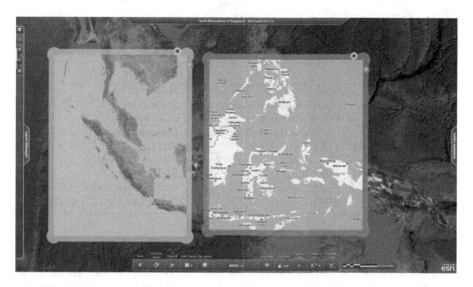

Fig. 6. Spatially registered overlay windows allow any of the different maps and layers to be displayed for a region of the current map area. Up to four of these 'X-ray' windows can be displayed, overlapped, resized, dragged into position and have their opacity adjusted at any time. When the base map is translated (dragged), the overlaid windows remain stationary on the display, but the area that they display will be translated accordingly to match the new part of the base map that they cover.

5.1   Data Sets and Presentation

GeoTouch-II contains a rich set of data from various sources, selectable for the main display (and for X-ray windows, which can display an overlay of different information). Table 2 shows the local and online data sources used in GeoTouch-II.

When adding new databases and scanned overlays, the main issue to solve is the registation of the overlaid area to the map geometry. This obviously implies that the same map projection method is used for the overlay as for the base map. At the present time, this scaling is not automatic, often requiring some conversion of data as it is incorporated into GeoTouch-II.

The current state of GeoTouch-II software is that it works extremely well for a global scale system, moving down into continental and regional scales. As the 'zoom' level increases, detail becomes much greater, and map retrieval time tends to slow (although the quanta of displayed information at a particular zoom level remains similar – relating to screen size and feature resolution – at higher zoom levels, data is extracted from deeper levels of hierarchical storage, and hit rates for cacheing strategies are reduced). The extent of the maps is similar to that found on Google maps, although some of the local data sets are of considerably higher resolution. Given the aims of GeoTouch and GeoTouch-II, it is not surprising that the tool begins to reach its limits at city scale. Whilst it can view neighbourhoods, even down to the detail of individual houses (a

Table 2. Data sets, both online and locally hosted, available at the fingertips (literally) for GeoTouch-II users

Online		Local
Google map	OpenStreetMap - Mapnik	SuGAr [21]
Google satellite	OpenStreetMap - Osmarender	Shaded relief
Google hybrid	OpenStreetMap - CycleMap	Fault lines
Google terrain	OpenStreetMap - No Name	Geological maps
Google terrain hybrid	ESRI Topography	SRTM
Bing road	ESRI Street	Tsunami animation
Bing aerial	ESRI Imagery	Bathymetry
Bing hybrid	ESRI Terrain	Christchurch faults (22/02/2011)
DeLorme World	ESRI Physical	Japan faults (11/03/2011)

favourite past-time of overseas visitors is to view their own home), the operating software is not optimised for this kind of viewing. It can therefore be seen that generic GeoTouch type visualisation matches the presentation and display needs of the digital urban modelling community, but lacks the finer detail and close-up interfaces that would truly be required by city planners, architects and developers. To state this differently, we can learn from the control, gesture and software methodologies of GeoTouch and most definitely from the social and technical analysis of the system, but for digital urban modelling and simulation, there may be opportunities to employ better optimised software for fine-detail viewing and manipulation.

5.2   GeoTouch-II Analysis

GeoTouch-II is located in an open alcove area (approximately $35m^2$) off the main thoroughfare through EOS. There is ample comfortable seating nearby, free coffee available from the pantry next door, and several tables upon which coffee cups can be placed. The floor is carpeted, and scattered but muted down lighting is provided. Next to GeoTouch-II is a frosted glass 'whiteboard', and the location is just a few steps away from the working area of most EOS researchers.

Being based upon an LCD display, GeoTouch-II is automatically turned on at 8am each morning, and turned off at 7pm in the evening. Thus, for most users, it is already powered, and displaying current map data whenever they walk past.

An informal survey has found that almost all of the 80 staff members in EOS have used GeoTouch-II or use it regularly, and all interviewed staff found it to be usable and useful. This does not mean that it has reached a state of perfection (the survey also identified several data sets that still need to be provided). Interestingly, surveys also revealed that GeoTouch-II is both more responsive, and also 'crisper' than the original device.

For use in interviews, by the media, GeoTouch-II acquits itself very well [5], and it is equally usable for education and collaboration. Unlike the original GeoTouch, which remains in its installed location and is rarely turned on,

GeoTouch-II is almost always occupied, in fact it is always in use during coffee breaks, and is often the location of lively discussions between scientists.

6   Digital Urban Modelling and Simulation

The use of GeoTouch and GeoTouch-II by earth scientists has revolved around the presentation of GIS data, linked to several ancillary data sets. The multi-touch aspect is widely used, but the features exploited from the available set of gestures, are limited. Digital urban modelling, in the sense of ValueLab [10], also revolves around the presentation of GIS data, however it has the very strong information architecture component. In fact, GeoTouch-II allied with city model scale data (such as CityEngine) could serve well as an urban planning tool.

The key to GeoTouch-II, as well as to ValueLab, has been to abstract the hardware away from the software interfaces. Thus it is unimportant whether capacitive touchscreens or LLP systems are in use – the actual information supplied to the applications is in a standard form and format. Thus the applications can be developed and tested on computers with small LCD displays, operated through a mouse.

The usefulness of any such system relies upon a number of factors:

- Responsiveness of the system: user preference dictates a system that acknowledges user input quickly and responds quickly (if not, it should give a visual indication). Rendering and data access latencies should also be kept low.
- Contrast and viewing angle: depending upon the location of users.
- Gestures supported: could be limited to standard mouse input types, or include custom multi-touch only gestures. These impact learning curve and may introduce familiarity issues.
- The data sets available: obviously the system is only as useful as the variety of data, and quality of data, available.
- The method of presenting/accessing the data: GeoTouch uses a geographically based display, in common with several similar systems (such as Google Earth), however it is equally possible to base the presentation methodology upon a different arrangement of data.
- Installation location: not just where in the building, but also how high on the wall, how far from users' desks, and how close to a thoroughfare (and is free coffee available nearby?).
- Customisation: how difficult would it be to add features, or upload additional data.

6.1   GeoTouch for Urban Planners

Fig. 7 illustrates the power of a GeoTouch-type tool for planners. The figure shows before and after images of the same location on Sentosa (the resort island at the South of Singapore), where very rapid development has taken place over the past couple of years to build Resorts World Sentosa. Similar before and after comparisons are particularly useful for observing the effects of tsunami, volcano and earthquake damage.

Fig. 7. Before and after imagery of the same location on the North shore of Singapore's Sentosa holiday island. This has been the site of rapid development during the period 2008 to 2010.

Apart from the obvious use of tools like this by urban planners who are examining GIS data, viewing urban models and so on, it is also possible to pose questions and examine answers. For example, one of the features of GeoTouch-II is an overlay that integrates a tsunami modelling system into the display. The question "what if a tsunami occurs here" can be answered through such tools that model the propagation of waves, displaying wave height in a rippling false-colour animation. In a similar way, city planners will be able to overlay visualisation of power networks, transport grids (particularly useful in megacity contexts), and model the dispersion of pollutants from industrial zones. The key to achieving this is in the interface between the GIS data, and the simulation tools: the benefit to the planners is in rapid and convenient access to such data, and yet this also solves an issue for those doing simulations - as to how they should best present their data.

6.2   Authoring

To date, GeoTouch and GeoTouch-II have primarily used multitouch interaction for the presentation of data: either static GIS overlays, frames of bitmapped graphics, video clips with sound, or simulation results. The freehand drawing system is perhaps the only part of the existing GeoTouch system that could truly be considered a multitouch authoring tool. In fact, a 'comprehensive' list of potential multitouch applications has been collated online [29], and considering this in relation to other published multitouch material, it appears that authoring – or knowledge creation – tools are significantly under-represented at present in favour of visualization/presentation tools. This has been explored recently by Burkhard et al. [4]. Furthermore, a consensus may be emerging that recent computer interaction systems, including multitouch, are significantly suboptimal in the sense of naturalness [25].

Overall, there can be little debate that multitouch systems are popular, and extremely useful, for a certain type of collaborative work at present. New multitouch applications and systems are created and published almost daily – in the digital urban modelling and visualization field, as well as in many other areas. However, it is not until these systems feel natural (either by the systems changing their capabilities or the users changing their expectations, or more likely some comination of both), that they will truly be ready for more widespread daily use. Most important may be a switch in perspective towards creative and authoring applications rather than simply visualization and presentation.

7 Conclusion

This chapter has surveyed general multitouch technology, for larger multitouch interaction systems that would suit uses ranging from education to corporate presentation, museum display and media interviews. The evolution of such systems from pioneering work in the 1970s, has been discussed, along with the convergence towards capacitive overlays for LCD flat panels.

The particular example of GeoTouch, and its descendent GeoTouch-II, have been discussed. These are relatively early examples of the application-driven use of multitouch interfaces in a non-research environment (i.e. not computer engineering/science research), and between them cover the two main hardware technology approaches to such displays. Both systems have experienced day-to-day use, and this information, stretching back nearly three years in the case of the original GeoTouch, has been analysed and presented here as a classification of features and usefulness, in particular as an aid to implementers of future multitouch systems in similar environments, such as urban planning and modelling for future cities.

It has also been noted that GeoTouch-type systems are predominatly tools to display and visualize existing data: relatively few multitouch systems appear to have found use for knowledge creation and authoring. For collaborative multitouch to have a greater impact in day-to-day work environments, further research may be necessary on developing natural authoring and knowledge creation tools, and assessing their effectiveness in work environments.

Acknowledgements. Thanks are given to Farzaneh Ahmadi for providing survey information relating to the adoption and use of GeoTouch, and to Google for pioneering the provision of online map data of good quality with fast access time. Similarly, the authors wish to acknowledge ESRI, Bing, Delorme World and OpenStreetMap for provision of good quality maps, and NASA for their SRTM data. Thanks are also due to GNS Science, USGS, LIPI (Lembaga Ilmu Pengetahuan Indonesia) and to Kerry Sieh, Paul Tapponnier, Chris Newhall for providing data used in GeoTouch, and to Lyou Chinmei for programming suggestions.

References

[1] Ang, L.M.: Multi-touch interfaces (final year project report). Tech. rep., Nanyang Technological University, School of Computer Engineering, Singapore (May 2008)
[2] Arrington, M.: Microsoft touchwall can inexpensively turn any flat surface into a multi-touch display (May 2008), http://www.crunchgear.com/2008/05/14/microsoft-touchwall-can-inexpensively-turn-any-flat-surface-into-a-multi-touch-display/
[3] Balagtas-Fernandez, F., Forrai, J., Hussmann, H.: Evaluation of User Interface Design and Input Methods for Applications on Mobile Touch Screen Devices. In: Gross, T., Gulliksen, J., Kotzé, P., Oestreicher, L., Palanque, P., Prates, R.O., Winckler, M. (eds.) INTERACT 2009, Part I. LNCS, vol. 5726, pp. 243–246. Springer, Heidelberg (2009)
[4] Burkhard, R., Schneider, C., Meier, M.: The ETH Value Lab and two software tools for knowledge creation in teams. In: International Conference on Information Visualisation, pp. 469–473 (2009)
[5] Channel News Asia: GeoTouch-II in action (March 2011), http://www3.ntu.edu.sg/CorpComms2/Documents/2011/Mar/CNA_110317_2130_Insight_Japan%20quake.wmv
[6] Dietz, P., Leigh, D.: Diamondtouch: a multi-user touch technology. In: Proceedings of the 14th Annual ACM Symposium on User Interface Software and Technology, UIST 2001, pp. 219–226. ACM, New York (2001), http://doi.acm.org/10.1145/502348.502389
[7] Ecole Nationale de l'Aviation Civile: A survey of available multitouch devices, includes linux driver information (April 2011), http://lii-enac.fr/en/architecture/linux-input/multitouch-devices.html
[8] Fu, C.-W., Goh, W.-B., Ng, J.A.: Multi-touch techniques for exploring large-scale 3d astrophysical simulations. In: Proc. 28th int. conf. Human Factors in Computing Systems (CHI 2010), pp. 2213–2222. ACM (2010)
[9] Greene, K.: A low-cost multitouch screen technology review (May 2008), http://www.technologyreview.com/Infotech/20827/page1/
[10] Halatsch, J.: Value lab: Collaboration in space. In: Int. Conf. Information Visualisation IV 2007, pp. 276–381 (2007)
[11] Han, J.Y.: Low-cost multi-touch sensing through frustrated total internal reflection. In: Proceedings of the 18th Annual ACM Symposium on User Interface Software and Technology, UIST 2005, pp. 115–118. ACM, New York (2005), http://doi.acm.org/10.1145/1095034.1095054
[12] Han, J.Y.: Multi-touch interaction wall. In: ACM SIGGRAPH 2006 Emerging Technologies, SIGGRAPH 2006. ACM, New York (2006), http://doi.acm.org/10.1145/1179133.1179159

[13] Izadi, S., Hodges, S., Butler, A., Rrustemi, A., Buxton, B.: Thinsight: integrated optical multi-touch sensing through thin form-factor displays. In: Proceedings of the 2007 Workshop on Emerging Displays Technologies: Images and Beyond: The Future of Displays and Interacton, EDT 2007. ACM, New York (2007), http://doi.acm.org/10.1145/1278240.1278246

[14] JazzMutant: JazzMutant - Lemur (May 2006), http://www.jazzmutant.com/lemur_overview.php

[15] Jordà, S., Geiger, G., Alonso, M., Kaltenbrunner, M.: The reactable: exploring the synergy between live music performance and tabletop tangible interfaces. In: Proceedings of the 1st International Conference on Tangible and Embedded Interaction, TEI 2007, pp. 139–146. ACM, New York (2007), http://doi.acm.org/10.1145/1226969.1226998

[16] Julian, T.: Talk about going viral, touchscreen (May 2008), http://www.sacbee.com/2010/10/14/3103164/talk-about-going-viral-touchscreen.html

[17] Kaltenbrunner, M., Bencina, R.: The design and evolution of fiducials for the reactivision system. In: Proceedings of 3rd International Conference on Generative Systems in the Electronic Arts (3rd Iteration 2005) (2005)

[18] Kasday, L.R.: Touch position sensitive surface (US patent no. 4484179)

[19] Mallos, J.B.: Direct television drawing and image (US patent no. 3846826)

[20] Matsushita, N., Rekimoto, J.: Holowall: Designing a finger, hand, body, and object sensitive wall. In: Proceedings of UIST 1997 (1997)

[21] McLoughlin, I., Tan, S.L., Wong, K.J.: Data collection, communications and processing in the Sumatran GPS array (SuGAr). In: Proc. Int. Conf. Wireless Networking 2011 (July 2011)

[22] Microsoft: Microsoft surface (April 2011), http://www.microsoft.com/surface

[23] Mueller, R.E.: Direct television drawing and image (US patent no. 3846826)

[24] NASA: NASA. worldwind Java SDK (April 2011), http://worldwind.arc.nasa.gov/java/index.html

[25] Norman, D.A.: Natural user interfaces are not natural. Interactions 17, 6–10 (2010), http://doi.acm.org/10.1145/1744161.1744163

[26] Rekimoto, J.: Smartskin: an infrastructure for freehand manipulation on interactive surfaces. In: Proceedings of the SIGCHI Conference on Human Factors in Computing Systems: Changing Our World, Changing Ourselves, CHI 2002, pp. 113–120. ACM, New York (2002), http://doi.acm.org/10.1145/503376.503397

[27] Schmitt, G.: Information architecture: basis and future of CADD. Birkhuser Basel (1999)

[28] Slater, J.A., Garvey, G., Johnston, C., Haase, J., Heady, B., Kroenung, G., Little, J.: The srtm data finishing process and products. J. Photogrammetric Engineering and Remote Sensing (3), 237–248 (2006)

[29] Tahir, Donovan, FoxOne, Hakon, Roftlol, nuiman, Black09, Jarno, Kamelisko, Scape, Ballentine, Jiang, Robin, Ruly, Scape, Black09, juan bran: Crystal: Ways to use multitouch (April 2011), http://wiki.nuigroup.com/index.php?title=Ways_to_use_multitouch&oldid=3153

[30] Topolsky, J.: Microsoft intros the touchwall – maps will never be the same again (May 2008), http://www.engadget.com/2008/05/15/microsoft-intros-the-touchwall-maps-will-never-be-the-same-ag/

[31] White, R.M.: Tactile sensor employing a light conducting element and a resiliently (US patent no. 4668861)

338 I.V. McLoughlin, L.M. Ang, and W.B. Goh

[32] Wilson, A.D.: Touchlight: an imaging touch screen and display for gesture-based interaction. In: Proceedings of the 6th International Conference on Multimodal Interfaces, ICMI 2004, pp. 69–76. ACM, New York (2004), http://doi.acm.org/10.1145/1027933.1027946

[33] Wilson, A.D.: Playanywhere: a compact interactive tabletop projection-vision system. In: Proceedings of the 18th Annual ACM Symposium on User Interface Software and Technology, UIST 2005, pp. 83–92. ACM, New York (2005), http://doi.acm.org/10.1145/1095034.1095047

[34] Wilson, T.V.: Howstuffworks: iphone touch screen (April 2011), http://electronics.howstuffworks.com/iphone1.htm

[35] Wu, M., Balakrishnan, R.: Multi-finger and whole hand gestural interaction techniques for multi-user tabletop displays. In: Proceedings of the 16th Annual ACM Symposium on User Interface Software and Technology, UIST 2003, pp. 193–202. ACM, New York (2003), http://doi.acm.org/10.1145/964696.964718

Testing Guide Signs' Visibility for Pedestrians in Motion by an Immersive Visual Simulation System

Ryuzo Ohno[1] and Yohei Wada[2]

[1] Department of Built Environment, Tokyo Institute of Technology
G3-4, 4259 Nagatsuta-cho, Midori-ku, Yokohama, Japan 226-8502
rohno@n.cc.titech.ac.jp
[2] Fujita Co. Ltd., Japan

Abstract. When we visit a complex public space such as a railway station or a large shopping mall for the first time, we must rely on guide signs to find our way. In crowded situations, we are called upon to read these signs while walking so as not to disturb pedestrian flow. The present study uses an immersive visual simulation system to examine the influence of observation conditions on sign detection and recognition. The experimental variables address the spatial layout of signs as well as the presence of other pedestrians. The results indicate some quantitative relationships between the above variables and readability and suggest effective layouts for signs in spaces where crowded conditions are unavoidable.

Keywords: observation conditions, detection, recognition, guide signs, pedestrians.

1 Introduction

Urban facilities are growing increasingly larger and more complex, often leading to difficulty and stress for people seeking to navigate them. When we visit a complex railway station or a large shopping mall, we rely on guide signs to find our destination. These are not always helpful, however, since the sheer number of signs around us may distract us from picking up the necessary information. The presence of other pedestrians also adds to the difficulty by blocking our view. In crowded situations where we cannot disturb pedestrian flow, we must moreover be able to read signs while walking and paying attention to the people ahead. With the above in mind, the present study uses an immersive visual simulation system to examine the influence of observation conditions on sign detection and recognition by pedestrians in motion.

Most previous research dealing with way-finding and guide signs (e.g., Tanaka and Sugawara, 2004) do not discuss the influence of observation conditions on sign detection and recognition from a quantitative viewpoint. Although many psychophysical studies (e.g., Hara, Namba and Noguchi, 2003) have focused on the readability of individual sign attributes, for example color and type of lettering as well as background contrast, most have been conducted using static targets in laboratory settings that exclude environmental factors. Yata and Uehara (1991) tested the visibility of signs in a real setting (a railway station), but again only under static observation conditions.

S. Müller Arisona et al. (Eds.): DUMS, CCIS 242, pp. 339–346, 2012.
© Springer-Verlag Berlin Heidelberg 2012

2   Method

Two experiments were performed for the present study. The first examined the readable range (readability threshold) of three types of sign lettering in motion. This served to determine conditions for the second experiment as well as to test the performance of the immersive visual simulation system known as the D-vision (see Fig. 1). The D-vision displays wide-angle images (180 degrees both vertically and horizontally) capable of filling viewers' peripheral vision; viewers may also gain stereoscopic vision through the use of polarizing glasses. The image's motion was controlled by the experimenter. The second experiment tested the influence of various observation conditions on sign detection and recognition.

Fig. 1. The immersive visual simulation system D-vision

(This system was developed by the Sato Laboratory, Tokyo Institute of Technology)

3   Experiment 1: Threshold of Sign Readability from an Observer While Walking

3.1   Objectives and Method

To obtain the perceptual threshold (readability) of signs in motion, a series of psychophysical experiments was conducted using D-vision. Three types of stimuli were used: I) Landolt rings, II) letters of the alphabet and III) Chinese characters. Eight different figures were provided for each type (see Fig. 2). The figures were printed at 2 different heights (150 mm and 225 mm) on square boards measuring 350 x 350 mm and 450 x 450 mm, respectively. The signs were put up in a virtual corridor 10 m wide and 5 m high at 4 positions combining 2 possible horizontal alignments (immediately in front of the viewer and 10 m to the side) with 2 vertical ones (2 m and 5 m high from the floor).

The subjects, 3 university students, participated in 6 sessions (3 types of figures x 2 sizes). For each session, subjects were asked to tap a keyboard when they detected the target figure (assigned from among the 8 figures possible) while moving through the virtual space at a walking speed (1.5 m/s). At the moment of response, the distance between the observation point and the target was recorded.

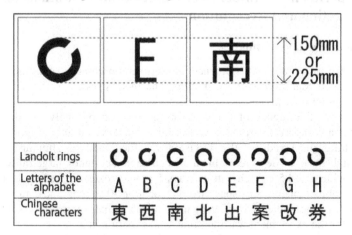

Fig. 2. Three types of targets

3.2   Results and Discussion

At each session, detection distances were recorded for all 8 figures in all 4 possible positions, resulting in a total of 32 measurements per session. Since there was no clear difference in data whether by subject or by sign position, the results were analyzed by calculating the average detection distance for each target (see Fig. 3). Although the absolute values have little meaning, given that they are based on data obtained in a virtually simulated space, they nonetheless indicate the relative readability of each figure: the farther the distance at which the target was detected, the easier it was to read. As expected, readability of figures fell along with increasing complexity. Interestingly, the readability of Landolt rings varied according to the position of the gap. Rings with a gap at the right, left, top, or the 45° positions in between tended to be detected at a farther distance, i.e., were easier to read, than those with the gap at

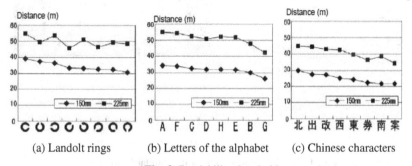

| (a) Landolt rings | (b) Letters of the alphabet | (c) Chinese characters |

Fig. 3. Readability thresholds
(Average distance at which each target was detected)

the bottom. While the readability of Landolt rings is supposedly the same regardless of where the gap is (the reason they are used as standardized symbols for testing vision), this does not seem to be the case for when they are in motion (see fig. 3a).

4   Experiment 2: Influence of Observation Conditions on Sign Detection and Recognition

4.1   Objectives and Method

Experiment 2 examined the influence of various observation conditions on sign detection and recognition while in motion. The factors tested were sign layout and presence of other pedestrians.

The degree of influence of a factor was determined by analyzing the detection distance for a comparison stimulus versus for a standard stimulus. Fig. 4 shows the virtual setting displayed by the D-vision for the standard stimulus. The main experimental space, made to resemble a concourse in a common large railway station, was 15 m wide and 3.5 m high with byways 5 m wide extending every 15 m on both sides. The subject entered this space from a corridor 30 m long and 5 m wide shown at the bottom. The subjects were 9 (4 male and 5 female) university students. The procedure for the experiment was the same as in experiment 1.

Two indicators of degree of influence were calculated from the data as follows:

(1)   Variation ratio (V)
     V = detection distance for comparison stimulus / detection distance for standard stimulus
(2)   Detection ratio (D)
     D = number of targets detected / number of targets displayed

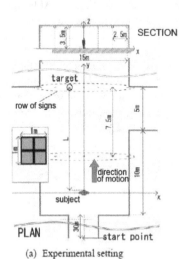

(a) Experimental setting

(b) Standard stimulus:

-   Seven Chinese-character signs displayed per every row placed 7.5 m apart in depth.

-   Five occurrences of the target (selected from the 8 characters in Figure 3c) randomly placed among 210 signs.

Fig. 4. Experimental setting for the standard stimulus

4.2   Influence of Signs' Layout

Density of Signs. Two comparison stimuli were used for this test: lower density (7 signs per row, rows placed 10 m apart) and higher density (7 signs per row, rows placed 5 m apart). As shown in Fig. 5, a significant difference ($P < 0.01$) in variation ratio was observed between the standard and higher-density stimuli, while the lower-density stimulus did not result in significant change ($P = 0.068$). The findings suggest that because the signs moved toward subjects at constant speed, the amount of visual information required to process grew as the density of signs increased, resulting in information overload and lowered performance after a certain level.

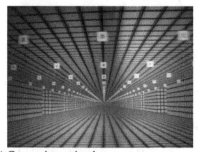

a) Comparison stimulus
(lower density: 7 signs/10 m)

(b) Comparison stimulus
(higher density: 7 signs/5 m)

Variation ratio

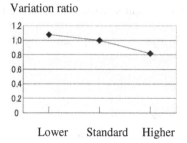

Lower   Standard   Higher

Detection ratio   = 0.98 (lower density)
= 0.93 (higher density)

Fig. 5. Influence of density of signs

Aggregation. In this comparison stimulus, 2 sign boards were paired above and below and placed at the same position as in the standard stimulus. To make the number of signs (i.e. the amount of information) per distance equal to that in the standard stimulus, the distance between rows was made twice as long (15 m). Two tests were conducted using signs of different sizes (150 mm and 225 mm). As shown in Fig. 6, the results obtained were inconsistent. With the smaller signs (150 mm), aggregation had a significantly negative effect on readability ($P = 0.023$), while for the larger signs the effect appeared positive, although the significance level was low ($P = 0.053$). These phenomena may be interpreted as follows. Since in the aggregated stimulus subjects were faced with 14 signs at once, it took them more time to complete searching for the target than with the standard stimulus, thus lowering performance. This effect was more remarked for the smaller signs because the distance at which subjects grew able to read the lettering was shorter and the movement of the signs away from view (optic flow) was therefore faster. As for the inconsistent effect seen for the larger signs, it may be that doubling the signs made them more noticeable, allowing subjects to know further in advance where they would need to look before the lettering actually became readable.

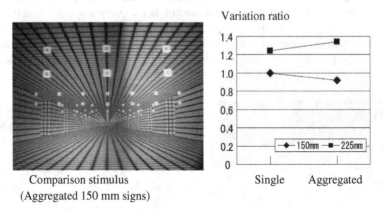

Comparison stimulus
(Aggregated 150 mm signs)

Fig. 6. Influence of aggregation of signs

Alignment. In this comparison stimulus, the sign boards were placed irregularly, i.e. they were shifted randomly from their original positions to the right and left and front and back within a range of 1.2 m as well as up and down within a range of 1.0 m. As shown in. 7. A significant difference ($p < 0.01$) in variation ratio was observed between standard and irregularly placed stimuli.

This may be because the lack of smoothness in eye movement caused by the irregular layout cost subjects more time while searching for the target.

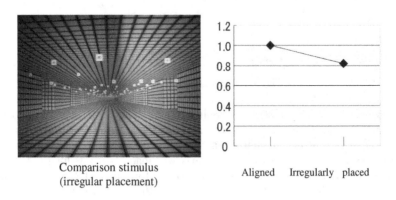

Comparison stimulus
(irregular placement)

Fig. 7. Influence of alignment of signs

4.3   Presence of Other Pedestrians

In a real setting such as a railway station, other people are usually also present and may affect readability of signs in at least 2 ways: as distracters of attention and as visual barriers.

Pedestrians Ahead. In this comparison stimulus, silhouettes of pedestrians ahead (see fig. 8) were added to the standard stimulus. Subjects were asked to use a handheld controller (see fig. 9) to change motion along with the silhouettes, which moved at uneven speeds. The hypothesis that pedestrians ahead would disturb detection of the target was supported by the drop in the variation ratio (P = 0.047) and the detection ratio (0.82).

This result may be explained by the allocation of subjects' limited resources of attention away from the task of searching for the target to keeping pace with others near them.

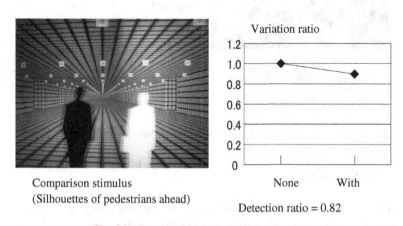

Comparison stimulus
(Silhouettes of pedestrians ahead)

Variation ratio

Detection ratio = 0.82

Fig. 8. Influence of other pedestrians ahead

Fig. 9. The controller

Density of Surrounding Crowd. In this comparison stimulus, silhouettes of a surrounding crowd (see Fig. 10) were added to the standard stimulus at 3 levels of density. Signs were also placed on the side walls in addition to the ones on the ceiling. The signs on the wall were hidden by the crowd from time to time, while the ones on the ceiling stayed always visible. The influence of crowd density on the readability of signs was not clearly evident from the variation ratio. However, the detection ratio of the signs on the ceiling dropped to 0.53 in highly crowded settings, while that of the signs on the wall remained at 0.97. It is interesting that the subjects tended to fail to detect the always visible signs on the ceiling while almost completely detecting the occasionally hidden signs on the wall. This result may also be related to allocation of attention.

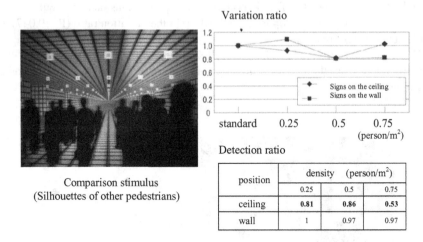

Comparison stimulus
(Silhouettes of other pedestrians)

Detection ratio

position	density (person/m^2)		
	0.25	0.5	0.75
ceiling	**0.81**	**0.86**	**0.53**
wall	1	0.97	0.97

Fig. 10. Influence of other pedestrians

5   Conclusions

The above experiments conducted revealed that the readability of figures viewed in motion may differ when they are viewed under static conditions. The following factors were found to be relevant to sign detection and recognition while in motion: I) density of signs (amount of visual information), II) smoothness of eye movement from one sign to another, and III) allocation of visual attention. Although the results were obtained in a virtual setting and the absolute numerical values have limited meaning, the results nonetheless clarify empirically some of the mechanisms involved in the detection and recognition of guide signs by pedestrians.

References

1. Tanaka, M., Sugawara, F.: The influence affect user with mixture environment of the sign for movement, and indoor advertising sign: A case of JR East Tokyo Station. Journal of Architecture, Planning and Environmental Engineering (585) (November 2004)
2. Hara, N., Namba, I., Noguchi, T.: Equivalent Luminance Contrast Representing the Relationship between Color Difference and Readability of Chromatic Documents. Journal of Light and Visual Environment 27(3), 165–171 (2003)
3. Yata, A., Uehara, K.: Hoko kukan ni okeru keiro tansaku no tokusei (Characteristics of way-finding behavior in pedestrian spaces). In: Proceedings of the AIJ (Architectural Institute of Japan) Annual Conference, pp. 689–690 (1991)

Author Index